AF720375

OXFORD STUDIES IN EUROPEAN LAW

Series Editors

PAUL CRAIG

Professor of English Law at St John's College, Oxford

GRÁINNE DE BÚRCA

Professor of Law at New York University School of Law

Private Regulation and the Internal Market

OXFORD STUDIES IN EUROPEAN LAW

Series Editors

Paul Craig, Professor of English Law at St John's College, Oxford and
Gráinne de Búrca, Professor of Law at New York University School of Law

The aim of this series is to publish important and original research on EU law. The focus is on scholarly monographs, with a particular emphasis on those which are interdisciplinary in nature. Edited collections of essays will also be included where they are appropriate. The series is wide in scope and aims to cover studies of particular areas of substantive and of institutional law, historical works, theoretical studies, analyses of current debates, as well as questions of perennial interest such as the relationship between national and EU law and the novel forms of governance emerging in and beyond Europe. The fact that many of the works are interdisciplinary will make the series of interest to all those concerned with the governance and operation of the EU.

OTHER TITLES IN THIS SERIES

The EU Deep Trade Agenda
Law and Policy
Billy A. Melo Araujo

Economic Governance in Europe
Comparative Paradoxes and Constitutional Challenges
Federico Fabbrini

The Human Rights of Migrants and Refugees in European Law
Cathryn Costello

An Ever More Powerful Court?
The Political Constraints of Legal Integration in the European Union
Dorte Sindbjerg Martinsen

The Concept of State Aid Under EU Law
From Internal Market to Competition and Beyond
Juan Jorge Piernas López

Justice in the EU
The Emergence of Transnational Solidarity
Floris de Witte

The Euro Area Crisis in Constitutional Perspective
Alicia Hinarejos

The European Fundamental Freedoms
A Contextual Approach
Pedro Caro de Sousa

National Identity in EU Law
Elke Cloots

The Constitutional Foundations of European Contract Law
A Comparative Analysis
Kathleen Gutman

The Criminalization of European Cartel Enforcement
Theoretical, Legal, and Practical Challenges
Peter Whelan

Religion and the Public Order of the European Union
Ronan McCrea

Fundamental Rights in Europe
Federico Fabbrini

The Principle of Loyalty in EU Law
Marcus Klamert

Constitutional Pluralism in the EU
Klemen Jaklic

EU Consumer Law and Human Rights
Iris Benöhr

The Principle of Mutual Recognition in EU Law
Christine Janssens

The Coherence of EU Free Movement Law
Constitutional Responsibility and the Court of Justice
Niamh Nic Shuibhne

European Law and New Health Technologies
Edited by Mark L Flear, Anne-Maree Farrell, Tamara K Hervey, and Thérèse Murphy

Private Regulation and the Internal Market

Sports, Legal Services, and Standard Setting in EU Economic Law

MISLAV MATAIJA

OXFORD
UNIVERSITY PRESS

OXFORD
UNIVERSITY PRESS

Great Clarendon Street, Oxford, OX2 6DP,
United Kingdom

Oxford University Press is a department of the University of Oxford. It furthers the University's objective of excellence in research, scholarship, and education by publishing worldwide. Oxford is a registered trade mark of Oxford University Press in the UK and in certain other countries

© M. Mataija 2016

The moral rights of the author have been asserted

First Edition published in 2016

Impression: 1

All rights reserved. No part of this publication may be reproduced, stored in a retrieval system, or transmitted, in any form or by any means, without the prior permission in writing of Oxford University Press, or as expressly permitted by law, by licence or under terms agreed with the appropriate reprographics rights organization. Enquiries concerning reproduction outside the scope of the above should be sent to the Rights Department, Oxford University Press, at the address above

You must not circulate this work in any other form and you must impose this same condition on any acquirer

Crown copyright material is reproduced under Class Licence Number C01P0000148 with the permission of OPSI and the Queen's Printer for Scotland

Published in the United States of America by Oxford University Press
198 Madison Avenue, New York, NY 10016, United States of America

British Library Cataloguing in Publication Data
Data available

Library of Congress Control Number: 2015959807

ISBN 978–0–19–874665–2

Printed and bound by
CPI Group (UK) Ltd, Croydon, CR0 4YY

Links to third party websites are provided by Oxford in good faith and for information only. Oxford disclaims any responsibility for the materials contained in any third party website referenced in this work.

Foreword

The author deserves our praise for putting together in concise form a framework to discuss private regulation within the framework of EU law. The outcome of his research is the first systematic attempt to bring under the same roof private regulation that occurs in different areas.

The arguments in favour of private regulation have largely to do with the possession of information about the specifics of a particular profession or transaction. At the antipodes, self-regulation could be hampered by capture, and could shift costs to other segments of society. It could even run counter to the public order where it operates. These are not easily managed trade-offs.

At the legislative level there is only so much that one can do. Indeed, if at all, law should encourage a private entrepreneur to come up with a more efficient production process. Did Bill Gates ever imagine, when working in his garage, that his software innovations would become the standard for the industry? Did not social welfare increase through the supply of simpler, better quality software that he managed to produce? The question is what to do once his inventions became the dominant model in the software industry, and whether sanctions against similar successes disincentivize (potential) innovators. And then there is the role of courts that will be called to adjudicate disputes against this background.

This last part is one of the focuses of this remarkable study. A 'unifying' theory is warranted, since otherwise there might be institutional 'negative' externalities: courts might be accused of favouring one type of private regulation over another. The quest for a similar theory though, is still on. Idiosyncratic elements of product or services markets have hindered a crowning success on this front. This research is one decisive step towards an approach that will help us discuss private regulation in a manner that will allow societies to reap gains from informed regulation, while minimizing the risks from self-regulation.

Adjudicators especially, but practitioners and academics as well, will be well-advised to ponder on the methodological tools offered, and the results of the analysis in this easy-to-read, well-informed volume.

Petros C Mavroidis
Edwin B. Parker, Professor at Columbia Law School (New York City)
& Professor of Law at the University of Neuchâtel (Switzerland)

Series Editors' Preface

We customarily conceptualize regulation in statist terms, with the relevant norms being produced by the state and partaking of the force of law. There is force in this view, and it is empirically grounded as the paradigm for regulatory behaviour in the old and new millennia. This regulatory paradigm has, however, never occupied the entire terrain. There has always been a significant body of private regulation, where the relevant norms emanate from a plethora of bodies, which are themselves situated in various fora, national, regional, or global.

This naturally generates important inquiries as to the legitimacy and accountability of such private regulation, with concerns as to whether public values can subsist in the context of such private or hybrid regulatory arrangements. This in turn leads to a host of more specific questions concerning the extent to which the state should be able to delegate certain functions to private parties, how far it should impose constraints thereon, and the nature thereof.

There is, however, no doubt that private regulation is here to stay. This is in part because the rationale for much private regulation mirrors that for public regulation, including in this respect its capacity to address market failure, externalities, free rider problems, and the like. It is in part because there may well be reasons why private regulation is regarded by the parties and the state as preferable to public regulation.

All of which means that the present book is especially timely, considering as it does how EU economic law deals with and is affected by private regulation. For the author, private regulation refers to non-state actors that, either jointly or independently, engage in standard setting, monitoring or enforcement of rules that govern access to markets and/or the behaviour of market participants. The decisions reached by such actors may be formally binding due to state delegation or ex-post recognition, but they may alternatively have a *de facto* or quasi-binding effect.

The study is conducted with a focus on three principal areas of private regulation: sports, the legal profession, and standard setting. The EU legal framework for the study of these sectors comprises competition law, free movement rules, and internal market legislation. The choice of sectors makes good sense given that private regulation is dominant and there are prominent regulatory concerns, while at the same time the sectors reveal the forces that drive the choice for private as opposed to public regulation.

The study provides an excellent opportunity to test the scope of application of prominent areas of EU law, competition, and free movement, to private actors, and to consider in some detail how far and in what ways EU legislation impacts on private actors. In addition, the analysis enables us to reflect on the ways in which these important bodies of EU law interact, and how far they can pull in opposing directions.

This book will be of interest to those whose primary focus is on regulation, but also to those whose principal concerns reside in competitition and free movement.

Paul Craig and Gráinne de Búrca

Acknowledgements

Writing a book is a solitary task, yet nobody does it on their own. In any event, this was the case here. Several institutions were generous enough to support the project in various ways. Family members, friends, mentors, and colleagues who have contributed in one way or another are too numerous to count. They should be blamed for none of the errors, but credited in large part for whatever may deserve praise.

The book began its life as a doctoral thesis at the European University Institute (EUI) in Florence, defended in 2013. While at the EUI, I benefited enormously from the guidance of two supervisors. Petros Mavroidis, from whom I have learned much ever since we first met at Columbia Law School in 2008, helped to see the project to its completion with confidence, encouragement, and good humour. Before him, Miguel Poiares Maduro supported me through the difficult early stages of the PhD, helping me to spot the ideas worth exploring. The comments of the examining committee members, Giorgio Monti, Allan Rosas, and Stephen Weatherill, were essential not only in finalizing the thesis but also in laying the groundwork for its adaptation into a monograph. I owe an equally great debt to the anonymous reviewers of this manuscript, whose comments and criticisms were instrumental in developing the final work.

The School of Law at King's College London was kind enough to invite me for a research stay, during which I benefited from the input of Alison Jones, Christopher Townley, and Richard Whish. This has formed the basis of Chapter III of this book. My work on the book was also shaped by an internship in the chambers of Judge Marko Ilešič at the Court of Justice of the EU, a research visit in the chambers of Advocate General Eleanor Sharpston, as well as by my collaboration with the European University Institute's Centre for Judicial Cooperation.

I benefited from the comments of various participants in conferences where parts of this work were presented: 'Contract and Regulation' at the EUI in 2015; the Harvard European Law Association conference in 2014; a lecture at the Court of Justice of the EU in June 2014; the 9th and 12th Jean Monnet Seminars in Dubrovnik, 2011 and 2014; the 2nd Workshop on Regulation at HEC Paris in 2012; 'Law and Boundaries' at Sciences Po in 2012; the Competition & Regulation and Transnational Law Working Groups at the EUI, 2011–12; the Council for European Studies conference in Montreal in 2010; and the UACES conference in Bruges in 2010. Chapter II is partly based on the paper 'The Public–Private Distinction, Autonomy and Free Movement: Unpacking the Assumptions' (2014) 13 Global Jurist 23, and Chapter III builds on my contribution to Alberto Alemanno and Amandine Garde (eds), *Regulating Lifestyle Risks: The EU, Alcohol, Tobacco and Unhealthy Diets* (Cambridge University Press 2015), entitled 'Competition Law Implications of Private Regulation in Lifestyle Policy'.

One must not forget those at home, and for me 'home', at least academically, will always be the European Public Law department at the University of Zagreb. Its current and past members, Nika Bačić, Melita Carević, Tamara Ćapeta, Iris Goldner Lang, Filip Kuhta, Tamara Perišin, Siniša Rodin, Goran Selanec, and Snježana Vasiljević were my closest colleagues during many of the stages of the work on this book. I must also thank the many students of EU law, internal market law, competition law, international and WTO law whom I have been lucky enough to teach and otherwise work with in Zagreb. Their ideas and questions have sharpened my thinking.

Thanks are also due to my excellent colleagues at the Legal Service of the European Commission, in particular those in the WTO and Trade Policy Team, in whose company I am becoming a better lawyer on a daily basis. Hopefully, some of that is reflected in this book.

At various points and in various capacities, many have helped me with their discussions, advice, comments, and criticism. I thank Alberto Alemanno, Loïc Azoulai, George Bermann, Maja Brkan, Gráinne de Búrca, Fabrizio Cafaggi, Gonçalo Coelho, Marise Cremona, Antoine Duval, Mateja Đurović, Amandine Garde, Damien Geradin, Damien Gerard, Rob Van Gestel, Christophe Giolito, Rob Howse, Ivana Isailović, Marko Jurić, Jindrich Kloub, Neil Komesar, Giuseppe Martinico, Hans Micklitz, Horatia Muir Watt, Fernando Pastor Merchante, Ernst-Ulrich Petersmann, Siniša Petrović, Jorge Piernas, Don Regan, Mirna Romić, Luca Rubini, Heike Schweitzer, Saša Sever, Sigmar Stadlemeier, Oana Stefan, Yane Svetiev, Paul Verbruggen, and Derrick Wyatt, among others.

The book would not be what it is without the diligence and professionalism of Elinor Shields and Natasha Flemming at Oxford University Press, the support of the staff at the European University Institute, including Marlies Becker, Angelika Lanfranchi, and Eleonora Masella, nor without the earlier linguistic help of Jason-Louise Graham.

Finally, a special thank you must go to the friends who made my years in Florence truly worthwhile: in particular, Chiara, Dorothy, Emilie, Fernando, Gonçalo, Jorge, Mateja, Neja, Tamara, and Teimur. Back in Zagreb, my parents Mirjana and Rafael and my brother Marko were in charge of the home base, tolerating my comings and goings for far too long without complaining. Most of all, my love and gratitude goes to Lea. She has not only put up with my many hours and days in isolation from the outside world, but has supported, advised, and encouraged me every step of the way. She continues to inspire everything I do, and this book is very much for her.

All views are personal. I aimed to account for the relevant legal developments as of July 2015.

Mislav Mataija

Brussels
5 November 2015

Table of Contents

Tables of Cases

COURT OF JUSTICE OF THE EUROPEAN UNION AND THE GENERAL COURT

OTHER JURISDICTIONS

EUROPEAN COMMISSION COMPETITION DECISIONS

Tables of Legislation

REGULATIONS

DIRECTIVES

OTHER LEGAL INSTRUMENTS AND SOFT LAW

List of Abbreviations

AG	Advocate General
Art	Article
CCBE	Council of Bar Associations of Europe
CEN	European Committee for Standardization
CENELEC	European Committee for Electrotechnical Standardization
CJEU	Court of Justice of the European Union
ECB	European Central Bank
ECJ	European Court of Justice
ECN	European Competition Network
ECR	European Court Reports
EFTA	European Free Trade Association
ESO	European standardization organization
ETSI	European Telecommunications Standards Institute
EU	European Union
Eurocontrol	European Organization for the Safety of Air Navigation
FA	Football Association
FIFA	Fédération Internationale de Football Association
FSC	Forest Stewardship Council
GC	General Court
IEC	International Electrotechnical Commission
IIA	Inter-institutional Agreement on Better Law-making
IMF	International Monetary Fund
IOC	International Olympic Committee
ISO	International Organization for Standardization
MSC	Marine Stewardship Council
n	note
NCA	National competition authority
NSB	National standardization body
nyr	not yet reported
OJ	Official Journal of the European Union
para	paragraph
SSO	Standard-setting organization
TBT	Technical Barriers to Trade
TFEU	Treaty on the Functioning of the European Union
TEU	Treaty on European Union
UEFA	Union of European Football Associations
WTO	World Trade Organization

I

Private Regulation and EU Economic Law

1. Introduction

The two building blocks of the EU's internal market are the free movement and competition rules. The first set of rules applies to the Member States, preventing protectionism and ensuring market access. The second disciplines the abuse of dominance or collusion among competitors in the marketplace. Behind both is the aim of facilitating cross-border trade and competition, while respecting as much as possible, in the first case, the regulatory autonomy of the Member States and, in the second case, the private autonomy of market participants.

What happens, however, when the Union of European Football Associations (UEFA), the European governing body of football, adopts rules restricting cross-border player transfers; when a bar association prohibits its members from partnering with accountants; or, when an organization in charge of standardizing construction products adopts a standard that works in favour of domestic producers? Should these be conceived as 'regulation' or as manifestations of a private actor's autonomy? Are they restrictions of competition in the marketplace governed by competition law, infringements of the free movement rights of others subject to the free movement rules, or both? Does it matter?

These cases fall within a broad category that can be described as private regulation. This phenomenon has given rise to debates about, for example, whether privately produced norms can be called 'law' and whether they are acceptable from the point of view of democratic legitimacy. This book focuses on a different but related set of questions. It discusses how EU economic law deals with and how it is affected by private regulation. In particular, I focus on three prominent areas of private regulation: sports, the legal profession, and standard setting.

Under EU economic law, I primarily mean the competition and free movement rules. To a lesser extent, the book will also address EU internal market legislation relevant for the three case studies, as the backdrop or context in which EU law is applied. I focus, however, on the difficulties that private regulation creates for competition and free movement doctrine, forcing the interpretation of the two sets of rules to adapt to a reality in which the public–private divide holds less and less explanatory power. A further source of complexity lies in the fact that the two sets of rules, generally seen as distinct, overlap when dealing with cases of private regulation.

This introductory chapter is structured as follows. First, I clarify the scope of the book, the meaning of key terms such as 'private regulation', and the kinds of issues the intersection of private regulation and economic law raises. Then, I discuss in more detail the emerging field of private regulation and the potential of EU economic law to address some of its costs while preserving its benefits. Finally, I outline the three main instruments of EU economic law that restrain the actions of private regulators: competition law, free movement law, and EU legislation. I conclude by describing the structure of the book.

1.1 The scope of the book

Controlling or influencing the behaviour of private actors through legal rules is not an unusual function of legal systems. What I aim to address is much more limited in relation, first, to the instruments that are used and second, to the types of private actors and actions that are controlled.

First, I am concerned only with the application of the free movement and competition rules, as well as internal market legislation to the extent described. Among the competition rules, I will only be looking systematically at the antitrust rules of Art 101 (agreements, concerted practices, and decisions of associations of undertakings) and Art 102 TFEU (abuse of dominance) as well as, to a limited extent, Art 106 on exclusive rights and services of general economic interest. The rules on mergers and state aids are addressed only incidentally.

Secondly, this book does not deal with all private action but only with private regulation. From the outset, it should be made clear that there is no precise definition of the terms 'private regulation' and 'private regulator'. In fact, as I will argue, the very public–private, State–market distinction on which many of the debates relevant for this book are premised is highly contestable. The cases of private regulation analysed here are better described as positioned somewhere along a spectrum of possibilities between the ideal notions of 'public' and 'private' that are used in legal debates. This means that calling a regulatory scheme 'public' or 'private' is, for these purposes, a heuristic exercise only.

With that caveat, I will attempt to describe 'private regulation' as referring to non-State actors that, either jointly or independently, engage in standard setting, monitoring or enforcement of rules that govern access to markets, and/or the behaviour of market participants. Their decisions can be formally binding due to State delegation or ex-post recognition. Alternatively, they can have a quasi-binding effect as a consequence of market power, like in the area of sports (see Chapter V). Private regulation can be embedded in 'co-regulatory' schemes that employ both State and private bodies, but it frequently has a significant impact on third parties even without State involvement.

In any event, not all private action is covered by the term. A clear *ex ante* definition of how private regulation differs from other kinds of private action is impossible to draw,[1] but to qualify as a 'private regulator', a private actor clearly needs to

[1] A borderline case is the use of 'gatekeepers': a regulatory scheme that imposes a distinct duty on a certain class of private actors vis-à-vis third parties. An example of this would be the common practice of requiring online intermediaries such as Internet service providers or search engines

have a modicum of authority or influence transcending that available to all private persons in the exercise of their autonomy.

Within the general question of how competition and free movement law (and, to a limited extent, internal market legislation) deal with private regulation, I will analyse three specific fields. These are the regulation of sports (Chapter V), regulation of the legal profession (Chapter VI), and standard setting (Chapter VII). All three are highly representative illustrations, for several reasons.

Firstly, the three case studies cover areas where private regulation is dominant. While sport is to some extent governed both by national and international law, sporting bodies have traditionally regulated their domains on their own, not only in terms of 'purely sporting' rules but more broadly: deciding on athlete and club licensing, setting disciplinary rules like those on doping, or co-ordinating commercial activities such as the sale of media rights. In the legal profession, while some of the bodies that decide on entry into the profession impose rules on pricing or advertising and enforce codes of professional conduct have public status, their decision-making process is usually autonomous. Even though standards are frequently taken over in legislation, public procurement or other State measures, their development is usually, by design, dominated by industry.

Secondly, all three case studies involve public interest regulatory concerns, meaning that both the exercise of private regulatory power and the EU law-based discipline that may be applied to it are contested. These regulatory objectives could relate to market failures like information asymmetries (the main justification for imposing quality standards in legal services, for example) or negative externalities (in the case of environmental or food safety standards). There can also be a public interest in controlling concentrations of market power, such as in the case of sporting bodies' joint selling of media rights or standard-setting bodies being used as a forum for collusion among competitors. Similarly, private regulation in all three fields raises the issue of conflicts of interest where a regulator is economically active in the same market that it is regulating (such as sporting bodies both licensing and organizing certain competitions,[2] professional bodies that both provide and regulate professional training,[3] or certification bodies that sell the same kind of products they are in charge of approving).[4]

to remove material that infringes intellectual property rights. For a more general discussion, see Henry Farrell, 'Regulating Information Flows: States, Private Actors, and E-Commerce' (2006) 9 Annual Review of Political Science 353; Frank Pasquale, 'Beyond Innovation and Competition: The Need for Qualified Transparency in Internet Intermediaries' (2010) Northwestern University Law Review 104; Jonathan Zittrain, 'Internet Points of Control' (2003) 43 Boston College Law Review 1.

[2] Case C-49/07 *Motosykletistiki Omospondia Ellados NPID (MOTOE) v Elliniko Dimosio* [2008] ECR I-4863.

[3] Case C-1/12 *Ordem dos Técnicos Oficiais de Contas v Autoridade da Concorrência* ECLI:EU:C:2013:127.

[4] Case C-18/88 *Régie des télégraphes et des téléphones v GB-Inno-BM SA* [1991] ECR I-5941.

Thirdly, these case studies show the advantages of resorting to private regulation in some circumstances, notably because of the informational disadvantages and complexities of achieving the same task through public command and control regulation. Standard setting is the classic example: the Member States have long resorted to national, and the EU to European standard-setting bodies, to set detailed requirements various products should satisfy. This can also be linked to broader concerns, such as the need to preserve the independence of the legal profession from the State for reasons of impartiality and sound administration of justice, or an element of tradition associated with the 'specificity' of sport.

Fourthly, the three case studies vary, to some extent, according to the role of the State. With the legal profession, State and private regulation are deeply intertwined. In sports, the role of the State is comparatively marginal. With standard setting, Member State or EU influence ranges between very low (market-based standardization) to quite high (harmonized standards developed by the European standardization bodies). This makes it possible to see how the varying role of the State is reflected in the application of free movement and competition law.

Finally, all three case studies present sufficient case law to study both the application of free movement and competition law in the sector, and to assess the relationship between them. Another interesting dimension is that significant EU internal market legislation governs the legal profession and standard setting, but sport has been largely free of direct EU legislative intervention.

1.2 Private regulation and economic law—reasons to consider their relationship

How economic law deals with private regulatory schemes is interesting for (at least) two reasons. First, private regulation is somewhat unique in that it can be reviewed or supervised under a wider variety of rules than is the case with State measures or ordinary marketplace behaviour. In addition to the fact that private actors are increasingly directly addressed through EU legislation, free movement and competition rules are both in principle applicable. Therefore, private regulatory schemes offer a good opportunity to test the relationship and limits of these different rules of EU economic law. Are free movement and competition law co-extensive? Can they be used interchangeably or be 'blended' in a single type of analysis? To what extent can they accommodate relevant policy choices and justifications? The first overriding issue is, therefore, how private regulation affects competition and free movement law.

The second reason why this topic is relevant has to do with private regulation itself. It is growing in significance and is frequently a part of the regulatory strategies of the EU and its Member States. At the same time, it poses risks: the lack of accountability, participation, and legitimacy and the high likelihood of capture. The free movement and competition rules were not drafted with those issues in mind. Nevertheless, they provide possibilities of judicially and administratively reviewing the behaviour of private regulators, something that is not always available in the legal orders of the Member States. As a by-product of protecting competition and trade, they could have the consequence of promoting better governance standards, inclusiveness, and openness.[5] The same is true of EU legislative or soft law[6] instruments: by addressing particular sectors where private regulation is prominent, they can directly or indirectly impose substantive or procedural requirements.

In a less optimistic reading, the application of EU economic law could have a chilling effect on the innovative potential of private regulation and dampen the benefits traditionally associated with it, such as expertise, flexibility, and lower costs. This is true on the national, but also on the transnational and European level. As States and international organizations increasingly involve private actors, for example by relying on them in implementation of publicly developed rules, the overzealous application of EU free movement or competition rules could prevent regulatory experimentation.[7]

2. Private Regulation—A Growing Phenomenon

Private regulation and private law-making have become a topical issue for legal scholars. Even though the first instances of private regulation such as guilds go back to the Middle Ages,[8] what brought private regulation to the fore of recent attention were the privatization and liberalization movements of the 1980s and the 1990s. Liberalization was followed by a shift to re-regulation that often, instead of relying on standard command-and-control approaches, involved private actors[9] which took over previously public tasks such as managing the telecommunications or transport infrastructure. In addition, private regulation is

[5] This idea has been explored at length in Harm Schepel, *The Constitution of Private Governance: Product Standards in the Regulation of Integrating Markets* (Hart 2005).

[6] See Commission, 'Guidelines on the applicability of Article 101 of the Treaty on the Functioning of the European Union to horizontal co-operation agreements' (Communication) (2011) OJ C 11 as an example of regulating the procedures and rules of private standard-setting bodies through a soft law measure that summarizes the requirements of competition law in a particular area. In the area of the liberal professions, there is extensive EU legislation related to the freedom to provide services and the freedom of establishment of professionals that also addresses the behaviour of professional bodies (see Chapter VI).

[7] See Erika Szyszczak, 'Competition and the Liberalised Market' in Niamh Nic Shuibhne (ed), *Regulating the Internal Market* (Edward Elgar 2006) 97–8: 'If private power is encumbered with the same obligations and duties as the state, there may be disincentives to provide certain services on the market and markets will not develop under normal competitive principles.'

[8] Fabrizio Cafaggi and Agnieszka Janczuk, 'Private Regulation and Legal Integration: The European Example' (2010) 12 Business and Politics 1, 2.

[9] ibid. In the US, the deregulation movement was underpinned by public choice and interest group theories that described the industry capture and rent-seeking associated with traditional regulation. On this, see Herbert Hovenkamp, *The Antitrust Enterprise: Principle and Execution* (Harvard University Press 2005) 238–40. As Hovenkamp points out, in many previously regulated sectors, 'it turned out that the principal beneficiaries of industry regulation were the regulated firms themselves, who were shielded from competition and guaranteed profit margins' (239).

nowadays relied upon as an important part of regulatory strategies in areas such as product or food safety,[10] emissions reduction,[11] and Internet infrastructure.[12]

Even outside traditional regulatory domains, scholars have described a number of cases where informally produced norms and enforcement mechanisms supersede or replace State institutions and courts. Bernstein's account of the diamond industry,[13] Ellickson's description of informal dispute resolution mechanisms[14] and Dixit's analysis of private ordering as a compensation mechanism for weak State institutions[15] have all shown that informal private ordering is common in practice and that it can have significant advantages over traditional legal mechanisms. It remains, however, in 'the shadow of'[16] the legal system, even if not directly constrained by it.

The important question is just how far that shadow should fall, or how the legal system should respond to the rise of private regulation. Which of the traditional tasks of the State can be delegated? What sort of judicial or administrative review can be applied to private action? How can public values be achieved in a proportionate and efficient way in the context of private or hybrid regulatory arrangements? Beyond those discussions, however, private regulation is a conundrum for legal theory. Can it be seen not just as one social phenomenon among many others, but as law in its own right—even if it is not formally recognized by the State or embedded in State measures in some way? What are the consequences for our implicit understandings of law, democracy, and the State of recognizing that private regulation can be 'law', in some sense of the word?

While increasingly frequent, this debate is not new. In his 1937 paper,[17] Louis Jaffe integrates these two levels of discussion by referring to a quote of Justice Sutherland of the US Supreme Court in *Carter v Carter Coal Co.*:

[10] Fabrizio Cafaggi, 'Product safety, private standard-setting and information networks' EUI Working Paper LAW 2008/17; Bernd van der Meulen (ed), *Private Food Law: Governing Food Chains Through Contract Law, Self-regulation, Private Standards, Audits and Certification Schemes* (Wageningen Academic Publishers 2011).

[11] See Patrick Ten Brink, *Voluntary Environmental Agreements: Process, Practice and Future Use* (Greenleaf Publishing 2002) and Martin Herberg, 'Global Legal Pluralism and Interlegality: Environmental Self-Regulation in Multinational Enterprises as Global Law-Making' in Olaf Dilling, Martin Herberg, and Gerd Winter (eds), *Responsible Business: Self-Governance and Law in Transnational Economic Transactions* (Hart 2008).

[12] See Christopher M Bruner, 'States, Markets, and Gatekeepers: Public–Private Regulatory Regimes in an Area of Economic Globalization' (2008) 30 Michigan Journal of International Law 125 and A Michael Froomkin and Mark A Lemley, 'ICANN and Antitrust' (2003) University of Illinois Law Review 1.

[13] Lisa Bernstein, 'Opting Out of the Legal System: Extralegal Contractual Relations in the Diamond Industry' (1992) 21 Journal of Legal Studies 115.

[14] Robert Ellickson, *Order Without Law: How Neighbors Settle Disputes* (Harvard University Press 1994).

[15] Avinash K Dixit, *Lawlessness and Economics: Alternative Modes of Governance* (Princeton University Press 2004).

[16] Robert N Mnookin and Lewis Kornhauser, 'Bargaining in the Shadow of the Law: The Case of Divorce' (1979) 88 Yale Law Journal 950.

[17] Louis L Jaffe, 'Law Making by Private Groups' (1937) 51 Harvard Law Review 201.

The difference between producing coal and regulating its production is, of course, fundamental. The former is a private activity; the latter is necessarily a governmental function, since, in the very nature of things, one person may not be entrusted with the power to regulate the business of another, and especially of a competitor ... [18]

This traditionally hostile view of private regulation is, as Jaffe claims, connected with a classic Austinian conception of law as a command of the sovereign.[19] Strikingly, the reaction of Justice Sutherland would still represent the majority view of the participation of private actors in regulation. The rising prominence of private regulation may, however, lead to a more tolerant stance that explores ways of improving private regulatory schemes instead of denying them legal validity.

On the theoretical level, it has indeed been noted that 'private government, private regulation and private justice are becoming central sources of law'.[20] The modern regulatory landscape has been described as a 'mixed, public–private, dynamic norm-creation process' in which national and transnational, public and private actors compete for authority and interact in complex ways.[21]

Teubner and Fischer-Lescano have discussed the emergence of 'autonomous private legal regimes' in various segments of the society and economy, such as *lex mercatoria* or Internet governance, as one of the features of legal pluralism. These regimes, they claim, do not derive their validity from delegation or other links to the State, but create their own law because of a 'demand for regulating norms which cannot ... be satisfied by national or international institutions'.[22] Bringing these regimes back into the fold of 'Austinian' hierarchical, State-centred law is, as they argue, a project unlikely to succeed. The best that law can do is to control their excesses, acting as a 'gentle civilizer of social systems'.[23] One of the central ideas to be explored by this book is whether, and to what extent, EU free movement and competition rules have taken up that role. Either of them could be destructive, preventing the development of private regulation as a danger to the public interest. They could also wash their hands, relying on a strong understanding either of private autonomy (free movement law) or of regulatory autonomy (competition law) to abstain from judgment on private regulation. The middle ground—extending the opportunities for judicial review while remaining broadly deferent in specific cases—is, as I will argue, closer to reality. Yet, it remains quite controversial doctrinally and theoretically.

[18] *Carter v Carter Coal Co.* 298 US 238 (1936) 311. Cited in Jaffe (n 17) 206.

[19] Jaffe (n 17) 207.

[20] Gunther Teubner, 'Global Private Regimes: Neo-spontaneous Law and Dual Constitution of Autonomous Sectors in World Society?' in Karl-Heinz Ladeur (ed), *Globalization and Public Governance* (Ashgate 2004) 75.

[21] Gralf-Peter Calliess and Peer Zumbansen, *Rough Consensus and Running Code: A Theory of Transnational Law-Making* (Hart 2010) 10. See also Peer Zumbansen, 'Neither "Public" nor "Private", "National" nor "International": Transnational Corporate Governance from a Legal Pluralist Perspective' (2011) 38 Journal of Law and Society 50.

[22] Andreas Fischer-Lescano and Gunther Teubner, 'Regime-Collisions: The Vain Search for Legal Unity in the Fragmentation of Global Law' (2003) 25 Michigan Journal of International Law 999, 1010.

[23] ibid 1045.

The importance of private regulation has also reverberated in private law scholarship. For example, industry codes of conduct are frequently referred to in contractual clauses. Contractual litigation may thus be forced to decide whether those codes have legal consequences and how they should be interpreted, for example in a dispute between a firm and a consumer. This may import certain regulatory notions into contract law. Similarly, private regulation may influence the interpretation of private law constructs, such as what may be considered as an implied term of a contract in English law.[24] National rules on torts may be faced with the problem of the liability of private regulators to third parties, notably consumers.[25] In that sense, the appropriate legal treatment of private regulation may be seen as one aspect of the broader debate on regulatory private law, or between instrumentalist and formalist, subjectivist and objectivist approaches to contract interpretation and private law more broadly.[26]

3. Distinctions, Taxonomies, and Definitions

This book does not take sides in the theoretical dispute on the legal nature of the rules and systems created by private and/or transnational actors. Pragmatically, one could simply say, along with Snyder, that 'there is something we should call law, that carries much of the effect of legislation or case-law, but that is privately made'.[27] A more careful theorist might prefer to highlight the difference between law and other social norms.[28] Regardless of where one stands, the reality is that private regulation is spreading as a useful mechanism for the achievement of public ends, or (depending on one's perspective) an effective tool for self-interested actors to capture the political process. It comes in many forms and takes place in a number of sectors: regulation of the liberal professions, rules of sporting bodies, product and service standards, private food

[24] Thus, 'the courts have suggested that the disciplinary power of an association to fine a member is subject to an implied term that the fine will not be unreasonable or excessive in all the circumstances'. Catherine Donnelly, 'The Response of English Public Law to Private Actors in Public Governance' in M Ruffert (ed), *The Public/Private Divide: Potential for Transformation* (BICL 2009) 200.

[25] An excellent example are the actions in tort brought by the victims of substandard breast implants against a German standard setting and certification body in French and German courts. See Barend van Leeuwen, 'PIP Breast Implants, the EU's New Approach for Goods and Market Surveillance by Notified Bodies' (2014) 3 European Journal of Risk Regulation 338.

[26] See, for example, Hans-W Micklitz, Yane Svetiev, and Guido Comparato (eds), 'European Regulatory Private Law—The Paradigms Tested' (2014) EUI Working Paper LAW 2014/4; Duncan Kennedy, 'A Transnational Genealogy of Proportionality in Private Law' in Roger Brownsword and others (eds), *The Foundations of European Private Law* (Hart 2011) 187: '... it seems possible that European private law theory has reached a kind of historic turning point and will now find itself merging into the more general debate in administrative, constitutional and European Union law, within which "proportionality" is both omnipresent and highly controversial.'

[27] David V Snyder, 'Private Lawmaking' (2003) 64 Ohio State Law Journal 371, 373.

[28] See, for example, Gralf-Peter Calliess and Moritz Renner, 'Between Law and Social Norms: The Evolution of Global Governance' (2009) 22 Ratio Juris 260.

safety certification, etc. The rules of private regulators are interlinked with or imported into traditional legal mechanisms through legislation, judicial recognition, or contractual references. Privately produced rules are often reinforced by private mechanisms for enforcement or dispute settlement. How exactly specific legal mechanisms, such as those of EU economic law, should respond to these phenomena seems to depend on their effects rather than their abstract 'legal nature'.

In order to understand the notion of private regulation, instead of providing either a very precise definition or a long list of unconnected examples, perhaps it is more helpful to start with some distinctions in order to highlight the different forms that it may take.

A first distinction might be between 'pure' self-regulation and other forms of private regulation. In pure self-regulation, the effects of the decisions of regulatory bodies are limited to their members. The term 'self-regulation' is frequently used to describe private regulation in general. However, as Cafaggi notes, it is better understood as referring only to situations where there is 'formal coincidence between regulators and the regulated',[29] such as the representatives of an industry agreeing on certain practices that only affect the industry itself.[30] The term 'private regulation', which will be used throughout, is broader because it reflects, firstly, the fact that State bodies as well as constituencies such as NGOs, academia, and organized labour can participate in a regulatory scheme and, secondly, the fact that a scheme can address or affect regulated entities ('targets') or beneficiaries that are different from the entities adopting the rules,[31] as well as have a significant positive or negative impact on third parties such as competitors or consumers.

The second important distinction is between purely private regulation and combinations of private and public regulation. It is increasingly common for public and private regulators to share responsibilities. Firstly, regulatory power can be *ex ante* delegated to private actors. Secondly, private regulation can be given effect *ex post* through a legislative reference or judicial recognition. A more complex form is co-regulation, where private regulators take part in the regulatory process by taking over one or some of its segments—standard setting, monitoring, enforcement, or dispute resolution. For example, private bodies may be in charge of setting standards which are then enforced publicly (as, for example, in the development of so-called *de facto* technical regulations; see Chapter VII section 2.1) or monitoring compliance with public standards (see, for example, private certification schemes attesting compliance

[29] Fabrizio Cafaggi, 'The Architecture of Transnational Private Regulation' EUI Working Paper LAW 2011/12 4.

[30] See Snyder (n 27) 387, referring to the 'self-regulatory misnomer'.

[31] Cafaggi (n 29) provides an example: 'In financial market transnational private regulation, investors and depositors can be considered intentional beneficiaries, taxpayers may be incidental beneficiaries or, as was the case in the financial crisis, those negatively affected by the drawbacks of the previous regulatory regimes.'

with legal requirements).[32] One could also speak of regulation *through* private actors, where public regulatory aims are achieved by imposing certain requirements on gatekeepers, private actors that control key inputs or facilities necessary for others to compete, as is the case with *ex ante* regulation of telecom incumbents.[33] In many of these cases, private actors are normally given not only additional responsibilities and powers but are required to structure their decision-making in line with certain requirements, such as transparency, openness, and non-discrimination.[34]

These hybrid arrangements are considerably more complex than outright delegation from the State to a private actor. Increasingly, 'not all governance or regulatory functions are necessarily performed by a single organization; rather, they may be dispersed amongst actors in a regulatory regime, including market actors, civil society organisations, non-state regulators … and international and national state-based actors, who are interrelated in a myriad of different ways.'[35] Julia Black uses the notion of a 'regulatory regime' to describe these complex regulatory schemes.[36] Thus, as Cafaggi notes, what is new is not private regulation in itself, but the 'integrated nature of the new regulatory models': private regulation is 'partly grounded on private autonomy, partly on delegation by public power'.[37]

In this book, the term 'co-regulation' will be used to describe hybrid public–private regulatory schemes with participation of both State and private actors. I will use it in a somewhat loose sense, however, not distinguishing it strictly from delegation or ex-post recognition.[38] The point is simply to highlight the participation of the State at some level of the scheme.

A further distinction can be made between transnational and national private regulation. Many of the common examples of private regulation involve actors organized along national lines, such as a professional association or a recognized

[32] See Fabrizio Cafaggi, 'Rethinking Private Regulation in the European Regulatory Space' EUI Working Paper LAW 2006/13 section 4 for a taxonomy of the different forms along the spectrum between public and private regulation.

[33] See n 1.

[34] See, for example, the Interinstitutional Agreement on Better Law-making [2003] OJ C321/1 para 17: 'The Commission will ensure that any use of co-regulation or self-regulation is always consistent with Community law and that it meets the criteria of transparency (in particular the publicising of agreements) and representativeness of the parties involved. It must also represent added value for the general interest …'

[35] Julia Black, 'Legitimacy and the Competition for Regulatory Share' LSE Law, Society and Economy Working Paper 14/2009, 4.

[36] Black defines it as 'a set of interrelated units which are engaged in joint problem-solving to address a particular goal; its boundaries are defined by the definition of the problem being addressed; and it has some continuity over time'. ibid 5.

[37] Cafaggi (n 32) 1–2. In his study of transnational commercial law, for example, Calliess similarly points out that while 'there in fact are instances of private legal systems, which operate largely outside the state', these are exceptions because 'transnational legal regimes depend on the formally organized administration of socio-economic sanctions'. Gralf-Peter Calliess, *Lex mercatoria* (2015) ZenTra Working Papers in Transnational Studies 52/2015.

[38] For a more careful definition of co-regulation, distinguishing it in particular from 'enforced self-regulation', see Colin Scott, 'Self-Regulation and the Meta-Regulatory State' in Fabrizio Cafaggi (ed), *Reframing Self-Regulation in European Private Law* (Kluwer Law International 2006) 138–9.

standard-setting body of a certain State. National private regulation is often a part of delegated or co-regulatory schemes, with private regulators working in close co-operation with governments and their rules co-opted into legislation. More recently, however, private regulation has also emerged on the European and transnational stage. Transnational regulation by firms, industry associations, standard-setting bodies, and NGOs has grown prominent in a number of sectors (environmental governance, food safety, sports regulation, Internet regulation, and others) and levels of regulation (law-making, standard setting, implementation, and enforcement). The drivers of these developments are, among others, 'weakening of national governments, the rise and professionalization of multinational corporations and supply chains, and the proliferation, diversification and internationalisation of new social movements and their strategies'.[39]

Other distinctions can be made according to the forms or effects of the activity of the private regulator. For example, an important issue is the extent to which different groups are included in the regulatory process. Pure self-regulation, where actors make rules for themselves, can be distinguished from increasingly prominent 'multi-stakeholder' initiatives, which involve different constituencies such as consumers, NGOs, and academia.[40] From a more technical perspective, private regulatory schemes can be distinguished according to whether or not their measures have binding legal effects and on what basis. Regimes of delegation or co-regulation in which the state is involved alongside private actors can lead to the creation of such binding effects. Even without such State involvement, however, private regulatory schemes can be much more than talking shops. Their rules can be enforced through private-law mechanisms like contract and tort and/or by relying on private dispute resolution mechanisms. The sanction for violating the rules of a private regulatory scheme can be exclusion from the marketplace, like in the case of athletes condemned for doping or professionals violating an ethical rule.

Finally, an important distinction is between 'monopolistic' and competitive private regulation. With competitive private regulation, multiple private regulatory schemes compete on the basis of price and quality. Professionals can, for example, be members of one among several professional bodies that are differentiated in terms of specialization, membership costs, the strictness of qualifications rules, etc.[41] Producers could certify their products for compliance with one of

[39] Ramses A Wessel and Jan Wouters, 'The Phenomenon of Multilevel Regulation: Interactions between Global, EU and National Regulatory Spheres' (2008) 4 International Organizations Law Review 259, 271.

[40] See Cafaggi, 'Rethinking Private Regulation in the European Regulatory Space' (n 32) 13–14. For more details on multi-stakeholder models of regulation, see David Vogel, 'Private Global Business Regulation' (2008) 11 Annual Review of Political Science 261 and Axel Marx, 'Global governance and the certification revolution: Types, trends and challenges' Leuven Centre for Global Governance Studies Working Paper No 53—November 2010.

[41] As Scott (n 38) notes, 'regulatees may be attracted to joining a regime which is more costly and stringent if its reputation is such that it can secure more customers and/or charge a higher price for its product' (142).

many quality standards of similar coverage. While competitive private regulation may reduce the risk of capture and encourage efficient as well as efficiently differentiated rules, it may also be less efficient than concentrated models, for instance if asymmetries of information lead consumers to select among the different standards purely on the basis of price.[42]

4. The Costs and Benefits of Private Regulation

While its rationales depend heavily on the sector, the potential benefits of private regulation can be divided into two groups. Firstly, private regulation can be justified on grounds similar to any other type of regulation. It can address market failures like asymmetries of information, positive or negative externalities, or 'free rider' problems associated with public goods,[43] and pursue interests such as environmental protection, human and animal health, product safety, preservation of cultural heritage, etc. In addition, there are benefits specific to private regulation, making it not only a useful element of the regulatory mix but perhaps even superior to State intervention.[44]

Firstly, private regulation is well-placed to take advantage of high levels of expertise. The direct involvement of industry players in highly technical sectors enables the most up-to date knowledge to be used. Secondly, private regulation is more flexible than traditional forms of State regulation, and less bound by rigid hierarchical limitations or elaborate decision-making procedures. This also enables it to be more innovative in devising new ways of responding to societal problems, which can then be fed back into the design of public regulation—what some scholars have called reflexive or experimentalist governance.[45] Thirdly, private regulation that involves a broad circle of interested actors can be seen as more legitimate, which in turn leads to greater compliance. This is especially true for

[42] Anthony Ogus, 'Rethinking Self-Regulation' (1995) 15 Oxford Journal of Legal Studies 97, 103. See also Ségolène Barbou des Places, 'Self-Regulation and the Professions: A Perspective from Regulatory Competition Theory' in Fabrizio Cafaggi (ed), *Reframing Self-Regulation in European Private Law* (Kluwer Law International 2006).

[43] See for example Cento Veljanovski, 'Economic approaches to regulation' in Robert Baldwin, Martin Cave, and Martin Lodge (eds), *The Oxford Handbook of Regulation* (Oxford University Press 2010).

[44] See for example Ogus (n 42) 97 et seq; Cafaggi, 'Rethinking Private Regulation in the European Regulatory Space' (n 32) 8–10; Robert Baldwin and Martin Cave, 'Self-Regulation' in Robert Baldwin and Martin Cave (eds), *Understanding Regulation: Theory, Strategy and Practice* (Oxford University Press 1999) 125 et seq; Giandomenico Majone, *Dilemmas of European Integration. The Ambiguities and Pitfalls of Integration by Stealth* (Oxford University Press 2005) 102–03.

[45] See for example CF Sabel and J Zeitlin, *Experimentalist Governance in the European Union: Towards a New Architecture* (Oxford University Press 2010) and, in the context of private regulation, Colin Scott, 'Reflexive Governance, Regulation and Meta-Regulation: Control or Learning?' in Olivier de Schutter and Jacques Lenoble (eds), *Reflexive Governance: Redefining the Public Interest in a Pluralistic World* (Hart 2010). Similarly, Snyder (n 27) 441 speaks of private lawmaking as 'molecular federalism' that achieves the benefits of diversity and experimentation.

multi-stakeholder forms of regulation where actors with clearly divergent interests and approaches are consulted.

Private regulation can, however, be seen through less rose-tinted glasses. Wouters, Marx, and Hachez note that 'the actions of private actors may lack transparency for the public and are not usually controlled by a system of checks and balances as are those of public authorities'.[46] Its domination by industry experts and insiders can lead to regulatory capture by well-organized groups with narrow but strong interests.[47] Its ability to show 'equal respect and regard for all relevant individuals and groups and their interests and concerns'[48] can be questionable because it tends to be specialized and compartmentalized, and even the cases when it does involve a wide variety of stakeholders can be regarded as mere window-dressing. Its flexibility can be equated with a lack of transparency or predictability of the rules and procedures applied.

In addition, just like any other kind of regulation, private regulation can be unreasonable, disproportionate, or economically inefficient. In Stewart's terms, it can show *disregard* either procedurally (by failing to seek or provide information, failing to provide access to decision-making procedures, or failing to reason their decisions) or substantively (by discriminating or ignoring relevant concerns).[49] In the EU context, these failings may also pose a risk for (market) integration. The risks may be more acute because private regulation is not always fully subject to legal controls such as legislative reform or judicial review, especially if it operates on a transnational level.[50]

An important question raised by the growth of private regulation is therefore how to preserve its benefits while ensuring accountability, transparency, participation, and due process.[51] Appropriate institutional design of the private regulator in line with good governance principles can go a long way, for example by ensuring a meaningful debate in its decision-making bodies, transparency, consultations, and mechanisms of appeal. Beyond that, however, it has been claimed that

[46] Jan Wouters, Axel Marx, and Nicolas Hachez, 'Private Standards, Global Governance and Transatlantic Cooperation: The Case of Global Food Safety Governance', Leuven Centre for Global Governance Studies Working Paper, 18. See also Julia Black, 'Constitutionalising Self-Regulation' (1996) 59 Modern Law Review 24.

[47] The concept of capture fits more easily with co-regulation, as private participants in the scheme can exercise a strong influence on the State bodies involved. Even within purely private regulatory schemes, however, one could speak of capture by a well-organized minority interest. On the difficulty of defining when capture has actually occurred, see M Elizabeth Magill, 'Courts and Regulatory Capture' in Daniel Carpenter, David A Moss (eds), *Preventing Regulatory Capture: Special Interest Influence and How to Limit it* (Cambridge University Press 2013).

[48] Richard B Stewart, 'Remedying Disregard in Global Regulatory Governance: Accountability, Participation, and Responsiveness' (2014) 108 American Journal of International Law 211, 212.

[49] ibid 224. [50] ibid 225.

[51] The Opinion of AG Maduro in Joined cases C-570/07 and C-571/07 *José Manuel Blanco Pérez and María del Pilar Chao Gómez v Consejería de Salud y Servicios Sanitarios* (C-570/07) *and Principado de Asturias* (C-571/07) [2010] ECR I-4629, para 20, points out a tension between the benefits of proximity to the subject matter of regulation and the resulting danger of regulatory capture, proposing a requirement of 'coherence and consistency' as part of the proportionality analysis.

more effective external controls, such as judicial review,[52] need to be placed on private regulators.

5. Private Regulation and EU Policies

The EU has proven to be fertile ground for private regulation. Starting from the 1980s and the so-called 'new approach to harmonisation', which lays down only general principles through legislation and leaves the details to EU-level standard-setting bodies, and especially after the Better Regulation Program of 2002,[53] private actors have often been given explicit roles in the shaping and implementation of EU policies. The Inter-institutional Agreement on Better Law-making of 2003 ('IIA') promotes the use of both co-regulation, 'whereby a Community legislative act entrusts the attainment of the objectives defined by the legislative authority to parties which are recognised in the field, such as economic operators, the social partners, nongovernmental organisations, or associations' and self-regulation, defined as 'the possibility for economic operators, the social partners, non-governmental organizations or associations to adopt amongst themselves and for themselves common guidelines at European level'. The IIA lays down the procedural and substantive conditions for using co-regulation and self-regulation in legislation and subjects it to review by the Commission.[54] It attempts, less than convincingly, to prohibit their use 'where fundamental rights or important political options are at stake' (when are they not?) or 'where the rules must be applied in a uniform fashion in all Member States'.

Internal market regulation in particular has embraced co-regulatory strategies. In that context, the Commission has welcomed 'flexible approaches to legislation', which 'involve national authorities and/or relevant sectors in deciding on regulatory detail, to ensure that regulation is designed as closely to the market as possible'.[55] It advocates the use of self- and co-regulation, including voluntary

[52] 'Depending on the institutional design [private regulation] can also produce legal disintegration if private rule-making monopolies arise in the absence of conflict of interest rules and without subjecting the private regulatory activity to effective judicial review.' Fabrizio Cafaggi, 'Private Regulation in European Private Law' EUI RSCAS WP 2009/31, 6. See also Black (n 46).

[53] Commission Action Plan 'Simplifying and improving the regulatory environment' (Communication) COM(2002) 278 final. See European Economic and Social Committee, 'The Current State of Co-Regulation and Self-Regulation in the Single Market' (2005) EESC Pamphlet Series for an assessment of actual examples of co- and self-regulation, and the Opinion of the European Economic and Social Committee on Self-regulation and co-regulation in the Community legislative framework (2015) INT/754 for a more recent review.

[54] Interinstitutional Agreement on Better Law-making (n 34) paras 18–23. At the time of writing, the Commission is about to propose a new IIA.

[55] Commission, 'Instruments for a modernised single market policy—Accompanying document to the Communication from the Commission to the European Parliament, the Council, the European Economic and Social Committee and the Committee of the Regions—A single market for 21st century Europe (Commission staff working document) SEC/2007/1518 final', section 2.2.

standard setting and industry codes of conduct, as an 'alternative or complement' to legislation. On the other hand, while it points out the advantages of private regulation such as adaptability, speed, diversity, and stakeholder inclusion, the Commission has also highlighted the risk of anti-competitive collusion or abuse, and the need to involve all relevant stakeholders in order to prevent regulatory capture.[56] Informal attempts at engaging with private regulators, such as the Commission's Community of Practice for better self- and co-regulation,[57] are also being used.

EU legislation increasingly relies on private actors for its implementation. The Services Directive provides for the adoption of European codes of conduct for various professions.[58] The Market Abuse Directive,[59] the General Product Safety Directive,[60] and the Audiovisual Media Services Directive,[61] among others,[62] also envisage a supporting role for private actors or a form of recognition of private regulation. Even when private regulation is not directly relied upon by EU legislation, CJEU case-law sometimes refers to it. In *Commission v Luxembourg* and *Wilson*, rules of the CCBE (Council of Bar Associations of Europe) on professional competence were invoked as a sufficient guarantee against the necessity of national laws requiring language tests for foreign-trained lawyers.[63]

In these ways, EU law legitimizes private regulation. Often, as in the Services Directive, it is highlighted that this political recognition comes at a price: even when helping achieve an EU public policy, self- and co-regulation must respect

The Lamfalussy process (a flexible regulatory method used in securities, banking, insurance, and pension sectors) and 'New Approach' standardization were mentioned as examples.

56 ibid, section 2.3.

57 See <https://ec.europa.eu/digital-agenda/en/community-practice-better-self-and-co-regulation-0>. The Community of Practice has developed Principles for Better Self- and co- Regulation, 'designed to offer guidance in cases where two or more actors (public or private) decide to work together to improve the status quo'.

58 Panagiotis Delimatsis, '"Thou Shall Not … (Dis) Trust": Codes of Conduct and Harmonization of Professional Standards in the EU' (2010) 47 Common Market Law Review 1049. See, in particular, Directive 2006/123/EC of the European Parliament and of the Council on services in the internal market [2006] OJ L376, recital 114 and Art 37/1.

59 Directive 2003/6/EC of the European Parliament and of the Council of 28 January 2003 on insider dealing and market manipulation (market abuse) [2003] OJ L96/16 Arts 11 and 12.

60 Directive 2001/95/EC of the European Parliament and of the Council on general product safety [2002] OJ L11/4. According to its Art 3/3, 'the conformity of a product to the general safety requirement shall be assessed by taking into account … (a) voluntary national standards transposing relevant European standards … (b) the standards drawn up in the Member State in which the product is marketed … (d) product safety codes of good practice in force in the sector concerned; (e) the state of the art and technology …'

61 Directive 2010/13/EU of the European Parliament and of the Council on the coordination of certain provisions laid down by law, regulation or administrative action in Member States concerning the provision of audiovisual media services [2010] OJ L95/1. Under Art 9/2, 'Member States and the Commission shall encourage media service providers to develop codes of conduct regarding inappropriate audiovisual commercial communications.'

62 For a recent, extensive list of examples, see Appendix II to the EESC Opinion on Self-regulation and co-regulation in the Community legislative framework (n 53).

63 Case C-193/05 *Commission v Luxembourg* [2006] ECR I-8673 and Case C-506/04 *Graham J. Wilson v Ordre des avocats du barreau de Luxembourg* [2006] ECR I-8613. See Chapter VI section 4.3.

the requirements of the competition and free movement rules.[64] Through this bargain, it can be argued, EU law attempts to discipline private regulation while preserving its benefits. This idea will reappear throughout the book, and will be explored in the following section.

6. EU Law and Scrutiny Over Private Regulation

The judicial supervision of private regulation is often not possible in national legal orders due to constitutional constraints or the prevailing legal doctrine. The divide between public and private law is highly relevant on the national level, and a regulatory role of private actors sits uneasily with the doctrines and mechanisms developed for the control of public bodies.[65] For example, the application of constitutional provisions to private parties in German law is limited to so-called 'mittelbare Drittwirkung', an interpretative duty for the courts.[66] In English law, as Donnelly notes, there are obstacles to judicially reviewing cases of delegation to private actors; in particular, 'where private actors exercise governance functions by virtue of legislation, public law provides virtually no control'.[67] Because of this, it is not always possible to apply principles such as legality, transparency, openness, statement of reasons, and judicial review to private regulation, making it difficult to address the problems discussed in section 4 on the national level.

To some extent, this can be compensated by the judicial and administrative review of private regulators at the level of the EU.[68] As described above, the EU has accepted private or hybrid regulatory forms as a part of its own regulatory mix, on the condition of compliance with free movement and competition disciplines. The case-law of the CJEU makes it clear that both competition law and free movement law are capable of being applied to private regulators, even when their actions are protected by some sort of legal autonomy under national law. These two sets of rules, then, have some potential in addressing the drawbacks of increased reliance on private regulation.

[64] Recital 113 states, inter alia: 'Those codes of conduct should comply with Community law, especially competition law. They should be compatible with legally binding rules governing professional ethics and conduct in the Member States.'

[65] Black (n 46) 24 notes: 'When faced with the question of whether and how to review the decisions of self-regulatory associations (SRAs), the [UK courts'] current response is based on where it draws the boundary between public and private law. [This] is notoriously uncertain, couched largely in procedural terms and dogged by tensions between the role of the body and the legal nature of its relations with its members [...]'

[66] See for example Joanna Krzeminska-Vamvaka, 'Horizontal Effect of Fundamental Rights and Freedoms—Much Ado About Nothing? German, Polish and EU Theories Compared After Viking Line' Jean Monnet Working Paper 11/09, especially section II.

[67] Donnelly (n 24) 177.

[68] 'EU level' can mean either judicial review before the Court of Justice or the General Court, or review by national courts in application of EU law, perhaps but not necessarily in the context of a ruling on a preliminary reference given by the ECJ. In competition law, review over private regulation is most frequently pursued by national competition authorities and the Commission, subject to judicial review by national courts or the General Court, but can also take place in a preliminary reference procedure.

Either as a cause or consequence of these case-law developments, the EU legal order is not based on a systematic distinction between private and public law.[69] As I will argue in more detail in Chapters II and III, the application of neither competition nor free movement law can be adequately explained by a simple version of a public–private divide. Insofar as EU law accepts a public–private distinction, it is a functional one. It is not so much about *ex ante* classifications of actors as public or private in an abstract, 'objective' sense, but rather a form of *ex post* justification for limiting the reach of its disciplines on a case-by-case basis.[70] This aligns neatly with the functionalist, effects-focused approach of EU law that disregards diverging national public–private law distinctions in order to ensure that EU rules are applied uniformly and to 'overcome formalism, doctrinalism and rule-centredness in comparative (private) law'.[71]

It should also not be disregarded that EU legislation can be used to discipline private regulators. Any legal act that can impose requirements on private actors is a kind of control mechanism. In the EU context that would clearly include regulations, but even a directive (which in principle cannot be invoked directly against a private party)[72] could fulfil that role, either through its indirect or interpretative effect,[73] or through its implementation into the national law of a Member State. However, what this book will address is narrower: EU legislation which is either motivated by the need to control the behaviour of private regulators, or which explicitly imposes requirements on private actors in their regulatory capacity. Chapters VI and VII provide several examples of such legislation in the context of the legal profession and standard setting.

In the best-case scenario, EU free movement and competition rules, together with legislation, have the potential not only to safeguard the internal market from private regulatory impediments to competition and trade, but also, as a side effect, to make private regulation more legitimate and more effective in the pursuit of goals such as health and safety or environmental protection. Of course, to what extent this ideal can actually be realized is a separate matter, and one that is likely to be highly sector- and case-specific.

[69] Loïc Azoulai, 'Sur un sens de la distinction public/privé dans le droit de l'Union européenne' in Sophie Robin-Olivier, Okeoghene Odudu, and Loïc Azoulai (eds), *The Public/Private Divide in European Union Law* vol WP 2010/7 (CEJEC 2010). For more details, see Chapter II section 3.

[70] As AG Ruiz-Jarabo Colomer remarked: '[T]he distinction between public and private undertakings, for the purposes of the Treaty, cannot be based merely on the identity of its various shareholders, but depends on the opportunity available to the State to impose specific objectives of economic policy other than the pursuit of the greatest financial gain which characterises private business.' Opinion in Case C-367/98 *Commission v Portugal* [2002] ECR I-4731, para 55.

[71] Constanze Semmelmann, 'The Public–Private Divide in European Union Law or an Overkill of Functionalism' (2012) Maastricht European Private Law Institute Working Paper 2012/12 14. See also Constanze Semmelmann, 'Theoretical Reflections on the Public–Private Distinction and their Traces in European Union Law' Oñati Socio-legal Series [online] 2(4) 25.

[72] Case C-91/92 *Paola Faccini Dori v Recreb Srl* [1994] ECR I-3325. See also Art 288 TFEU on the effect of regulations and directives.

[73] This would require national courts to interpret domestic legislation in light of the provisions of directives, even those that do not satisfy the conditions for direct effect. See Case 14/83 *Sabine von Colson and Elisabeth Kamann v Land Nordrhein-Westfalen* [1984] ECR 1891.

In this sense, EU law instruments can become a kind of 'meta-regulation' of private regulators. Meta-regulation refers to 'ways that outside regulators ... seek to induce targets to develop their own internal, self-regulatory responses to public problems'.[74] It involves shifting some discretion to private regulators, which can be justified in particular by their informational advantages.[75] From the point of view of the private regulator, meta-regulation can be attractive as it facilitates conditional recognition of their practices by public actors.[76] As I will explore in later chapters, this trade-off is highly relevant to the legal analysis of private regulation in both free movement and competition law. The general recognition of their legitimacy, as well as frequent deference to their measures on a case-by-case basis, goes hand-in-hand with exposure to judicial review and other forms of legal control.

In the following sections, I will briefly explain how the three control mechanisms I have identified—competition law, free movement law, and EU legislation—can be used to scrutinize private regulation.

6.1 Competition and free movement: An uncertain relationship

A number of doctrines developed in free movement and competition law facilitate their application to private or co-regulatory arrangements. The free movement rules can be applied directly to private actors (so-called 'horizontal effect') in a rather unclear set of circumstances which includes a number of cases of private regulation. Competition law, on the other hand, can be applied to co-regulatory schemes or even directly to the measures of the Member States. This has been described as the 'publicisation' of competition law and 'privatisation' of free movement law.[77] This extension of their functions has led to an overlap between them, of which cases of private regulation constitute a major part.

This development would not likely have been foreseen by the initial drafters of the EC Treaties. The conventional point of view is that there is a clear dividing line: private restraints to cross-border competition are covered by the competition rules and public restraints by the free movement rules.[78] In this reading, the

[74] Cary Coglianese and Evan Mendelson, 'Meta-regulation and Self-regulation' in Martin Cave, Robert Baldwin, and Martin Lodge (eds), *The Oxford Handbook of Regulation* (Oxford University Press 2010) 150.

[75] ibid 152–53. 'When problems are highly complex or poorly understood, or when regulatory targets are sufficiently diverse that one-size rules do not fit all, regulators might find the best option is to adopt a meta-regulation strategy or simply allow self-regulation to flourish on its own' (ibid 163).

[76] Jacco Bomhoff and Anne Meuwese, 'The Meta-regulation of Transnational Private Regulation' (2011) 38 Journal of Law and Society 138, 139.

[77] See Denis Waelbroeck, 'Les rapports entre les règles sur la libre circulation des marchandises et les règles de concurrence applicables aux entreprises dans la CEE' in Francesco Capotorti and Pierre Pescatore (eds), *Du droit international au droit de l'intégration: liber amicorum Pierre Pescatore* (Nomos 1987) 786, as well as Robert Lane, 'The internal market and the individual' in Shuibhne Niamh Nic (ed), *Regulating the Internal Market* (Edward Elgar 2006) 246.

[78] See for example Wolf Sauter and Harm Schepel, *State and Market in European Union Law: The Public and Private Spheres of the Internal Market Before the EU Courts* (Cambridge University Press 2009) 103. For more details, see Chapter II section 3.

threshold question in borderline or overlap cases would be the classification of certain conduct as public or private. After all, the Court itself frequently points out that the competition rules are directed at actions of undertakings, and the free movement provisions at the actions of the Member States.[79]

The case-law, however, clearly shows the limits of such a bright-line approach. In the actual assessment of measures under the free movement and competition rules, the Court follows a functional approach that focuses on the specific activity that is being challenged, rather than on the public or private status of the regulator. In free movement analysis, the broad understanding of what constitutes Member State measures[80] enables the capture of a wide variety of conduct. In competition analysis, the analogous device is the flexible reading of the concepts of 'undertaking' and 'economic activity'.[81] The definitions of economic activity are somewhat different under the two sets of rules,[82] but they would still allow a wide variety of conduct to fall under either. The overlap between the two sets of rules is also favoured by the broad understanding of what constitutes a restriction. On the one hand, the free movement rules are more than a ban on discriminatory or protectionist measures. They also protect market access 'under conditions of effective competition'[83] and thus, to some extent, overlap with the functions of competition law. On the other hand, the competition rules are strongly influenced by the ideal of market integration, disciplining restrictions on parallel trade.[84] Thus, they overlap with the functions of free movement.

For these reasons, the spheres of application of the two sets of rules cannot be clearly separated, at least not in the case of private regulation. The public–private divide is of little help in addressing that overlap since it merely restates the original questions with which either of those sets of rules struggles when deciding its own limits.

In the subsequent sections, I will separately address in some more detail the specificities of competition and free movement law as applied to private regulators. These will serve as a brief introduction. The rules will be discussed in Chapters II and III, and the relationship between them will be the subject of Chapter IV.

[79] See for example Joined cases 177 and 178/82 *Criminal Proceedings Against Jan van de Haar and Kaveka de Meern BV* [1984] ECR 1797, paras 11–14.

[80] Sauter and Schepel (n 78) 43 et seq.

[81] ibid 75 et seq. Famously, the Court has held that the concept of an undertaking encompasses *'every entity engaged in an economic activity, regardless of the legal status of the entity and the way in which it is financed'* (Case C-41/90 *Klaus Höfner and Fritz Elser v Macrotron GmbH* [1991] ECR I-1979, para 21).

[82] See for example Okeoghene Odudu, 'Economic Activity as a Limit to Community Law' in Catherine Barnard and Okeoghene Odudu (eds), *The Outer Limits of European Union Law* (Hart 2009).

[83] Case C-565/08 *Commission v Italy* [2011] ECR I-2101, para 51.

[84] See for example Joined cases C-468/06 to C-478/06 *Sot. Lélos kai Sia EE and Others v GlaxoSmithKline AEVE Farmakeftikon Proïonton, formerly Glaxowellcome AEVE* [2008] ECR I-7139.

6.2 Competition law

Competition law in the EU and elsewhere walks the line between protecting competition by disciplining abuses of market power and preserving free markets by limiting its own intervention. This reflects unease about the capacity of decision-makers to decide which market practices are beneficial and which are not, as well as a desire to protect private autonomy. As a consequence, both the most aggressive applications and the most reluctant abstentions of competition law can be justified by the need to protect free markets. As Amato writes:

> Here, then, is the dilemma. How can private power be prevented from becoming a threat to the freedoms of others? But at the same time, how can power conferred on institutions for this purpose be prevented from itself enlarging to the point of destroying the very freedoms it ought to protect?[85]

This unease is magnified when private regulation is concerned because the discussion is not just about 'private autonomy' in the strict sense. With private regulation, competition law has to address the various regulatory objectives pursued by private actors, that is deal with a sort of 'regulatory autonomy'. Thus, while controlling the concentration of economic power in the hands of private actors is a task of the competition rules, private regulation was probably not a concept their initial drafters had in mind. Nevertheless, private regulation with an impact in the marketplace was quickly seen to fall under the rules. They were applied, for example, to the sporting bodies,[86] bar associations,[87] private standard-setting bodies,[88] copyright collecting societies,[89] a European association of broadcasters,[90] self-regulation in the cognac, wine,[91] and beef industries,[92] etc.

On reflection, regulatory activity of private actors may be particularly apt for competition law scrutiny. When private regulators bring together a number of competitors in a certain sector, such as in the cases of professional associations, sports leagues, or industry standard-setting bodies, they do so in order to agree

[85] Giuliano Amato, *Antitrust and the Bounds of Power: The Dilemma of Liberal Democracy in the History of the Market* (Hart 1997) 3.

[86] See Chapter V. [87] See Chapter VI. [88] See Chapter VII.

[89] Case 127-73 *Belgische Radio en Televisie and société belge des auteurs, compositeurs et éditeurs v SV SABAM and NV Fonior* [1974] ECR 51; Joined cases 110/88, 241/88, and 242/88 *François Lucazeau and others v Société des Auteurs, Compositeurs et Editeurs de Musique (SACEM) and others* [1989] ECR 2811; Case C-52/07 *Kanal 5 Ltd and TV 4 AB v Föreningen Svenska Tonsättares Internationella Musikbyrå (STIM) upa* [2008] ECR I-9275.

[90] Joined cases T-185/00, T-216/00, T-299/00, and T-300/00 *Métropole Télévision SA (M6)* (T-185/00), *Antena 3 de Televisión, SA* (T-216/00), *Gestevisión Telecinco, SA* (T-299/00) *and SIC - Sociedade Independente de Comunicação, SA* (T-300/00) *v Commission* [2002] ECR II-3805.

[91] Case 123/83 *Bureau national interprofessionnel du cognac v Guy Clair* [1985] ECR 391.

[92] Case C-209/07 *Competition Authority v Beef Industry Development Society Ltd and Barry Brothers (Carrigmore) Meats Ltd* [2008] ECR I-8637. This case is a borderline example: while it could be described as a form of industry self-regulation, it may be more correct to say it is a straightforward cartel. For more on this uncertain (and perhaps not entirely helpful) distinction, see Imelda Maher, 'Competition Law and Transnational Private Regulatory Regimes: Marking the Cartel Boundary' (2011) 38 Journal of Law and Society 119.

on some common rules or co-ordinate the activities of members. This is close to the definition of a cartel, or at least a 'horizontal agreement' under Art 101 TFEU. When a powerful single actor, whether a firm or an industry association (often the difference is not clear, as an entity can have both a regulatory role in controlling access to a market and compete in that same market),[93] is able to adopt rules affecting its competitors, it is likely to be seen as having or even abusing a dominant position.

Competition law has, on the other hand, had to adapt to private regulation, especially co-regulation, in a number of ways. Firstly, the Court has developed a doctrine under which the competition rules can be applied to the Member States when they facilitate or require anticompetitive behaviour.[94] In co-regulation, therefore, both the private actors and the public bodies involved, or even the Member State as such, can be liable. Secondly, competition law has found ways of leaving some policy space to private and co-regulatory schemes. Certain disputes about private regulation were thus resolved under an open-ended proportionality analysis, on the basis of the so-called 'inherent restriction' test (see Chapter III section 3.1.3). Private regulators might also, under certain conditions, avail themselves of the rules on services of general economic interest (Art 106/2 TFEU). A measure of deference to private regulation may be found even under the more conventional tests of Art 101/3 or 'objective justification' under Art 102, especially if economic arguments in favour of regulation, such as market failures, are used.[95]

6.3 Free movement law

In the EU context, apart from the competition rules, the rules on the free movement of goods, services, persons, capital, and the freedom of establishment may also be used as a mechanism for the scrutiny of private regulators, at least in some circumstances.

In comparison to the competition rules, the free movement rules are even more broadly formulated, in terms of both prohibitions and justifications.[96] Unlike competition law, they do not require a detailed economic or factual assessment, nor do they usually allow justifications on purely economic grounds. Proving the existence of market power, or showing a link between the market position of the measure's originator and its capacity to actually restrict market entry, is not normally an issue under the free movement rules. The Member States, whom the rules usually address, are always assumed to be capable of distorting competition.

Nevertheless, just as the competition rules are intended to cover marketplace behaviour but have spread to some forms of regulatory (and even State) action,

[93] See *MOTOE* (n 2). [94] See Chapter III section 3.2.

[95] See Chapter III section 3.1.5.

[96] This does not, however, mean that the free movement rules are always broader. See Chapter IV section 6.1.2.

the free movement rules are primarily addressed to Member State action but also cover some private conduct. This is usually called 'horizontal effect'.[97]

The extent to which the free movement rules can impose obligations on individuals is not clear. Certainly, the rules have caught a number of private regulators connected to the State through delegation or ex-post recognition (such as in the case of bar associations, whose regulations are often approved by the state,[98] or recognized standard-setting bodies whose standards are referenced in legislation).[99] An explicit supporting role of the State is, however, not necessary, as the case of sporting bodies shows.[100] The Court has long recognized the possibility of applying free movement rules not only 'to the action of public authorities but ... also to rules of any other nature aimed at regulating in a collective manner gainful employment and the provision of services'.[101] Private actors that effectively legislate for a certain sector despite having no clear connection to the State, such as sporting bodies, fall within that group. The private actor does not, however, even need to be in a quasi-legislative position. In *Laval* and *Viking Line*, trade unions engaged in collective bargaining and collective actions were caught by the free movement provisions.[102] Less clear (but, thankfully, also less of a concern for this book) is to what extent the free movement rules can be relied upon against private actors that have no regulatory role or other position of power.[103]

Based on the notion that private autonomy would be endangered by applying the free movement rules directly to private parties, it is frequently claimed that 'horizontal effect' should be limited. One of the suggestions is to only apply the rules to those private actors that are in fact in a position to restrict free movement,[104] for example by being able to create specific negative effects for cross-border (as opposed to intra-State) economic activity. Similarly, it has been argued that an impact-based *de minimis* test, tolerating restrictive conduct that does not have great market-distorting effects, should be adopted in free movement law, and especially (perhaps only) for private

[97] For criticism of the term 'horizontal direct effect' in this context, see Julio Baquero Cruz, *Between Competition and Free Movement: The Economic Constitutional Law of the European Community* (Hart 2002) 106–08.

[98] See Chapter VI. [99] See Chapter VII. [100] See Chapter V section 3.

[101] See Case 36-74 *BNO Walrave and LJN Koch v Association Union cycliste internationale, Koninklijke Nederlandsche Wielren Unie and Federación Española Ciclismo* [1974] ECR 1405, paras 17–18 and Case C-415/93 *Union royale belge des sociétés de football association ASBL v Jean-Marc Bosman, Royal club liégeois SA v Jean-Marc Bosman and others and Union des associations européennes de football (UEFA) v Jean-Marc Bosman* [1995] ECR I-4921, paras 82–83. See also Paul Verbruggen, 'The Public–Private Divide in Community Law: Exchanges Across the Divide' (2009) EUI Working Paper LAW 22/2009, 4–6.

[102] C-341/05 *Laval un Partneri Ltd v Svenska Byggnadsarbetareförbundet, Svenska Byggnadsarbetareförbundets avdelning 1, Byggettan and Svenska Elektrikerförbundet* [2007] ECR I-11767 and C-438/05 *International Transport Workers' Federation and Finnish Seamen's Union v Viking Line ABP and OÜ Viking Line Eesti* [2007] ECR I-10779.

[103] See Chapter II sections 2.3 and 2.4. A different line of case-law concerns the Member States' failure to prevent restrictions of free movement created by individuals (Case C-265/95 *Commission v France* [1997] ECR I-6959).

[104] See the Opinions of AG Maduro in *Viking Line* (n 102) and Case C-58/08 *The Queen, on the application of Vodafone Ltd and Others v Secretary of State for Business, Enterprise and Regulatory Reform* [2010] ECR I-4999.

actors.[105] Others have argued, for example, that the responsibility of private actors should be limited to non-discrimination, intentional action, etc.[106]

These limits are important, because private actors should be able to predict with some level of certainty when they will be subject to free movement rules and when not. As I will argue in Chapter II, however, clarifying the definition of a restriction and the possibilities of justification, in a way that does not simply revert to the dogma of the public–private divide, would provide ample possibilities for filtering out private conduct that does not harm the internal market. In addition, the case-law shows flexibility at the justification stage when private actors are concerned, granting private regulators a relatively broad policy space as long as they uphold good governance, participation, and non-discrimination standards. This reflects a more general argumentative shift from private to regulatory autonomy (see Chapter II section 4.2).

6.4 EU legislation

Finally, legislation can be and has been used to bind private regulators to EU law requirements. There are several examples of regulations and directives that, while primarily addressed to the Member States, also discipline private action.

The Services Directive, for example, explicitly states that it applies to 'the rules of professional bodies, or the collective rules of professional associations or other professional organizations, adopted in the exercise of their legal autonomy'.[107] Thus, while it is largely the Member States who are subject to the Directive's requirements, it specifically addresses private regulation as a potential entry barrier. It also provides for the adoption of EU-wide private Codes of Conduct in particular sectors, pointing out the need for them to be aligned with competition law.[108]

In the scope of the case studies analysed in this book, there are further examples of legislation that either specifically or incidentally address private regulators. In the area of the legal profession, two sector-specific and two general directives[109]

[105] See Pernilla Lindh, 'The Influence of Competition Law on Free Movement Rules' in Heikki Kanninen, Nina Korjus, and Allan Rosas (eds), *EU Competition Law in Contest: Essays in Honour of Virpi Tiili* (Hart 2009).

[106] See Chapter II section 4.1 for more details.

[107] More specifically, see Services Directive (n 61) Arts 3/7, 3/9, and 10.

[108] See also the Common Regulatory Framework for Electronic Communications, that is Directive 2002/21/EC of the European Parliament and of the Council on a common regulatory framework for electronic communications networks and services ('Framework Directive') [2002] OJ L108/33 and its various amending directives and regulations. The Framework addresses undertakings with significant market power (telecom incumbents), even though national regulatory agencies bear the supervisory responsibility.

[109] These are: Council Directive 77/249/EEC of 22 March 1977 to facilitate the effective exercise by lawyers of freedom to provide services (1977) OJ L78/17, Directive 98/5/EC of the European Parliament and of the Council of 16 February 1998 to facilitate practice of the profession of lawyer on a permanent basis in a Member State other than that in which the qualification was obtained [1998] OJ L77/36, Directive 2005/36/EC of the European Parliament and of the Council on the recognition of professional qualifications [2005] OJ L255/22 and the Services Directive (n 61). See Chapter VI section 4.

govern the practices of professional bodies, in particular those regulating the entry of attorneys from other Member States into their market. In standard setting, the recognized standard-setting bodies are subject to a set of procedural and reporting rules by a regulation,[110] and some of their standards are adopted in order to implement various EU legislative instruments[111] and referenced in the Official Journal accordingly.

At this point, another interesting question that this book will not discuss in detail should also be flagged: whether the actions of private regulators that impede cross-border competition and trade could in themselves trigger EU legislative action. Since a growing segment of regulatory tasks is performed by private actors, one might argue that it would not fully reflect reality to read Art 114 TFEU, the traditional legal basis for EU internal market legislation which enables the 'the approximation of the provisions laid down by law, regulation, or administrative action in Member States which have as their object the establishment and functioning of the internal market', as referring only to Member States' measures.

Of course, the case-law makes clear that the EU does not have 'a general power to regulate the internal market'.[112] Normally, Art 114 TFEU can be a legal basis for EU legislation when the differences in the laws of the Member States create appreciable distortions of competition,[113] or at least if there is a danger that divergent laws will arise if the EU does not act.

In *Vodafone*, however, AG Maduro suggested that private restrictions to free movement—and therefore to the establishment of the internal market—could in themselves provide the EU with harmonization competence. As he put it: 'if the Community can prohibit a certain action by a private party it should be competent to simply regulate that action'.[114] The Court did not follow this approach. On the other hand, it did not explicitly reject it either, and its reappearance in future cases is not excluded.[115]

[110] Regulation (EU) No 1025/2012 of the European Parliament and of the Council of 25 October 2012 on European standardisation [2012] OJ L316/12. The notification obligations for 'de facto' technical regulations under Directive 98/34/EC of the European Parliament and of the Council of 22 June 1998 laying down a procedure for the provision of information in the field of technical standards and regulations and of rules on Information Society services [1998] OJ L 204/37 may also be relevant for private regulators. See Chapter VII section 2.1.

[111] For example, the Regulation (EU) 305/2011 of the European Parliament and of the Council of 9 March 2011 laying down harmonised conditions for the marketing of construction products and repealing Council Directive 89/106/EEC [2011] OJ L88/5. For more details, see Chapter VII section 2.2.

[112] Case C-376/98 *Germany v European Parliament and Council* [2000] ECR I-8419, para 83.

[113] *Tobacco Advertising* (n 112) paras 106–08.

[114] Opinion of AG Maduro in *Vodafone* (n 104) para 22. While the AG did not clarify in general terms the circumstances that could give rise to such EU intervention, he deemed excessive differences in prices between local and roaming calls to be sufficient, because they have a direct negative impact on cross-border activity.

[115] For a discussion, see Martin Brenncke, 'Case C-58/08, *Vodafone Ltd and Others v. Secretary of State for Business, Enterprise and Regulatory Reform*, Judgment of the Court of Justice (Grand Chamber) of 8 June 2010' (2010) 47 Common Market Law Review 1793.

It is true that this case did not deal with private regulation under any definition of the term. In themselves, the pricing decisions of Vodafone, Telefonica, and other telecoms are ordinary market behaviour. However, if independent pricing decisions could suffice to bring about internal market legislation that regulates roaming prices, one would expect that private regulation that covers entire sectors of industry or engages in partnerships with the Member States can be covered *a fortiori*. The case-law on EU competences may, thus, be a source of interesting future developments.

7. Outline and Methodology

The book will be structured as follows. The first several chapters will be general in their approach. Chapter II will look at the application of free movement to private regulation, focusing specifically on two issues: the limits of horizontal effect and the specificities of the legal tests, in particular justifications, when dealing with private actors. I will discuss the judgments of the Court where the free movement rules were applied to private actors, focusing on the different regulatory roles of the actors that were challenged.

Chapter III looks at competition law, arguing that EU antitrust law applies a broad approach that rarely excludes private regulation from scrutiny, but nevertheless opens up possibilities for exonerating regulatory practices even if they lead to inefficient outcomes. This broad approach is traced through decisions of the General Court and Court of Justice as well as Commission decisions in various sectors. I distinguish the application of competition law directly to private regulators and to the State through the 'effet utile' doctrine or the rules on special and exclusive rights. Bringing together diverse strains of case-law on Art 101, Art 102, special and exclusive rights and services of general economic interest, I will look at the attempt of EU competition law to internalize potential conflicts between competition and other regulatory objectives.

Chapter IV builds on Chapters II and III in order to address the problem of overlap between competition and free movement law. By looking at the judgments and Commission decisions where the two sets of rules were or could have been applied simultaneously, I discuss to what extent they are or should be convergent or if, conversely, we should strictly separate them to prevent overlap. The Court's strategy, I find, is somewhere in between, treating them as clearly distinct legal tests but tolerating overlap and even using hybrid arguments that show the two sets of rules influencing each other.

The final three chapters deal with the case studies already discussed in this introductory chapter: sport (Chapter V), the legal profession (Chapter VI), and standard setting (Chapter VII). In these case studies, I follow a similar methodology. I first look separately at the enforcement of competition law and free movement law against private regulation in the sector by the Court, the Commission, and, to a limited extent, by national competition authorities. I also look at internal market legislation that is relevant for private regulators in the legal profession and standard setting. In the area of sports, where there is little directly relevant legislation, I focus on various policy documents and soft law. Then, I look at the overlap and interplay of free movement and competition in cases specific to those sectors.

All three case studies will examine to what extent EU competition and free movement law challenge or, rather, defer to the substantive decisions of private regulators. All three will also look at the important role of institutional[116] and procedural concerns in explaining the extent of application of competition and free movement, and not just the 'objective' requirements of legal doctrine. Finally, Chapter VIII presents some general conclusions.

[116] See, for example, Cass R Sunstein and Adrian Vermeule, 'Interpretation and Institutions' University of Chicago Law & Economics, Olin Working Paper No 156 and Neil K Komesar, *Imperfect Alternatives: Choosing Institutions in Law, Economics, and Public Policy* (University of Chicago Press 1994).

II

Free Movement and Private Regulation

1. Introduction: Horizontal Effect and the *Effet Utile* of EU Law

The behaviour of private actors holding market power is normally scrutinized by antitrust law. In EU law, however, there is a peculiarity: the potential application of the free movement rules. These rules of the Treaty prohibit restrictions on the free movement of goods, services, capital, persons, and the freedom of establishment, enabling challenges to measures that discriminate or impede market access in the Member States. They relate primarily to the actions of the Member States themselves, such as laws or administrative measures. Their wording does not seem to exclude private actors and measures,[1] but it does not explicitly address them either, and the vast majority of free movement claims are brought against the Member States. In a number of judgments of the Court of Justice, however, the free movement rules were interpreted as creating duties for private actors, which is usually described as 'horizontal effect'.[2]

The traditional justification for this is the useful effect of EU law. EU law's ability to reach individuals directly, not just through the medium of the Member States, is a major element of the process of its constitutionalization.[3] Famously, the 'vigilance of individuals' in protecting their own rights was cited

[1] TFEU Art 34: 'Quantitative restrictions on imports and all measures having equivalent effect shall be prohibited between Member States'; Art 45: '1. Freedom of movement for workers shall be secured within the Union; 2. Such freedom of movement shall entail the abolition of any discrimination based on nationality between workers of the Member States as regards employment, remuneration and other conditions of work and employment'; Art 49: 'Within the framework of the provisions set out below, restrictions on the freedom of establishment of nationals of a Member State in the territory of another Member State shall be prohibited'; Art 56: 'Within the framework of the provisions set out below, restrictions on freedom to provide services within the Union shall be prohibited in respect of nationals of Member States who are established in a Member State other than that of the person for whom the services are intended'; and Art 63/1: 'Within the framework of the provisions set out in this chapter, all restrictions on the movement of capital between Member States and between Member States and third countries shall be prohibited.'

[2] For criticism of the term 'horizontal direct effect', see Julio Baquero Cruz, *Between Competition and Free Movement: The Economic Constitutional Law of the European Community* (Hart 2002) 106–08.

[3] See Robert Lane, 'The Internal Market and the Individual' in Shuibhne Niamh Nic (ed), *Regulating the Internal Market* (Edward Elgar 2006) 245.

in *Van Gend & Loos*[4] both as an argument in favour of direct effect of EU law and as a way of guaranteeing its effectiveness. For similar reasons, the Court developed the *Francovich* doctrine of Member State liability for damages caused to individuals by violations of EU law,[5] as well as the *Courage* principle that competition law violations must be followed by adequate and dissuasive sanctions.[6]

It may seem natural, then, to say that where there is a right there should also be duties.[7] The application of the free movement to private actors is usually justified by more specific reasons, however.

Firstly, if individuals could not rely on EU law against the Member States, action by the Commission or the other Member States would be necessary. If individuals could not rely on EU law against other individuals, the consequences would be less obvious, but still damaging. In such a scenario, the only recourse would be to raise a claim against the Member State for tolerating a private restraint. That claim, however, might not be possible under domestic procedural rules, or there might be evidentiary hurdles (eg showing a causal link between Member State inaction and the actual infringement of EU law).[8] Bringing the case to the EU level would be doubly difficult, since the Commission would have to be persuaded to raise a dispute between individuals to the level of an infringement action against a Member State.

Secondly, in the free movement context, the 'useful effect' of EU law is expressed as the need to achieve market integration by removing regulatory barriers. As the case law confirms, these barriers may come in different guises: legislation and other legal acts, unwritten administrative practices, non-binding measures,[9] or simple failures to act.[10] This functionalist[11] approach, focusing on the effects instead of the legal form of a measure, is easily transposed from the question of

[4] Case 26-62 *NV Algemene Transport—en Expeditie Onderneming Van Gend & Loos v Netherlands Inland Revenue Administration* [1962] ECR 1, section B.

[5] Joined cases C-6/90 and C-9/90 *Andrea Francovich and Danila Bonifaci and others v Italian Republic* [1991] ECR I-5357. See also, among others, Joined cases C-46/93 and C-48/93 *Brasserie du Pêcheur SA v Bundesrepublik Deutschland and The Queen v Secretary of State for Transport, ex parte: Factortame Ltd and others* [1996] ECR I-1029 and Case C-224/01 *Gerhard Köbler v Republik Österreich* [2003] ECR I-10239.

[6] Case C-453/99 *Courage Ltd v Bernard Crehan and Bernard Crehan v Courage Ltd and Others* [2001] ECR I-6297.

[7] On this parallelism between rights and obligations for individuals, see Lane (n 3), 251 et seq. In fact, already in *Van Gend & Loos* (n 4), section B, the Court noted that 'independently of the legislation of Member States, Community law … not only imposes obligations on individuals but is also intended to confer upon them rights which become part of their legal heritage'.

[8] At the same time, this would not fully immunize private action from free movement scrutiny: to the extent that actions of individuals can be translated to liability of the Member State (such as in *Spanish Strawberries*, Case C-265/95 *Commission v France* [1997] ECR I-6959), there is no complete legal autonomy of individuals, but only an obstacle in the way of redress.

[9] Case C-470/03 *A.G.M.-COS.MET Srl v Suomen valtio and Tarmo Lehtinen* [2007] ECR I-2749.

[10] *Spanish Strawberries* (n 8).

[11] Wolf Sauter and Harm Schepel, *State and Market in European Union Law: The Public and Private Spheres of the Internal Market Before the EU Courts* (Cambridge University Press 2009) 23, 45.

what sort of measure restricts free movement to the question of *whose* measures restrict free movement. From a market integration standpoint, a Member State, one of its administrative bodies, or local entities, or a private actor involved in a co-regulatory scheme is equally capable of erecting barriers to free movement. In *Walrave*, one of the first cases of horizontal effect, the Court noted that working conditions can, depending on the Member State in question, be regulated either by laws or by 'agreements and other acts concluded or adopted by private persons'.[12] A Member State could thus deliberately avoid scrutiny by delegating. This anti-circumvention argument led the Court to impose obligations on a non-State cycling federation.[13]

The logic of 'useful effect', however, is simplistic and one-sided. It does not tell us how far the application of the free movement rules to private parties should go or whether it should be nuanced in comparison to the standard case of applying the rules to the Member States.[14]

This chapter will begin by outlining the different groups of cases where 'horizontal effect' was found to exist so far (section 2), after which I will make two main arguments. The first argument is that extending free movement scrutiny to some private actors, especially those that can be referred to as private regulators, is justified, not just due to the anti-circumvention argument just described but even when

[12] Case 36-74 *B.N.O. Walrave and L.J.N. Koch v Association Union cycliste internationale, Koninklijke Nederlandsche Wielren Unie and Federación Española Ciclismo* [1974] ECR 1405, para 19. This is all the more important given that the extent of participation of private actors in the regulatory 'mix' varies across Member States. See for example Catherine M Donnelly, *Delegation of Governmental Power to Private Parties: A Comparative Perspective* (Oxford University Press 2007).

[13] The Court was worried that 'the abolition of barriers of national origin could be neutralized by obstacles resulting from the exercise of their legal autonomy by associations ... which do not come under public law'. *Walrave* (n 12) paras 17–18; Case C-415/93 *Union royale belge des sociétés de football association ASBL v Jean-Marc Bosman, Royal club liégeois SA v Jean-Marc Bosman and others and Union des associations européennes de football (UEFA) v Jean-Marc Bosman* [1995] ECR I-4921, paras 82–83.

[14] The extent to which the free movement rules can impose obligations on individuals is not clear and has been the subject of many journal articles and even treatises over the years. See, inter alia, Derrick Wyatt, 'Horizontal Effect of Fundamental Freedoms and the Right to Equality after Viking and Mangold, and the Implications for Community Competence' (2008) 4 Croatian Yearbook of European Law and Policy 1; Baquero Cruz (n 2); Sacha Prechal and Sybe de Vries, 'Seamless Web of Judicial Protection in the Internal Market?' (2009) 34 European Law Review 5; GR Milner-Moore, 'The Accountability of Private Parties under the Free Movement of Goods Principle' (1995) Jean Monnet Working Paper 9/95; Aline-Maria Lengauer, *Drittwirkung Von Grundfreiheiten* (Springer 2011); Nicholas MacGowan and Mary Quinn, 'Could Article 30 Impose Obligations on Individuals?' (1987) 12 European Law Review 163; Harm Schepel, 'Constitutionalising the Market, Marketising the Constitution, and to Tell the Difference: On the Horizontal Application of the Free Movement Provisions in EU Law' (2012) 18 European Law Journal 177; Jukka Snell, 'Private Parties and the Free Movement of Goods and Services' in Mads Andenas and Wulf-Henning Roth (eds), *Services and Free Movement in EU Law* (Oxford University Press 2002); Christoph Krenn, 'A Missing Piece in the Horizontal Effect "Jigsaw": Horizontal Direct Effect and the Free Movement of Goods' (2012) 49 Common Market Law Review 177; Joanna Krzeminska-Vamvaka, 'Horizontal Effect of Fundamental Rights and Freedoms—Much Ado About Nothing? German, Polish and EU Theories Compared After Viking Line' Jean Monnet Working Paper 11/09; Lorna Woods, *Free Movement of Goods and Services within the European Community* (Ashgate 2004) ch 3; Malcolm Jarvis, 'Scope: Persons Bound' in Peter Oliver (ed), *Oliver on Free Movement of Goods in the European Union* (Hart 2010).

those actors exercise regulatory power without outright delegation (section 3). The chapter will attempt to move away from the standard approach of legal literature, which is based on a set of often unworkable versions of the public–private distinction and an ill-defined notion of private autonomy in order to either completely oppose or fully support the application of the free movement rules to private parties. Instead, I argue, the interpretation of the rules should adapt.

Building on that point, the second argument addresses when and how this scrutiny should apply. I will claim that the existing legal tests, elaborated in a more detailed way that takes into account the context of private regulation, are sufficient to protect the interests usually associated with the claim of private autonomy. I will also claim that EU free movement law has already engaged with private regulators in a way that reflects the regulatory nature of their activities, thus going beyond a simple public–private, regulation–market divide (section 4).

Before entering into those arguments, one issue must first be clarified. It concerns the difference between imposing duties—such as the duty not to discriminate or to enable market access—on private actors under the free movement rules (the substantive aspect of 'horizontal effect') and simply invoking them in a dispute between private parties (the procedural aspect).

The procedural aspect, in itself, does not raise the difficulties associated with the substantive one. Let us imagine a national law which prohibits the marketing of all imported beef. An imaginary plaintiff, a domestic beef producer, relies on that law to claim damages for lost business from a beef importer. Assuming—almost certainly correctly—that the law is contrary to Art 34 TFEU on the free movement of goods, could the national court ignore EU law because the parties are private? The answer is no. The law is an act of the legislature of a Member State, clearly bound by Art 34. As a violation of EU law, it has to be disapplied by the national court. This does not mean that distinct obligations are imposed on the domestic beef producer.[15] It is the Member State that infringed EU law by adopting legislation contrary to Art 34 TFEU.[16]

The difficulty, then, lies in the substantive version of horizontal effect: the ability of the free movement rules to directly impose duties on private actors. In the example from above, let us assume that the ban on marketing imported beef was imposed by an association covering the entire domestic retail industry. From the

[15] The position is different for directives, on which an individual may directly rely only against the State (this may be qualified by case law such as Case C-144/04 *Werner Mangold v Rüdiger Helm* [2005] ECR I-9981 and Case C-555/07 *Seda Kücükdeveci v Swedex GmbH & Co. KG* [2010] ECR I-365, where disputes between individuals were solved on the basis of fundamental rights of which a directive was a 'reflection'). But that can be explained by the particular nature of directives as measures that have to be transposed by the Member States, as opposed to the Treaty and regulations as directly effective sources of law. This distinction between directives and the Treaty is sometimes obscured by the use of similar language of 'horizontal effect' (see Baquero Cruz, n 2).

[16] Eleanor Spaventa, 'The Horizontal Application of Fundamental Rights as General Principles of Union Law' in Anthony Arnull and others (eds), *A Constitutional Order of States?: Essays in EU Law in Honour of Alan Dashwood* (Hart Publishing 2011) 209–10. Spaventa uses a similar example with the same outcome. For her, the question is whether the Treaty or secondary law give a free-standing cause of action against a private actor or not.

point of view of the importer, the market effects may be the same as with restrictive legislation. But is the legal situation different? Can an industry association not freely decide what kind of beef its members should be selling? Does the answer to that question depend on the market shares held by the associations' members? Does anything change if the association is somehow sponsored, authorized, or supervised by the state? This is where the interesting questions lie.

2. A Taxonomy of Private Action Under the Free Movement Rules

This section will provide a descriptive overview of the cases in which free movement scrutiny was applied to private actors so far.

Ever since *Walrave*, the Court has recognized the possibility of applying free movement rules not only 'to the action of public authorities but ... also to rules of any other nature aimed at regulating in a collective manner gainful employment and the provision of services'.

These early statements reveal most of all a concern with private actors in regulatory roles, setting *de facto* or *de iure* binding rules for accessing a profession or another economic activity. As the case law developed, however, it became clear that a 'quasi-legislative' role such as that played by the cycling association is not necessary.[17] Regulation, of course, involves more than rule-setting, and the free movement rules have been applied to cases far removed from the archetype of a 'private legislator'.

Instead of a chronological overview of the case law, therefore, it seems more helpful to classify the cases according to their regulatory character. The categories I use are co-regulation, private regulation, pure private relationships, and finally, private action based on restrictive legislation.[18] These distinctions, it should be

[17] See C-438/05 *International Transport Workers' Federation and Finnish Seamen's Union v Viking Line ABP and OÜ Viking Line Eesti* [2007] ECR I-10779, para 64: '... it does not follow from the case-law that [the possibility of relying on the free movement rules by a private undertaking against a trade union] applies only to quasi-public organisations or to associations exercising a regulatory task and having quasi-legislative powers.' Krzeminska-Vamvaka (n 14) 28–29. Contrary to some criticisms (eg Harm Schepel, 'Who's Afraid of the Total Market? On the Horizontal Application of the Free Movement Provisions in EU law' in Ioannis Lianos and Okeoghene Odudu (eds), *Regulating Trade in Services in the EU and the WTO—Trust, Distrust and Economic Integration* (Cambridge University Press 2012) 301, 306), this statement should not be read as a departure from *Walrave*, because 'collective regulation' or 'regulatory function' are broader concepts than 'quasi-legislation' or collective rule-setting.

[18] Different classifications have been proposed. Vassilis Hatzopoulos, *Regulating Services in the European Union* (Oxford University Press 2012) 302, distinguishes between the 'organizational rationale', 'object rationale', and 'effect rationale' of extending free movement scrutiny to private actors, and Peter Oliver and Wulf-Henning Roth, 'The Internal Market and the Four Freedoms' (2004) 41 Common Market Law Review 407 between 'collective private regulation' and 'purely private action'. Loïc Azoulai, 'The Court of Justice and the Social Market Economy: The Emergence of an Ideal and the Conditions for its Realization' (2008) 45 Common Market Law Review 1335, 1344 distinguishes between actions that can be imputed to the State, collective regulation of employment or self-employment, and discrimination in access to employment.

noted, are not watertight and should be seen as heuristic devices. Some cases will have some elements of both public and private regulation, or feature private actors in positions of power that may but need not be described as regulatory.

After discussing these categories in turn, I will touch upon the horizontal applicability of the rules on free movement of goods. I will treat that issue separately because of the traditional view—that I believe to be misplaced—that goods are a special case.

2.1 Co-regulation

As described in more detail in Chapter I, co-regulation in the broadest sense refers to public and private actors regulating together. The State can delegate tasks to private actors, recognize their decisions *ex post* through legislation, administrative, or judicial decisions. Alternatively (in the narrow understanding of co-regulation) the distribution of tasks between the State and private actors can be more complex, and it is not necessarily the State that takes the initiative. In all of these cases, the private regulator's link to the State amounts to more than simply being subject to its laws. The argument can be made that it is precisely that link to the State that triggers free movement scrutiny. This is the reason why horizontal direct effect in this group of cases has traditionally been the easiest to accept.[19]

In addition, this category of cases is by far the largest, although this is sometimes obscured by the fact that many of them are commonly not recognized as 'horizontal' cases, but rather as State restrictions of free movement. Despite this distinction, it is clear that non-State actors involved in co-regulatory schemes themselves, and not just the Member States as their 'guardians', are required to respect the free movement rules.

Some cases in this category concern straightforward delegation. In *Buy Irish*, the rules on free movement of goods were applied to a company formed in order to promote the Irish government's policy of import substitution, with the State subsidizing it, appointing its management board, and setting the broad aims of the pro-Irish goods campaign it conducted.[20] In *Apple & Pear Development Council*[21] and *Commission v Germany*,[22] regulatory authority was partly delegated to hybrid public–private actors. A ministerial decision (in the former) or law (in the latter) established these bodies and granted them powers such as charging mandatory membership fees to producers, collecting information, promoting product standardization, research, and advertising. On the other hand, both bodies were mostly

[19] See for example Stefan Leible, 'Fundamental Freedoms and European Contract Law' in Stefan Grundmann (ed), *Constitutional Values and European Contract Law* (Kluwer Law International 2008) 68, 74.

[20] Case 249/81 *Commission v Ireland* [1982] ECR 4005. The fact that the campaign 'formed part of a government programme' was considered to distinguish it from a purely private, non-binding advertising scheme (paras 15, 25–26).

[21] Case 222/82 *Apple and Pear Development Council v K.J. Lewis Ltd and others* [1983] ECR 4083.

[22] Case C-325/00 *Commission v Germany* [2002] ECR I-9977.

composed of representatives of private producers. Moreover, in *Commission v Germany*, the body had the legal form of a private company, and the certificate of 'German quality product' that it issued to producers was used on the basis of private licensing contracts. Thus, both schemes had a strong private element, even if their design could be traced back to the State.[23]

This private element did not exclude a restriction of the free movement of goods. In fact, it was precisely the hybridity of the regulatory scheme and the possibility of capture by producers that was suspect. In both cases, the industry body was 'obliged to respect the basic rules of the Treaty on the free movement of goods when it sets up a scheme, open to all undertakings of the sectors concerned, which can have effects on intra-Community trade similar to those arising under the scheme adopted by the public authorities'.[24] The bodies cannot 'enjoy the same freedom' as producers themselves or voluntary producers' organizations which, presumably, would not be held liable under the free movement rules.[25]

In *Royal Pharmaceutical Society* and *Hünermund*, similar findings were made in relation to professional bodies of pharmacists that were incorporated by the State and authorized to perform regulatory roles, such as maintaining mandatory registers of professional pharmacists and imposing disciplinary measures.[26]

More controversial are the cases where the level of State control over private actors was lower. Examples of this are *Laval* and—to a limited extent—its sibling *Viking Line*, where the free movement rules were applied to trade unions engaged in collective negotiation that led to strikes and boycotts.[27] An important aspect of these judgments was the Nordic labour tradition in which collective agreements negotiated by trade unions substitute for aspects of what would be, in many States,

[23] See also Case 29/82 *F. van Luipen en Zn BV against a disciplinary measure adopted against it* [1983] ECR 151, on the issue of mandatory membership in a similar private body.

[24] *Commission v Germany* (n 22) para 18.

[25] ibid. According to Snell (n 14) 220–21, the link with the Member State—by which he means 'all bodies through which the State is able to achieve a protectionist effect'—is key to these cases. Otherwise, 'actions of individuals or voluntary associations do not fall within the scope of the provision'. This test is fraught with difficulties. Firstly, it is clear that the free movement rules do not apply only to binding measures (*Buy Irish* (n 20), para 28). Therefore, the mere fact that membership in an association is voluntary cannot, as such, be enough to exclude a scheme from the free movement rules. After all, even a State body can have voluntary membership. Moreover, the 'protectionist effect' criterion assumes that the free movement rules themselves only cover protectionist measures, which decades of case law disproves.

[26] Joined cases 266/87 and 267/87 *The Queen v Royal Pharmaceutical Society of Great Britain, ex parte Association of Pharmaceutical Importers* [1989] ECR 1295, paras 14–16 and Case C-292/92 *Ruth Hünermund and others v Landesapothekerkammer Baden-Württemberg* [1993] ECR I-6787, paras 14–16. State controls on key appointments, the ability to issue binding instructions and approve the budget of a body also suffice to subject a body that is not formally part of the State apparatus to the free movement rules. Case C-302/88 *Hennen Olie BV v Stichting Interim Centraal Orgaan Voorraadvorming Aardolieprodukten and State of the Netherlands* [1990] ECR I-4625, paras 13–16.

[27] C-341/05 *Laval un Partneri Ltd v Svenska Byggnadsarbetareförbundet, Svenska Byggnadsarbetareförbundets avdelning 1, Byggettan and Svenska Elektrikerförbundet* [2007] ECR I-11767; *Viking Line* (n 17). See Azoulai (n 18), 1344–46 and ACL Davies, 'One Step Forward, Two Steps Back? The Viking and Laval Cases in the ECJ' (2008) 37 Industrial Law Journal 126, 135–36.

dealt with by labour legislation, such as setting a minimum wage for a particular sector. This regulatory role of trade unions is clear in *Laval*, where Sweden relied on trade unions to implement, through case-by-case negotiations, its minimum labour law requirements for posted workers under the eponymous Directive.[28]

The *Viking* judgment is more ambiguous, as it does not concern the implementation of a Directive.[29] On the one hand, it seems to be a straightforward private dispute between ship operators and trade unions. Following the 'State action is always present'[30] line, one could point out the fact that the unions were acting on the basis of specific Finnish rules protecting collective bargaining,[31] which also put collective agreements in a position different from standard contracts, regulating their applicability, the negotiation and conciliation process, etc. More interestingly, the 'flag of convenience' policy of the International Transport Workers' Federation allowed its members to conclude collective agreements only for vessels beneficially owned in their state and was effectively enforced by boycotts and collective action, amounting to a kind of transnational private regulation. These circumstances separate the situation from a simple private dispute, but do not rise to the level of co-regulation. In fact, it is questionable whether the situation in *Viking Line*—at least as far as only the local trade union's strike is concerned—creates the kind of effects that should give rise to free movement scrutiny under the test I will describe in this chapter.[32]

Putting *Viking Line* to one side, however, it is clear that co-regulation will as a rule give rise to free movement scrutiny, whether directly over the State, or over the hybrid or private bodies participating in the regulatory scheme.

2.2 (Purely) private regulation

In other regulatory schemes, the role of the State is not decisive. A private regulator of this kind,[33] such as a non-recognized standard-setting organization or a sporting body, does not owe its regulatory position to delegation or exclusive rights granted by the State, but to the consent of the relevant stakeholders. In market integration terms, the formal absence of links to the State is of little

[28] Directive 96/71/EC of the European Parliament and of the Council concerning the posting of workers in the framework of the provision of services [1997] OJ L18.

[29] The Court's own rationale for applying the free movement rules is not entirely clear, given that the Court simultaneously cites the non-circumvention argument from *Walrave* and the *Defrenne* reference to the 'mandatory nature' of Treaty provisions. See Loïc Azoulai, 'Sur un sens de la distinction public/privé dans le droit de l'Union européenne' in Sophie Robin-Olivier, Okeoghene Odudu, and Loïc Azoulai (eds), *The Public/Private Divide in European Union Law* WP 2010/7 (CEJEC 2010) 25. In any case, *Viking Line* makes it clear that the free movement rules apply in particular to 'all agreements intended to regulate paid labour collectively' (para 58).

[30] Cass R Sunstein, 'State Action Is Always Present' (2002) 3 Chicago Journal of International Law 465, 465–66.

[31] Paragraph 35.

[32] For the opposite view, see Azoulai (n 18) 1346.

[33] As explained in Chapter I, I prefer not to use the more common term 'self-regulation' in this context, as I also deal with schemes in which the targets of regulation are not the same as the regulators.

consequence. The withdrawal of an authorization to enter international sporting competitions or exclusion from participating in a standard can have just as much—or more—bite when imposed by a private regulator as through equivalent legislative restrictions.

Walrave and *Bosman* are two well-known examples.[34] In these judgments, the Court found both that the sporting associations' rules concern economic activity and that they restrict free movement. In *Deliège*, both points were confirmed even in relation to the rules of an amateur sport.[35] Sports regulation can sometimes come close to co-regulation, given that sport is frequently regulated by the Member States, at least to some extent. Importantly, however, such links with the State are not relied upon by the Court in its reasoning.

There are examples of purely private or self-regulation in other contexts as well. In *Ferlini*, an EU official was asked to pay a higher rate for the medical services than persons affiliated with the national insurance scheme. This discriminatory price was voluntarily fixed by an association assembling all Luxembourg hospitals.

Applying today's Art 18 TFEU, the general prohibition of discrimination based on nationality, the Court rephrased its case law from *Walrave* and *Bosman* in a very strong way:

> According to the case-law of the Court, the first paragraph of [Art 18] also applies in cases where a group or organisation ... exercises a certain power over individuals and is in a position to impose on them conditions which adversely affect the exercise of the fundamental freedoms guaranteed under the Treaty ...[36]

The key consideration, therefore, was the *de facto* power exercised by the association over individuals and its ability to affect their free movement rights. Links with the State did not seem to be a decisive factor, even though, as in most cases, they could have been found: in Luxembourg at the time, the prices fixed among the hospitals were part of a system that was at the very least co-organized by the State,[37] and even the association that actually charged Mr Ferlini the higher price, the CHL (Centre Hospitalier de Luxembourg), was a public body created by law and financed by the State.

[34] In *Lehtonen*, a case concerning the Finnish Basketball Association's implementation of the rules of its international counterpart FIBA, the Court summarized the test: '[P]rovisions on freedom of movement for persons and freedom to provide services do not only apply to the action of public authorities but extend also to rules of any other nature aimed at regulating gainful employment and the provision of services in a collective manner.' Case C-176/96 *Jyri Lehtonen and Castors Canada Dry Namur-Braine ASBL v Fédération royale belge des sociétés de basket-ball ASBL (FRBSB)* [2000] ECR I-2681, para 35.

[35] Joined cases C-51/96 and C-191/97 *Christelle Deliège v Ligue francophone de judo et disciplines associées ASBL, Ligue belge de judo ASBL, Union européenne de judo* (C-51/96) and *François Pacquée* (C-191/97) [2000] ECR I-02549, paras 45–48.

[36] Case C-411/98 *Angelo Ferlini v Centre hospitalier de Luxembourg* [2000] ECR I-8081, para 50.

[37] The prices of various medical services were either fixed by a Grand-Ducal Regulation, or were supposed to be fixed in mandatory collective agreements between the Association of Sickness Funds and service providers. While Mr Ferlini was not covered by any Luxembourg social security scheme and was therefore not directly caught by those rules, the hospitals' price-fixing agreement was clearly part of a broader co-regulatory scheme.

Both *Ferlini* and the sports cases show that the line between pure self-regulation and co-regulation is difficult to draw. Some involvement of the State usually exists. The key point is that in these cases the Court seems to be willing to impose free movement obligations on private regulators regardless of the involvement of the State in some aspect of the regulatory scheme: the central criterion is the effect of their actions on others.[38]

2.3 Pure private relationships

In some cases, the free movement rules were applied to private actors with little or no reference to either a regulatory role or any connection to the State. These cases mostly had to do with the free movement of persons, and more specifically discrimination against workers or other persons on the basis of nationality. This case law, while based on the free movement rules, is inspired by separate but related Treaty non-discrimination provisions which have long been applicable in private relationships. This personal right to non-discrimination clearly has a fundamental right aspect and is supported by both EU and national fundamental rights guarantees.[39]

In *Angonese*, an Italian bank's recruitment scheme required job applicants to produce a specific type of Italian and German language proficiency certificate issued by the regional authorities of the bilingual region of Bolzano.[40] Mr Angonese, an Italian national who studied in Vienna and could prove that he was bilingual by other means, disputed the requirement and the ECJ agreed with him.

The Court saw no difficulty in stating that (today's) Art 45 TFEU on the free movement of workers precludes such a requirement. This was justified, firstly, by the *Walrave* and *Bosman* proposition that the Treaty discrimination ban covers rules on working conditions, and secondly, by the *Defrenne*[41] judgment which extended the Treaty provision on equal pay for men and women[42] to contracts

[38] Thus, the more recent examples of linking horizontal effect directly to the effects of a particular measure, notably in AG Maduro's Opinion in *Viking Line* (n 17) and in Case C-171/11 *Fra.bo SpA v Deutsche Vereinigung des Gas- und Wasserfaches eV (DVGW)—Technisch-Wissenschaftlicher Verein* (ECJ, 12 July 2012) certainly have precursors. See also Case 90-76 *S.r.l. Ufficio Henry van Ameyde v S.r.l. Ufficio centrale italiano di assistenza assicurativa automobilisti in circolazione internazionale (UCI)* [1977] ECR 1091 where insurance companies' organizational rules were held to be covered by the provisions on free movement of services regardless of any link with public authority, as collective business regulation.

[39] In that spirit, see Baquero Cruz (n 2) 115. As Prechal and de Vries (n 14) 17 note, 'the nexus between economic integration and non-discrimination on grounds of nationality is getting weaker and weaker', as the rationale of non-discrimination guarantees moves from market unification to the protection of human dignity.

[40] Case C-281/98 *Roman Angonese v Cassa di Risparmio di Bolzano SpA* [2000] ECR I-4139. Interestingly, the requirement was actually based on a collective agreement between banks. Had the test been required by the collective agreement (it only gave banks the opportunity to unilaterally adopt testing rules), the Regulation (EEC) 1612/68 of the Council on freedom of movement for workers within the Community (1968) OJ L257 would have been applicable. In any event, had the Court been so inclined, the existence of the collective agreement could have provided an argument for extending the free movement rules, similarly to *Ferlini*.

[41] Case 43-75 *Gabrielle Defrenne v Société anonyme belge de navigation aérienne Sabena* [1976] ECR 455.

[42] Today's Art 157 TFEU.

between individuals. The Court read Art 45, like the general prohibition of discrimination in Art 18 TFEU, as being designed 'to ensure that there is no discrimination on the labour market'.[43] This was enough to hold that, insofar as Art 45 TFEU prohibits discrimination on grounds of nationality, it applies to private persons as well as to public authorities.

Angonese has seen relatively little follow-up. In *Raccanelli*, a PhD researcher claimed that, by not allowing him to choose between an employment contract and a grant contract, the Max-Planck Society (a private law association) in effect discriminated against him on the basis of nationality and violated the Treaty rules on free movement of workers. The Court confirmed that, since Art 45 TFEU is 'worded in general terms and is not addressed specifically to the Member States or to bodies governed by public law',[44] since it 'lays down a fundamental freedom and … constitutes a specific application of the general prohibition of discrimination', it applies not only to all agreements collectively regulating paid labour but also to 'contracts between individuals'.[45] More recently, in *Erny*, the Court made it quite clear that both Art 45 TFEU and rules of secondary law[46] prohibit clauses in individual contracts and collective agreements that discriminate against workers on the basis of nationality.[47]

There was public or State involvement in all of these cases.[48] In *Angonese*, much like in *Ferlini*, the disputed rule was based on a collective agreement among regional banks, and the test it required was normally used by public authorities. The Max Planck Society, while private, is a network of largely publicly funded research institutes. In *Erny*, the defendant employer's salary calculation method was taken over from German law. These points, however, did not seem to be decisive.[49]

The judgments show that, regardless of the regulatory nature of certain private restraints or their impact on market access, the EU free movement rules, complemented by the general prohibition contained in Art 18 TFEU as well as by secondary legislation, prohibit employers from discriminating against workers on the basis of nationality.

The free movement of services can also be relevant in this context. For example, the *Haug-Adrion* judgment suggests that this broad non-discrimination rationale

[43] *Defrenne* (n 41) para 35.

[44] Case C-94/07 *Andrea Raccanelli v Max-Planck-Gesellschaft zur Förderung der Wissenschaften eV* [2008] ECR I-5939, para 42.

[45] ibid para 45.

[46] Article 7/4 of Regulation 1612/68 (n 40), as well as its successor, Regulation (EU) 492/2011 of the European Parliament and of the Council on freedom of movement for workers within the Union (2011) OJ L141/1, provide unambiguously that 'any clause of a collective or individual agreement or of any other collective regulation concerning eligibility for employment, employment, remuneration and other conditions of work or dismissal shall be null and void in so far as it lays down or authorises discriminatory conditions in respect of workers who are nationals of the other Member States'.

[47] Case C-172/11 *Georges Erny v Daimler AG - Werk Wörth* EU:C:2012:399.

[48] Prechal and de Vries (n 14) 15–16.

[49] In that sense, see the Opinion of AG Kokott in Case C-379/09 *Maurits Casteels v British Airways plc* EU:C:2010:675, at n 62.

could also apply to recipients of services.[50] The notion that every service provider is fully bound by the free movement provisions could have wide-ranging consequences. On the other hand, prohibiting service providers from blatantly discriminating against consumers on the basis of nationality or residence, without objective business justification, is not controversial. In fact, Art 20/2 of the Services Directive does just that.[51] In any event, however, the Court has never really explored the consequences of *Haug-Adrion* further, and to this day the judgment seems like something of an outlier.

2.4 Private action based on restrictive legislation

Finally, in a separate line of 'horizontal' free movement cases, individuals were prevented from relying on a contract or an intellectual property right against other individuals on the basis of the free movement provisions. A close look reveals that these judgments do not truly impose duties on private parties. They only hold that private parties are prevented from relying on certain rights granted to them under national legislation when that legislation, or its interpretation adopted by a court, infringes the free movement rules. For our purposes, therefore, a brief outline will suffice.

In *Dansk Supermarked*, the plaintiff relied on a Danish law to block the re-import of a product for which, under a contract with the producer, it was to be the exclusive seller in Denmark. The Court found that interpreting the Danish marketing legislation in such a way that it prevents re-importation violates the free movement rules.[52] Had it stopped there, not much about this case would be remarkable. In the following paragraph, however, the Court added that it is 'impossible' for 'agreements between individuals … to derogate from the mandatory provisions of the Treaty on the free movement of goods'.[53] This may be read

[50] Mr Haug-Adrion, a German working in Belgium, claimed that he was discriminated against by his German insurance company when it charged him a higher insurance price because he had a car with customs plates. The Court considered that the prohibition of discrimination reflected in the free movement of workers and services applied to this relationship. Those provisions, as well as the general prohibition of discrimination (today's Art 18 TFEU), 'are intended to eliminate all measures which, in the fields of free movement of workers and freedom to provide services, treat a national of another Member State more severely or place him in a situation less advantageous, from a legal or factual point of view, than that of one of the Member State's own nationals in the same circumstances'. Case 251/83 *Eberhard Haug-Adrion v Frankfurter Versicherungs-AG* [1984] ECR 4277 para 14. The Court eventually concluded that there was no discrimination because the rules were 'based on objective actuarial factors' and because they could also have affected German nationals (paras 16–17).

[51] 'Member States shall ensure that the general conditions of access to a service, which are made available to the public at large by the provider, do not contain discriminatory provisions relating to the nationality or place of residence of the recipient, but without precluding the possibility of providing for differences in the conditions of access where those differences are directly justified by objective criteria.' Directive 2006/123/EC of the European Parliament and of the Council on services in the internal market [2006] OJ L376.

[52] Case 58/80 *Dansk Supermarked A/S v A/S Imerco* [1981] ECR 181; see para 11.

[53] ibid para 17. Therefore, a contractual re-importation ban 'may not be relied upon … in order to classify the marketing of such goods as an improper or unfair commercial practice'.

as saying that the rules on free movement of goods apply directly to agreements between individuals. The real target for the Court, however, was a judicial interpretation of Danish law that would consider parallel imports to be contrary to 'approved commercial usage' because of a private contract.

Later case law made it clear that ordinary contractual clauses do not as such restrict the free movement of goods. A good example is *Bayer v Süllhöfer*, concerning a no-challenge clause in a patent licensing agreement. The Court was quick to dismiss that claim: the case concerns essentially the validity of a contractual clause and not 'the application of national legislation relating to the exercise of an industrial property right likely to form a barrier to the free movement of goods between Member States'.[54]

2.5 Limits? The case of goods

So far, I have discussed the horizontal effect of the free movement rules largely without distinguishing the different fundamental freedoms—goods, services, establishment, workers, and capital. Actions of private or semi-private bodies have been assessed under almost all of the fundamental freedoms—services (*Walrave*), establishment (*Viking Line*), workers (*Angonese*), and goods (*Apple & Pear Development Company*, *Dansk Supermarked*). The sole exception so far, for lack of cases and not because of any point of principle, seems to be the free movement of capital.[55]

For some time, however, the orthodox position has been that the rules on free movement of goods, unlike those on workers and services, do not have horizontal effect.[56] Indeed, the Court has stated on several occasions that those rules are intended to catch State measures and not the ordinary conduct of undertakings.

Two judgments are especially important in this respect. *Sapod Audic*[57] concerned a co-regulatory scheme under which producers had to subscribe to a waste management system run by an authorized private company and 'identify' the packaging of products covered by the system. One producer, Sapod, tried to avoid paying the fees it owed to Eco-Emballages, the waste management company, by

[54] Case 65/86 *Bayer AG and Maschinenfabrik Hennecke GmbH v Heinz Süllhöfer* [1988] ECR 5249, para 12. See also Jukka Snell, *Goods and Services in EC Law: A Study of the Relationship Between the Freedoms* (Oxford University Press 2002) 131–35 and Baquero Cruz (n 2) 110.

[55] A leading treatise on the subject recognizes the possibility of horizontal effect of the provisions on capital, but does so by analogy with the case law on the other freedoms. Steffen Hindelang, *The Free Movement of Capital and Foreign Direct Investment: The Scope of Protection in EU Law* (Oxford University Press 2009) 210–12. On the far-reaching consequences that this extension might have (and reasons for thinking that it might be forthcoming), in particular in the context of 'golden share' cases, see Schepel (n 14).

[56] See Leible (n 19) 75; Krenn (n 14) 181–83; Oliver and Roth (n 18) 422; Johan Willem Van de Gronden, 'The Internal Market, the State and Private Initiative: A Legal Assessment of National Mixed Public–Private Arrangements in the Light of European Law' (2006) 33 Legal Issues of Economic Integration 105, 116; Arthur S Hartkamp, 'Fundamental Rights, Fundamental Freedoms and Contract Law' in Stefan Grundmann (ed), *Constitutional Values and European Contract Law* (Kluwer Law International 2008) 90–91.

[57] Case C-159/00 *Sapod Audic v Eco-Emballages SA* [2002] ECR I-5031.

claiming that the contractual duty to affix a green logo to the packaging restricted the free movement of goods. The Court dismissed the free movement claim primarily because the duty arising from French law to *identify* the packaging (and not necessarily to affix a logo on it) was a selling arrangement and not a rule on product characteristics.[58] It then added that, since the specific duty to affix a logo arises out of a private contract and not out of the French law itself, it 'cannot be regarded as a barrier to trade for the purposes of [Art 34 TFEU] since it was not imposed by a Member State but agreed between individuals'.[59]

Vlaamse Reisbureaus concerned a law prohibiting travel agencies from giving rebates to consumers, thus creating a price support for tour operators. The case was largely dealt with under competition law, and in any case, the Court concluded that it concerned services and not goods. Nevertheless, it added that 'since Articles [34 and 36 TFEU] concern only public measures and not the conduct of undertakings, it is only the compatibility with those Articles of national provisions of the kind at issue in the main proceedings that need be examined'.[60] In several other judgments, while not technically dealing with the issue of horizontal effect, the Court similarly pointed out that Art 34 TFEU relates to 'measures of the Member States' and 'national provisions'.[61]

Sweeping statements excluding private action from the scope of the free movement of goods were not necessary to solve either *Sapod Audic* or *Vlaamse Reisbureaus*. Addressing the question of horizontal effect may therefore have indicated a desire by the Court to pre-emptively close its doors to contractual litigation between private parties.[62] Still, the judgments were sufficiently ambiguous to allow for a future change of course.

This is what seems to have happened in the *Fra.bo* judgment,[63] where the rules on free movement of goods were extended to a standard-setting organization,

[58] Under the distinction established by Joined cases C-267/91 and C-268/91 *Criminal proceedings against Bernard Keck and Daniel Mithouard* [1993] ECR I-6097, rules that relate to selling arrangements are generally excluded from the scope of today's Art 34 TFEU. A rule that would require affixing a logo on the packaging would be related to product characteristics and clearly within the scope of Art 34.

[59] Paragraph 74.

[60] Case 311/85 *ASBL Vereniging van Vlaamse Reisbureaus v ASBL Sociale Dienst van de Plaatselijke en Gewestelijke Overheidsdiensten* [1987] ECR 3801, para 30.

[61] Joined cases 177 and 178/82 *Criminal proceedings against Jan van de Haar and Kaveka de Meern BV* [1984] ECR 1797, para 30.

[62] The existence of Council Regulation (EC) 2679/98 on the functioning of the internal market in relation to the free movement of goods among the Member States [1998] OJ L337/8 which explicitly deals with private restraints to the free movement of goods by imposing obligations on the Member States—inspired by the *Spanish Strawberries* judgment—might be said to explain the reluctance to apply the Treaty provisions on goods directly against private actors. On the other hand, the duties imposed by the Regulation are rather weak, and there has been no significant case law on it. See Baquero Cruz (n 2) 113 and Snell (n 14) 239.

[63] *Fra.bo* (n 38). See Chapter VII for an extended discussion of *Fra.bo*. This judgment may go some way towards addressing the concern for inequality across the freedoms expressed by Stephen Weatherill, 'The Elusive Character of Private Autonomy in EU Law' in Dorota Leczykiewicz and Stephen Weatherill (eds), *The Involvement of EU Law in Private Law Relationships* (Hart 2013) 13.

DVGW, whose standards are recognized as granting a presumption of conformity with German product safety legislation and constitute the only practical way into the German market. Due to the way the national court's questions were posed, the Court did not address the issue of whether or not there was actually a restriction, nor how it could be justified, but simply found that the rules on free movement of goods apply to DVGW's refusal to certify certain products of Fra.bo, an Italian manufacturer.

At first blush, this may seem like a co-regulatory scheme that would easily qualify for free movement scrutiny, even under the logic of *Buy Irish* or *Apple and Pear Development Council*. On two points, however, the judgment was innovative, not just in terms of the rules on goods.

Firstly, the case was not about the German legislation that, arguably, constituted a restriction of free movement in itself by not providing a meaningful alternative to DVGW standards. The judgment directly addressed the practices of DVGW: the standard itself and the refusal to recognize conformity checks performed by a non-certified laboratory.[64]

Secondly, continuing the line from AG Maduro's Opinion in *Viking Line*,[65] *Fra.bo* seems to show a growing convergence around the effects of a restraint on free movement, and not links to the State, as the main criterion for the applicability of the free movement rules to private parties. DVGW, according to the Court, is subject to the free movement rules in its standardization and certification activities because it 'in reality holds the power to regulate the entry into the German market'.[66] Admittedly, it is not quite as simple as that. The judgment points out the legal context within which DVGW operates, especially the presumption of conformity with product safety laws. It also points out that DVGW's measures give rise to restrictions 'in the same manner'—whatever that means—as State measures.[67] On its own, however, legal form cannot explain the extension of the free movement rules to DVGW. Under this effects-based approach that is also attuned to the legal and economic context, it is quite possible that, out of two superficially similar measures adopted by two regulators, be they private or public, one will fall under the free movement rules and the other will not.

Was *Fra.bo* a reversal of precedent? Arguably, the special status of the free movement of goods in relation to individual measures was always overestimated. *Sapod Audic* can be read as merely saying that contracts between individuals that do not restrict a firm's general market access opportunities fall outside of the rules on free movement of goods.[68] Goods may not be a special case at all, except to the extent

[64] The judgment even explicitly plays down the links between DVGW and Germany: '... the DVGW is a non-profit, private-law body whose activities are not financed by the Federal Republic of Germany ... that Member State has no decisive influence over the DVGW's standardisation and certification activities, although some of its members are public bodies.' *Fra.bo* (n 38), para 24.

[65] See n 38. [66] *Fra.bo* (n 38), para 31. [67] ibid para 26.

[68] Gareth Davies, 'Freedom of Movement, Horizontal Effect, and Freedom of Contract' (2012) 3 European Review of Private Law 805, 814.

that they are less likely than the rules on workers or services to involve the fundamental rights concerns that motivated the Court in cases like *Angonese*.

2.6 Alternative techniques: Member State liability and indirect effect

Horizontal effect has two important alternatives. The first is to impose liability on the Member States for tolerating actions of individuals that infringe the free movement rights of others. The two classic examples here are *Spanish Strawberries*, where France's failure to prevent farmers from repeatedly and violently attacking distributors and sellers of imported fruit was held to violate the free movement of goods, and *Schmidberger*, where permitting an environmentalist protest on an important highway was considered to be a restriction of the free movement of goods, but justified as a legitimate exercise of the freedom of assembly and expression.[69]

These cases can be seen as a part of the same trend that led to the imposition of free movement scrutiny on individuals. Alternatively, they could be viewed as an adequate substitute that makes it unnecessary to apply the free movement rules to private actors.[70] In truth, they are probably best seen as two separate avenues. There is no evidence that this kind of Member State liability excludes private liability. Both a private regulator and a Member State could be concurrently liable, if not for precisely the same conduct, then for different aspects of a restrictive co-regulatory scheme. In addition, there are many private restraints of free movement for which the State normally bears no responsibility, such as the rules of sporting bodies.

Yet another alternative way of conceptualizing horizontal effect would be to focus on the duty of Member State bodies, especially courts, to respect the free movement rules when adjudicating private disputes. This would be a version of indirect effect[71] (*mittelbare Drittwirkung*) in German constitutional

[69] *Spanish Strawberries* (n 8); Case C-112/00 *Eugen Schmidberger, Internationale Transporte und Planzüge v Republik Österreich* [2003] ECR I-5659.

[70] For a recent argument along those lines, see Barend van Leeuwen, 'Private Regulation and Public Responsibility in the Internal Market' (2014) 33 Yearbook of European Law 277. See also Baquero Cruz (n 2) 111, in relation to the rather non-obvious example of *Bosman* (arguably, if *Bosman* could be construed as a case of (only) Member State liability, the same could be true of any horizontal case). See also Schepel (n 17) 311, Tonia Novitz, 'The Impact of Viking and Laval: Contesting the Social Function and Legal Regulation of the Right to Strike' in Edoardo Ales and Tonia Novitz (eds), *Collective Action and Fundamental Freedoms in Europe: Striking the Balance* (Intersentia 2010) 257 and ACL Davies (n 27) 142. Oliver and Roth (n 18) 427 also favour applying the free movement rules to the duty of the Member States to supervise private actors (in most cases, apparently, instead of direct private liability).

[71] In section 1, I mentioned the distinction between procedural (a dispute between private parties in which the issue is a Member State's violation of the free movement rules), and substantive horizontal effect (an individual's violation of the free movement rules). This is not the same as the distinction between indirect and direct horizontal effect. Both with indirect and direct horizontal effect, the background issue is a legal requirement placed on an individual: the duty to respect the free movement rules, whether imposed directly or construed on the basis of the duties of the adjudicator. The term 'indirect horizontal effect' has been used both to refer to what I call 'procedural horizontal effect' as well as to a version of *Drittwirkung*. See Monica Claes, 'The European Union, its Member States and their Citizens' in Dorota Leczykiewicz and Stephen Weatherill (eds), *The*

law.[72] This doctrine holds that, even though constitutional rights cannot form the basis for a direct claim by an individual against another individual, they 'radiate' across the legal system, requiring courts to reinterpret the rights and obligations of the parties, as opposed to the outcome that would otherwise be dictated by the law (eg by national contract law).

While this idea was referenced before the CJEU on several occasions,[73] there are at least two problems with using it in the free movement context.

Firstly, as Kumm has argued, *mittelbare Drittwirkung* is largely equivalent to applying constitutional requirements directly on private actors (*unmittelbare Drittwirkung*). In both cases, the content of rights and obligations is changed in comparison with what the law would otherwise require.[74] Following this line of argument, it is not clear what would be gained by justifying horizontal effect on the basis of interpretative duties of courts, instead of simply saying that the free movement rules can bind individuals directly.

Secondly, the analogy between the free movement rules and national constitutional rights is imperfect at best. It is true that the free movement rules are seen as quasi-constitutional guarantees: perhaps not fundamental rights, but at least 'fundamental freedoms'.[75] They are all directly effective and national courts and other authorities are required to respect them. Still, it is a stretch to say that they have a

Involvement of EU Law in Private Law Relationships (Hart 2013) 42. It is also useful to highlight the difference between indirect horizontal effect and Member State liability under *Spanish Strawberries* and *Schmidberger*. In the second case, it is a distinct Member State violation—consisting in allowing or facilitating private conduct—that gives rise to liability. Individuals responsible for that conduct are not party to the proceedings, and even if they were, their liability could be constructed either around the logic of indirect effect or on some other grounds, independently of Member State liability.

[72] The doctrine was initially developed in the German Federal Constitutional Court judgment *Lüth* (1958) BVerfGE 7, 198. On the intellectual history of the extension of proportionality analysis into private relations, see Alec Stone Sweet and Jud Mathews, 'Proportionality Balancing and Global Constitutionalism' (2008) 47 Columbia Journal of Transnational Law 68, 111–12. See also Jacco Bomhoff, 'Lüth's 50th Anniversary: Some Comparative Observations on the German Foundations of Judicial Balancing' (2008) 9 German Law Journal 121 and Eric Engle, 'Third Party Effect of Fundamental Rights (Drittwirkung)' (2009) 5 Hanse Law Review 165; Krzeminska-Vamvaka (n 14) section II. Unlike Prechal and de Vries (n 14) 116, I use the term 'indirect horizontal effect' only in this sense, and not to encompass for example direct actions against the State for tolerating private infringements, like in *Spanish Strawberries* (n 8).

[73] Most famously, see Opinion AG Maduro in *Viking Line* (n 17) para 39. See also Case 248/83 *Commission v Germany* [1985] ECR 1459, para 15; Opinion of AG Van Gerven in Case C-262/88 *Douglas Harvey Barber v Guardian Royal Exchange Assurance Group* [1990] ECR I-1889, para 53; and Opinion of AG Trstenjak in Case C-80/06 *Carp Snc di L. Moleri e V. Corsi v Ecorad Srl* [2007] ECR I-4473, para 69.

[74] As Kumm summarizes, 'under the guise of interpreting the general clause [of the civil code] the judge is required to make exactly the kind of determination that he would have been required to make were he to directly adjudicate competing constitutional rights claims'. Kumm (n 76) 356.

[75] For the language of 'fundamental freedoms', see *Angonese* (n 40) para 35. More recent examples are Case C-589/10 *Janina Wencel v Zakład Ubezpieczeń Społecznych w Białymstoku* (CJEU, 16 May 2013) para 69 and Joined cases C-197/11 and C-203/11 *Eric Libert and Others v Gouvernement flamand* (C-197/11) *and All Projects & Developments NV and Others v Vlaamse Regering* (C-203/11) (CJEU, 8 May 2013) para 38.

'radiating' effect. Even with the Charter of Fundamental Rights, the Treaties are not a fully-fledged constitution that governs the totality of the Member States' legal orders. This is important because the *mittelbare Drittwirkung* doctrine assumes that disputes between individuals are grounded in statutory rules such as contract or tort law that are an elaboration of, and not just connected to, broader constitutional values.[76] To transpose the German doctrine to the EU level, it would be necessary to conceptualize these national rules as reflecting the general values outlined by the EU Treaties. This seems like a rather unnatural exercise given that many of these rules do not fall under EU competence at all. The only way that EU law enters the frame is through a direct conflict with the individual practices deemed to violate free movement, and not as the value-background of whatever legislation a national court is applying.

3. Free Movement Between Public and Private

As we have seen, the free movement rules have been applied to a number of actors and actions that could be described as private. The question is whether this is justified and how far it should go. On this point, many scholars make two connected claims. The first one rests on the public–private divide and claims that the free movement rules are addressed only to the Member States, while the competition rules are addressed to private actors. The second claim is that the free movement rules should not apply to private actors because of the need to protect private autonomy. Private autonomy would be jeopardized, it is argued, by subjecting private actors to the same kind of free movement discipline as the Member States.

In this simple form at least, these claims are unhelpful. The public–private distinction on which they are premised, in all its incarnations (public actors versus private actors, public law versus private law, public interest versus private interest,[77] regulatory versus market behaviour),[78] is unsatisfactory in the descriptive sense.[79] Trying to decide what constitutes State action has always been a difficult task because, in one way or another, 'State action is always present'.[80] Indeed,

[76] Mattias Kumm, 'Who is Afraid of the Total Constitution?: Constitutional Rights as Principles and the Constitutionalization of Private Law' (2006) 7 German Law Journal 341, 355–56.

[77] Constanze Semmelmann, 'The European Union's Economic Constitution Under the Lisbon Treaty: Soul-Searching Shifts the Focus to Procedure' (2010) 35 European Law Review 516, 529.

[78] 'The distinction between the public power of regulation and the private freedom of action—which constitutes the liberal State—is becoming less apparent.' Azoulai (n 18) 1345. This debate is particularly relevant to the question whether the free movement rules should apply to conduct that is also covered by the competition rules. See for example Okeoghene Odudu, *The Boundaries of EC Competition Law: The Scope of Article 81* (Oxford University Press 2006) 30–33 and Okeoghene Odudu, 'Economic Activity as a Limit to Community Law' in Catherine Barnard and Okeoghene Odudu (eds), *The Outer Limits of European Union Law* (Hart 2009) 263 et seq.

[79] See Chapter I. See Claes (n 71) 43–45, also making the point that the EU version of the public–private divide may not coincide with national versions.

[80] Sunstein (n 30) 465–66. As Tushnet points out, the issue of state action or horizontal effect arises when we notice that 'the people or corporations exercising "private" power are actually exercising power conferred on them by laws creating and regulating market behaviour'. Mark

one would be hard-pressed to find a single case of horizontal application of the EU free movement rules that could not be explained by some sort of link to the State, facilitation by the State, or at least by the similarity of a particular action to something that the State might be expected to do or has done before.[81] The latter category is especially inconclusive since, as Choper points out, 'any governmental function can in theory be done privately'.[82] Especially given the complexity of today's regulatory landscape, it makes little sense to criticize the extension of EU free movement rules to some private actors by simply invoking the principle that the private sphere is autonomous and purely voluntary.[83] To be convincing, a public–private distinction would have to take into account a range of contextual factors of each particular scheme, resembling a spectrum more than a divide between two categories.[84] The discussion over horizontal effect might therefore be

Tushnet, 'The Issue of State Action/Horizontal Effect in Comparative Constitutional Law' (2003) 1 International Journal of Constitutional Law 79. One could go even further and show that a State acts even by deciding not to act in some contexts, such as in the classic US Supreme Court judgment in *Miller v Schoene*, 276 US 272 (1928). L M Seidman, 'The State Action Paradox' (1993) 10 Constitutional Commentary 379, 397. Even more broadly, one could claim that 'all private action ultimately rests on the state's willingness to enforce the civil and criminal rules that facilitate that action'. Jesse H Choper, 'Thoughts on State Action: The Government Function and Power Theory Approaches' (1979) Washington University Law Quarterly 757, 791; in that spirit; see also Harold W Horowitz, 'The Misleading Search for State Action under the Fourteenth Amendment' (1956) 30 Southern California Law Review 208; and Robert J Glennon Jr and John E Nowak, 'A Functional Analysis of the Fourteenth Amendment State Action Requirement' (1976) Supreme Court Review 221.

[81] With a bit of creativity, one could explain every case where horizontal effect was discussed in terms of State action. To take two examples, even *Sapod Audic* and *Vlaamse Reisbureaus*, where the Court found that no free movement liability can arise from a contract between private parties, were actually about State action: legislation that either imposed a duty to contract with a third party (*Sapod Audic*) or required travel agencies to honour existing pricing agreements (*Vlaamse Reisbureaus*). See section 2.5.

[82] Choper (n 80) 779.

[83] This could be restated in a deeper theoretical sense as well. The traditional public–private distinction in legal debates is based on the simplest of several possible notions of public and private: the one conceived in classic liberalism. Thus, 'public' refers simply to the State, and 'private' refers to the market as a 'sphere of formally voluntary relations'. Jeff Weintraub, 'The Theory and Politics of the Public/Private Distinction' in Jeff Weintraub and Krishan Kumar (eds), *Public and Private in Thought and Practice: Perspectives on a Grand Dichotomy* (University of Chicago Press 1997) 7 et seq. It is questionable whether relying on that particular distinction to delineate the ways in which power in society is limited and controlled makes sense outside the context of a hierarchical, nation-State legal system. For debates on the impact of private regulatory regimes on law and governance, see Andreas Fischer-Lescano and Gunther Teubner, 'Regime-Collisions: The Vain Search for Legal Unity in the Fragmentation of Global Law' (2003) 25 Michigan Journal of International Law 999; G Teubner, 'Global Private Regimes: Neo-Spontaneous Law and Dual Constitution of Autonomous Sectors in World Society?' in Karl-Heinz Ladeur (ed), *Globalization and Public Governance* (Ashgate 2004); Gralf-Peter Calliess and Peer Zumbansen, *Rough Consensus and Running Code: A Theory of Transnational Law-Making* (Hart 2010); Nico Krisch, *Beyond Constitutionalism: The Pluralist Structure of Postnational Law* (Oxford University Press 2010). Deeper challenges to the public–private distinction in law have been made, far beyond the scope of private regulation and other 'in-between' scenarios. See, for example, Clare Dalton, 'An Essay in the Deconstruction of Contract Doctrine' (1985) 94 Yale Law Journal 997.

[84] Duncan Kennedy, 'The Stages of the Decline of the Public/Private Distinction' (1982) 130 University of Pennsylvania Law Review 1349.

better served by direct arguments explaining why particular activities of private actors should be scrutinized or not, rather than by the often distracting search for links to the State. This is especially true in the context of co-regulatory schemes, where almost any action can be partly viewed as State action.

Simply redrawing the public–private divide by, for example, extending the 'public' box to certain powerful actors, would also not do justice to this growing regulatory complexity. It is too simple to say that certain private actors[85] have power while others do not, because power depends on the relationship we choose to scrutinize.[86] It may be, for example, that a sporting body has regulatory power when licensing competitions, outside of which it is more like a run-of-the-mill industry group, advocating for its members, organizing meetings and joint initiatives. This makes it very difficult to draw useful *ex ante* distinctions between public and private, or even to single out a category such as 'collective regulation' as an appropriate target for free movement scrutiny, as opposed to other sorts of private activity.

Moreover, treating the public–private divide as a question that can be answered objectively *ex ante* disregards a basic legal realist insight: the designations 'public' and 'private' are not natural or inevitable, but reflect political choices made on the basis of their jurisdictional or substantive consequences. In other words, we tend to define activities as public or private not because we feel that they are objectively either of the two, but because we prefer the legal consequences of doing so to the consequences of doing the opposite.[87] Thus, arguments couched in terms of a public–private distinction are often about something else, such as about the institutions that we think should properly handle certain types of issues[88] or, even more simply, about the desirability of whatever practices are subject to legal scrutiny.[89]

[85] Choper (n 80), in the context of whether there is State action for the purpose of applying the US Constitution, proposes a focus on the power of the private actor. Under this approach, even a private actor that has not been delegated or granted a governmental function, but has for example a natural monopoly in the provision of a basic service would fall under the scope of state action. A similar argument in the EU context has been made by Prechal and de Vries (n 14) 24.

[86] '… the Corporate Power thesis conceives of Power as though it were Mercantilist gold bullion-physically piled on someone's desk, infinitely fungible unit for unit, and indifferently expendable to achieve any result. Yet all our experience is squarely to the contrary. Power to do A is not power to do B.' Bayless Manning, 'Corporate Power and Individual Freedom: Some General Analysis and Particular Reservations' (1960) 55 Northwestern University Law Review 38, 44. As Manning concludes (46): 'In any society, important economic and political decisions must be made and someone has to make them. The tough problem is how to allocate decision-making power on particular kinds of issues to the persons or institutions most likely to exercise it to produce the policy results we want … The question is not Power; it is policy.' See also Paul M Schoenhard, 'A Three-Dimensional Approach to the Public–Private Distinction' (2008) Utah Law Review 635.

[87] William J Nowak, 'Public–Private Governance: A Historical Introduction' in Jody Freeman and Martha Minow (eds), *Government by Contract: Outsourcing and American Democracy* (Harvard University Press 2009) 36, referring to Morris R Cohen, 'Property and Sovereignty' (1927) 13 Cornell Law Quarterly 8 and Robert L Hale, *Freedom Through Law: Public Control of Private Governing Power* (Columbia University Press 1952).

[88] cf the discussion in Neil K Komesar, *Imperfect Alternatives: Choosing Institutions in Law, Economics, and Public Policy* (University of Chicago Press 1994) 196–97.

[89] In the EU context, one might argue that the *Viking Line* judgment (see section 2.1) is an unjustified extension of horizontal effect going against private autonomy. Others might argue the

Finally, two features of EU law make it even less fruitful to discuss limits to the applicability of its disciplines in terms of a public–private divide. Firstly, the idea of a public–private distinction or of a divide between public and private law does not translate well into EU law.[90] There is no limited sphere of public law to which EU law is relevant, to the exclusion of a sphere of private law subject to Member State regulation. Free movement law in particular is dominated by functionalism, which tends to disregard such distinctions, even when they are based on centuries of Member State legal tradition.[91]

Secondly, while the issue of 'horizontal effect' is heavily contested in comparative constitutional law, the relevance of that debate for EU law is questionable. In the traditions of many states, constitutions cannot directly impose duties on private persons, notwithstanding some marginal doctrines that allow, for example, a broad interpretation of what 'State' means. National constitutions, however, have a better claim to being addressed solely to the State and its bodies than do the EU Treaties. This is not (just) a matter of constitutional theory. A number of Treaty provisions have been designed to impose, or subsequently interpreted as imposing, obligations on individuals. The competition rules, prohibiting anti-competitive agreements and abuses of dominant positions, are an obvious example.[92] Article 157 TFEU on equal pay for men and women has for decades been interpreted as binding individuals,[93] despite the fact that it is expressly addressed to the Member States, unlike any of the free movement rules.[94] The general prohibition of discrimination on grounds of nationality has been interpreted as binding non-State actors,[95] and the same has been held for the general principle of non-discrimination as 'reflected' in secondary law.[96] Article 95 TFEU, under the heading 'Transport Policy', prohibits carriers from imposing discriminatory rates for carriage of goods on account of their origin or destination and Art 97 requires that 'charges or dues in respect of the crossing of frontiers which are charged by a carrier in addition to the transport rates shall not exceed a reasonable level'.

same for the *Angonese* judgment (see section 2.3), because free movement law has no business interfering with employers' decisions on how language testing for new employees should be arranged, even if they are discriminatory. If those two groups do not overlap, the consistency of the arguments is questionable. This is not to say that the arguments are wrong—only that they are not explicit about their assumptions, and that they would do much more work in championing their cause if posed directly as an argument about how certain activities, in their political and economic context, should be treated under EU law, rather than as arguments invoking the public–private distinction.

[90] Azoulai (n 29) contrasts the French with the EU notion of the distinction between public and private law. See also Claes (n 71) 33. Among the various national traditions, EU law has been much less of an irritant to those that put less stock in the distinction to begin with, such as in English law. Carol Harlow, '"Public" and "Private" Law: Definition Without Distinction' (1980) 43 Modern Law Review 241; Dawn Oliver, *Common Values and the Public–Private Divide* (Butterworths 1999); John WF Allison, *A Continental Distinction in the Common Law: An Historical and Comparative Perspective on English Public Law* (Oxford University Press 2000); Matthias Ruffert (ed), *The Public–Private Law Divide: Potential for Transformation?* (BICL 2009).

[91] Sauter and Schepel (n 11). [92] See in particular Arts 101 and 102 TFEU.

[93] *Defrenne* (n 41). [94] See n 1. [95] *Ferlini* (n 36).

[96] See inter alia *Mangold* (n 15), *Kücükdeveci* (n 15); and Joined cases C-297/10 and C-298/10 *Sabine Hennigs* (C-297/10) *v Eisenbahn-Bundesamt* and *Land Berlin* (C-298/10) *v Alexander Mai* (CJEU, 8 September 2011).

There is nothing, therefore, in the character of the Treaties that would prevent them from addressing individuals. If there is a reason not to apply the free movement rules to (some) private actors, it must have to do with those particular rules, rather than with the nature of the legal document in which they are contained. What this means is that the much-belaboured issue of horizontal effect may not be a grand constitutional question, but a much humbler one: what should be considered to impede free movement and what should not.

3.1 The many meanings of 'private autonomy'

The flipside of the public–private distinction is the argument for private autonomy. As Tushnet puts it, the fear is that 'applying all the constitutional norms that bind public actors to private actors, through the construction of private law totally responsive to constitutional norms, would put an end to private autonomy'.[97] This argument is frequently applied to the context of the free movement rules. Like the public–private distinction more generally, however, it is too blunt an instrument for drawing the boundaries of those rules with regard to private action.

To be sure, I do not claim that liberty and private autonomy are illegitimate concerns. The private autonomy claim, however, tends to be presented as self-explanatory even though it tends to collapse into a number of diverse, more specific claims. Those claims would be better addressed directly, instead of serving as unstated assumptions[98] of the private autonomy argument.

Importantly, those claims are usually not purely about liberty, that is freedom from legal control. If they were, one would expect them to extend also to other forms of law—such as national law or EU secondary law—that imposes duties on private actors similar to those imposed, in this context, by the free movement rules. Yet, a national law or an EU regulation prohibiting certain forms of collective action, while likely to be heavily criticized from the point of view of labour rights or (in the latter case) EU competences, will not be contested on the same grounds as a substantially identical judicially imposed rule based on the EU free movement provisions.[99] Of course, many would argue that freedom of assembly and the right to strike are too important to tolerate limits. Few would, however, claim that limiting collective action is unjustified because laws should not intrude into the affairs of private persons.

What are some of the substantive arguments that 'private autonomy' is shorthand for? They may, for example, concern the autonomy of private law, which is primarily an area of Member State competence. In other words, they might relate

[97] Tushnet (n 80) 84 and the sources cited therein. In relation to the EU free movement rules, this argument is ubiquitous: Prechal and de Vries (n 14) 18, for example, while eventually coming to a very different overall conclusion (24), make it almost in passing, claiming that extending the horizontal effect of the free movement rules to all situations would be 'a disproportionate interference with and permanent risk for the exercise of contractual freedom of private parties'.

[98] See also Claes (n 71) 47–51.

[99] *Viking Line* (n 17).

to the need to protect the discipline from encroachment by EU law.[100] Leible has, for example, argued against direct horizontal effect on the basis of the need to prevent 'direct interference with the national systems of private law'.[101]

Secondly, the autonomy argument may have to do with legal certainty and an implicit preference for rules over standards.[102] Private law is often seen to be governed by clear rules, and juxtaposing or overriding them with standard-like free movement provisions may seem to be an undue intrusion.

Connected to the distrust of standards, the private autonomy argument can be based on a distrust of judicial review. The open-ended nature of the free movement rules can be seen as an invitation for judicial law-making. Balancing the different values and interests that may come into play when adjudicating private disputes should, the argument goes, be left to legislatures and not judges.[103]

Private autonomy may also stand for the problem of liability allocation (why should private persons be liable for breaches of the free movement rules instead of the Member States, for example through infringement actions?)[104] or over-enforcement (the existence of alternative legal mechanisms means that the likelihood of private conduct being condemned will unduly rise).[105] In the EU context, these alternative legal mechanisms may consist of directly applicable secondary law (regulations) or of Treaty-based competition law; moreover, national

[100] Kumm (n 76) 360; Claes (n 71) 32.

[101] Leible (n 19) 83. Cherednychenko has similarly claimed that '[t]he values underlying fundamental rights must certainly be respected within contract law, but contract law must preserve its key role in accommodating its values within its own fabric. Fundamental rights must therefore influence rather than govern contract law.' Olha Cherednychenko, 'Subordinating Contract Law to Fundamental Rights: Towards a Major Breakthrough or Towards Walking in Circles?' in Stefan Grundmann (ed), *Constitutional Values and European Contract Law* (Kluwer Law International 2008) 60, 68. Leible considers that 'rules that the parties may waive can never have the effect of restricting trade because the parties are free to draft their contract otherwise' and that it is only the Member States that need to 'fashion their rules of private law in such a way that restrictions are impossible' (84). It is important to distinguish private action from private law, such as legislation on contracts. Still, private law is often seen as the guarantor of contractual freedom and thus interfering with it is seen as an encroachment into the private sphere (cf the notion of a 'private law society'—the classic here being Franz Böhm, 'Privatrechtsgesellschaft und Marktwirtschaft' (1966) 17 ORDO 75). See also Stefan Grundmann, 'The Concept of the Private Law Society: After 50 Years of European and European Business Law' (2008) 4 European Review of Private Law 553. For a different perspective, see Claudio Michelon, 'The Public Nature of Private Law?' in Cláudio Michelon and others (eds), *The Public in Law: Representations of the Political in Legal Discourse* (Ashgate 2012).

[102] Duncan Kennedy, 'Form and Substance in Private Law Adjudication' (1976) 89 Harvard Law Review 1685, 1687–88.

[103] Claes (n 71) 32. See Duncan Kennedy, 'A Transnational Genealogy of Proportionality in Private Law' in Roger Brownsword and others (eds), *The Foundations of European Private Law* (Hart 2011) 217–19 for a discussion of judicial value-balancing in private law.

[104] Leible (n 19); Spaventa (n 16) 216–17. This argument, of course, implies that the Member States bear ultimate responsibility for any restraint on free movement, even when committed by private actors, which may not be true if we assume that duties are placed directly on private actors.

[105] In the US context, Michelman has pointed out that 'a perception that persons ... generally have available to them a sufficient range of "exit" choices "and" the belief that general background law tends to protect persons against abuses of power by others' lead to objections to the horizontal application of constitutional rules. Frank I Michelman, 'W(H)ither the Constitution' (1999) 21 Cardozo Law Review 1063, 1077.

administrative law, national competition law, consumer law, or other rules could be claimed to sufficiently scrutinize private actors.[106]

Finally, an especially frequent version of the private autonomy argument is based on federalism, that is on the division of powers between the national and EU levels.[107] The legislatures of the Member States, as well as of the EU—in the latter case, at least when adopting regulations—are perfectly capable of restricting individual autonomy in the very same way as would be achieved by applying the EU Treaties directly to that individual.[108] Indeed, as Davies notes, 'the most obvious and substantial impact of the internal market on party autonomy ... results from the mass of secondary legislation regulating standards, qualifications, and consumer rights'.[109] It is therefore unclear whether the private autonomy argument assumes that there is something specific to regulating individual conduct through free movement rules as opposed to those other rules, or if the claim is merely disputing the level at which a decision is made, arguing that it would infringe the division of powers between the EU and the Member States.

Each of these arguments would have to bear its own weight, depending on the context. My point is not to disprove them, but merely to note that blanket invocations of private autonomy, just like blanket invocations of the public–private distinction, are not convincing arguments against free movement scrutiny. Whether the free movement rules should prohibit certain conduct, and how exactly their application to private actors should work, requires a more nuanced answer. I will begin to sketch such an approach in the following section.

3.2 The institutional context: When judicial scrutiny might make sense

So far, I have argued that the extent to which the free movement rules impose duties on individuals is unlikely to be decided by simple divides, such as the one between public and private, or state and market. What are, then, the circumstances in which free movement scrutiny might be appropriate?

The first step is to take into account the institutional context.[110] For example, courts in general, and the CJEU in particular, can be well-placed to impose

[106] See for example Prechal and de Vries (n 14) 18 and Snell (n 14) 232.

[107] As Choper notes in the US context: 'The primary purpose of the state action requirement [...] is not to protect individual autonomy; that is, it is not meant to guarantee individuals immunity from all governmental regulation. Rather, the state action requirement serves to allocate power within the federal system; it limits the power of the national government vis-á-vis the states.' Choper (n 80) 757 et seq.

[108] cf ibid 757–58. [109] Davies (n 68) 806–07.

[110] Most notably, Komesar (n 88) and Neil K Komesar, *Law's Limits: The Rule of Law and the Supply and Demand of Rights* (Cambridge University Press 2001). In the EU law context, see Miguel Poiares Maduro, *We the Court: The European Court of Justice and the European Economic Constitution: A Critical Reading of Article 30 of the EC Treaty* (Hart 1998). For an application of institutional analysis to the question of State action in US constitutional law, see Christian Turner, 'State Action Problems' (2013) 65 Florida Law Review 281.

checks on the actions of private regulators when neither the market forces nor the political process on the EU or national level can effectively prevent the exclusionary consequences of private regulation.[111]

First and foremost, this will be the case in co-regulatory schemes that, because of their hybrid public–private character, are neither adequately disciplined by the market nor by the political process.[112] In these cases, a private actor such as an industry association is endowed with a regulatory authority that cannot be eliminated through market competition. Bar associations fixing prices without effective oversight[113] are an example of this. More broadly, domestic political processes could be captured or influenced by private associations in less direct ways.[114] A self-regulating minority has high stakes and high returns on participating in the political process, while consumers and potential competitors may not be sufficiently organized to challenge the dominance of the private regulator.

Other situations of a monopoly of a private regulator in a Member State could also be good candidates for judicial oversight, even when that monopoly was not acquired through an act of the State. Free movement scrutiny could be useful when sports associations limit the access of foreign athletes to competitions[115] or when standard-setting organizations whose standards are *de facto* indispensable for market access impose quality standards that favour their own members.[116] The outcome of such regulation, with no oversight, is likely to be biased in favour of the actors involved in setting and enforcing the rules. Market discipline may be an insufficient control mechanism, especially when the individual stakes of consumers and potential competitors are small, making it difficult for them to negotiate around a monopolistic regulatory scheme or develop a competing scheme of their own. Network effects and high transaction costs

[111] The differences in institutional context may also help explain why the US equivalent to the free movement rules, the so-called dormant commerce clause of the Constitution, has not been applied against private regulation. For a rare attempt at making the analogy between State and private restrictions on interstate commerce, see Alfred L Brophy and Shubha Ghosh, 'Whistling Dixie: The Invalidity and Unconstitutionality of Covenants Against Yankees' (1999) 10 Villanova Environmental Law Journal 57, 86–88.

[112] Miguel Poiares Maduro, 'The Chameleon State: EU Law and the Blurring of the Private/Public Distinction in the Market' <http://ssrn.com/abstract=1575542>, 10–11.

[113] Case C-35/99 *Criminal Proceedings Against Manuele Arduino, Third Parties: Diego Dessi, Giovanni Bertolotto and Compagnia Assicuratrice RAS SpA* [2002] ECR I-1529, Joined cases C-94/04 and C-202/04 *Federico Cipolla v Rosaria Fazari, née Portolese* (C-94/04) *and Stefano Macrino and Claudia Capoparte v Roberto Meloni* (C-202/04) [2006] ECR I-11421 and Case C-565/08 *Commission v Italy* [2011] ECR I-2101.

[114] In the case law of the ECJ, there are a number of examples where private or hybrid bodies were placed, by the political process, in situations of conflict of interest. See, for example, *Apple and Pear Development Council* (n 21), Case C-506/04 *Graham J. Wilson v Ordre des avocats du barreau de Luxembourg* [2006] ECR I-8613 and Case C-49/07 *Motosykletistiki Omospondia Ellados NPID (MOTOE) v Elliniko Dimosio* [2008] ECR I-4863.

[115] *Bosman* (n 13).

[116] Even though it was a challenge under the competition rules, and an unsuccessful one at that, Case T-432/05 *EMC Development AB v Commission* [2010] ECR II-1629 could provide some food for thought. See Chapter VII for a broader discussion.

may also make it difficult for alternatives to the *de facto* monopoly of a private regulator to appear.[117]

All of these difficulties increase if the area being regulated is highly complex and if information on the pertinent issues is not readily available at low cost—which is often the main reason for the emergence of private regulation in the first place.

For these reasons, a private association that is either formally or informally in the position of regulating a certain area on the level of a Member State can be a rather poor candidate for supervision either through market competition or through the (domestic) political process.

In these circumstances, courts, and the ECJ in particular, may indeed need to step in. Litigation can provide effective redress for harmed individuals, especially competitors that may have high enough of a stake to pursue it. Moreover, the CJEU may be in a much better position to review private regulators than are national courts, given that it is not burdened by a jurisdictional public–private law divide which often complicates judicial review in the Member States. In addition, the free movement rules and the proportionality test provide a relatively simple yet flexible framework for analysis[118] that does not entail significant decision costs for judges—especially in the case of the CJEU which often gives merely general legal guidance to the fact-finding national court.[119]

Of course, just because there are problems in the functioning of markets or political processes, it does not follow that courts are the right alternative.[120] Many of the same problems that affect markets or political processes plague courts as well: limited resources, high costs, difficulties with highly complex issues, etc. This means that the interventionist role of courts should be limited.

Arguably, these limits are already recognized in the case law. The CJEU has shown little desire to use the free movement rules to deeply supervise the behaviour of private actors, even private regulators. Judging by the oft-repeated fears of an assault on private autonomy by way of the free movement rules, one would expect the case law to be positively brimming with private suits in which, for example, a debtor would be trying to get out of a contract by invoking the free movement rules. That, however, has not happened. There have been few cases—certainly, no more than a fraction of the total number of free movement cases—imposing obligations on private actors, and almost all of them have to do with

[117] For some of the market failures associated with private regulation, see Avery Katz, 'Taking Private Ordering Seriously' (1996) 144 University of Pennsylvania Law Review 1745, 1749–53. For a discussion in the context of the liberal professions, see Tinne Heremans, *Professional Services in the EU Internal Market: Quality Regulation and Self-Regulation* (Hart 2012) 66–85.

[118] Stone Sweet and Mathews (n 72) 162.

[119] See *Cipolla* (n 113) paras 65–69 or Case C-368/95 *Vereinigte Familiapress Zeitungsverlags- und vertriebs GmbH v Heinrich Bauer Verlag* [1997] ECR I-3689, paras 27–32 for examples of proportionality guidance that puts a number of difficult questions to the national court.

[120] This is why Komesar focuses on comparative institutional analysis, rather than what he calls 'single institutional analysis' that criticizes a particular institution while assuming other institutions are preferable. Komesar (n 88) 38, 147, and 205.

private regulation, not ordinary market transactions.[121] Even where free movement scrutiny has been applied, the Court has tended to show deference to private regulators, as will be discussed below. The Court tends to justify most private restraints, even when it does not a priori reject jurisdiction.

The restrained application of the free movement rules on private actors makes sense from an institutional perspective. A large number of cases in which individuals challenge the practices of other individuals would exert considerable pressure on the Court's resources.[122] The efficacy of the market solution—allowing private actors a significant scope of autonomy and leaving it to competition to rectify any restrictive or discriminatory practices—varies depending on the context. A shop refusing to stock foreign goods could simply be driven out of the market, with no particular need for judicial or legislative intervention.[123] If there are several competing private regulatory schemes, the market can be expected to perform well in eliminating those that are unnecessarily restrictive.[124] Along those lines, the case law shows that ordinary contracts between individuals largely fall outside the scope of the rules on free movement of goods.[125] On the other hand, discrimination against persons on the basis of nationality is subject to judicial review under the free movement rules, even in the case of a single employment relationship.[126] This difference could be explained not just by the sensitive fundamental rights at issue in the second case, but also by the greater likelihood that normal market forces will dis-incentivize private contracts restricting trade in goods.

The Court has also reacted to the likelihood that checks and balances will be imposed on a private regulator by the political process. For co-regulation on the national level, it has shown a level of deference in cases where there is effective supervision of the private regulator by his public counterpart in the co-regulatory scheme.[127] The EU political process can also be used to constrain or even directly

[121] As Davies, notes: 'Private contractual preferences do not, in general, appear to be seen as restrictions on free movement.' He adds that 'the mere fact that there are so few [cases] may be one of the most powerful arguments that free movement is not understood by the Court, or courts, to regulate private contractual preferences as such, outside of a private regulatory context'. Davies (n 68) 806 and 818.

[122] Komesar (n 88) 141. As Komesar suggests, courts are likely to react to constraints on resources by interpreting the law in a way that reduces likelihood of plaintiff success: introducing deference, standing or jurisdictional obstacles. ibid 165 et seq.

[123] See the Opinion of Maduro in *Viking Line* (n 17) para 42. Snell (n 14) 229 et seq. claims that applying the free movement rules to private undertakings in such circumstances 'would ... amount to inefficient and unnecessary public intervention'.

[124] See Anthony Ogus, 'Self-regulation' in *Encyclopedia of Law and Economics*, vol. 5 (2000) 594–96 and Ségolène Barbou des Places, 'Self-Regulation and the Professions: A Perspective from Regulatory Competition Theory' in Fabrizio Cafaggi (ed), *Reframing Self-Regulation in European Private Law* (Kluwer Law International 2006) for discussions of competitive self-regulation. See also Chapter I section 3.

[125] *Sapod Audic* (n 57) para 74.

[126] *Angonese* (n 40).

[127] In *Commission v Italy* (n 113) para 53, Italian regulation of lawyers' fees was considered not even to restrict free movement, in part because courts could depart from the prices set by the bar association and confirmed by the government. Moreover, numerous competition cases such as *Arduino* and *Cipolla* (n 113) show significant deference to governmental supervision of co-regulatory schemes.

address private actors, including private regulators.[128] In these cases, judicial intervention on the basis of the free movement rules may not be as necessary. Let us take the example of the recognition of professional qualifications of lawyers by bar associations. Instead of leaving bar associations free to recognize only the qualifications they deem appropriate and hoping that cross-border competition would compel them to be fair about it, and instead of expecting domestic courts and the ECJ to examine their rules on a case-by-case basis, the EU could legislate on the issue, requiring recognition and perhaps a level of uniformity of professional qualifications across the Member States. In practice, there were in fact cases of deep free movement scrutiny that were followed by EU legislation.[129] While free movement cases still come to the Court, the earlier cases do seem to show a more activist approach with less explicit deference to bar associations. Scrutiny is also much more likely against national than against transnational or EU-level private regulation, as there is a market-partitioning element at play. There are very few examples of free movement scrutiny without such a link to market-partitioning.

Finally, one objection to the analysis so far should be addressed: the possibility of using other legal techniques to supervise abuse of private regulatory power. In particular, competition law has often been claimed to be sufficient, making free movement scrutiny of private actors unnecessary.[130] The relationship between free movement and competition law will be the subject of Chapter IV. For now it is sufficient to say that these rules will not necessarily achieve the same outcomes nor, more importantly, can they do justice to the same set of considerations. Moreover, while there may be cases where both free movement and competition law apply, there are other cases where one of them does not.[131] Thus, competition law may be unavailable or unsuitable for protecting market integration from some private restraints. As I will try to show in Chapter IV, the differences between these two sets of rules and the complexities arising from their relationship suggest that both should, in principle, be available.

4. The Legal Test(s) for Private Action Under the Free Movement Rules

We have seen that private regulatory regimes have been subjected to the free movement rules in a variety of circumstances. In fact, if we can speak of private actors with regulatory roles, it is a safe assumption that the free movement rules will apply. This is certainly true in relation to co-regulatory regimes, where the well-worn *Walrave* formulation seems wide enough to subject them to free movement

[128] Two very different examples are the Directive 2006/123/EC of the European Parliament and of the Council on services in the internal market [2006] OJ L376 (see point 114 in the preamble and Art 37/1) and the Regulation (EC) 717/2007 of the European Parliament and of the Council on roaming on public mobile telephone networks within the Community and amending Directive 2002/21/EC [2007] OJ L171. See Chapter I section 6.4.

[129] See Chapter VI. [130] Snell (n 14) 232. [131] ibid.

rules. Even purely self-regulatory schemes with significant *de facto* effects on third parties such as consumers and market entrants will in most cases invite free movement scrutiny.

Nevertheless, there is still considerable controversy over the extent of the obligations imposed on private actors. When such obligations are imposed, the Court relies on a number of distinct narratives, without an overriding logic.[132] *Effet utile* and the need to prevent circumvention of the free movement rules (*Walrave*), the 'inequality' that would result from applying free movement to public, but not to equivalent private regulation (*Bernard*,[133] *Bosman*), attribution of action to the State (*Buy Irish*, *Apple & Pear Development Council*), and the universal nature of non-discrimination as a fundamental right (*Defrenne*, *Angonese*) have all been relied upon. Sometimes, these different narratives are cited together even when they do not seem to fit the context, such as in *Angonese* or in *Viking Line*.[134] Moreover, we are not yet sure what the consequences of passing that threshold are. Is the scrutiny that is applied to private actors the same as that applied to State bodies? Are the justifications that can be applied different in the two cases?

As I argued above, the discussion on the horizontal effect of the free movement rules does not have to be brought up to the level of a 'grand dichotomy'[135] of public and private. The Court today seems open to extending free movement scrutiny to private actors when their actions, seen in the legal and economic context, are capable of impeding or restricting free movement, and not only when they are structurally linked to the State. It may, therefore, be worth exploring whether this simple question could provide the overriding narrative—is the private regulator capable of impeding free movement or not?[136]

Simplifying the question in this way leads to new problems, of course. For one thing, it may assume that we have a much clearer idea of what it means to 'impede free movement' than we actually do.[137] This point must be conceded. The benefit of this approach, however, is at least that these issues can be addressed more directly than by relying on a dogmatic version of the public–private distinction.

Secondly, it might be argued that this approach is a radical overextension of the free movement rules. It does not need to be that way, however. Subtle

[132] Krenn (n 14) 215 uses the metaphor of 'a jigsaw puzzle waiting for pieces to fall into place'.

[133] Case C-325/08 *Olympique Lyonnais SASP v Olivier Bernard and Newcastle UFC* [2010] ECR I-2177, para 31.

[134] See n 29.

[135] Norberto Bobbio, *Democracy and Dictatorship: The Nature and Limits of State Power* (Polity 1989) ch 1.

[136] This would bring EU law to the stage that Kennedy would call 'continuumisation': the troublesome public–private distinction ends up being replaced by a balancing process taking into account a variety of factors to decide whether the effects of a private restraint merit scrutiny. This is not a hugely original suggestion. Indeed, Kennedy would describe this as merely one of the predictable stages of the decline of the public–private distinction as one of the bedrocks of classic nineteenth-century legal thought. Kennedy (n 84) 1352–53.

[137] As Seidman points out, reformulating the public–private distinction in 'pragmatic' terms presupposes that we have goals we are trying to accomplish. Since those goals are in and of themselves questionable, most of the troubling questions on the actual extent of scrutiny simply reappear. Seidman (n 80) 401.

modifications of the existing test can suffice to prevent over-enforcement. In most cases, private actors would not be found to restrict free movement even when they make economic decisions that favour actors from their own Member State. Moreover, even when private actors are found to restrict free movement, they normally have an easier job justifying their measures than do the Member States.

Even now, the doctrine surrounding the free movement rules allows for plenty of ways to dampen the impact of the free movement rules on private action. One example is the notion of 'uncertain and indirect effect'. Even where a measure impedes market access, it is sometimes not considered to be a restriction of free movement because it is marginal or because its impact is difficult to predict. This legal construct could rescue a number of cases of private regulation.[138] For example, if one private regulator is in competition with others, so that its restrictive rules can be avoided, the construct of 'uncertain and indirect effects' of his measures to free movement could be used to avoid scrutiny.

Another factor which excludes quite a number of cases from free movement challenges is the principle that the free movement rules do not apply to internal situations confined to a single Member State—for example national private regulation that affects no cross-border interests. Although this is a highly imprecise and problematic filter,[139] it may accomplish one goal: limit the application of the free movement rules to cases that are serious enough to incentivize cross-border litigation.

In addition, it has been argued that an impact-based *de minimis* test, tolerating restrictive conduct that does not have great market-distorting effects, should be adopted in free movement law, and especially (perhaps only) for private actors.[140] So far, the Court has resisted this, perhaps in order to avoid complex case-by-case assessments. This rejection is probably justified for most Member State measures, which can usually be assumed to create restrictive effects. For private restrictions, however, there is a better argument for examining their actual market effects more closely. This could be achieved through a form of special *de minimis* test for private actors, or could be folded into the definition of a restriction.

[138] These cases mostly exempt measures which could lead to the imposition of additional costs on new entrants, but those costs are either so low or so improbable that they unlikely to bear on a decision to invest or trade. The classics are Case C-69/88 *H. Krantz GmbH & Co. v Ontvanger der Directe Belastingen and Netherlands State* [1990] ECR I-583, para 11, Case C-190/98 *Volker Graf v Filzmoser Maschinenbau GmbH* [2000] ECR I-493, para 25, and Case C-379/92 *Criminal proceedings against Matteo Peralta* [1994] ECR I-3453, para 24; see also Case C-211/08 *Commission v Spain* [2010] ECR I-5267, para 72 and Case C-291/09 *Francesco Guarnieri & Cie v Vandevelde Eddy VOF* [2011] ECR I-2685, para 17 for two recent examples.

[139] See for example Alina Tryfonidou, *Reverse Discrimination in EC Law* (Kluwer Law International 2009); Mislav Mataija, 'Internal Situations in Community Law: An Uncertain Safeguard of Competences within the Internal Market' (2010) 5 Croatian Yearbook of European Law and Policy 31.

[140] Pernilla Lindh, 'The Influence of Competition Law on Free Movement Rules' in Heikki Kanninen, Nina Korjus, and Allan Rosas (eds), *EU Competition Law in Contest: Essays in Honour of Virpi Tiili* (Hart 2009) 17–27.

In the following sections, I will further explore the issue of how the notion of a restriction of free movement should apply to private actors. I will also discuss how the justification test can be used as a way of exonerating much private action and protecting private autonomy as well as regulatory diversity.

4.1 The scope of the free movement rules and the definition of a restriction

The best safeguard against an overextension of the free movement rules is a clearer definition of a restriction of free movement. This can allow ample room for showing that ordinary private conduct, such as a contract between individuals or a refusal to contract with another individual, does not create barriers to trade in the first place.

In simplified terms, the legal test for a restriction to any fundamental freedom is either that the measure is discriminatory (eg favouring domestic over imported goods) or that it restricts market access by impeding or making less attractive the use of one's free movement rights.[141]

In practice, little private action will actually be restrictive under the latter test—especially when it comes to private action in general, not just private regulation. A restraint must be such as to impede, at least as far as a court can predict, market access of products, persons, services, capital, etc. This analysis is somewhat hypothetical in that it does not require a detailed market assessment showing, for example, reduced sales to be a consequence of a certain measure or action. It is still demanding enough to filter out simple private relationships, such as the proverbial shopkeeper who only sells domestic goods. Even if his decision is discriminatory,[142] it simply does not restrict anyone's market access, as long as there are alternative distribution channels in place. Since the Court defines a restriction on the basis of effects, it is possible to exclude behaviour that does not adversely impact free movement.[143] It is not necessary to invent an entirely new legal test: under a contextually sensitive, effects-focused test, this is already the main question to be asked about all restraints, public or private.

That same question may legitimately be answered differently when different kinds of actors adopt measures that appear to be similar, depending on the context. We can usually assume that legislation—if discriminatory or restrictive—will adversely affect market access, simply by virtue of its character as a binding measure with the power of the State behind it. For private measures, that may not be the case. Let us take the example of a ban on the advertising of alcohol. Such bans introduced through legislation have been considered to be restrictions on the free movement of goods, because of the assumption that they make it more difficult for a foreign producer, assumed to be a new entrant, to gain a foothold

[141] For a more detailed discussion, see Catherine Barnard, *The Substantive Law of the EU: The Four Freedoms* (3rd edn, Oxford University Press 2010).

[142] Thus, if subject to 'normal' free movement scrutiny, it would fail the *Keck* test for selling arrangements (see n 58).

[143] See also Davies (n 68) 812–13.

in the marketplace.[144] What if that same measure was adopted by an advertising industry association? The economic effects could be comparable, but could also be negligible. To actually show a restriction of free movement before a court, it should be necessary to make the additional effort of showing why this particular measure produces restrictive effects of the sort normally contemplated by the free movement rules. This should be done on a case-by-case basis and the evidentiary burden should be higher than in the case of clearly public restraints. The question we are asking is the same; it is just that with clearly public measures the way to the answer is shorter.

Two objections are possible at this point. One of them is that this approach tends to blend the issue of scope and the issue of the definition of a restriction (or, in different terms, the personal and material scope of the provisions).[145] This should be conceded. In defence, it could be remarked that the Court itself rarely draws a bright line between these two issues. The various steps of the free movement analysis do not necessarily pose fundamentally different questions. Rather, they are a sequence of filtering devices, ranging from relatively simple (scope) to relatively detailed (the necessity test) analytical steps that structure a judge's thinking on, essentially, a single question: what violates the right to free movement? Whether certain cases of private regulation are filtered out at the scope stage, the restriction stage, or even at the justification stage matters only if it affects the predictability of the outcome or the difficulty of the decision. Actors prefer to escape the free movement rules before the justification stage because of its perceived unpredictability; the differences between the issues of scope and restriction, in this sense, are much less pronounced.

The second and more difficult objection is that, if the criterion is simply based on the effects of a measure, any refusal to deal in a cross-border situation will be seen as restricting the other party's free movement rights. Refusing an offer to import goods, refusing to provide services to cross-border clients, complaining about the noise from a (foreign-owned) bar down the street—all of these, in some sense, impact someone's free movement rights. Strictly following the logic that is usually applied to Member State restrictions, they would be considered *prima facie* restrictive and would have to be justified—arguably, an overreaching and inefficient judicial intervention. This problem is behind the criticism of those who object to an effects-based approach to the free movement rules that would rely on the 'ability to obstruct' as its guiding criterion.[146]

The way to overcome that problem would be—building on AG Maduro's proposal in *Viking Line*[147]—to take a broader perspective on the issue of when private

[144] Case C-405/98, *Konsumentombudsmannen (KO) v Gourmet International Products AB (GIP)* [2001] ECR I-1795, para 21.

[145] See Harm Schepel, 'Freedom of Contract in Free Movement Law: Balancing Rights and Principles in European Public and Private Law' (2013) 5&6 European Review of Private Law 1211, 1214.

[146] See for example Schepel (n 17) 307.

[147] '... provisions on freedom of movement apply to private action that, by virtue of its general effect on the holders of rights to freedom of movement, is capable of restricting them from exercising those rights, by raising an obstacle that they cannot reasonably circumvent' (para 48).

actors are actually in a position to restrict free movement. Instead of *prima facie* condemning every private action that makes a particular exercise of free movement of another private party more difficult, only those actors that are generally (but still in context of a certain class of actions, measures, or powers, and not in the abstract) in a position to affect free movement should be caught. This will be the case when their measures or actions constitute obstacles to accessing a market[148] in a Member State that cannot be overcome, or can be overcome only with significant costs or difficulties. Such scenarios are relatively rare, and would mostly boil down to private regulators in a position of *de facto* or *de iure* monopoly, or at least a position of significant power, in regulating or facilitating the access to a market. Situations where there are alternatives in the marketplace or where there is competitive private regulation would largely be filtered out.

Whether the type of actions a particular defendant can take, given the legal and economic context, rises to the level that merits free movement scrutiny, should therefore be analytically separate from the question of whether the particular action had an adverse impact on the plaintiff's single exercise of freedom of movement. This might be translated into two questions within the legal test: first, is the defendant in such a position, due to the legal and economic context, that it is able to impose barriers to free movement that cannot be reasonably circumvented and, second, has there actually been a restriction on the free movement rights of the plaintiff? This threshold for applying the free movement rules to private actors is, in most cases at least, likely to be higher than that for the application of the competition rules.[149]

It is true that this proposal poses evidentiary obstacles and boundary issues.[150] Arguably, however, the same is true with most existing interpretations, but without the benefit of addressing the underlying issues in a direct manner. This test would also lead to a seemingly paradoxical consequence. While, with State restrictions,

[148] For an example of the Court's definition of barriers to market access, see Case C-518/06 *Commission v Italy* [2009] ECR I-3491: even though the measure 'leaves intact the right of access to the Italian market', it affects market access by 'leading to significant additional costs': 'if they wish to enter the Italian market under conditions which comply with Italian legislation, such undertakings will be required to re-think their business policy and strategy, inter alia, by considerably expanding the range of insurance services offered'. This makes access to the Italian market less attractive and, even if access is obtained, 'reduces the ability of the undertakings concerned to compete effectively ... against undertakings traditionally established in Italy' (paras 65–70).

[149] On the standards for applying competition law to dominant actors in general, see Einer Elhauge and Damien Geradin, *Global Competition Law and Economics* (Hart 2011) section 3B; Renato Nazzini, *The Foundations of European Union Competition Law: The Objective and Principles of Article 102* (Oxford University Press 2011) ch 10; Richard Whish and David Bailey, *Competition Law* (7th edn, Oxford University Press 2012) 179–89. Even in competition law, higher levels of scrutiny may apply to 'super-dominant' undertakings (see ibid 187–89). By analogy, free movement scrutiny need not apply to each and every case of market dominance; equally, a private regulator may be in a position of power that is not a dominant position at all, in the meaning given to that term in competition law. See Chapter IV on the relationship of free movement and competition law.

[150] See Gareth Davies, 'Freedom of Contract and the Horizontal Effect of Free Movement Law' in Dorota Leczykiewicz and Stephen Weatherill (eds), *The Involvement of EU Law in Private Law Relationships* (Hart 2013) 57–58; Krzeminska-Vamvaka (n 14) 47–48.

the free movement rules primarily catch discrimination and, only in addition to that, non-discriminatory[151] measures that impede market access, the primary focus here is on whether or not there is an impediment. If no impediment to market access arises out of a particular class of actions of a particular private actor, then that private actor could also be free to discriminate—unless there is another legal rule, such as secondary EU law or consumer law,[152] that prevents it. This would apply to the example of the shopkeeper, who is free not to stock imported goods if he so chooses, or the neighbour who objects to the opening of a nightclub that happens to be run by a subsidiary of a firm from another Member State.[153]

A number of commentators, it should be pointed out, have argued the exact opposite: private actors should not be able to discriminate, but should be able to impose non-discriminatory barriers.[154] In my view, this would be an overly rough transposition of the free movement test applicable to States. When a Member State discriminates, it normally also restricts the market access of the discriminated goods, services, etc. Beyond that, the State can affect market access by non-discriminatory measures. When we think about private actors, however, it becomes clearer that discrimination and impediment to market access are only partially overlapping categories: one can discriminate without affecting market access (the example of the shopkeeper), and one can also affect market access without discriminating (for example, the claim advanced by the plaintiff in *Fra.bo*).

There is one important caveat, however. Regardless of general effects in the marketplace, discrimination should not be permissible in situations such as those in *Angonese* or *Raccanelli*; specifically, when discrimination against persons—primarily as workers, but in some cases perhaps also as self-employed persons, providers, and even recipients of services—is at stake.[155] Admittedly, these cases do not fit into the test just outlined. The extension of the free movement rules to such situations, primarily discrimination of persons based on nationality, follows a different rationale linked to fundamental rights and should be retained as such. This would do

151 See, however, Gareth Davies, 'Understanding Market Access: Exploring the Economic Rationality of Different Conceptions of Free Movement Law' (2010) 11 German Law Journal 671, 674, making the argument that 'measures which affect all market actors equally do not in fact hinder market access'. This debate is beyond the scope of this chapter. It suffices to say that the general view is that at least some measures that are not even indirectly discriminatory (ie they do not have a disparate impact) but substantially affect market access fall under the scope of the free movement rules. See for example Barnard (n 141) 164, 264.

152 See the examples of secondary law referred to in section 2.4.

153 See Davies (n 150) 56–57. Davies argues for the exclusion of situations such as these on different grounds: according to him, the free movement rules are essentially about protecting the freedom of contract, so that only measures of third parties that impact the contracting freedom of others are caught; a party to a contract does not restrict the free movement rights of the other party.

154 Oliver and Roth (n 18) 426, Milner-Moore (n 14) summary of section C, Prechal and de Vries (14) 17–18.

155 See for example Norbert Reich, 'The Impact of the Non-discrimination Principle on Private Autonomy' in Dorota Leczykiewicz and Stephen Weatherill (eds), *The Involvement of EU Law in Private Law Relationships* (Hart 2013) 257–62.

justice to a rift in the free movement rules between their more traditional, economic aspects, and aspects related to citizenship and fundamental rights.[156]

Schepel, among others, has criticized this approach by pointing to an apparent contradiction with *Bosman*, where the Court made clear that the free movement rules also apply to non-discriminatory restrictions.[157] What is set apart by *Angonese*, however, is not the abstract technique of discriminating between different categories, but actual discrimination against persons entitled to rely on free movement rights. It does not follow from *Angonese* that all private actions, whether discriminatory or not, that affect the movement of an individual good or service, have to be prohibited by the free movement rules.

There is an even simpler way to explain what looks like a contradiction between the approach in *Angonese* and the effects-based approach to private restrictions of market access. Discrimination against workers on the basis of nationality is already prohibited by directly applicable secondary law, namely Regulation 492/2011.[158] Thus, not only does EU law treat it distinctly, but private autonomy arguments clearly cannot exempt it from scrutiny.

4.2 Justifying private regulation

It is often argued that private actors, because of private autonomy or because of the freedom of association, should not be required to justify their actions under the strict proportionality test as is applied to Member State measures.[159] The proportionality test can, however, adapt. Indeed, the case law shows that, by and large, private parties can justify restrictions that the Member States cannot. Even where their actions are considered to restrict free movement, private parties still enjoy a comparatively wide margin for justification as well as a more flexible proportionality test.

Famously, the *Bosman* case made it clear that there are no strict limits on the ability of private actors to invoke public interest justifications, including those listed in the Treaty.[160] In subsequent cases, private actors were allowed to plead a wide range of justifications. This was a significant step since, even to this day, it is not uncommon for scholars to argue that private parties should not be able

[156] See section 2.3 and n 39 in particular. The reading of the fundamental freedoms as being, at least in some contexts, equivalent to fundamental rights could, however, be read as an argument for convergence rather than differentiation. See, for example, Alina Tryfonidou, 'Further Steps on the Road to Convergence Among the Market Freedoms' (2010) 35 European Law Review 41: '... although the market freedoms continue to have as their sole aim the construction and maintenance of an internal market, when read in the light of Union citizenship they are also considered to be fundamental rights in the economic sphere to which all Union citizens are entitled ... In other words, all market freedoms now form part of a general right for Union citizens to pursue an economic activity in a cross-border context.'

[157] Schepel (n 17) 308. [158] See n 46.

[159] See, for example, Norbert Reich, 'Balancing in Private Law and the Imperatives of the Public Interest: National Experiences and (Missed?) European Opportunities' in Roger Brownsword, Hans-W Micklitz, Leone Niglia, and Stephen Weatherill (eds), *The Foundations of European Private Law* (Hart 2011) 221, 245–46 and Schepel (n 145) 1221 et seq.

[160] *Bosman* (n 13) para 86.

to invoke public policy as a way of justifying their measures at all, or at least that there is something incongruous to that idea.[161]

Even beyond *Bosman*, however, EU law has adapted to private regulation in ways that facilitate the justification of private restraints.

Firstly, arguments usually associated with private autonomy can be explicitly recognized in addition to whatever substantive justification the private party invokes. A good example, while not truly a 'horizontal' case, is *Schmidberger*, the case on environmental protesters blocking the highway. Austria did not invoke environmental protection to justify permitting the protests. It was not necessary to show that there was a real reason to be worried about pollution on that highway, or that the protests might somehow contribute to the preservation of nature, or that they were consistent with other aspects of Austrian policy. The protests were justified by relying on freedom of expression of the protesters—an aspect of private autonomy.[162] One could imagine other rights, such as the freedom of contract, freedom of assembly and association, freedom of entrepreneurship, etc., being used in a similar way.[163] For example, an industry body that sets vehicle emission standards could argue that its measures are protecting the environment, but also that they are an aspect of freedom of association. Sometimes, a private regulator may get a double, mutually reinforcing set of justifications: the substantive justification and a justification connected to a notion of private autonomy.[164]

[161] 'Private acts ... serve individual interests (or, in case of a class of persons, the collective interests), which are typically of an economic nature. A limitation of a freedom, however, can only be justified ... by grounds of common interest that are "non-economic" in nature. This structural incongruence ... already puts the thesis of direct horizontal effect into doubt.' Leible (n 19) 76. K Mortelmans, 'Towards Convergence in the Application of the Rules on Free Movement and on Competition?' (2001) 38 Common Market Law Review 613, 642 argues that the ability of private parties to justify restrictive measures should be limited not just in principle, but through the necessity and proportionality test as well—arguably, the opposite of the direction taken by the case law. More broadly, Semmelmann (n 77) 536–37 notes the intellectual origin of proportionality as a way of limiting State intervention, and wonders whether its application to private action shows that it has morphed into a more generic 'functional instrument' for weighing policy goals. Schepel (n 17) 311 argues that broad justification would 'be at the detriment of the robustness and coherence of the justification regime'.

[162] *Schmidberger* (n 69) para 66.

[163] AG Trstenjak in her Opinion in *Fra.bo* (n 38) paras 36–39, 55–57, and 60, suggested that private parties could justify their measures, along with the written and unwritten justifications available to Member States, also by 'special grounds in the private interest', an example of which would be the objective of encouraging the training of young players recognized in *Bernard* (n 133) 'objective considerations' that she considers to be a special category recognized in *Angonese* (n 40) or, finally, a right recognized by the Charter of Fundamental Rights, such as the right to conduct a business (Art 16). While it is questionable whether the distinctions between 'public interest justifications', 'special grounds in the private interest', and 'objective considerations' are valid, the Opinion clearly makes the point that the scope for private parties to invoke various justifications is quite a bit broader than with Member State measures.

[164] The distinction between these two categories of justifications is largely a heuristic device. For example, were the justifications invoked by the trade unions in *Viking Line* (n 17) paras 75–86 substantive (protection of workers) or procedural (protection of the negotiating ability of trade unions)? Were they based on the autonomy granted to trade unions or on the 'public interest' of social protection? Except for the purpose of discussion, these various aspects of the trade unions' argument cannot be fully separated.

Such 'double-dip' justifications are unlikely to go far, however. In relation to private regulators, there is a trade-off between their ability to defend measures on the basis of private autonomy and what can be described as 'regulatory autonomy'. Regulatory autonomy involves deferring to private regulators by granting them a wide margin of discretion, in some cases even wider than in the case of Member States, to pursue a legitimate policy by means of their own choosing. The price to be paid for that privilege, however, is that private autonomy claims, whether those arguing for broad exclusion from EU law or those relying exclusively on freedom of contract, association, or assembly, lose force.

This can be described along a scale. At one end of the scale are arguments invoking full private autonomy, claiming that private action, even regulatory, can never fall under the scope of the free movement rules.[165] Given that they call for broad *ex ante* exclusion of private action from scrutiny, these claims have not really been tenable for some time.

The next mode of justification can be described as autonomy-based balancing. It is also based on the idea of a protected sphere of conduct that should not be disciplined by EU law, but it does not demand blanket exemptions. Instead, it either asks for a more permissive standard of review due to the particularities of private regulation,[166] or offsets values such as the freedom of association or assembly against the restrictive effects of private regulation in the balancing stage.[167]

As the regulatory nature of private measures becomes more apparent, however, the usefulness of these arguments, standing on their own, recedes. There are several reasons for that. Firstly, whenever the measures of private regulators have effects beyond the circle of actors that set the rules, third parties do not benefit from the regulators' freedom of association. Secondly, it is unclear what weight should be given to values of autonomy in different contexts if no account is taken of the substantive aims pursued and tools used.[168]

[165] *Walrave* (n 12) para 15, *Viking Line* (n 17) paras 39, 42, and 48 (arguing that trade union actions, in particular because of the fundamental right to strike, fall outside the scope of the free movement rules), *Fra.bo* (n 38) para 14.

[166] The arguments of the UEFA and Germany in *Bosman* (n 13) are a good illustration: 'UEFA argued ... that it is extremely difficult to distinguish between the economic and the sporting aspects of football and that a decision of the Court ... might call in question the organization of football as a whole. For that reason, even if [Art 45 TFEU] were to apply to professional players, a degree of flexibility would be essential because of the particular nature of the sport' (para 71); 'The German Government ... referring to the freedom of association and autonomy enjoyed by sporting federations under national law [argued that] by virtue of the principle of subsidiarity, taken as a general principle, intervention by public, and particularly Community, authorities in this area must be confined to what is strictly necessary' (para 72). See also *Bernard* (n 133) para 40.

[167] Notes 162 and 163. See also *Commission v Germany* (n 22) para 26 for an attempt at justifying a restriction of free movement of goods on grounds of protecting industrial and commercial property.

[168] cf the Opinion of AG Lenz in *Bosman* (n 13) para 216, where he argues that, while sporting bodies could certainly invoke their freedom of association as a fundamental right, the focus of the balancing exercise should be on 'imperative reasons in the general interest', that is specific substantive justifications.

This is why the analysis naturally drifts towards substantive justification, that is whether a private regulator's measure is necessary and proportionate for the achievement of a legitimate aim.[169] While this analysis can work in a similar way as with Member State measures, the case law shows that, even here, the Court tends to follow a more deferential approach to private regulators. In *Deliège*, for example, it emphasized that adopting a certain system of selecting participants in a sports tournament 'must be based on a large number of considerations unconnected with the personal situation of any athlete, such as the nature, the organization and the financing of the sport concerned',[170] issues which 'fall naturally to the bodies concerned, such as ... sports federations'.[171] This shows the openness of the Court to taking into account the structural features of private regulation and its informational advantages, in order to preserve the way in which a particular sector is regulated.

In all three of the case studies addressed in Chapters V–VII, there are examples of this. The need to preserve the 'European sports model', the reluctance to challenge the bar associations' authority over the legal profession in the administration of disciplinary and ethical rules, and the broad recognition and deference to recognized standards bodies can all be seen as ways of preserving the autonomy of private regulators in deciding not only on their internal organization but also on substantive issues—stopping short, however, of granting them absolute authority over sectors of the economy. This flexibility could also have been used, for example, in *Laval* and especially *Viking Line*, in order to allow more space for trade union action.[172]

Deference to the structural or organizational features of private regulators is connected to another tendency: focusing the proportionality analysis on procedural issues. The analysis of private regulatory restrictions to free movement may focus on issues such as the decision-making procedure, composition of the decision-making bodies, transparency, fair hearing, opportunities for judicial review, etc.[173] It is difficult to lay down in advance a list of relevant features, but

[169] The justification could be based on explicit Treaty provisions, as in ibid (n 115) para 86, or on any number of legitimate grounds that the Court recognizes in its case law (whatever the term used; see n 163), such as in *Bernard* (n 133) paras 38–39.

[170] *Deliège* (n 35), para 65.

[171] ibid para 67.

[172] See for example Christian Joerges, 'A Renaissance of the European Economic Constitution' in Ulla B Neergaard, Ruth Nielsen, and Lynn M Roseberry (eds), *Integrating Welfare Functions into EU Law: From Rome to Lisbon* (Djoef Publishing 2009) 29, 46–52 and in particular the citation of Alexander Somek at 51.

[173] See Sacha Prechal, 'Free Movement and Procedural Requirements: Proportionality Reconsidered' (2008) 35 Legal Issues of Economic Integration 201 for an extensive overview of the ways in which procedural criteria, including judicial review, have been relevant to the free movement proportionality analysis. Of these, Case 222/86 *Union nationale des entraîneurs et cadres techniques professionnels du football (Unectef) v Georges Heylens and others* [1987] ECR 4097, paras 13–16 (duty to state reasons and judicial review are necessary to protect fundamental rights in the context of a diploma recognition procedure, which could also apply to a professional body that decides on those issues) and Case C-18/88 *Régie des télégraphes et des téléphones v GB-Inno-BM SA* [1991] ECR I-5941, paras 35–37 (the lack of a hearing or judicial review of telephone equipment type approval decisions by the telecom incumbent speak against the justification of a restriction to free movement of goods) are particularly relevant for private regulators. *Wilson* (n 114)

broadly speaking, if some benchmark of procedural fairness is achieved, it is less likely that the Court of Justice would enter into a substantive re-assessment of the private regulator's decision. The price to be paid for that, however, is the willingness to engage with EU law and accept its potential applicability, that is letting go of the idea of full autonomy.

Finally, the necessity test contained in the proportionality analysis, asking whether there is a less restrictive alternative that achieves the same legitimate aim, can work to the advantage of private regulators. Since private regulators are not a part of the State, they cannot be assumed to have the full range of hypothetical regulatory alternatives at their disposal. Their toolbox may be limited to a certain narrow sector or one particular level of regulation (eg only enforcement, but no standard setting). Therefore, their measures might be easier to justify if the test takes into account only the alternatives available to the specific regulator. The evidence is scant, but it could be claimed that the ECJ has responded to this problem with a certain level of deference,[174] meaning that the necessity test may in fact be easier to satisfy for private actors.[175]

Another question worth asking is whether private actors might be allowed to invoke certain substantive justifications that are unavailable to Member States. Notably, the Member States are usually not allowed to invoke economic arguments to justify restrictive measures. Some have pointed out that this would mean that private actors would, as well, be precluded from defending their actions on the basis of their 'best economic interest'.[176]

paras 43–62 discusses a similar issue (whether the system of review over bar admission decisions is in line with fair trial guarantees) in the context of a specific rule of the Lawyers' Establishment Directive (Directive 98/5/EC of the European Parliament and of the Council to facilitate practice of the profession of lawyer on a permanent basis in a Member State other than that in which the qualification was obtained [1998] OJ L77/36). In the context of competition law, see Harm Schepel, 'Delegation of Regulatory Powers to Private Parties Under EC Competition Law: Towards a Procedural Public Interest Test' (2002) 39 Common Market Law Review 31, 50: 'Self-regulatory arrangements are to be protected from antitrust if they can make a plausible claim to put the "public interest" over narrow private interests. The "public interest" is defined neither substantively nor institutionally: [it] is defined procedurally.'

[174] See, by analogy, Case C-309/99 *J. C. J. Wouters, J. W. Savelbergh and Price Waterhouse Belastingadviseurs BV v Algemene Raad van de Nederlandse Orde van Advocaten, intervener: Raad van de Balies van de Europese Gemeenschap* [2002] ECR I-1577, discussing whether the bar association was 'entitled to consider' that there was a risk of conflicts of interest (para 105) and finding that the measure could 'reasonably be considered to be necessary' (para 107). This is reminiscent of the light level of scrutiny that would in US law be called a 'rational basis' or 'means/end rationality' test. Joel P. Trachtman, 'Trade and ... Problems, Cost-Benefit Analysis and Subsidiarity' [1998] 9 European Journal of International Law 32, 35.

[175] In *Erny* (n 47), however, the Court refused Daimler's argument that the salary calculation method that would have been in line with EU law is difficult to administer, saying that it had already rejected such justifications when advanced by the Member States and that 'neither the scope nor the content of those grounds of justification is in any way affected by the public or private nature of the disputed provisions' (para 48). This is perhaps idiosyncratic: it is not clear why calculating a salary top-up would be too difficult for an average employer. The paragraph could, in fact, be read as saying that the scope of other grounds of justification could be affected by the public or private nature of the restraint.

[176] Schepel (n 17) 313.

What the Member States are normally prevented from relying on under the heading of 'economic arguments' are, in fact, self-serving protectionist objectives. Arguments that a certain policy improves social welfare or that it addresses a certain market failure can still be used. What about private actors? While profit-seeking undertakings that engage in ordinary marketplace behaviour will not normally be caught by the free movement rules (excluding discrimination of the *Angonese* variety), and could in any event rely on justifications such as the freedom to conduct a business, private regulators could legitimately be required not to impede free movement for pure profit-seeking reasons. Nevertheless, the resources of private actors are normally more limited than those of the Member States, making economic arguments more persuasive. In addition, many private regulatory schemes are connected to the pursuit of commercial ends (such as, for example, a sporting body that regulates the very competitions from which it derives income). Some additional room should therefore be made for economic arguments than is the case with State measures. For example, a private regulator that does not dispose of State-like resources should be able to show that a hypothetical alternative measure is not economically feasible.

5. Conclusion

In this chapter, I have claimed that judicial supervision of private regulators under the free movement rules is justified at least in some circumstances. Broadly speaking, the judiciary should step in when neither markets, nor domestic and EU political processes are able to control the exercise of private power capable of restricting free movement. The legal test best able to capture this idea is one focused on the effects of a private regulator's activities on free movement. Indeed, the case law, especially after *Fra.bo*, seems to be moving in that direction. I nuanced this, however, by proposing a more general evaluation of effects: a restriction of free movement, when private regulators are concerned, should not simply be an action that makes another person's particular exercise of free movement more difficult. Instead, the analysis should ask whether that private regulator, when engaging in the type of activity or measure as the one scrutinized, and keeping in mind the legal and economic context, is in a position to impede free movement. The situations that can satisfy that test largely boil down to a *de iure* or *de facto* regulatory monopoly over a certain sector that creates market-partitioning effects.

Two aspects of this test are important. First, this case-by-case scrutiny has to consider the legal context, including links to the State such as co-regulation, delegation, or exclusive rights. The existence of those links would, in general, argue in favour of scrutiny. I have, however, argued against basing the legal test directly on a public–private divide, simply classifying actors into 'public' or 'private', 'regulatory' or 'economic', 'public interest' or 'private interest' boxes. It is not just that the borders between these categories are unclear; I have argued also that they are theoretically unsound and, more often than not, based on previously formed but unstated political preferences. There is an entire level of discussion behind classifying an actor or action as public or private, and the test I have proposed does a better job of bringing that discussion to light.

The second important aspect of my proposal is that it adapts to the context of private regulation. In terms of the scope and definition of a restriction to free movement, it would generally require a more demanding analysis than in the case of straightforward State measures. In terms of justifications, it would be more permissive, both in terms of the aims that can be invoked and in terms of how demanding the proportionality and necessity test would be. The latter adaptation can already, to a great extent, be traced in the case law. In particular, I have argued that private regulators have benefited from a certain level of deference, not just to the substantive regulatory choices they make but also to their structure and organization (regulatory autonomy). This implies, however, a general openness to free movement scrutiny and a limited ability to invoke pure private autonomy arguments such as freedom of association and assembly.

III

Competition Law and Private Regulation

1. Introduction

In addition to the free movement rules, the competition rules make up the second part of the EU's 'economic constitution'.[1] Unlike with the former, there is nothing remarkable in applying the latter, in particular Arts 101 and 102 TFEU,[2] to private regulation. After all, even a blatant price-fixing agreement 'regulates' the behaviour of its participants. Similarly, many private initiatives that are not purely self-serving could be described as agreements or decisions under Art 101 or as dominant positions in the market under Art 102. The very fact that a private actor is in a role that can be described as regulatory may indicate a level of market power that triggers antitrust scrutiny. As Maher points out, 'it is not contradictory to treat cartels as both potentially vulnerable to one form of regulation (competition law) while also performing important regulatory functions themselves'.[3]

As the importance of private regulation on both the national and transnational stage grows, however, its tension with competition law becomes more apparent. The tension is exacerbated by modern competition law's focus on economic efficiency,[4] as expressed in the 'more economic approach' of the European Commission. The notion that private restraints of competition should be preserved because of their

[1] On the notion of the European economic constitution, see Miguel Poiares Maduro, *We the Court: The European Court of Justice and the European Economic Constitution: A Critical Reading of Article 30 of the EC Treaty* (Hart 1998); Julio Baquero Cruz, *Between Competition and Free Movement: The Economic Constitutional Law of the European Community* (Hart 2002); Christian Joerges, 'A Renaissance of the European Economic Constitution' in Ulla B Neergaard, Ruth Nielsen, and Lynn M Roseberry (eds), *Integrating Welfare Functions into EU Law: From Rome to Lisbon* (Djoef Publishing 2009); Gralf-Peter Calliess, Jens Mertens, and Moritz Renner, 'Privatizing the Economic Constitution—Can the World Market Reproduce its own Institutional Prerequisites?' Osgoode CLPE Research Paper 11/2012 <http://ssrn.com/abstract=2056625>. Historically, the term traces its lineage to German ordoliberalism (see, eg Franz Böhm, 'Privatrechtsgesellschaft und Marktwirtschaft' (1966) 17 ORDO 7). See also Giuliano Amato, *Antitrust and the Bounds of Power: The Dilemma of Liberal Democracy in the History of the Market* (Hart 1997) 100.

[2] Article 101 TFEU deals with agreements, concerted practices, and decisions of associations of undertakings which have the object or effect of restricting competition, and Art 102 TFEU with abuses of dominant positions. National competition laws contain similar provisions.

[3] Imelda Maher, 'Competition Law and Transnational Private Regulatory Regimes: Marking the Cartel Boundary' (2011) 38 Journal of Law and Society 119, 122.

[4] Karen Yeung, 'Competition Law and the Public/Private Divide' in Jean-Bernard Auby and Mark Freedland (eds), *The Public Law/Private Law Divide: une entente assez cordiale?* (LGDJ 2004) 142.

role in, for example, creating jobs, implementing industrial policy objectives, or ensuring product safety is losing traction.[5]

At the outset, it should be made clear that there is no single, overriding approach that competition law takes in cases of private regulation. The issue is rarely even discussed in those terms. Instead, competition law scholarship frequently debates the specificity of sectors in which private regulation is prominent. Some of those sectors are sports,[6] the liberal professions,[7] and standard setting,[8] which I cover in Chapters V–VII. This chapter will attempt to generalize on some questions that recur in those specialized debates. To what extent can competition law be used as a mechanism for the *review* of regulation, and how does it adapt to that task? Should the competition rules take into account a multitude of regulatory aims, is it legitimate and practical for them to do so?

While, as explained, a broad range of restrictions to competition could in some sense be described as regulatory, this chapter will take a somewhat narrower focus, conscious, however, of all the definitional uncertainties that involves. It will not portray all anticompetitive co-ordination as a form of regulation. Rather, it will primarily discuss private schemes that claim to pursue general, public-interest aims and/or are addressed at persons (targets or regulatees) who are not parties to the scheme. This covers not only delegation or co-regulation, but also other

[5] Giorgio Monti, *EC Competition Law* (Cambridge University Press 2007) 89–91; Maher (n 3) 125. Historically, the existence of EU competition law is in part a response to the fact that cartels were 'the preferred means of industrial ordering' in Europe before the Second World War. Maher (n 3) 124. See also Amato (n 1) 39–40. For more on this, in the broader context of the history of European competition law(s), see G Marenco, 'The Birth of Modern Competition Law in Europe' in *European Integration and International Co-ordination: Studies in Honour of Claus-Dieter Ehlermann* (2002), David J Gerber, *Law and Competition in Twentieth Century Europe: Protecting Prometheus* (Oxford University Press 2001) and Yeung (n 4) 137.

[6] See Chapter V as well as Stephen Weatherill, *European Sports Law: Collected Papers* (1st edn, T.M.C. Asser Press 2007); Erika Szyszczak, 'Competition and Sport' (2007) European Law Review; Alfonso Rincón, 'EC Competition and Internal Market Law: On the Existence of a Sporting Exemption and its Withdrawal' (2007) 3 Journal of Contemporary European Research; Michael H LeRoy, 'The Narcotic Effect of Antitrust Law in Professional Sports: How the Sherman Act Subverts Collective Bargaining' (2011) 86 Tulane Law Review 860; and Oliver Budzinski, 'The Institutional Framework for Doing Sports Business: Principles of EU Competition Policy in Sports Markets' University of Southern Denmark Department of Environmental and Business Economics—Markets and Competition Working Paper No 2011-0124 <http://ssrn.com/abstract=1746948>.

[7] See Chapter VI, as well as *European Competition Law Annual 2004: The Relationship Between Competition Law and the (Liberal) Professions* (Claus-Dieter Ehlermann and Isabela Atanasiu (eds)) (Hart 2006); Tinne Heremans, *Professional Services in the EU Internal Market: Quality Regulation and Self-regulation* (Hart 2012); Ida E Wendt, *EU Competition Law and Liberal Professions: an Uneasy Relationship?*, vol 2 (Martinus Nijhoff Publishers 2012); and Panagiotis Delimatsis, '"Thou Shall Not ... (Dis) Trust": Codes of Conduct and Harmonization of Professional Standards in the EU' (2010) 47 Common Market Law Review 1049.

[8] See Chapter VII, as well as ABA Section on Antitrust Law, *Handbook on the Antitrust Aspects of Standards Setting* (American Bar Association 2004); Herbert Hovenkamp, 'Standards Ownership and Competition Policy' (2007) 48 Boston College Law Review 87; Harm Schepel, *The Constitution of Private Governance: Product Standards in the Regulation of Integrating Markets* (Hart 2005); and Heike Schweitzer, 'European Standard-Setting Policy and the Role of Competition Law' in Carl Baudenbacher (ed), *Current Developments in European and International Competition Law 15th St Gallen International Competition Law Forum (ICF) 2008* (Helbing & Lichtenhahn 2009).

instances of private regulation that has a legitimate claim to be more than a simple profit-seeking cartel.

In the context of private regulation, optimal competition law enforcement would maximize the benefits of private regulation (such as expertise, flexibility, lower costs, and its ability to address various market failures) while minimizing its cost (rent-seeking, capture, lack of transparency and accountability, and of course straightforward reductions in output, increases in price, and other economic inefficiencies associated with barriers to entry, price-fixing, market-sharing, etc.).[9] This enterprise is immediately complicated by the fact that the existence of private regulation may, in itself, be proof of the fact that markets do not always work well. From an institutional economic point of view, private regulation could be described as a response to the high transaction costs of atomistic market contracting through the establishment of a 'hierarchy', such as a standard-setting body.[10] Private regulation, like other forms of regulation, can be a response to market failures such as information asymmetry,[11] negative externalities,[12] the existence of public goods, and free-rider problems,[13] or, for example, create positive network effects.[14] Some sectors tend to be regulated even in the absence of obvious market failures. In sports, for example, this is due to the necessity of co-operation and credible sporting competition, as well as the long-standing tradition of global 'pyramid' governing structures and built-in redistributive mechanisms.[15]

The arguments of economic theories of regulation, such as the need to respond to market failures or the trade-off between the efficiencies of co-operation and the welfare loss caused by higher prices,[16] could be accommodated in traditional competition analysis. Going beyond them is more difficult. Controversies arise either when competition law internalizes regulatory aims and values that are not

[9] Maher (n 3) 132–33; Avery Katz, 'Taking Private Ordering Seriously' (1996) 144 University of Pennsylvania Law Review 1745, 1746–48.

[10] Calliess, Mertens, and Renner (n 1) 8–10.

[11] For example, regulating entry into the liberal professions may be seen as a response to the adverse selection and moral hazard that come about because of consumers' inability to distinguish between high and low quality services; Heremans (n 7). Labelling standards are another example of responding to high information costs. Ian Sheldon, 'Food Standards and International Trade' in Jutta Roosen, Jayson L Lusk, and Jason F Shogren (eds), *The Oxford Handbook of the Economics of Food Consumption and Policy* (Oxford University Press 2011) 394.

[12] An environmental sustainability standard can be described as a response to negative externalities. Suzanne Kingston, 'Integrating Environmental Protection and EU Competition Law: Why Competition Isn't Special' (2010) 16 European Law Journal 780, 800.

[13] See for example Iain Paterson, Marcel Fink, and Anthony Ogus, *Economic Impact of Regulation in the Field of Liberal Professions in Different Member States* (IHS Research Report—Study for the European Commission, DG Competition, 2003) 16. Heremans (n 7) points out that the public goods argument has limited weight in settings where the free rider problem is not particularly strong, such as in legal services.

[14] A compatibility standard creates positive network externalities by increasing the value of a system (eg the telephone network) with the rise in the number of users. Knut Blind, *The Economics of Standards: Theory, Evidence, Policy* (Edward Elgar 2004) 14–18.

[15] Of course, there are economic arguments for the specificity of sport as well. See Budzinski (n 6).

[16] Oliver E. Williamson, *Economies as an Antitrust Defense: The Welfare Tradeoffs* (1968) 58 The American Economic Review 18.

in some sense economic, or when it defers to the choices of private regulators without clearly showing the off-setting economic benefits of their measures—granting a kind of 'margin of appreciation' to private actors. This is where competition law struggles with its own limits.[17]

Another complication is the fact that, as discussed in Chapters I and II, private regulation is often sanctioned, sponsored, or even required by the State. These co-regulatory schemes can also be challenged under competition law. This may result in certain activities being immunized or exempt due to their link with the political process, often with rather unpredictable results.[18] In the EU context, moreover, it is not just the Member States that sometimes favour or require private regulation, but the EU institutions themselves. Standardization under the New Approach[19] is one example among many[20] of EU legislation delegating the production of norms to (partly) private actors. On top of that, private regulation may have links with international organizations or even semi-private transnational organizations—such as in the area of sports.[21] The presence of these links with State, EU, international, or transnational authorities is reflected in the competition law analysis of private regulators. Similarly to the free movement cases discussed in Chapter II, however, this rarely amounts to full *ex ante* exemptions from scrutiny.

The uneasiness of applying competition law to regulatory measures is reflected in the scholarly discussion. The application of competition law to private regulation, including co-regulation, is often presented as an exercise in distinguishing 'public' from 'private' conduct, or conduct in the 'public interest' from conduct in the 'private interest', as if those categories are self-explanatory. This sort of pigeonholing, however, is no more helpful in competition law than in free movement law. A simple understanding of the public–private divide, where private market actors do the competing, focused only on offering better products at lower prices, and public actors do the regulating,[22] is at odds with reality and can lead to distortive results. It shifts attention from the more central question of which instances of private regulation should be scrutinized and which should not, depending on the aims we believe competition law should pursue. Instead, it focuses on a search for links to the State which almost inevitably becomes formalistic and inconclusive, since most private action is in some sense 'authorized' by the State and most State action either benefits some private actors or could be performed by private actors.[23] Whether the 'publicness' of regulation is, as such, the right benchmark

[17] See Damien M B Gerard, 'A Global Perspective on State Action' in Ioannis Lianos and D Daniel Sokol (eds), *The Global Limits of Competition Law* (Stanford University Press 2012) 100.

[18] See for example Wolf Sauter and Harm Schepel, *State and Market in European Union Law: The Public and Private Spheres of the Internal Market Before the EU Courts* (Cambridge University Press 2009) 104–19.

[19] See Chapter VII section 2.2.

[20] See Chapter I sections 5 and 6.4.

[21] See Chapter VI.

[22] See n 194.

[23] As Elhauge notes, discussing the US antitrust state action doctrine: 'Purely formal concepts of state action are ... incapable of striking the rough compromise necessary to accommodate conflicting interests without reference to those interests. The principal problem is the absence of formal grounds for satisfactorily determining which exercises of authority created or enforced by the state

is not a foregone conclusion. In standard setting, for example, it is precisely the private interests of participating market actors that incentivizes the development of high-quality standards leading to economic benefits.[24]

The chapter will proceed as follows. Firstly, I will make a distinction between a 'broad' (internalizing) and a 'narrow' (externalizing) reading of competition law—a choice the necessity of which cases of private regulation highlight (section 2). Secondly, I will highlight the specificities of private regulation as the object of antitrust scrutiny (section 3.1), distinguishing the application of competition law to private actors and to the Member States (section 3.2). Section 4 concludes.

2. Competition Law and Regulation—Two Competing Visions

Competition law, at least as it has been traditionally understood, has trouble adapting to the task of supervising (private) regulatory schemes that base their legitimacy on something more than simply the merits of competing in the market. An important reason for this is that it is intellectually grounded in the idea of an unregulated marketplace.

When states choose to open a sector to competition, for example by privatizing or liberalizing, they do so believing that market forces will deliver not only low prices, but also an appropriate level of quality and availability of products and services. That aim may have previously been pursued through public ownership or command-and-control regulation, supported by a legal exemption from antitrust scrutiny. Therefore, as Hovenkamp puts it, 'the natural effect of deregulation is to enlarge the domain of antitrust by removing or narrowing antitrust immunities'.[25] In this picture, competition law is a substitute for regulation: it keeps liberalized markets true to their beneficial role by preventing the build-up and abuse of private power. If deregulation is followed by a move to private regulation, however, this increases the likelihood of conflict between competition law and sectorial regulation that was perhaps previously avoided, thanks to some sort of state action or regulatory immunity doctrine.

The notion that competition law and regulation cannot coexist is too simplistic and has been rejected by the Court of Justice and other institutions.[26]

should be deemed state action and which should not. Every restraint resulting from the exercise of such authority cannot be viewed as state action immune from antitrust review, for whenever businesses restrain trade they are exercising authority created or enforced by the state.' Einer R Elhauge, 'The Scope of Antitrust Process' (1991) 104 Harvard Law Review 667, 679–80.

[24] Schepel (n 8) 291–92.

[25] Herbert Hovenkamp, *The Antitrust Enterprise: Principle and Execution* (Harvard University Press 2005) 244.

[26] Joined cases 40–48, 50, 54–56, 111, 113, and 114–73 *Coöperatieve Vereniging 'Suiker Unie' UA and others v Commission* [1975] ECR 1663 established only that competition law withdraws when a national regulatory scheme leaves undertakings with no freedom of action (paras 65–72). When that is not the case, the Court usually sees no problem, in principle, in applying competition law on top of sector-specific regulation. See Case T-271/03 *Deutsche Telekom AG v Commission* [2008] ECR II-477, paras 263–66. Pablo Ibáñez Colomo, 'On the Application of Competition Law as

Competition law can be applied in the presence of sector-specific regulation. They can be seen as complementary, rather than antagonistic.[27] It is undeniable, however, that there can be tensions between the aims they pursue, or between the priorities of competition agencies and those of sectorial regulators. These tensions have spawned a literature[28] that sometimes speaks critically of 'regulatory antitrust'. It argues that 'antitrust law ... is directed at removing the obstacles to the competitive working of the market deriving from private behaviour, but it should not aim at attaining a particular result',[29] like shaping market structure in order to achieve market integration, innovation, energy security, or some other policy objective.[30] The debate is often, rather imprecisely,[31] framed in terms of a tension between *ex ante* (sector-specific) regulation and *ex post* (antitrust) intervention.

The 'competition and regulation' debate, of course, is not directly concerned with the application of competition law to the activities of *regulators* (be they public or private). It deals with the parallel application of the competition rules and regulatory rules, usually by different authorities, and with potentially divergent results. This chapter, on the other hand, asks how competition law deals with a regulatory scheme that is the *object* of scrutiny. The essential problem is similar, however: should competition law defer to other forms of regulation, or at least modify its approach when faced with regulatory arrangements?

One response would be to say that antitrust should have the same purpose as law or regulation in general: correcting market failures in pursuit of efficiency. Following this line, the idea of adapting competition law to regulation would be meaningless, because regulation that does not conform to economic efficiency should not exist. On this premise, antitrust could be used to replace regulatory measures (private or not) with more efficient outcomes.[32]

This chapter, however, will assume that competition law follows—and should follow—a more moderate line, and adapts to the regulatory context of the cases

Regulation: Elements for a Theory' [2010] Yearbook of European Law 261, 282. See also, more generally, John Temple Lang, 'European Competition Policy and Regulation: Differences, Overlaps, and Constraints' in Howard A Shelanski and François Lévêque (eds), *Antitrust and Regulation in the EU and US* (Edward Elgar 2009); Joël Monéger, 'Competition, Regulation and System Coherence' in Hanns Ullrich (ed), *The Evolution of European Competition Law: Whose Regulation, Which Competition?* (Edward Elgar 2006); D Geradin, *Remedies in Network Industries: EC Competition Law vs. Sector-Specific Regulation* (Intersentia Publishers 2004); and Pierre Larouche, *Competition Law and Regulation in European Telecommunications* (Hart Publishing 2000).

27 Hovenkamp (n 25) 227.

28 See n 26.

29 Alberto Pera, 'Changing Views of Competition, Economic Analysis and EC Antitrust Law' (2008) 4 European Competition Journal 127, 129.

30 Giorgio Monti, 'Managing the Intersection of Utilities Regulation and EC Competition Law' (2008) 4 Competition Law Review 123, 140.

31 Ibáñez Colomo (n 26) shows a number of instances where competition law was applied in an 'ex ante' manner (section 2.1).

32 The concept of economic efficiency can, of course, be understood in different ways. Louis Kaplow and Steven Shavell, *Fairness versus Welfare* (1st edn, Harvard University Press 2002), for example, argue that the only factor that should be given weight in legal decisions is their impact on individual welfare. Others consider that a broad range of legitimate regulatory objectives could be captured in an efficiency or market failure-based approach (Ibáñez Colomo (n 26) 560–61).

it scrutinizes. Under that assumption, however, the dilemma of *how* to adapt to regulation can lead to two competing visions of competition law: a narrow or 'externalizing' approach and a broad or 'internalizing' one.

The narrow vision is exclusively or mostly based on economic efficiency, similarly to the response I just discarded. What is different, however, is that a narrow competition law limits itself in order to avoid clashes with areas of law or regulation that are not necessarily based on economic efficiency objectives. To make up for the narrow justifications it allows for restrictive conduct, it chooses to be relatively narrow in scope. An efficiency-driven competition law would thus tend to be excluded from certain segments of the economy.[33] In this sense, a narrow approach to competition law 'externalizes' the decision on the acceptability of a private regulatory measure to other institutions or areas of law, such as to a legislator, or indeed to private regulators themselves.

Advocates of the narrow vision of competition law would not necessarily be against a salary cap in professional sports, or a food industry scheme limiting fat content in children's foods. They might, however, rather immunize those practices from competition law through some sort of judicially developed exemption doctrine or through a political decision, than move away from an efficiency-based analysis.[34] US state action doctrine, for example, prevents (notwithstanding many uncertain cases at the margin) the application of antitrust to State regulatory action. While more open than EU law to antitrust exemptions for State bodies, US antitrust law is less tolerant of private regulators that attempt to justify conduct in terms of broad public interest objectives. Famously, in *National Society of Professional Engineers*, a claim that a ban on competitive bidding among construction engineers is justified by public safety and professional ethics was described as a 'frontal assault on the basic policy of the Sherman Act'.[35] This distinction is in line, for example, with Elhauge's reading of the state action doctrine: financially interested actors can never be trusted to 'determine which restraints are in the public interest and which are not' because 'competition is the sole means

[33] A good example of the differences in approach between the two visions of competition law can be seen in Townley's comments on a discussion paper of the UK Office for Fair Trading. Christopher Townley, 'Which Goals Count in Article 101 TFEU? Public Policy and its Discontents: The OFT's Roundtable Discussion on Article 101(3) of the Treaty on the Functioning of the European Union' (2011) 32 European Competition Law Review 441, 445.

[34] One example of such exemptions is the US approach to professional sports. Joint selling of broadcasting rights is exempt by the Sports Broadcasting Act of 1961 (15 USC § 1291—Exemption from antitrust laws of agreements covering the telecasting of sports contests and the combining of professional football leagues), and major league baseball is subject to an even broader antitrust exemption thanks to a string of Supreme Court judgments starting with *Federal Baseball Club v National League* 259 US 200 (1922).

[35] *National Society of Professional Engineers v United States* (1978) 435 US 679 section B. Tellingly, the Court adds that 'the purpose of the analysis is to form a judgment about the competitive significance of the restraint; it is not to decide whether a policy favoring competition is in the public interest ... Subject to exceptions defined by statute, that policy decision has been made by Congress' (section A). See also *FTC v Indiana Federation of Dentists* (1986) 476 US 447, as well as the other cases discussed in Einer Elhauge and Damien Geradin, *Global Competition Law and Economics* (Hart 2011) chapter 2 section F.

approved by antitrust law for harnessing self-interested market actions for the public good'.[36] If the decision was genuinely made by public authorities, however, antitrust should step back.

The narrow view could even take the more extreme position of disregarding whether or not the State was involved and entirely exempt all regulatory action, whether public or private—transposing state action immunity to functionally equivalent private action. For example, one could say that private codes governing the entry into a profession restrict competition, but that competition authorities do not have the competence to deal with them because they are regulatory, not market behaviour.[37]

The narrow vision of competition rules as limited instruments seems attractive because it conforms to notions of judicial and agency self-restraint which are quite influential in modern antitrust scholarship. Limiting the scope of antitrust might thus be justified by the claim that false positives are more harmful than false negatives,[38] as well as by arguments connected to private autonomy, such as the freedom of contract. As Pera points out, 'antitrust rules should be applied parsimoniously ... antitrust law should be basically a marginal kind of intervention, which is relatively rare, and generally concerns large distortions of competition'.[39]

The second, broad vision allows competition authorities and courts in competition cases to take into account a wide set of values, regulatory aims, and justifications. It 'internalizes' the debate on the acceptability of private regulation, the substantive regulatory objectives it pursues, and the way in which it pursues them. This approach grants a broader scope to the competition rules, coupled with broad justifications for *prima facie* restrictive conduct. A restrictive agreement could, for example, avoid condemnation because of the benefits it produces for public health. Private regulators could be granted a measure of deference because of their links with public regulation or because they represent a broad constituency of stakeholders and employ transparent and fair procedures.

The broad approach could go even further. When dealing with private regulation, it could turn competition analysis into a form of re-regulation and impose certain substantive (eg successful promotion of public health) and procedural requirements (eg fair procedures and the right to appeal) as a way of avoiding antitrust scrutiny.[40] Rather than simply remedying harm to competition, this version

[36] Elhauge (n 23) 706–09.

[37] While not addressing purely private regulation, Odudu seems to argue for a version of such an approach: 'A regulatory regime that does not pursue efficiency cannot be seen as anti-competitive since efficiency is not necessarily the criterion by which regulatory regimes should be assessed: the competition rules are simply an inappropriate lens through which to view regulation.' Okeoghene Odudu, *The Boundaries of EC Competition Law: The Scope of Article 81* (Oxford University Press 2006) 31.

[38] 'Judicial errors that tolerate baleful practices are self-correcting, while erroneous condemnations are not.' Frank H Easterbrook, 'Limits of Antitrust' (1984) 63 Texas Law Review 1, 3.

[39] Pera (n 29) 133.

[40] Schepel and others have argued that competition law has been used to impose good governance standards on private regulators. See, for example, Schepel (n 8) 338, noting 'the potential competition law has for subjecting private transnational governance to a more or less coherent set of procedural requirements that are cut loose from hierarchical conceptions of legitimacy'.

of competition law can be understood as a kind of accountability mechanism[41] or administrative law for private regulators, based on the idea that 'as regulatory functions are in essence public in nature, they should be subject to the sorts of constraints imposed on the exercise of public power'.[42] In a sense, this leads to a reallocation of regulatory authority among different actors in the Union: the EU and its institutions, the Member States, and private actors.[43]

The substantive problem with this approach is that it is more complex and less predictable. The institutional problem is that it gives much greater discretion and flexibility to competition authorities and courts, which may be claimed to be illegitimate.[44] The first, cleaner approach may also seem preferable in terms of reducing decision and error costs. This may not be the case, however. The broad reading might allow decision-makers, for example, to forgo a detailed analysis of the market effects of a restraint in favour of a more flexible proportionality test, such as in *Wouters* or *Meca-Medina* (see section 3.1.3). The time and expense needed to conduct that kind of analysis are relatively low.[45] It is also not obvious whether the broad approach is overall more or less strict, that is whether it leads to over- or under-enforcement. All the broad approach does is place a broader range of conduct within the scope of the rules; in practice, the justifications could be applied in a way that finds fewer violations than in the narrow reading.

While mainstream competition law scholarship largely follows the first approach, various features of EU law show that it often—at least when private regulation is concerned—leans in the direction of the broad reading. EU competition law is thus complicated by its potential application to the State, the *Wouters/Meca-Medina* proportionality analysis, the rules on services of general economic interest, and relatively flexible justifications more generally (see section 3).

Speaking of the application of competition law to Member States, he points out a 'process requirement' which 'transforms antitrust into a kind of administrative law for private regulation ... what antitrust protects here is not a competitive market [but] democratic governance' (331).

41 Yeung (n 4) 132.

42 See Erika Szyszczak, 'Competition and the Liberalised Market' in Niamh Nic Shuibhne (ed), *Regulating the Internal Market* (Edward Elgar 2006) 99, arguing that 1990s case-law such as *Höfner* (Case C-41/90 *Klaus Höfner and Fritz Elser v Macrotron GmbH* [1991] ECR I-1979) places the 'values inherent in free movement and competition law in relation to values of good governance'.

43 Maher (n 3) 59 argues that by prohibiting cartels 'the EU ensures that it decides to what extent and in what circumstances and under what conditions such potentially powerful transnational private regulatory regimes should be permitted to operate'. Competition law significantly affects 'to whom and how private regulatory power should be allocated' (62).

44 Okeoghene Odudu, 'The Wider Concerns of Competition Law' (2010) 30 Oxford Journal of Legal Studies 599, 607–09.

45 Arndt Christiansen and Wolfgang Kerber, 'Competition Policy with Optimally Differentiated Rules Instead of "Per Se Rules vs Rule of Reason"' (2006) 2 Journal of Competition Law and Economics 215 argue, based on a model that compares the costs of rule differentiation and the benefits of fewer errors, that simple rules based on economic theory should be used more frequently than a 'case by case' approach balancing the procompetitive and anticompetitive features of a restraint. A proportionality test based on public interest objectives, however, does not present the same decision costs as an economic rule of reason, and may in fact reduce errors that would come about in subjecting regulation to a narrow efficiency analysis.

The narrow and broad approaches differ mostly along two issues. Firstly, what values and aims can be relevant in competition analysis? Secondly, which institutions (in the broad sense) are appropriate for dealing with those aims and values? In the following section, I will discuss these differences in more detail.

2.1 The aims of competition law between the two approaches

For a number of commentators, the aim of competition law is economic efficiency, understood as either consumer or total welfare.[46] Others argue either for a more inclusive approach to economic concepts,[47] or more explicitly for the inclusion of non-economic aims, such as environmental protection, food safety, etc.[48] An important tradition of European competition scholarship, with its roots in ordoliberalism, also highlights 'economic freedom' or 'freedom to compete' as the central aim, leading to a focus on competitive market structures.[49]

Since the 'more economic approach' was introduced,[50] the Commission and national authorities have devoted more analytical attention to economic arguments and concepts such as consumer welfare, market definition, market power, etc.[51] There is, of course, controversy about their precise meaning. The argument for economic efficiency differs with regard to the choices between static and dynamic analysis, the balance between allocative, productive, and dynamic efficiency, consumer welfare or total welfare approaches, and the use of neoclassical or behavioural economics. It is also disputed to what extent any one school of

[46] The most influential proponent of that view is Robert H Bork, *Antitrust Paradox: A Policy at War with Itself* (Simon & Schuster 1993). For a critical approach to Bork's influence and to the way consumer welfare is defined, see Barak Orbach, 'The Antitrust Consumer Welfare Paradox' (2011) 7 Journal of Competition Law & Economics 133. In the EU context, see Odudu, *The Boundaries of EC Competition Law* (n 37) and Odudu, 'The Wider Concerns of Competition Law' (n 44)

[47] Oliver Budzinski, 'Monoculture Versus Diversity in Competition Economics' (2008) 32 Cambridge Journal of Economics 295 and Wolfgang Kerber, 'Should Competition Law Promote Efficiency? Some Reflections of an Economist on the Normative Foundations of Competition Law' in Josef Drexl, Laurence Idot, and Joël Monéger (eds), *Economic Theory and Competition Law* (Edward Elgar 2007).

[48] Christopher Townley, *Article 81 EC and Public Policy* (Hart 2009), Kingston (n 12), Witt (n 82); Laura Parret, 'Shouldn't We Know What We are Protecting? Yes We Should! A Plea for a Solid and Comprehensive Debate about the Objectives of EU Competition Law and Policy' (2010) 6 European Competition Journal 339; Maurice E Stucke, 'Reconsidering Antitrust's Goals' (2012) 53 Boston College Law Review 551. See also, in general, Ben Van Rompuy, *Economic Efficiency: The Sole Concern of Modern Antitrust Policy?* (Kluwer Law International 2012).

[49] See Heike Schweitzer, 'Efficiency, Political Freedom and the Freedom to Compete—Comment on Maier-Rigaud' in Daniel Zimmer (ed), *The Goals of Competition Law* (Edward Elgar 2012).

[50] The 'more economic approach' can be tracked in particular through a number of block exemption regulations, starting with Commission Regulation 2790/1999 on the application of Article 81(3) of the Treaty to categories of vertical agreements and concerted practices (1999) OJ L336/21. A fuller list is given in Ioannis Lianos, 'Competition Law in the European Union after the Treaty of Lisbon' in Diamond Ashiagbor, Nicola Countouris, and Ioannis Lianos (eds), *The European Union after the Treaty of Lisbon* (Cambridge University Press 2012) 265, at n 3.

[51] Pera (29) 131. See also Ioannis Lianos, '"Lost in Translation": Towards a Theory of Economic Transplants' Jean Monnet Working Paper 08/09 <http://ssrn.com/abstract=1485378>.

thought can guide competition law.[52] The focus on economic efficiency as the central issue of antitrust, however, is hardly controversial. Eliminating other policy goals, according to Odudu, has the advantage of legitimacy and justiciability.[53] Ibáñez Colomo has argued that the main problem with the broad 'regulatory antitrust' approach is that it creates a risk 'that the law is instrumentalised to meet the objectives of sector-specific regimes' and that 'it may alter the expected standards of intervention by the authority'.[54]

There is an institutional aspect[55] to this narrower reading: public interest objectives should, the argument goes, be dealt with in the political process, not before competition authorities or courts. Hovenkamp, for example, has claimed: 'On the question of which markets should be regulated, and by what means, legislatures have the final say ... Antitrust law takes as given a market's existing regulatory structure, warts and all, and tries to prevent injuries to competition that the regulatory process leaves untended.'[56] Even if competition law does need to be applied, it cannot take into account aims beyond consumer welfare because 'correcting flaws in political processes is not an antitrust task'.[57] The discussion on error costs in antitrust also touches upon the limited ability of decision-makers to deal with complex objectives. Easterbrook, for example, argues for judicial restraint where the economic effects are ambiguous, due to the limited expertise of courts.[58] In the private regulation context, the decision costs may be particularly high as the need for special expertise can be the reason for the very existence of private regulation.

A second difficulty is the decentralized enforcement of EU competition law after Regulation 1/2003.[59] With the competition agencies and courts of the Member States all required to directly apply Arts 101 and 102, including justification under Art 101/3 which used to be the sole prerogative of the Commission, coherence is more difficult to achieve. For private regulation, this means that the variety of goals and concerns that the broad approach takes into account would have to be accommodated by a number of authorities whose approaches are likely

[52] Budzinski (n 47) has, for example, suggested that there are advantages to maintaining diversity in competition analysis, and Stucke (n 48) has advocated an even more broadly diversified approach.

[53] See n 44.

[54] Ibáñez Colomo (n 26) 277. It should be noted that this approach purports to know what the 'expected standards of intervention' are, which is precisely the main question.

[55] See Neil K Komesar, *Imperfect Alternatives: Choosing Institutions in Law, Economics, and Public Policy* (University of Chicago Press 1994).

[56] Hovenkamp (n 25) 231.

[57] ibid 234. The *Trinko* judgment of the US Supreme Court is a good example of this type of thinking: if there is a competing regulatory scheme in place, if it broadly addresses competition, and if errors are likely if antitrust law is superimposed, then the antitrust rules should not apply. *Verizon Communications Inc. v Law Offices of Curtis V. Trinko, LLP* 540 US 398 (2004). See also Pierre Larouche, 'Contrasting Legal Solutions and the Comparability of EU and US Experiences' in François Leveque and Howard Shelanski (eds), *Antitrust and Regulation in the EU and US: Legal and Economic Perspectives* (Edward Elgar 2009).

[58] See Easterbrook (n 38) 12 et seq.

[59] Council Regulation (EC) 1/2003 of 16 December 2002 on the implementation of the rules on competition laid down in Articles 81 and 82 of the Treaty [2003] OJ L1/1.

to diverge. Schweitzer, among others, has claimed that only a centralized system of individual exemptions operated by the Commission[60] could enable a balancing of public policy values. She claims that, after decentralization, taking into account a broad set of public policies under Art 101/3 would be illegitimate, non-justiciable, and even contrary to the conditions for direct effect.[61] Whether national competition authorities and courts are appropriate venues for broad supervision of private regulators will also depend on their guarantees of independence from political pressure.[62]

Some commentators have acknowledged that EU competition law pursues objectives that go beyond efficiency, but can still be described as 'broadly' economic. Monti, for example, identifies the three core aims of EU competition policy as efficiency, economic freedom, and market integration.[63] In certain cases, these aims may clash. The best example is the conflict between efficiency and market integration—sometimes, economically efficient exercises in market segmentation such as distribution networks may be blocked by the application of the principle that 'the Treaty aims at abolishing the barriers between States and could not allow undertakings to reconstruct such barriers'.[64]

Certainly, the range of arguments that could fit into either economic efficiency or the broader category of 'economic' justification is wide.[65] To what extent is it nevertheless possible to go beyond that and directly consider broader public policy arguments in competition law? For example, some authors have suggested that environmental protection should be seen as one of the aims of competition law. In practice, this would mean that some restraints that would otherwise be considered illegal should be tolerated because of their environmental benefits.[66] Conversely, it might be argued that the harmful environmental effects of a restraint should, on top of the harm it creates for competition, argue in favour of a prohibition under competition law. For example, competition law has been held not to prevent

[60] Council Regulation No 17 of 21 February 1962: First Regulation implementing Articles 85 and 86 of the Treaty [1962] OJ 13/204.

[61] Heike Schweitzer, 'Competition Law and Public Policy: Reconsidering an Uneasy Relationship: The Example of Art. 81' EUI Working Papers LAW No 2007/30.

[62] See, similarly, Petros C Mavroidis and Damien J Neven, 'The White Paper: A Whiter Shade of Pale—Of Interest and Interests' in Claus-Dieter Ehlermann and Isabela Atanasiu (eds), *Competition Law Annual 2000: The Modernisation of EC Antitrust Policy* (Hart 2001), in particular section 5.4.

[63] Giorgio Monti, 'Article 81 EC and Public Policy' (2002) 39 Common Market Law Review 1057, 1059 et seq.

[64] Joined cases 56 and 58-64 *Établissements Consten S.à.R.L. and Grundig-Verkaufs-GmbH v Commission* [1966] ECR 299, 240 and more recently, for example, Joined cases C-468/06 to C-478/06 *Sot. Lélos kai Sia EE and Others v GlaxoSmithKline AEVE Farmakeftikon Proïonton, formerly Glaxowellcome AEVE* [2008] ECR I-7139, para 37.

[65] See Townley (n 48) 177, who differentiates between using public policy outside ('mere balancing') and within ('market balancing') the efficiency assessment.

[66] In that sense, see Kingston (n 12) and Hans HB Vedder, 'Voluntary Agreements and Competition Law: What Are, and What Should be the Boundaries to VA's Imposed by Competition Law?' FEEM Working Paper No 79/2000 <http://ssrn.com/abstract=253333>, as well as Luc Gyselen, 'The Emerging Interface Between Competition Policy and Environmental Policy in the European Union' in James Cameron, Paul Demaret, and Damien Geradin (eds), *Trade and the Environment: The Search for Balance* (Cameron May 1996).

manufacturers of washing machines from agreeing to a binding energy efficiency standard, even if that increases prices.[67] But if they were to agree to only make inefficient machines that are cheaper to produce, perhaps the harm to the environment could be an additional factor, on top of the harm to consumer welfare, supporting a finding of a breach of Art 101 TFEU.[68]

The notion that broader aims should be taken into account in the application of competition law is supported by policy linking clauses in the Treaties requiring the Union, generally, to 'ensure consistency between its policies and activities, taking all of its objectives into account' (Art 7 TFEU)[69] and specifically, to take, among others, environmental protection (Art 11 TFEU), consumer protection (Art 12 TFEU), a high level of employment and social protection, human health, education, and training (Art 10 TFEU), gender equality and non-discrimination (Art 8 TFEU), and animal welfare (Art 13 TFEU) into account when defining and implementing its policies.

Even the more progressive proposals on the inclusion of public policy aims in competition analysis acknowledge, however, significant limitations. For example, Townley excludes public policy from Art 101/1 (finding of a restriction). Using such arguments there, he claims, would generate 'too much uncertainty and involve too much cost, for insufficient return'. Moving on to Art 101(3), he interprets its indispensability requirement as meaning that 'only where an objective could not be achieved by anyone in any way (to the appropriate level) more efficiently than by distorting competition would the agreement be exempted'. Townley also points out a number of situations where public policy arguments might be less relevant for competition analysis, for example when there was recent legislative action in the field or when the impact on public policy goals is not appreciable.[70]

The benefits of the broad approach come into sharper focus when private regulation is concerned. If we assume (we do not have to)[71] that some regulation can legitimately pursue outcomes that cannot be defended on efficiency grounds (because they sacrifice total welfare and/or are simply redistributive),[72] that some of that regulation can be performed by private parties and that those private parties can be challenged under competition law, then competition law has to find a way to adapt. In other words, if the only legitimate aim of competition law is economic efficiency, and such a competition law is applied to scrutinize regulatory conduct in a sector which is dominated by private regulation, this will in effect impose economic efficiency as the overarching aim of regulation in that sector.[73]

[67] CECED (Case IV.F.1/36.718) Commission Decision 2000/475/EC [1999] OJ L187/47.

[68] There seems to be more support for such interests to be used as a defence than as an aspect of the prohibition (among the exceptions is Yeung (n 4) 144, criticizing the focus on efficiency in both defences and prohibitions).

[69] This provision was added by the Treaty of Lisbon. See, generally, Lianos (n 50) 265–66.

[70] Townley (n 48) 311–14.

[71] See for example Stephen Breyer, *Regulation and Its Reform* (Harvard University Press 1984), who proceeds on the assumption that market failures are what justifies regulation.

[72] Louis Kaplow, 'On the Choice of Welfare Standards in Competition Law' in Daniel Zimmer (ed), *Goals of Competition Law* (Edward Elgar 2012) 7 et seq.

[73] See, similarly, Yeung (n 4) 156.

As even scholars who favour economic efficiency as the only relevant benchmark would probably acknowledge, this should not be the role of competition law.[74] Such an approach would also come into tension with the growing acceptance of private regulation.

Institutional arguments may sometimes speak in favour of the broad approach as well. Townley has argued that legislation may not be the best way to achieve public policy aims because for example of a 'lack of Parliamentary time'.[75] More generally, Komesar has pointed to a number of reasons why the political process may not work well, for example because of a bias in favour of a well-connected minority (often the very group in charge of regulating a certain sector).[76] The answer could perhaps lie in a comparison between institutional alternatives,[77] instead of assuming that one is automatically preferable to others.[78] EU competition law may even be the only avenue through which the practices of some private regulators, especially transnational private regulators, could be challenged. For example, Member State legislatures can realistically do very little to change the regulatory practices of an international sporting body, and the EU legislature does not have the competences to do so. This is not, in itself, an argument in favour of antitrust intervention, but it shows that effective institutional alternatives to which various regulatory objectives could be externalized may not exist.

The broader approach, therefore, internalizes the debate by accepting a wider set of arguments into the competition analysis. *Prima facie* restrictive private regulation can, of course, often be exonerated by an efficiency-driven analysis that sees market failures as the only legitimate reason for regulation.[79] In the liberal professions sector, for example, one can attempt to justify restrictive entry and conduct rules such as mandatory registration, price-fixing, and advertising bans by the existence of information asymmetries and negative externalities.[80]

[74] See for example Hovenkamp (n 25) 229–30: 'We undoubtedly regulate many more markets than require regulation, and we regulate many things that need not be regulated, assuming that the goal of regulation is economic efficiency. The last point, however, is important. The neoclassical economic critiques of regulation all rest on the premise that efficient allocation of resources is the only goal of regulatory policy. But policy making in a democratic society has always incorporated varied and sometimes even inconsistent goals ... regulatory policy has to one degree or another incorporated ideas about wealth distribution along with its concerns for efficiency.'

[75] Townley (n 33) 447. Townley's argument is more nuanced, however: he implies that competition authorities are not always the best place to consider public policy arguments and allows that either institution (competition authorities or legislators) might be better placed to handle certain issues in different circumstances.

[76] Komesar (n 55) 26–27.

[77] ibid 6, 20 et seq.

[78] In claiming, for example, that the institutional set-up accompanying antitrust law is not capable of taking into account broad regulatory aims, it is assumed that the political process (Hovenkamp, n 25) or the market (Easterbrook, n 58) is preferable, whereas it is possible that all of these institutional mechanisms suffer from their own problems in certain circumstances.

[79] See, for example, Michal S Gal and Inbal Faibish, 'Six Principles for Limiting Government-Facilitated Restraints on Competition' (2007) 44 Common Market Law Review 69, section I.1.

[80] Roger Van den Bergh and Peter Camesasca, *European Competition Law and Economics: A Comparative Perspective* (2nd edn, Sweet & Maxwell 2006) 182–85. For a more detailed analysis, see Heremans (n 7) 26–44. See also the reference to the *California Dental Association* judgment in n 174.

Secondly, private regulation can be justified by arguments of a broadly economic nature that do not necessarily, at least not explicitly, rely on efficiency, such as those that relate to employment, industrial policy, or market integration. Finally, in some cases private regulation could be justified by broad regulatory aims that may or may not be economically beneficial in the case at hand, such as health and safety, environmental protection, solidarity, etc. Of course, there is no firewall between these aims. Many regulatory objectives can be shown, in some sense, to contribute to consumer welfare. The question is whether a benefit to consumer or total welfare must always, and independently, be shown in order for private regulation to pass muster under the competition rules. The broad approach would be inclined to give a negative answer to that question and adapt to cases of private regulation, for example by introducing a sort of balancing mechanism.

Clearly, any such adaptation will create costs. Kaplow has, for example, singled out poor targeting and inefficiency as obstacles for the use of competition law to achieve redistribution.[81] Competition law is certainly a blunt instrument for redistribution, both in Kaplow's limited sense (redistribution between producer and consumer welfare) and in the broader sense of furthering objectives other than competition. When competition authorities analyse private regulation, however, they are not necessarily creating new policy or disregarding competition considerations. They are reviewing a measure already created by the private regulator, perhaps in partnership with State bodies. They are not required to define the right balance between competition and other objectives, but to decide whether the private regulator overstepped some permissible margin of discretion. As I will show, this sort of judgment more frequently focuses on considerations of procedure and good governance than on the substance of various policies. It is too simple to say that a broader approach, which would internalize some debate on public interest objectives, is the same as giving competition agencies a mandate to freely decide on any policy that comes before them.

On the other hand, the broader approach does enable competition law to be indirectly used or leveraged in pursuit of objectives that cannot be fully achieved in the EU political process. While the Commission in general supports a more narrow, efficiency-based approach,[82] it has used competition law as a tool for re-regulation, whether addressed at the structural/organizational features of private regulators (eg the requirement to structurally separate commercial from regulatory activities in the *FIA* case),[83] the procedural

[81] Kaplow (n 72) 8–14.

[82] Anne C Witt, 'Public Policy Goals Under EU Competition Law—Now is the Time to Set the House in Order' (2012) 8 European Competition Journal 443, contrasts the Commission's economic approach with the broader approach of the Court. See also Richard Whish and David Bailey, *Competition Law* (7th edn, Oxford University Press 2012) 116: 'The Commission today takes a much narrower view of what is meant by a restriction of competition for the purpose of Article 101(1); and it also has a narrower approach to the circumstances in which Article 101(3) is satisfied.'

[83] See the press-release IP/01/1523 (2001) 'Commission Closes its Investigation into Formula One and Other Four-Wheel Motor Sports' <http://europa.eu/rapid/press-release_IP-01-1523_en.htm>.

standards followed by private bodies (eg the requirements of openness and non-discrimination imposed on standard-setting bodies),[84] or even the actual substance of regulation.

A number of legal instruments allow the Commission, as well as national competition authorities, to pursue this 're-regulatory' or 'strategic'[85] approach. Soft law and sector inquiries offer a flexible, non-binding way of directing the action of private bodies. Commitment decisions and behavioural remedies allow the Commission to agree on requirements—on a voluntary basis, but under the threat of sanction—that go beyond simple invalidity and fines as sanctions for infringing conduct. The case studies discussed in Chapters V–VII show a number of examples where competition law is used, in particular by the Commission, to push private regulators towards reforms, largely focused on good governance and procedure. For example, the Commission has frequently spoken of good governance as a condition for the autonomy of sporting bodies from competition and free movement scrutiny, and its soft law documents have used the *Meca-Medina* judgment as a way of imposing a general requirement of proportionality on their measures.[86] The General Court has, on its part, used an Art 102 case to express a concern that private regulation of sports may lead to a 'violation of civil and economic liberties'.[87] In the legal profession, the Commission has had some success in pushing for liberalization and relaxation of regulation, despite having achieved very little in terms of actual enforcement. Again, the *Wouters* test was read as a general requirement of proportionality for professional bodies.[88] Standard-setting bodies have been required to develop policies on intellectual property and ensure transparency, openness, and accessibility of the standard development process.[89] Importantly, this use of competition law as an instrument for reform, in sectors where private regulators are dominant, is linked to the construction of a more general EU policy. The reason why competition law is used to this end is because it provides flexible and effective tools, especially in settings where the EU has limited legislative competence (such as sports) and where private actors, as potential targets of competition law, are the ones that in fact regulate a particular sector. In that sense, the commonly held view that the Commission, as antitrust enforcer, is entirely focused on a narrow, efficiency-dominated reading of competition law[90] should be qualified.

[84] Commission, 'Guidelines on the Applicability of Article 101 of the Treaty on the Functioning of the European Union to Horizontal Co-Operation Agreements' (Communication) (2011) OJ C11, section 7.

[85] Wulf-Henning Roth, 'Strategic Competition Policy: A Comment on EU Competition Policy' in Hanns Ullrich (ed), *The Evolution of European Competition Law: Whose Regulation, Which Competition?* (Edward Elgar 2006).

[86] See Chapter V.

[87] Case C-171/05 P *Laurent Piau v Commission* [2006] ECR I-37.

[88] See Chapter VI.

[89] See Chapter VII.

[90] See, for example, Witt (n 82) 469: 'Since the early 2000s, the Commission has taken the view that the interpretation of the competition rules should be insulated from non-competition values, and that such aims should be pursued independently by means of regulation, unless they can be translated into economic benefits.'

3. The Application of Competition Law to Private Regulation

So far, I have argued that competition law doctrine can adapt to private regulation either by following a broader approach, entrusting competition agencies and courts with a more flexible balancing task, or a narrower one, more focused on economic efficiency, but removing certain areas of (public and private) regulation from the ambit of competition law.

In the following sections, I will show the ways in which EU law has followed a relatively broad approach, including not only the possibility to apply it directly to Member States and specific rules on services of general economic interest (see section 3.1.5) but also a somewhat flexible interpretation of Art 101/3 (see section 3.1.4) and a judicially developed proportionality test within Art 101/1 (see section 3.1.3). This is certainly not enough to describe EU competition law as a completely open balancing exercise, but it does show a departure from the narrow approach.

As in the previous chapter, it is useful to keep in mind the difference between co-regulation and purely private regulation. With private regulation that does not involve State actors, the applicability of competition law is usually not an issue,[91] but the nature of the scrutiny may be affected by the regulatory nature of a restraint in different ways. Co-regulatory schemes, on the other hand, are sometimes exempted from the competition rules altogether in order to protect the political choices of the Member States. If this is not the case, however, legal challenges to co-regulation can be addressed not only to the private regulator but also to the Member State. Moreover, the provisions on services of general economic interest, as well as the doctrine of immunity for private actors that are left no freedom of action by public rules,[92] may also be relevant.

For the sake of simplicity, however, in the following section I will not follow the distinction between purely private or self-regulation and co-regulation. Instead, I will adopt the simpler and more conventional distinction between challenging private actors directly and challenging the State.

3.1 Applying the competition rules directly to private regulators

In the practice of the Commission and of the EU Courts, there have been many direct challenges against private regulators under Art 101 or Art 102 TFEU. The competition rules were invoked against the rules of sporting associations,[93] bar associations,[94] standard-setting bodies,[95] an international

[91] See, however, Case C-67/96 *Albany International BV v Stichting Bedrijfspensioenfonds Textielindustrie* [1999] ECR I-5751 and related case law.

[92] See n 26, as well as Joined cases C-359/95 P and C-379/95 P *Commission and France v Ladbroke Racing Ltd* [1997] ECR I-6265, paras 33–34.

[93] See Chapter V. [94] See Chapter VI. [95] See Chapter VII.

air-traffic control organization,[96] copyright collecting societies,[97] a European association of broadcasters,[98] self-regulation in the cognac and wine industry,[99] and others.

There is no specific test that competition law applies to private regulation, as opposed to other private action. Generally speaking, the steps in the analysis under Arts 101 and 102 TFEU are well known and will not be explored here in detail, except to point out the different ways in which the regulatory nature of conduct may be relevant at different points.

As a preliminary point, it should be noted that Art 101 has been, by and large, more significant in this context than Art 102, even though in principle both could be applied to private regulators.[100]

3.1.1 The scope of the EU competition rules

The fact that a certain activity is regulatory is not generally a reason for the exclusion of competition law. An 'undertaking' in EU competition law is 'any entity engaged in an economic activity, regardless of its legal status and the way in which it is financed'.[101] Offering goods and services on a market is an economic activity.[102] This applies to State and non-State bodies, and certainly private regulators as well. At least in some aspects of their activities, private regulators are undertakings themselves.[103] In addition, the Court has classified professional associations

[96] Case C-364/92 *SAT Fluggesellschaft mbH v Eurocontrol* [1994] ECR I-43 and Case C-113/07 P *SELEX Sistemi Integrati SpA v Commission of the European Communities and Organisation européenne pour la sécurité de la navigation aérienne (Eurocontrol)* [2009] ECR I-2207.

[97] Case 127-73 *Belgische Radio en Televisie and société belge des auteurs, compositeurs et éditeurs v SV SABAM and NV Fonior* [1974] ECR 313; Joined cases 110/88, 241/88, and 242/88 *François Lucazeau and others v Société des Auteurs, Compositeurs et Editeurs de Musique (SACEM) and others* [1989] ECR 2811; Case C-52/07 *Kanal 5 Ltd and TV 4 AB v Föreningen Svenska Tonsättares Internationella Musikbyrå (STIM) upa* [2008] ECR I-9275.

[98] Joined cases T-185/00, T-216/00, T-299/00, and T-300/00 *Métropole Télévision SA (M6)* (T-185/00), *Antena 3 de Televisión, SA* (T-216/00), *Gestevisión Telecinco, SA* (T-299/00) and *SIC—Sociedade Independente de Comunicação, SA* (T-300/00) *v Commission* [2002] ECR II-3805.

[99] Case 123/83 *Bureau national interprofessionnel du cognac v Guy Clair* [1985] ECR 391.

[100] A case in point is Case C-309/99 *J. C. J. Wouters, J. W. Savelbergh and Price Waterhouse Belastingadviseurs BV v Algemene Raad van de Nederlandse Orde van Advocaten, intervener: Raad van de Balies van de Europese Gemeenschap* [2002] ECR I-1577, where the Bar Association was examined as an association of undertakings under Art 101 rather than as an undertaking in a dominant position under Art 102.

[101] See, in particular, *Höfner* para 21, Joined cases C-159/91 and C-160/91 *Christian Poucet v Assurances Générales de France and Caisse Mutuelle Régionale du Languedoc-Roussillon* [1993] ECR I-637, para 17 and Case C-35/96 *Commission v Italy* [1998] ECR I-3851, para 36.

[102] This is also true for Member State bodies acting in the market. Case 118/85 *Commission v Italy* [1987] ECR 2599, para 7.

[103] An association that does not itself compete in a market but restricts itself to setting rules will not be considered an undertaking, which means that Art 102 cannot be applied, and that Art 101 may be applicable only under the notion of 'association of undertakings'. *Wouters* (n 100), paras 111–15. While setting rules may, in itself, be 'non-economic', related aspects can constitute economic activity. For example, an SSO's activity of setting standards will be viewed as an activity of an association of undertakings, rather than an offer of goods or services on the market. Selling access to the very same standards, however, would almost certainly be an economic activity in itself.

in highly (co-)regulated sectors as associations of undertakings, either when they facilitate collusion between their members or when they compete on a market themselves.[104]

Like the free movement rules, the scope of Arts 101 and 102 is defined in a functionalist way: what matters is the nature of the activity, and not its (national) legal classification.[105] Moreover, even if an entity is not an undertaking in some aspect of its activities, competition law will still govern its other, 'severable', activities.[106] Associations of undertakings are subject to Art 101 even when some of their members are not undertakings, but either employees in other undertakings or simply other interested parties.[107]

All this shows that the scope of the EU competition rules is defined relatively broadly and that private regulatory measures will, as a rule, be subject to them.

The situations where they could be wholly exempt from competition law fall into two main categories: (1) social functions based on solidarity; and (2) activities connected, due to their 'nature, aim and rules by which they are governed' to the exercise of 'powers which are typically those of a public authority'.[108] At first sight, these categories seem broad and difficult to define. In practice, however, both have been applied with restraint.

The first group includes cases of social security funds such as those in *Poucet and Pistre*,[109] where the applicants claimed that mandatory membership to a particular social security scheme for self-employed persons, because of the inability to select a private sector alternative, was a violation of competition law. These funds are non-profits and their only function is redistribution. The key criterion, for the Court, is whether the 'principle of solidarity' prevails over the principle of capitalization.

[104] *Wouters* (n 100) and Case C-1/12 *Ordem dos Técnicos Oficiais de Contas v Autoridade da Concorrência* ECLI:EU:C:2013:127 are two examples. See Tristan Baumé, 'Notion of Undertaking and Association of Undertakings, Exercise of the Powers of a Public Authority and Application of the *Wouters* Derogation to a Regulatory Measure Adopted by a Professional Association' (2013) Journal of European Competition Law & Practice, published online 19 May 2013 <http://jeclap.oxfordjournals.org/content/early/2013/05/19/jeclap.lpt023.full>. For standard-setting bodies, see Horizontal Co-operation Guidelines (n 84) para 258.

[105] *SAT Fluggesellschaft* (n 96) para 19.

[106] See, in that sense, Case 107/84 *Commission v Germany* [1985] ECR 2655 paras 14–15 and Case T-128/98 *Aéroports de Paris v Commission* [2000] ECR II-3929 para 108. See, however, *SELEX* (2009) (n 96) paras 76–77, showing that areas that are 'closely linked' to public authority-like activities will not be considered severable.

[107] In Case T-23/09 *Conseil national de l'Ordre des pharmaciens (CNOP) and Conseil central de la section G de l'Ordre national des pharmaciens (CCG) v European Commission* [2010] ECR II-5291, paras 73–77, it was made clear that, as long as a certain number of its members are undertakings, an association falls under Art 101. Conceivably, an association composed almost exclusively of non-undertakings might be excluded, but this is not often the case with professional associations. See also Joined Cases T-217/03 and T-245/03 *FNCBV and Others v Commission* [2006] ECR II-4987, para 55, as well as Case C-413/13 *FNV Kunsten Informatie en Media v Staat der Nederlanden* ECLI:EU:C:2014:2411, para 28.

[108] *Wouters* (n 100) para 57. The Court distinguished those functions from the Bar's rules, which are 'the expression of the intention of the delegates of the members of a profession that they should act in a particular manner in carrying on their economic activity' (para 64).

[109] *Poucet and Pistre* (n 101).

Clearly, this raises a number of boundary issues,[110] but it is clear that not every entity active in the area of social policy can benefit from this exemption.

Examples of the second group[111] are air traffic control (*Sat Fluggesellschaft*),[112] maritime anti-pollution surveillance (*Diego Calì*),[113] and tax collection on behalf of the State (*Altair Chimica*).[114] In these cases, the Court asks, regardless of whether an entity is formally a part of the State apparatus, whether its activities fall 'within the essential prerogatives of the state'[115] or, as AG Jacobs put it in Albany, whether it 'could, at least in principle, be carried on by a private undertaking in order to make profits'.[116] Both of these are question-begging exercises that, taken literally, could encompass very many (since most things traditionally performed by the State could be performed by non-state actors for profit) or very few cases (since most things could be claimed to be an essential prerogative of a particular state). Perhaps as a consequence of that, the case law sees a variety of factors as relevant but no single one as decisive.[117]

Overall, there are relatively few cases where a regulator was able to escape competition law scrutiny, and most of them concern activities that are quite close to the 'public' end of the spectrum, where it is either difficult to imagine a market at all, or where Member States were successful at 'cordoning off' an area from competition by adopting a clear *ex ante* decision against competition in a particular sector.[118] Such decisions can affect private actors in connected markets, so that

[110] Joined cases C-180/98 to C-184/98 *Pavel Pavlov and Others v Stichting Pensioenfonds Medische Specialisten* [2000] ECR I-6451, para 118. See Ivo Van Bael and Jean-François Bellis, *Competition Law of the European Community* (5th edn, Kluwer Law International 2009) 899.

[111] Odudu labels this group as dealing with public goods. Okeoghene Odudu, 'Economic Activity as a Limit to Community Law' in Catherine Barnard and Okeoghene Odudu (eds), *The Outer Limits of European Union Law* (Hart 2009) 233.

[112] *SAT Fluggesellschaft* (n 96).

[113] Case C-343/95 *Diego Calì & Figli Srl v Servizi ecologici porto di Genova SpA (SEPG)* [1997] ECR I-1547.

[114] Case C-207/01 *Altair Chimica SpA v ENEL Distribuzione SpA* [2003] ECR I-8875. See also Commission, 'Services of general interest, including social services of general interest: a new European commitment' accompanying the Communication on 'A single market for 21st century Europe' (Communication) COM (2007) 725 final, section 2.4. For a more detailed discussion, see Vassilis Hatzopoulos, 'The Economic Constitution of the EU Treaty and the Limits between Economic and Non-economic Activities' (2012) 23 European Business Law Review 973, 982–84.

[115] Monti, *EC Competition Law* (n 5) 486.

[116] Opinion of AG Jacobs in *Albany* (n 91) para 311.

[117] See the lengthy analysis of AG Jacobs, ibid, paras 306–48, as well as the judgment in *SAT Fluggesellschaft* paras 18–32. Especially telling is para 30 of the latter, where the Court concludes that 'taken as a whole, Eurocontrol's activities, by their nature, their aim and the rules to which they are subject, are connected with the exercise of powers relating to the control and supervision of air space which are typically those of a public authority' and not 'of an economic nature justifying the application of the Treaty rules of competition'.

[118] The case law on the application of competition law to the Member States (see section 3.2) seems to reflect this idea as well: a Member State can exempt certain private regulatory activities from competition law if the decision-making largely remains in the hands of public authorities or their representatives (or, in some cases, independent experts) and if the scheme has to pursue public interest criteria. See *Pavlov* (n 110) para 87 and C-208/13 *API - Anonima Petroli Italiana SpA v Ministero delle Infrastrutture e dei Trasporti and Ministero dello Sviluppo economico* ECLI:EU:C:2014:2147 paras 33–41.

their activities that could otherwise be described as economic are excluded from competition law because they are closely linked to the activities of a public authority. In *SELEX*, the Court of Justice overruled the General Court's interpretation according to which one activity (providing assistance to governments) of an international flight control organization was declared economic, while others (including standard setting) were not: for the Court, these were too closely linked to be assessed separately.[119] More recently, in *Compass-Datenbank* the Court similarly excluded from the competition rules the seemingly economic activity of collecting fees for access to public data because it was too closely connected to the non-economic activity of data collection and database maintenance.[120]

This does create an opening for certain private regulators, as participants in a co-regulatory scheme, to avoid competition law scrutiny: if their activity is closely linked to a measure that can be described as stemming from a 'public authority' (for example, a delegating act that fully defines the private regulator's task, fees that can be charged etc.),[121] and if there is no actual market at the root of the co-regulatory scheme,[122] its measures could fall under the 'exercise of the powers of a public authority'.[123]

There is also a separate line of case law according to which conflict with public policy aims included in the Treaty may justify the blanket exclusion of certain categories of conduct from competition law scrutiny. Thus, in *Albany*, the fact that the Treaty requires the EU to have a 'policy in the social sphere' and encourages social dialogue enabled the Court to exempt collective agreements from what is now Art 101(1) TFEU.[124] This category has so far been restricted to collective agreements

[119] See n 106.

[120] Case C-138/11 *Compass-Datenbank GmbH v Republik Österreich* ECLI:EU:C:2012:449 paras 40–49. This shows how the notion of severability can be manipulated in different ways to exclude or include conduct from the reach of the rules—not just by considering certain activities to be inseparable, but also by defining what those 'separate' activities are in the first place.

[121] In that sense, see also Case 30/87 *Corinne Bodson v SA Pompes funèbres des régions libérées* [1988] ECR 2479, para 18.

[122] One reason for the Court's holding in *Compass-Datenbank* could be the difference between that case and standard refusal to deal cases such as Case C-418/01 *IMS Health GmbH & Co. OHG v NDC Health GmbH & Co. KG.* [2004] ECR I-5039: the absence of an upstream market. That is to say, if Austria withdraws an area from the market completely (by only collecting data itself on a clearly defined legislative basis and for clearly defined purposes), it can also prevent the emergence of a secondary market linked to that activity (by preventing any further commercial use of the data from the register).

[123] These are largely the same features that can be used to obtain an exemption under the rules on services of general economic interest. See section 3.1.5.

[124] '[T]he social policy objectives pursued by such agreements would be seriously undermined if management and labour were subject to [Art 101/1] of the Treaty when seeking jointly to adopt measures to improve conditions of work and employment.' *Albany* (n 91) paras 59–60. See also Case C-222/98 *Hendrik van der Woude v Stichting Beatrixoord* [2000] ECR I-7111. In Case C-271/08 *Commission v Germany* [2010] ECR I-7091, AG Trstenjak argued that only agreements that are negotiated collectively and adopted with a view to improving work and employment conditions are exempt (paras 58 et seq). The judgment in that case (para 49) seemed to suggest that the exemption only relates to conduct that 'affects the essence of the right to bargain collectively'. In *FNV Kunsten* (n 107), the Court found that Art 101 still applies to collective agreements concluded to protect the working conditions of self-employed persons, who are considered to be undertakings unless the facts suggest that they are actually workers ('false self-employed').

between trade unions and employers,[125] even though it may expand as a result of the greater variety of substantive EU policy goals after the Lisbon Treaty.

Finally, private regulatory schemes may be outside the scope of the EU competition rules because of the trade effects doctrine or because they are *de minimis*. Firstly, Arts 101 and 102 only apply to restrictions that 'affect trade between Member States'. National private regulation can still be caught because the trade effects test does not depend on factual cross-border elements; indeed, if a scheme covers the whole of a Member State it is especially exposed to scrutiny, as it has a market-segmenting effect.[126] Schemes may fall below the radar if, for example, they are exposed to substantial regulatory competition in the Member State or if they cover only a small part of that Member State's market. Unlike in free movement law, there is no conceptual problem with scrutinizing transnational private regulation—it is likely to fulfil the trade effects criterion if it has transnational effects.[127] Secondly, a possible way out is the *de minimis* doctrine, according to which an agreement has to have an appreciable effect on competition. This could enable some agreements among small and medium undertakings to benefit from a safe harbour.[128]

3.1.2 The notion of a restriction of competition under Arts 101 and 102

The circumstances in which private regulatory schemes will actually restrict competition under Art 101/1 and/or Art 102 TFEU are as diverse, or almost as diverse, as with any other type of conduct.

Private regulators such as professional associations or industry groups have engaged in horizontal price-fixing, which is, at least without governmental blessing,[129] likely to be considered a restriction by object without an elaborate market analysis.[130] Private regulators are also the common venue for various

[125] There might be overlap between the first category of cases discussed *supra* (pension schemes based on solidarity) and this exclusion from competition law. Joined cases C-115/97 to C-117/97 *Brentjens' Handelsonderneming BV v Stichting Bedrijfspensioenfonds voor de Handel in Bouwmaterialen* [1999] ECR I-6025 (paras 80–84) and Case C-219/97 *Maatschappij Drijvende Bokken BV v Stichting Pensioenfonds voor de Vervoer- en Havenbedrijven* [1999] ECR I-6121 (paras 70–74), however, show that a pension scheme that does not fall within the solidarity exemption because it is based on capitalization, can still benefit from the *Albany* exception.

[126] *OTOC* (n 104) para 66.

[127] Some examples of private or hybrid regulation on the European, international, or transnational level are Case T-432/05 *EMC Development AB v Commission* [2010] ECR II-1629, *SELEX* (2009) (n 96) and Case C-519/04 P *David Meca-Medina and Igor Majcen v Commission* [2006] ECR I-6991.

[128] See the Commission Notice on agreements of minor importance which do not appreciably restrict competition under Art 81(1) of the Treaty establishing the European Community (de minimis) (2001) OJ C368 and the Commission notice—Guidelines on the effect on trade concept contained in Arts 81 and 82 of the Treaty (2004) OJ C101.

[129] See, for example, Case T-513/93 *Consiglio Nazionale degli Spedizionieri Doganali v Commission* [2000] ECR II-1807 and *Anonima Petroli Italiana* (n 118). Comprehensive governmental control can change the outcome quite significantly. See section 3.2.1 and Chapter VI.

[130] Joined cases T-374/94, T-375/94, T-384/94, and T-388/94 *European Night Services Ltd (ENS), Eurostar (UK) Ltd, formerly European Passenger Services Ltd (EPS), Union internationale des*

horizontal co-operation agreements, such as those on standard setting,[131] production, advertising, selling,[132] joint purchasing,[133] or information exchange,[134] all of which can be a part of industry-wide codes of conduct or similar documents. Finally, some private or hybrid associations such as professional (Chapter VI) and sporting bodies (Chapter V) are challenged under Art 101 because of their power to regulate the entry into or the conduct of a profession.

Article 102 on abuse of dominance may also be relevant. A single undertaking that can be described as a private regulator is likely to be in a position of dominance, generally defined as 'a position of economic strength' which enables it to prevent effective competition by behaving 'to an appreciable extent independently' of its competitors and consumers.[135] Private regulators can be in a position

chemins de fer (UIC), NV Nederlandse Spoorwegen (NS) and Société nationale des chemins de fer français (SNCF) v Commission [1998] ECR II-3141, para 136; and Case C-209/07 *Competition Authority v Beef Industry Development Society Ltd and Barry Brothers (Carrigmore) Meats Ltd* [2008] ECR I-8637, paras 15–23. In rare circumstances, such agreements may be justified under Art 101/3. See Whish and Bailey (n 82) 121. For an argument in favour of the possibility of justifying price-fixing by public interest objectives, see Townley (n 33) 444.

[131] Both product and process standards are potentially problematic from the point of view of competition, but are generally recognized to also lead to significant efficiencies and are useful to consumers. See n 8 and, more broadly, Chapter VII.

[132] For example, a group of food manufacturers could agree on lowering the fat content in their food. It could be argued that this is a pure cartel, similar to a quota, as it 'limits or control production' (Art 101/1b). See, however, Horizontal Co-operation Guidelines (n 84) para 330, where the Commission considered a similar hypothetical, but with governmental encouragement, unlikely to restrict competition. Agreements restricting selling or advertising (commercialization agreements), where for example manufacturers agree not to sell unhealthy foods in schools or advertise them to children, could be held to eliminate competition in one segment of the market and reduce the volume of sales. Agreements on the method of advertising could avoid Art 101/1 scrutiny if they are held to for example improve brand image—but this is unlikely to help straightforward agreements to refrain from a particular kind of advertising. The GC's judgment in EPI has dealt with an agreement among patent agents to prohibit comparative advertising, finding it to be a restriction of Art 101/1 but justified under Art 101/3—Case T-144/99 *Institute of Professional Representatives before the European Patent Office v Commission* [2001] ECR II-1087.

[133] An example of this might be a retailers' agreement not to stock low-quality high alcohol content drinks. This might be anticompetitive because it creates foreclosure in the purchasing market, reducing the range of products offered. As in several of the examples above, there is something counterintuitive to applying Art 101 here, however: the joint purchasing agreements usually considered under competition law are cases of leveraging buyer power to reduce the purchasing price or benefit the purchasers in some other way, not of competing retailers agreeing not to stock a certain product on health grounds. See the Horizontal Co-operation Guidelines (n 84) paras 194–224. See, however, Case C-205/03 P *Federación Española de Empresas de Tecnología Sanitaria* (*FENIN*) *v Commission* [2006] ECR I-6295, where the Court found that the purchasing activity of a medical insurance fund was not an economic activity.

[134] Producers might exchange information on the content or manufacturing process of products, allowing them to co-ordinate market behaviour, including prices. For more complex forms of information exchange, an effects analysis would have to be undertaken, and the finding of a restriction would hinge on the nature of the information exchanged, its effects on marketing strategy, purpose, conditions of participation in it, etc. Case C-238/05 *Asnef-Equifax, Servicios de Información sobre Solvencia y Crédito, SL v Asociación de Usuarios de Servicios Bancarios* (*Ausbanc*) [2006] ECR I-11125, paras 52–54. See also Whish and Bailey (n 82) 539–47.

[135] Case 27/76 *United Brands Company and United Brands Continentaal BV v Commission* [1978] ECR 207, para 65 and Case 85/76 *Hoffmann-La Roche & Co. AG v Commission* [1979] ECR 461, para 37. See Damien Geradin, Anne Layne-Farrar, and Nicolas Petit, *EU Competition Law and*

of dominance precisely because of their ability to regulate entry to the market, that is impose regulatory barriers to entry,[136] based either on a grant of special or exclusive rights by the State,[137] other forms of co-regulation, or simply because of the circumstances of a particular market, like in the case of sports.

Importantly, unlike Art 101, Art 102 does not cover 'associations of undertakings'. It does not apply to industry associations that do not themselves compete in the relevant market, since they are not undertakings. On the other hand, competitors that take part in private regulatory schemes could be caught by the notion of 'collective dominance'. For example, in *Piau*, football clubs were, as members of FIFA, held to be in such a position due to the close structural links between them that enabled collusion.[138]

Under Art 102, private regulators can be challenged both for exclusionary (foreclosure as a result of imposing regulatory restrictions on entry or conduct of competitors)[139] and exploitative abuses, including a number of traditional price and non-price restraints: exclusive dealing, refusal to supply, price discrimination, unfair trading conditions, alterations of the market structure,[140] or limiting production, markets, or technical development.[141] Some examples of Art 102 cases raised against private regulators are *Piau*[142] (FIFA's practices in licensing players' agents), *MOTOE*[143] (an Art 106/1 and Art 102 case against a Greek sporting body that licensed motorcycling races while also organizing them itself), and a number of cases against standard-setting bodies, especially for conduct related to patent rights (see Chapter VII). Overall, however, Art 101 has in practice been more important in terms of dealing with the specificities of private regulation.[144]

Economics (Oxford University Press 2012) 186–93. Indeed, the notion that dominant undertakings have a 'special responsibility' not to impair competition (*Hoffmann-La Roche* para 57) may carry particular weight as far as private regulators are concerned.

[136] See Commission, 'Guidance on the Commission's enforcement priorities in applying Article 82 of the EC Treaty to abusive exclusionary conduct by dominant undertakings' (Communication) (2009) OJ C45 para 17.

[137] Co-regulatory schemes may lead to the joint application of Art 102 and Art 106/1 against the Member State for facilitating or creating an abuse of a dominant position. See section 3.2. The Commission can adopt decisions against the Member State for such violations under Art 106/3. It is also possible to simultaneously apply Art 102 against the private party in the co-regulatory scheme. See, by analogy, the discussion on *CNSD II* (n 129) and a related infringement case against Italy in Heremans (n 7) 275–76.

[138] Piau (n 87) and Geradin, Layne-Farrar, and Petit (n 135) 198–99.

[139] Guidance on abusive exclusionary conduct (n 136) para 19.

[140] Bellamy & Child, *European Community Law of Competition* (Peter Roth and Vivien Rose (eds)) (6th edn, Oxford University Press 2008) 1023–24, 1026. See for example Joined cases T-191/98, T-212/98 to T-214/98 *Atlantic Container Line AB and Others v Commission* [2003] ECR II-3275.

[141] Case C-179/90 *Merci convenzionali porto di Genova SpA v Siderurgica Gabrielli SpA* [1991] ECR I-5889. Bellamy & Child (n 140) 1029–30.

[142] Piau (n 87).

[143] Case C-49/07 *Motosykletistiki Omospondia Ellados NPID (MOTOE) v Elliniko Dimosio* [2008] ECR I-4863.

[144] In some cases, a measure can fall under both Arts 101 and 102, such as 'where an agreement ... simply constitutes the formal measure setting the seal on an economic reality characterized by the fact that an undertaking in a dominant position has succeeded in having the tariffs in question

The Art 101 cases in particular reveal an interesting dynamic: when private regulation is concerned, competition law is forced to deal with claims of restrictions that might not normally be contemplated. Measures are claimed to restrict competition not because they economically benefit the regulator, but because they are excessive, biased, unfair, or badly designed. In *Meca-Medina*,[145] for example, the application of doping sanctions to two swimmers was examined as a restriction of Art 101. Ultimately, the measure was exonerated by application of the 'inherent restriction' doctrine (see section 3.1.3), but this still acknowledged the possibility that anti-doping rules—a far cry from the restrictions in output, market sharing, price-fixing, and similar restraints which clearly have a self-serving motivation to the detriment of competition—could infringe Art 101 simply by being overly strict against individual athletes (by setting either unjustifiably low thresholds for violations or disproportionately strict sanctions). There is no discussion of how such unreasonable anti-doping rules might reduce consumer welfare.

In this way, competition law seems to turn into a broader enquiry into the fairness and coherence of private regulatory measures, as well as the governance features of the private regulator, such as the composition of its bodies and the procedures it applies. Decision-making without appropriate safeguards to protect the interests of regulatees and third parties could be described as a restriction of competition even if its actual impact on the market as a whole—and not just on the interests of a single adversely affected competitor—is not obviously harmful.

3.1.3 The 'inherent restriction' test

From this brief overview, it seems as though many industry initiatives would in fact be considered *prima facie* restrictive of competition under Art 101/1 or Art 102 TFEU, and could only be saved in the subsequent step of justification under Art 101/3 or through 'objective justification' under Art 102. There is, however, one more possibility: the 'inherent restriction' or 'regulatory ancillarity'[146] test, first outlined by the Court in *Wouters*,[147] a case about a bar association's prohibition on multidisciplinary partnerships between lawyers and accountants. This test has been the subject of quite a lot of scholarly speculation.[148] Arguably, by now the

applied by other undertakings'. See Case 66/86 *Ahmed Saeed Flugreisen and Silver Line Reisebüro GmbH v Zentrale zur Bekämpfung unlauteren Wettbewerbs e.V* [1989] ECR 803, para 37.

145 See n 127. 146 Whish and Bailey (n 82) 130–36.

147 *Wouters* (n 100). See Chapter VI for more details.

148 Some authors have read *Wouters* as introducing a US-style 'rule of reason' within Art 101. R O'Loughlin, 'EC Competition Rules and Free Movement Rules: An Examination of the Parallels and their Furtherance by the ECJ Wouters Decision' (2003) 24 European Competition Law Review 62, 67–68. More broadly, see n 146, Hans Gilliams, 'Competition Law and Public Interest: Do We Need to Change the Law for the (Liberal) Professions?' in Claus-Dieter Ehlermann and Isabela Atanasiu (eds), *European Competition Law Annual 2004: The Relationship Between Competition Law and the (Liberal) Professions* (Hart 2006) and Alison Jones, 'Regulating the Legal Profession: Article 81, the Public Interest and the ECJ's Judgment in *Wouters*' (2008) 19 European Business Law Review 1079.

case law shows that *Wouters* was not a freak occurrence[149] but a fully-fledged doctrine and an additional way of exonerating certain private regulatory schemes.[150]

In *Wouters*, *Meca-Medina*, *OTOC*,[151] *Consiglio nazionale dei geologi*,[152] and *Anonima Petroli Italiana*[153] the Court applied the competition rules to the measures of private regulators,[154] but also gave them the benefit of a relatively broad proportionality test. This 'inherent restriction' test takes into account the overall context in which a decision was taken and asks whether it could have been 'reasonably considered necessary' to achieve a legitimate regulatory objective (so far, these have included the 'proper practice of the legal profession', 'healthy rivalry between athletes', 'the quality of the services offered by chartered accountants', 'providing necessary guarantees to consumers of geologists' services', and road safety). Even though a measure has a restrictive effect on competition,[155] Art 101/1 is not infringed when the restriction is 'inherent' in the achievement of such an objective.

Crucially, this is not a simple cost-benefit analysis, balancing the anticompetitive effects against the benefits to the public interest objective. Rather, it asks whether the measure was an acceptable use of the private regulator's margin of discretion: whether it could reasonably have been considered necessary to achieve its aim.[156] Moreover, the necessity test it entails may turn out to be more flexible than the free movement justification test as applied to States. In *Wouters*, for example, the Bar could not have been asked to adopt a less restrictive measure (eg impose substantive guarantees of independence on accountants) if it did not

[149] See Ian S. Forrester, 'Where Law Meets Competition: Is Wouters Like a Cassis de Dijon or a Platypus?' in Ehlermann and Atanasiu (n 148).

[150] The *Wouters* test was also influenced by a string of cases on 'ancillary restraints': contractual clauses that seem restrictive but are not considered to fall foul of Art 101/1 because they pursue a legitimate commercial objective. Some examples are: Case C-250/92 *Gøttrup-Klim e.a. Grovvareforeninger v Dansk Landbrugs Grovvareselskab AmbA* [1994] ECR I-564; Case 161/84 *Pronuptia de Paris GmbH v Pronuptia de Paris Irmgard Schillgallis* [1986] ECR 353; and Case 258/78 *L.C. Nungesser KG and Kurt Eisele v Commission* [1982] ECR 2015. See also K Mortelmans, 'Towards Convergence in the Application of the Rules on Free Movement and on Competition?' (2001) 38 Common Market Law Review 613, 628–29. In addition, two Commission decisions in the area of sports, *ENIC* and *Mouscron* (see Chapter V), seem to have followed a similar approach even before the *Wouters* jurisprudence was developed.

[151] *OTOC* (n 104).

[152] Case C-136/12 *Consiglio nazionale dei geologi v Autorità garante della concorrenza e del mercato and Autorità garante della concorrenza e del mercato v Consiglio nazionale dei geologi* ECLI:EU:C:2013:489.

[153] *Anonima Petroli Italiana* (n 118).

[154] In *Wouters*, Dutch bar association rules banning partnerships between lawyers and accountants; in *Meca-Medina*, the International Olympic Committee's anti-doping rules; in *OTOC*, the Portuguese chamber of accountants' rules on professional training; in *Consiglio nazionale dei geologi* and *Anonima Petroli Italiana*, professional rules on fees. To date, there have been no equivalent cases under Art 102. It is not clear, however, why the same principle could not apply to unilateral abuses of dominance as well.

[155] In all of the cited cases, the Court found the defendants to be associations of undertakings (and thus, in principle, within the scope of the competition rules) and their practices to have effects restrictive of competition. See, for example *OTOC* (n 104) paras 82–83 and 89–92.

[156] *Wouters* (n 100) paras 105–08.

have the power to do so—the range of alternatives available to it is more narrow than in the case of a public regulator.[157]

As in free movement law, incoherent or disproportionately restrictive measures will fail the test. At the time of *Wouters*, it was not yet fully clear in what circumstances that would be the case. Later cases provided some clarifications. In *Meca-Medina,* the Court conducted a more thorough proportionality analysis, making it clearer that restrictive measures must be 'limited to what is necessary'.[158] In *OTOC*, the Court completed the arc. Unlike *Wouters* and *Meca-Medina*, the Court here explicitly followed three steps similar to the free movement justification test: whether there is a legitimate aim, whether the measure is appropriate to achieve the aim, and whether it is necessary (with the twist of explicit deference that remained from *Wouters*, still asking whether the measure could 'reasonably be regarded' as necessary and not whether it is necessarily the least restrictive option).[159]

OTOC was also the first case where a measure actually failed the test. In truth, this was not a surprise: like in *MOTOE* (an Art 102 and Art 106/1 case), the Court noted that OTOC, a professional association of accountants, was in a conflict of interest being simultaneously a competitor and regulator in the same market, and that its rules on professional training 'do not ensure equality of opportunity' for competitors.[160] While the Court broadly recognized OTOC's authority to regulate, the specific restrictions it imposed on firms wishing to provide training services (a market in which OTOC itself competed) did not seem necessary for the quality of training[161] and failed to follow minimal good governance criteria: they were drafted in vague terms and no express limits or review mechanisms were imposed on refusals.[162] For the Court, a less restrictive alternative could consist of a 'monitoring system organised on the basis of clearly defined, transparent, non-discriminatory, reviewable criteria likely to ensure training bodies equal access to the market in question'.[163] The Court does not directly balance the harm to competition against a benefit to the quality of accountants' services. Presumably, the regulation could be more or less strict, and could even increase

[157] Paradoxically, this may mean that if the private regulator is given limited powers and resources, it will be easier for it to justify restrictive measures. For a criticism of the use of a 'least restrictive alternative' test in antitrust, see Alan Devlin, 'Antitrust as Regulation' (2012) San Diego Law Review 823, section I.C.

[158] *Meca-Medina* (n 127) para 47. For a critical approach to *Meca-Medina*, see Petros C. Mavroidis and Gianni Infantino, 'Inherit the Wind: A Comment on the *Bosman* Jurisprudence' in Miguel Poiares Maduro and Loïc Azoulai (eds), *The Past and Future of EU Law: The Classics of EU Law Revisited on the 50th Anniversary of the Rome Treaty* (Hart 2010).

[159] *OTOC* (n 104) paras 94–96.

[160] ibid paras 88–89.

[161] In effect, OTOC artificially segmented the training market in two parts, keeping one (short training sessions) only for itself, meaning that 'competition was eliminated on a substantial part of the market'. In using that phrase, the Court seems to be inspired by Art 101/3. See para 97. Even in the part that remained, its competitors had to go through a rather demanding approval procedure in which access was sometimes refused.

[162] Paragraphs 91–92.

[163] Paragraph 99.

prices and reduce welfare. As long as it is designed in a reasonable, coherent, and non-discriminatory way, however, private regulation will pass muster.

Similarly, in *Anonima Petroli Italiana*, the Court rejected an attempt to justify price-fixing for road haulage services by vague references to road safety. According to the Court, the challenged measure did not show how price-fixing is appropriate to protect that objective. The measure was also considered to be incoherent because it exempted certain categories of services for unclear reasons, and it went beyond what was necessary because it did not enable carriers to prove that they satisfy safety standards regardless of lower prices.[164] Again, the Court does not claim that restricting output in pursuit of road safety is inefficient, but it does take issue with poorly designed measures that are not genuinely connected with the objective they claim to pursue.

The *Wouters* test is often seen as an oddity in competition law. Article 101/1 is usually thought of as a *prima facie* prohibition of restrictive conduct, which can then be justified through Art 101/3 (see section 3.1.4). This may explain why the test was initially used rather sparingly before the Court, even though the Commission has used it quite prominently in some of its soft law documents (eg in the area of sports).[165]

What remains unclear, however, is when exactly the test applies. Recent case-law such as *Anonima Petroli Italiana* and *Consiglio nazionale dei geologi*, both on fee scales, shows that the Court is not particularly selective. It would certainly go too far to subject any Art 101 case to the *Wouters* test, circumventing the usual avenue of justification under Art 101/3. A further source of complexity is the fact that the *Wouters* test leaves considerable discretion to national courts and agencies. This was made clear by *Consiglio nazionale dei geologi*, where the Court left it to the referring court to decide whether, in light of the overall context, a rule of a geologists' code of conduct that refers to the 'dignity of the profession' as a criterion in setting prices (apparently leading to the uniform application of a 'recommended' fee scale in practice), may be regarded as 'necessary for the implementation of the legitimate objective of providing guarantees to consumers'.[166] Not only is this task vague, but it conflicts with the judgment in *Anonima Petroli Italiana* mentioned above, and potentially stretches the *Wouters* justification too far. Any price-fixing agreement could be said to 'provide guarantees to consumers': the guarantee of a fixed price. The Court does not discuss how the 'dignity of the profession' is a legitimate regulatory issue, or what actual legitimate regulatory objective price-fixing serves in the market for geologists. Meanwhile, on the opposite end of the scale, the General Court has more recently seemed to interpret the *Wouters* exception as only applying within the strict confines of outright legislative delegation.[167]

[164] *Anonima Petroli Italiana* (n 118) paras 50–55.

[165] See Chapter V.

[166] *Consiglio nazionale dei geologi* (n 152) para 56.

[167] Case T-90/11 *Ordre national des pharmaciens (ONP) and Others v European Commission* ECLI:EU:T:2014:1049 para 327 ('In the absence of a regulatory power in that sphere, the Association ought to have acted within the strict framework of the law.'). On this judgment, see Wolf Sauter,

To make matters more complex, it is conceivable that a similar test could be introduced by analogy into Art 102, even outside the area of services of general economic interest where the Treaty requires a proportionality test.[168] In addition, in *Anonima Petroli Italiana* the Court applied the *Wouters* test directly to a legislative measure (see section 3.2.1), and not to a private regulator's measure that was legally recognized by the State.

The increasing use of the *Wouters* test could be explained by the two main limitations of justification under either Art 101/3 or Art 102. One is the ability to invoke public policy justifications without anchoring them in economic reasoning. The second is the ability to explicitly recognize a margin of discretion: that is not just to approve of a regulatory measure in substantive terms, but to acknowledge that (private) regulators are entitled to choose among a variety of measures, some of which may be less efficient than others, as long as certain good governance criteria are followed.

On both of these points, the *Wouters* test is a more flexible tool. It is likely to be used[169] in cases of private regulation where Art 101/3 seems too rigid to take into account the regulatory context, its aims, and other features. In this sense, *Wouters* and its progeny show that the Court follows a broader approach to competition law, allowing some, relatively rare cases of private regulation to benefit both from broad possibilities of justification and an explicit margin of discretion instead of declaring their measures to be non-economic and exempting them from scrutiny. In this sense, the inherent restriction doctrine internalizes the conflict between competition and other regulatory objectives into the competition analysis. The conflict is not, however, resolved by openly weighing and balancing competition against other interests. Instead, the Court tackles the problem through a least-restrictive means test, coupled with open deference to private regulators and a strong emphasis on procedural and governance issues. Similarly to the free movement rules (see Chapter II), the Court is unlikely to challenge the substance of regulatory choices that it considers were made in an appropriate and unbiased way.

While the *Wouters* test had for years been used quite sparingly, however, more recent case law may tempt defendants to invoke it in a wide range of circumstances. The Court would do well to limit its availability, for example to cases where private regulators can show some level of legitimacy in pursuing legitimate regulatory objectives. This need not necessarily depend on their links to the State.

'Containing Corporatism: EU Competition Law and Private Interest Government' (2015) 36 European Competition Law Review 187.

[168] See section 3.1.5. As Rousseva points out, 'nothing in the *Wouters* judgment prevents the transposition of the reasoning to the assessment of conduct under [Art 102]'. Ekaterina Rousseva, *Rethinking Exclusionary Abuses in EU Competition Law* (Hart 2010) 268.

[169] It should be pointed out that this assumes that there is a conscious decision-maker choosing in which circumstances the *Wouters* test applies. This disregards a number of contingencies, such as what parties actually claim before courts. For example, *OTOC* may have been handled under Art 101/3 had the national referring court not specifically posed a question regarding the *Wouters* test.

3.1.4 Justifying regulatory restrictions under Art 101/3 or Art 102

Article 101/3 and 'objective justification' under Art 102 are the avenues through which defendants most commonly attempt to defend *prima facie* anticompetitive measures. Both of these loosely resemble a proportionality test.[170] They are, however, construed in a way that is narrower than the *Wouters* test, both because of the limited aims that can be invoked and because they leave no explicit room for deference: undertakings accused of restricting competition are not normally 'entitled to consider' that those restrictions are beneficial.

Article 101/3 allows for the exemption of restraints under four cumulative conditions: that they (1) improve the production or distribution of goods or promote technical or economic progress; (2) allow consumers a fair share of the resulting benefit; (3) do not impose restrictions which are not indispensable to achieving those objectives; and (4) do not eliminate competition in a substantial part of the market.[171]

It is clear that this allows for a number of justifications that have to do with efficiency, possibly including the correction of market failures and other pro-competitive aims. Private regulators could claim that their rules are indispensable for product or service quality, for example.[172] A narrower approach to competition law would stop here. US antitrust law, for example, has been rather strict with instances of professional regulation that attempted to invoke broad public policy aims as justification,[173] but relatively open to those that could be portrayed as economically beneficial, such as an agreement prohibiting misleading advertising (*California Dental Association*).[174]

What is less clear is whether Art 101/3 can go any further, by accommodating broader policy choices. Some of the features of Art 101/3 may be particularly problematic in that respect. For example, the requirement to show benefits to consumers, if interpreted narrowly, could be read as only contemplating identifiable short-term consumer benefit, or as excluding cases where the level of protection of, for example, public health sought by the regulator goes beyond what would be required by consumers in a competitive marketplace.[175] Notably, the Commission's Art 101/3 Guidelines require that 'the group of consumers affected by the restriction and benefiting from the efficiency gains are substantially the same', seemingly excluding redistribution among different groups of regulatees.[176]

[170] See for objective justification *United Brands* (n 135) 189 et seq.

[171] Bellamy & Child (n 140) 189–226.

[172] See pp. 78 and 91.

[173] See section 2, and in particular the discussion around n 35.

[174] *California Dental Association v FTC* (1999) 526 US 756. Justice Souter's opinion relied on information asymmetries to justify restrictions on advertising methods for dentists: 'the difficulty for consumers or potential competitors to get and verify information about the price and availability of services magnifies the dangers to competition associated with misleading advertising' (772).

[175] For an example of a narrow view of 'consumer benefit' under Art 101/3, see Case T-111/08 *MasterCard, Inc. and Others v Commission* ECLI:EU:T:2012:260 para 228.

[176] See Lianos (n 50) 265–66, as well as Commission, 'Guidelines on the application of Article 81(3) of the Treaty' (Communication of 27 April 2004) OJ C101/97 para 43.

The prohibition on eliminating competition in substantial parts of the market could also be an issue. How would it relate, for example, to a sporting body banning amateur clubs from accepting commercial sponsorship, while allowing it to professional clubs?

In practice, however, the four conditions are used in a somewhat flexible way. Firstly, the Commission accepts that goals pursued by various Treaty provisions can be taken into account, albeit only 'to the extent that they can be subsumed under the four conditions' of Art 101/3.[177] Both before the Commission and the Court, this has meant that public policy aims have been considered. Their impact, however, has been limited, especially as regards the Commission, which has increasingly focused its interpretation of Art 101/3 on economic efficiency.[178]

In *Métropole*, the General Court dealt with a Commission Art 101/3 exemption decision granted to media rights purchasing agreements and to the restrictive membership rules of the European Broadcasting Union (EBU). The Commission's arguments were partly based on the idea that EBU members were public broadcasters with a 'public mission' to ensure universal access to culturally significant content regardless of commercial considerations.[179] While it eventually found against the Commission on this point, the General Court acknowledged that 'in the context of an overall assessment', the Commission can 'base itself on considerations connected with the pursuit of the public interest' under Art 101/3.[180] More recently, the Commission's *CISAC* decision[181] took into account, but largely rejected on the facts, the argument of copyright collecting societies that the market segmentation created by their representation agreements should be justified on cultural grounds, as reflected in Art 151/4 TFEU.[182] The Court have also made forays into broader readings of Art 101/3.

[177] Commission, Art 81/3 Guidelines (n 176) para 42. See also Case T-17/93 *Matra Hachette SA v Commission* [1994] ECR II-595, para 139.

[178] See Witt (n 82) sections B and C. On the other hand, the application of Art 101/3 by national competition authorities and courts may lead to different results.

[179] See, however, *VBBB/VBVB* (Case IV/428) Commission Decision 82/123/EEC (1981) OJ L54/36VBBB-VBVB para 60, refusing an attempt to justify a book cartel on cultural grounds: 'The Commission also takes the view that it is not for undertakings or associations of undertakings to conclude agreements on cultural questions, which are principally a matter for government.' Mortelmans (n 150) 116.

[180] *Métropole* (n 98) para 118. The arguments actually used by the Commission were inspired by the case law on services of general economic interest. The General Court, however, found that 'inasmuch as, according to the Decision … [Art 106/2] is not applicable, factors coming essentially within the ambit of that article cannot in this case constitute a criterion for the application of [Art 101/3] in the absence of other justification' (paras 116–17).

[181] *CISAC* (Case COMP/C2/38.698) Commission Decision (2008) OJ C323/12. A full version of the Decision can be found at <http://ec.europa.eu/competition/antitrust/cases/dec_docs/38698/38698_4567_1.pdf> paras 93–99. The General Court did not examine this issue (Case T-442/08 *International Confederation of Societies of Authors and Composers (CISAC) v European Commission* ECLI:EU:T:2013:188).

[182] Article 151(4) of the Treaty: 'The Community shall take cultural aspects into account in its action under other provisions of this Treaty, in particular in order to respect and to promote the diversity of its cultures.'

In *Piau*, the General Court accepted under Art 101/3 an argument that sounds redistributive: the need to license players' agents in order to protect players from poorly negotiated contracts.[183]

Article 101/3 was successfully deployed to justify agreements on grounds that, while not necessarily linked to efficiency, could in broad terms be described as economic, such as the preservation of jobs (*Metro*, *Stichting Baksteen*, *Synthetic Fibres*),[184] industrial policy and market integration (*Ford/VW*, *Olivetti*).[185] Environmental benefits have had some sway as well.[186] In *CECED*, for example, an agreement to standardize the production of washing machines into categories of energy consumption and stop producing high-consumption machines was justified not only by the economic benefits to individual consumers, but also to some extent by the benefits to society as a whole for reducing energy consumption and pollution.[187] *CECED* also shows that the indispensability condition can be read similarly to a least restrictive alternative test: three regulatory alternatives to an agreement not to produce high-consumption washing machines (industry-wide targets, information campaigns, and labelling) were proposed, and all three were rejected as ineffective.[188]

As this analysis shows, Art 101/3 is not as flexible as the *Wouters* test, and not entirely conducive to invoking public policy arguments. Firstly, while giving a nod to public policy arguments, the Art 101/3 Guidelines and similar documents, such as the Horizontal Guidelines, are 'drafted explicitly in terms of economic efficiency'.[189] Secondly, before the Commission and the Court, parties were more successful in justifying agreements under Art 101/3 when they could link their broader arguments to efficiencies, or the pro-competitive aspects of a restraint. According to Monti, this shows that Art 101/3 requires a finding of efficiency gains prior to, or in addition to, the benefits to other values such

[183] Piau (n 87) paras 100 et seq.

[184] Case 26-76 *Metro SB-Großmärkte GmbH & Co. KG v Commission* [1977] ECR 1875, para 43; *Stichting Baksteen* (Case IV/34.456) Commission Decision 94/296/EC (1994) OJ L131/15, para 43; *Synthetic fibres* (Case IV/30.810) Commission Decision 84/380/EEC (1984) OJ L207/17, para 37; Monti, 'Article 81 EC and Public Policy' (n 63) 1071. For the field of state aids, see C Semmelmann, 'The European Union's Economic Constitution Under the Lisbon Treaty: Soul-Searching Shifts the Focus to Procedure' (2010) 35 European Law Review 516, 537–38.

[185] *Ford Volkswagen* (Case IV/33.814) Commission Decision 93/49/EEC (1992) OJ L20/14 para 36: '... the Commission also takes note of the fact that the project constitutes the largest ever single foreign investment in Portugal ... It therefore contributes to the promotion of the harmonious development of the Community and the reduction of regional disparities ... It also furthers European market integration by linking Portugal more closely to the Community through one of its important industries. This would not be enough to make an exemption possible unless the conditions of Article 85(3) were fulfilled, but it is an element which the Commission has taken into account.' See also *Metro* para 43.

[186] For an overview, see Witt (n 82) 459–60.

[187] Then Art 174 EC on environmental protection was also cited (para 55). See Mortelmans (n 150) 641–42.

[188] CECED (Case IV.F.1/36.718) Commission Decision 2000/475/EC [1999] OJ L187/47, paras 58–63. See also Van Bael and Bellis (n 110) 81.

[189] Yeung (n 4) 145; Whish and Bailey (n 82) 157. See also Witt (n 82).

as environmental protection.[190] Of course, it is difficult to draw a bright line between 'economic' and 'non-economic' values. Yet it seems clear that Art 101/3 was traditionally applied with a view to ensuring the efficient operation of markets.

Similarly, there is little indication so far that the judicially developed concept of 'objective justification' under Art 102 can be used as a public policy-based balancing exercise. Rather, objective justification has mostly been used as an element in the definition of an abuse, asking whether there are legitimate explanations for certain conduct from a commercial point of view or whether the only plausible motivation was to exclude competitors. The test can exonerate conduct that can be explained by the 'legitimate business interests' of the dominant undertaking,[191] as long as the restraint is proportionate to them. Its practical significance lies in the shifting of the burden of proof to the undertaking.[192] It has in general been interpreted narrowly, and attempts at justification were only successful where they invoked external circumstances over which an undertaking had no control.[193]

To date, there have been no cases where a clear public policy argument managed to exonerate an abuse under the 'objective justification' test. In fact, in *Hilti* and *Tetra Pak II*, attempts to justify restrictions on intra-brand competition by invoking health, safety and consumer protection were rejected without hesitation: '[T]he remedy must lie in appropriate legislation or regulations, and not in rules adopted unilaterally by manufacturers.'[194] It may be, however, that a case dealing with private regulation pursuing a legitimate public policy objective in a proportionate way—whether as part of a co-regulatory scheme or not—could lead the Court to soften its approach. AG Kokott in *MOTOE* seemed to suggest that the 'interests of sport' such as uniform rules and timetables could be an objective justification for abuses under Art 102, but not if 'used arbitrarily to promote the organisation's own economic interests', as was the case there.[195] Whether a different kind of case would lead to an adaptation of the 'objective justification' test, perhaps through the introduction of a *Wouters*-like proportionality analysis, remains a matter for speculation.

[190] Monti, 'Article 81 EC and Public Policy' (n 63) 1077–78.

[191] See the Opinion of AG Jarabo Colomer in *Sot. Lélos kai Sia* (n 64) para 99. See also Robert O'Donoghue, 'Verbalizing a General Test for Exclusionary Conduct under Article 82 EC' in Claus-Dieter Ehlermann and Mel Marquis (eds), *European Competition Law Annual 2007: A Reformed Approach to Article 82 EC* (Hart 2008) 347 and Rousseva (n 168) 131, reading objective justification largely as an efficiency defence.

[192] See Case T-201/04 *Microsoft Corp. v Commission* [2007] ECR II-3601 688 et seq for an unsuccessful attempt to rely on objective justification in the context of intellectual property.

[193] Rousseva (n 168) 263–65.

[194] Case T-83/91 *Tetra Pak International SA v Commission* [1994] ECR II-755 para 84. See also Case T-30/89 *Hilti AG v Commission* [1991] ECR II-1439 para 118: '... it is clearly not the task of an undertaking in a dominant position to take steps on its own initiative to eliminate products which, rightly or wrongly, it regards as dangerous or at least as inferior in quality to its own products.' Rousseva (n 168) 266.

[195] Opinion of AG Kokott in *MOTOE* (n 143) para 96.

3.1.5 Private regulation under Article 106/2—do private regulators perform services of general economic interest?

Under certain conditions, co-regulatory schemes can benefit from the Art 106/2 exemption from the competition rules for services of general economic interest (SGEIs). Undertakings entrusted by a Member State with providing an SGEI can only be subject to the competition rules insofar as that would not obstruct the performance of the tasks assigned to them.[196] This exemption must not affect the development of trade to an extent contrary to the interests of the Union.[197] Article 106/2 'seeks to reconcile the Member States' interest in using certain undertakings ... as an instrument of economic or fiscal policy with the Community's interest in ensuring compliance with the rules on competition and preservation of the unity of the common market'.[198] Over the years, the importance of this provision has grown, in part because of the growing role of private actors in delivering services that were once the sole province of governments.[199]

Not all private regulation can benefit from Art 106/2. The provision will be relevant only for some co-regulatory schemes, as it explicitly requires an act of the State entrusting an undertaking with the operation of SGEIs. This should be an act of official authority, such as legislation or other formal decision,[200] but it can also be a contract or a concession agreement.[201] The service may have been initially proposed or developed by the undertaking, not necessarily by the public authority.[202]

Moreover, the definition of a 'service of general economic interest', while rather open-ended, would not cover all forms of private regulation. The services have to be of an economic nature, but also in some sense 'exhibit special characteristics' as compared to other economic activities.[203] They have to relate to specific public service obligations 'in the general interest'.[204] This excludes, for example, collective

[196] Article 106/2 is applicable to undertakings. This means that it assumes that what is at stake is not 'exercising powers typical of a public authority'. This may lead to some confusion, as the question of whether there is economic activity and the question whether an undertaking has been entrusted, by an act of an official authority, with the performance of a SGEI, is similar.

[197] Bellamy & Child (n 140) 11.054; Whish and Bailey (n 82) 241. For an elaboration, see AG Léger in *Wouters* (n 100) para 157 et seq.

[198] AG Mengozzi in Case C-437/09 *AG2R Prévoyance v Beaudout Père et Fils SARL* [2011] ECR I-973, para 102, *Brentjens* (n 125) para 103.

[199] Commission, 'A Quality Framework for Services of General Interest in Europe' (Communication) COM/2011/900 final para 3. In general, see Tony Prosser, 'Competition Law and Public Services: From Single Market to Citizenship Rights?' (2005) 11 *European Public Law* 543 as well as T Prosser, *The Limits of Competition Law: Markets and Public Services* (Oxford University Press 2005) ch 2.

[200] Bellamy & Child (n 140) 1062–63. See *MOTOE* (n 143) paras 45–46 and Case T-289/03 *British United Provident Association Ltd (BUPA), BUPA Insurance Ltd and BUPA Ireland Ltd v Commission* [2008] ECR II-081, para 181.

[201] Case T-17/02 *Fred Olsen, SA v Commission* [2005] ECR II-2031, para 188.

[202] Commission, 'Communication on the application of the European Union State aid rules to compensation granted for the provision of services of general economic interest' (2012) OJ C8/4 paras 52–53.

[203] *OTOC* (n 104) para 105.

[204] Bellamy & Child (n 140) 1063–65.

rights societies,[205] trade unions, or charities.[206] On the other hand, water supply,[207] postal services,[208] ambulance transport,[209] supplementary healthcare funds,[210] and pension funds,[211] among others, were found to provide an SGEI. This does not mean, however, that undertakings that fall within those groups would *always* be exempted from the competition rules. Whether Art 106/2 can be invoked depends on the specific task,[212] and each case has to be judged on its own merits.

Most importantly, even where Art 106/2 is applicable, the measure has to pass a proportionality test. This test has traditionally been construed relatively strictly. While it is not necessary that the undertaking's existence would be jeopardized without the exclusive right, it is not enough that its public service task could be made more difficult by subjecting it to competition. It must be shown at least that competition would obstruct the task, or even—in one version—'that the undertaking ... has no other technically and economically feasible means of performing its particular task'.[213] In *Corbeau*, the Court also limited the possibility of compensating an SGEI provider for its public service obligation by granting it a monopoly in a related, but separate market.[214]

3.1.6 The three avenues for justification

It is clear from the case law outlined above that, in some circumstances at least, private regulators can rely on three overlapping possibilities of justifying their conduct: Art 101/3 or the 'objective justification' under Art 102, the *Wouters* test, and the rule on services of general economic interest from Art 106/2. There is no straightforward answer concerning what the relationship is between the three.

Clearly, similar arguments can be used in all of them. In *OTOC*, for example, the Court found the training regulation to fail the *Wouters* test as it went beyond what was necessary. It then, in a few brief sentences, relied on the same arguments to decide that the scheme could not be justified by Art 101/3 (the restrictions are not essential and they eliminate competition from a substantial part of the market),[215] nor by Art 106/2 (even if there was a service of general economic interest, which does not seem to be the case, the rules would

[205] Case 127-73 *Belgische Radio en Televisie and société belge des auteurs, compositeurs et éditeurs v SV SABAM and NV Fonior* [1974] ECR 51, paras 18–23.

[206] Commission, 'Services of general interest in Europe' (Communication) 2001/C/17/04 para 30.

[207] *NAVEWA-ANSEAU* (Case IV/29.995) Commission Decision 82/371/EEC (1982) OJ L 167/39 para 65.

[208] Case C-320/91 *Criminal Proceedings Against Paul Corbeau* [1993] ECR I-2533, para 15.

[209] Case C-475/99 *Firma Ambulanz Glöckner v Landkreis Südwestpfalz* [2001] ECR I-8089, para 56 et seq.

[210] *BUPA* (n 200) para 161 et seq.

[211] *Albany* (n 91) para 103 et seq.

[212] *Nungesser* (n 150) paras 8–9 and *Corbeau* (n 208) para 19.

[213] *NAVEWA-ANSEAU* (n 207) para 66. See also Whish and Bailey (n 82) 238–39.

[214] Whish and Bailey (n 82) 239–40.

[215] Paragraphs 102–03.

go beyond what is necessary to perform the tasks assigned to the OTOC).[216] Failing one of the tests on proportionality grounds, therefore, is likely to also result in failing the others.

This does not necessarily mean that the three justifications are identical. They differ in a number of specific ways and should not be easily conflated. Rather, they are meant to complement each other. The purpose of Art 106/2 is precisely to exclude certain activities from the logic of competition, as well as from the need for justification on the basis of economic efficiency. The *Wouters* test was formulated, in part at least, as a response to the limitations of Art 101/3—either procedural (due to the fact that, at the time, Art 101/3 could not be applied directly by the referring court),[217] or substantive (given that Art 101/3 is a relatively more demanding type of justification driven by economic arguments).

Broadly speaking, however, all three end up dealing with similar questions when faced with private regulation. In practice, this means that there are likely to be cases where the same conduct could be justified under any of the tests. For example, an imaginary 'light' version of the training regulation in OTOC, one that was free of conflicts of interest and that placed a reasonable and clearly outlined registration requirement for training providers could have been justified under Art 101/3 (as an economically efficient and narrowly circumscribed way of promoting quality services which benefits consumers—especially in light of information asymmetries and the public good aspect of some accountants' services), the *Wouters* exception (as an appropriate and least restrictive means 'inherent' in achieving the legitimate aim of the quality of accountants' services) or the Art 106/2 exception (the statutory authority to certify accountant training providers could—albeit at a stretch—be claimed to be a case of entrustment with an SGEI).

3.2 Private regulation and state action

Co-regulatory arrangements may also be subject to antitrust scrutiny. For example, the decisions of an industry association may be given binding effect through national legislation. In these cases, the application of competition law is complicated by the possibility of applying EU competition law to the Member State—the so-called '*effet utile*' doctrine, as well as to the private regulator. These two tests should be distinguished.

The same co-regulatory scheme—for example statutory delegation of the authority to fix prices to a professional association—could be disputed by a claim against the State that delegated or against the association that implemented the scheme. In principle, whether such a scheme should be allowed to stand should not depend on that procedural choice, but on whether we believe the legislator should be allowed to make such a decision despite its restrictive effects. This would

[216] Paragraphs 104–07.

[217] See the discussion of *Wouters* in Chapter VI section 5.1.1.

be the position under the US antitrust state action doctrine.[218] As Hovenkamp summarizes, it boils down to questions such as: is there a lawful regulatory regime in place? Does it leave the firms discretionary space and if so, is the state able and willing to supervise that conduct?[219] If that is the case, antitrust law withdraws, deferring to the political decision to exclude competition from certain markets (and, in relation to the states, respecting the principle of federalism).

In EU law, however, the situation is more complex. The Court has chosen to retain an explicit role in supervising State activities under competition law—again, in line with a broad reading of competition law.[220] At the same time, however, this review is limited in practice to cases of rather blatant capture and conflict of interest. This might be so because the resources of the Court (and other EU institutions) are too small to police all of the Member States' economic policies under the standards of competition law.[221] Moreover, applying an efficiency-driven competition law to Member States would subject democratic decision-making to a constitutional standard most of them would view as going beyond what is required by the Treaties.

As a consequence, the Court has seriously reviewed the national political process under the competition rules only in cases of clear capture—where, for example, the Member State government rubberstamps an existing cartel. While any State measure can in principle be challenged under the competition rules, if, on the facts, the regulatory scheme broadly seems like a reflection of a legitimate political choice, competition law withdraws (the free movement rules, however, can still kick in, as in the *Cipolla* judgment).[222]

[218] Under the 'state action doctrine', if the scheme is a result of a genuine governmental policy, it would be exempt from antitrust law regardless of who the defendant is. The state action doctrine is shorthand for the express (*Hughes Tool Co v Trans World Airlines, Inc* 409 US 363 (1973)) or implied immunity of federal regulation (*In re Stock Exchanges Options Trading Antitrust Litigation,* 317 F3d 134 (2d Cir 2003)), the immunity of state action (eg *Parker v. Brown* 317 US 341 (1943)), and the immunity granted to petitions to the government (*Eastern Railroad Presidents Conference v Noerr Motor Freight Inc.* 365 US 127, 135 (1961) and *United Mine Workers v Pennington* 381 US 657, 670 (1965)). A distinct, but clearly connected line of case law is the one arising from *Trinko* (n 57), holding that antitrust law should not be applied in the presence of a distinct regulatory regime that takes into account competition considerations, such as in telecoms. While the US approach seems to be more friendly to state action, the recent judgment in *FTC v Phoebe Putney Health System* 568 US (2013, nyr) is somewhat more restrictive, requiring states to 'clearly articulate an affirmative state policy to displace competition with a regulatory alternative'. For more details, see Elhauge (n 23); Hovenkamp (n 25) ch 10; Robert P Inman and Daniel L Rubinfeld, 'Making Sense of the Antitrust State-Action Doctrine: Balancing Political Participation and Economic Efficiency in Regulatory Federalism' (1996) 75 Texas Law Review 1203; Timothy J Muris, 'State Intervention/ State Action—A U.S. Perspective' George Mason University School of Law Law & Economics Working Paper Series <http://ssrn.com/abstract_id= 545163>.

[219] Hovenkamp (n 25) 237.

[220] See also Szyszczak (n 42) 93.

[221] As Marenco put it, 'a Community directly in charge of all economic problems arising here and there without the screen of the state governments would be a giant with clay feet, weakened rather than strengthened by the minutiae of its responsibilities'. Giuliano Marenco, 'Competition between National Economies and Competition between Businesses—A Response to Judge Pescatore' (1987) 10 Fordham International Law Journal 420, 442.

[222] Joined cases C-94/04 and C-202/04 *Federico Cipolla v Rosaria Fazari, née Portolese* (C-94/ 04) *and Stefano Macrino and Claudia Capoparte v Roberto Meloni* (C-202/04) [2006] ECR I-11421.

3.2.1 *The EU state action doctrine: Applying competition law to Member State measures*

The EU state action doctrine consists of two lines of case law that are not always seen as a coherent whole. The first one is the *Ladbroke* doctrine, which holds that undertakings do not violate Arts 101 and 102 TFEU if either Member State or EU legislation strictly governs their conduct, either 'requiring anticompetitive conduct' or 'creating a legal framework which itself eliminates any possibility of competitive activity on their part'.[223] This is not explicitly justified by the need to defer to the national or EU legislators' political choices to exclude competition from certain markets, but by a more formalistic reason: in those circumstances, the anticompetitive conduct is not 'attributable' to the undertakings.[224]

In practice, however, it is rather difficult for private regulators or other undertakings to rely on this exemption, as long as the legislation at issue leaves at least some scope for autonomous conduct. For example, if a law grants a professional association the power to fix prices, but does not set the level of those prices or the way in which they can be imposed, the association will still be subject to competition law.[225] Thus, the fact that public bodies are, for example, authorized to review the measures of the professional association would not in itself free the undertakings from liability.

This brings us to the second 'ingredient' of the EU state action doctrine: applying competition law to control the actions of the Member States. A Member State can be challenged through a combination of Arts 101 or 102 (depending on whether the anticompetitive behaviour of the private actors can be described as an agreement or an abuse of a dominant position)[226] and the loyalty clause of today's Art 4/3 TEU.[227]

Under this '*effet utile*' or '*useful effect*' doctrine, the Member States are prohibited from 'rendering the competition rules ineffective' by inducing or facilitating anticompetitive behaviour. More precisely, as the Court has been restating the test since *Van Eycke*,[228] the Member State can be challenged either for 'requiring or favouring the adoption of agreements, decisions or concerted practices contrary to Article 101 TFEU', 'reinforcing their effects', or for 'divesting its own rules of the

[223] See nn 26 and 92, as well as Case C-280/08 P *Deutsche Telekom AG v Commission* [2010] ECR I-9555, para 80.

[224] ibid. [225] *CNSD II* (n 129) paras 59 et seq.

[226] Cases based on Art 101 are much more frequent, but an Art 102 challenge is also possible under the same legal construct. See, for example *Ahmed Saeed* (n 144) para 52.

[227] Traditionally, this case law also cited the former Art 3(1)g EC which proclaimed competition to be one of the aims of the Treaty. The removal of this provision from the text of the Lisbon Treaty and its relegation to the Protocol No 27 on Internal Market and Competition has not, however, had significant effect in this sense. See Lianos (n 50) 264 and Ben Van Rompuy, 'The Impact of the Lisbon Treaty on EU Competition Law: A Review of Recent Case Law of the EU Courts' (2011) 1 CPI Antitrust Chronicle 8–9.

[228] Case 267/86 *Pascal Van Eycke v ASPA NV* [1988] ECR 4769 para 16.

character of legislation by delegating to private economic operators responsibility for taking decisions affecting the economic sphere'.[229]

The rise of this doctrine was followed by keen interest from scholars.[230] Apart from cases where there is literally an illegal agreement or abuse of a dominant position that is supported by the Member State, however, this line of case law no longer seems to have the bite that was predicted (and perhaps feared).[231] In *Meng* and *OHRA*,[232] the Court formulated a requirement that, in order to show that a Member State required, favoured, or reinforced Art 101 violations, in principle there should be a link between separate and identifiable conduct of undertakings[233] and the Member State measure. State regulation that creates anticompetitive effects on its own would thus be safe from scrutiny. A case in point is *Doulamis*, where a law banning the advertising of dental clinics was held to be out of reach of the competition rules.[234]

In the private regulation context, the second 'leg' of the *Van Eycke* test ('delegating the responsibility for taking decisions affecting the economic sphere') is particularly interesting. On the face of it, this test seems to allow challenges to any decision to delegate, as such, even without proof of a separate infringement by undertakings. There have, however, hardly been any cases of such a violation—unlawful delegation was only ever established in addition to a separate finding that the State required, favoured, or reinforced anticompetitive agreements.[235]

In principle, the liability of a Member State under the delegation test depends on the extent to which it imposes public interest criteria on undertakings (the

[229] Case C-185/91 *Bundesanstalt für den Güterfernverkehr v Gebrüder Reiff GmbH & Co. KG* [1993] ECR I-5801, para 14 and Case C-198/01 *Consorzio Industrie Fiammiferi (CIF) v Autorità Garante della Concorrenza e del Mercato* [2003] ECR I-8055, paras 45–6.

[230] See, among others, Ulla Boegh Henriksen, *Anti-competitive State Measures in the European Community: An Analysis of Decisions of the European Court of Justice* (Copenhagen Business School Press 1994); F Castillo de la Torre, 'State Action Defence in EC Competition Law' (2005) 28(4) World Competition 407; Harm Schepel, 'Delegation of Regulatory Powers to Private Parties under EC-Competition Law: Towards a Procedural Public Interest Test' (2002) 39 Common Market Law Review 31.

[231] Norbert Reich, 'The "November Revolution" of the European Court of Justice: Keck, Meng and Audi Revisited' (1994) 31 Common Market Law Review 459.

[232] Case C-2/91 *Criminal proceedings against Wolf W. Meng* [1993] ECR I-5751, paras 15–19 and Case C-245/91 *Criminal proceedings against Ohra Schadeverzekeringen NV* [1993] ECR I-5851, paras 11–14.

[233] For an example, see *Ahmed Saeed* (n 144) paras 48–9. For an early argument against this reading, see Denis Waelbroeck, 'Les rapports entre les règles sur la libre circulation des marchandises et les règles de concurrence applicables aux entreprises dans la CEE' in Francesco Capotorti and Pierre Pescatore (eds), *Du droit international au droit de l'intégration: liber amicorum Pierre Pescatore* (Nomos 1987) 788. « Nous pensons que la tentative de réduire la portée de l'arrêt a une simple condamnation de mesures étatiques favorisant des comportements interdits aux entreprises doit être rejetée ». A more recent argument along those lines can be found in the Opinion of AG Trstenjak in Case C-531/07 *Fachverband der Buch- und Medienwirtschaft v LIBRO Handelsgesellschaft mbH* [2009] ECR I-3717, paras 159–65.

[234] Case C-446/05 *Criminal proceedings against Ioannis Doulamis* [2008] ECR I-1377 paras 21–22.

[235] See, in more detail, Heremans (n 7) 270–71. The most recent example of this is *Anonima Petroli Italiana* (n 118).

substantive aspect) and supervises their conduct (the procedural aspect)—the latter being far more important in practice.[236] Specific legal provisions on the public interest criteria that need to be taken into account by the scheme, the ability of public bodies to supervise or participate in the decision-making, and mechanisms for the prevention of conflicts of interest such as the use of independent experts or committees, would all speak against liability. In practice, however, the Member States have been able to get away with anticompetitive arrangements as long as the power of review in the last instance is kept by the State. Thus, even schemes in which industry representatives adopted decisions limiting competition, without the significant decision-making participation of independent experts and public officials, or effective rules on transparency, accountability, and the public interests that should be taken into account have passed muster.[237] The Court has been willing to discipline only delegation that involved no public controls or public interest criteria whatsoever, granting a blank cheque to the industry—such as the law authorizing the Italian customs agents' association CNSD to fix prices.[238]

The reluctance to take this line of case law further can be explained by the potentially destructive effect it could have for the economic policies of the Member States.[239] Here, similarly as with the notion of 'economic activity', the Court seems to be trying, in a not entirely articulated way, to exempt from scrutiny specific activities that Member States have removed from the logic of competition through a clearly formulated policy, while retaining the power of supervision. Due to the complex nature of the legal tests, however, this exemption is rather opaque.

A further layer of complexity has been created by the *Anonima Petroli Italiana* judgment, which seems to allow Member State measures, challenged through the *effet utile* doctrine, to be justified through the *Wouters* proportionality test even if they fail to satisfy the criteria for exemption under the *effet utile* case law (that is, even if there is unlawful delegation and/or reinforcement of illegal agreements). The Court did not actually justify the particular measure, and it even hedged its findings saying that there is 'no need to consider whether the [*Wouters* case law] is applicable to national legislation' because the legislation is disproportionate anyway.[240] Still, were future judgments to take up the Court's suggestion,

[236] Miguel Poiares Maduro, 'The Chameleon State: EU Law and the Blurring of the Private/Public Distinction in the Market' <http://ssrn.com/abstract=1575542>, 7–8.

[237] This can be seen in Case C-35/99 *Criminal proceedings against Manuele Arduino, third parties: Diego Dessi, Giovanni Bertolotto and Compagnia Assicuratrice RAS SpA* [2002] ECR I-1529, paras 39–43 and *Reiff* paras 21–23. There are, however, some signs of a more active approach in Case C-250/03 *Giorgio Emanuele Mauri v Ministero della Giustizia and Commissione per gli esami di avvocato presso la Corte d'appello di Milano* [2005] ECR I-1267, paras 30–38.

[238] *Commission v Italy* (n 101) para 57. Even in that case, however, the Court found a separate infringement of Art 101 by CNSD, as well as a violation of the 'first leg' of *Van Eycke*—the improper delegation was found only in addition to those.

[239] See Van Bael and Bellis (n 110) 894–95. The arguments of Germany in *Wouters* (n 100) show that the application of competition law to regulation is much more than a technical issue. For Germany, the decision to delegate the adoption of universally binding rules is an issue of national sovereignty and, as they term it, 'institutional autonomy' (para 54).

[240] *Anonima Petroli Italiana* (n 118) para 49.

there would be quite a change of approach. The Court had previously refused to follow the arguments of AG Jacobs and AG Léger that, instead of searching for links between State measures and the conduct of undertakings, the *effet utile* case law should simply require Member States to justify, in terms of legitimate policy objectives, measures that in themselves restrict competition.[241] Yet, introducing a *Wouters*-type test could mean just that. Alternatively, if *Anonima Petroli Italiana* means that such a proportionality test will be *additional* to the existing test for state action, this would weaken the *effet utile* doctrine even further, because Member States would receive two separate avenues for justification—a procedural and a substantive one.

3.2.2 *The relationship of state action immunity and the useful effect doctrine*

A question that is sometimes neglected—perhaps because of the Court's formalistic language in state action cases, which frames state action immunity as a question of to whom certain conduct should be 'attributed'—is how the immunity of undertakings relates to the possibility of Member State liability under the useful effect doctrine.

Firstly, if an undertaking (the private regulator in a co-regulatory scheme, for our purposes) is independently liable under Art 101 or Art 102, what does that mean for the liability of the Member State? Is it superfluous, or, on the contrary, implied? The answer will depend on the case, because the Court sees these two tests as independent: all outcomes are possible.[242] A good example is provided by the two *CNSD* cases, on compulsory tariffs for customs agents. In these cases, both the state and the association were separately held to violate Art 101.[243] This is not, however, automatic—it would be possible to imagine a case where the professional association violates the competition provisions, but there is simply not enough of a link with Member State conduct to find liability on the part of the State.

More vexing is the opposite problem: what if the undertaking/private regulator succeeds (despite the odds) in obtaining *Ladbroke* immunity, and the State is subsequently challenged? Here, as well, one could say that these are two independent tests and that all outcomes are possible. The useful effect doctrine, however, usually seems to indicate that Member State liability hinges on a *separate* violation of competition law by the undertaking(s). If the *Ladbroke* immunity applies,

[241] Opinion of AG Jacobs in *Pavlov* (n 110) paras 161–63; Opinion of AG Léger in *Arduino* (n 237) paras 86–91.

[242] This is implied by the Court in *Fiammiferi* (n 229): '… it is of little significance that, where undertakings are required by national legislation to engage in anti-competitive conduct, they cannot also be held accountable for infringement of [Arts 101 and 102 TFEU] … Member States' obligations under [ex Art 3/1g EC, Art 4/3 TEU, and Arts 101 and 102 TFEU], which are distinct from those to which undertakings are subject under [Arts 101 and 102 TFEU], none the less continue to exist and therefore the national competition authority remains duty-bound to disapply the national measure at issue.' (para 51).

[243] See Heremans (n 7) 274–77 for a discussion of this case.

however, there is no violation by the undertakings, presumably meaning that the Member State will not be liable either.

There is a Catch-22 here. If there is indeed no Member State liability in such situations, this would mean that all an anticompetitive co-regulatory scheme has to do to avoid scrutiny under the competition rules is to limit the autonomy of the private parties as much as possible by leaving them no scope for competition whatsoever. *Wouters* seems to describe such a scenario: if a Member State delegates regulatory power while strictly defining the 'public-interest criteria' and 'essential principles' of the scheme, as well as maintaining ultimate decision-making authority, the measure would be considered a 'State measure', not attributable to the undertaking.[244] Indeed, this is the same idea that we have seen in the case law on the definition of an undertaking: a State should be able to reserve an area from the reach of competition law if it does so coherently and completely (see the discussion of *Compass-Datenbank*, section 3.1.1).

Finding Member State liability in such cases would amount to saying that Member States can violate the competition rules independently of the conduct of undertakings—precisely what the established doctrine seeks to avoid. Nevertheless, *Fiammiferi* seems to imply that exact outcome: even if the undertakings that participate in a co-regulatory scheme are free from competition law scrutiny because of State measures leaving them no scope for competition, the national competition authority still has to disapply national legislation that restricts competition.[245] It is not clear, however, how that legislation can infringe Arts 101 or 102, especially if one keeps in mind the *Wouters* holding which seems to allow a State to cordon off an area from the reach of competition law.

3.2.3 *Special and exclusive rights*

A similar form of scrutiny to the 'useful effect' test[246] arises where the grant of special and exclusive rights to a private actor is claimed to lead to an abuse

[244] *Wouters* (n 100) para 67. What would, then, happen if the State was challenged under the competition rules? *Arduino* (n 237), a case on legal professional regulation decided on the same day, provides the answer: even though the Italian measures granting legally binding effect to lawyers' fees were not based on public interest criteria, substantive or procedural guarantees against conflict of interest, the State was still not liable under the competition rules because it had not 'waived the power to make decisions of last resort or to review implementation of the tariff' (paras 38–43).

[245] See n 242. AG Jacobs also seems to notice this contradiction in his Opinion in *Pavlov* (n 110) para 161: 'I must confess that I do not find [the] automatic link between the legality of a private and a Member State's measure very satisfactory ... the [professional body's] decision is not caught by [Art 101/1] because any restrictive effects are the result of subsequent State intervention; that State intervention in turn is not caught by [the loyalty clause] because the LSV's decision as such is not restrictive enough. Therefore, neither ... can be challenged under Community competition law although the Minister could not have restricted competition without prior concertation by economic actors.'

[246] See *Ahmed Saeed* (n 144) para 50, showing the connection between Art 106/1 and the 'useful effect' case law based on a combination of either Art 101 or Art 102 and the loyalty clause.

of dominant position. In these cases, the Member State is challenged through a combination of Arts 102 and 106/1 on special and exclusive rights.[247] While the combination of Arts 102 and 106/1 does not prevent the mere creation of dominance, there is a violation where the undertaking is led to abuse the dominant position, where the exclusive rights are 'liable to create' such a situation or where they put the undertaking at an obvious advantage over its competitors, without subjecting its exclusive right to restrictions, obligations, and public review.[248] In these situations, it is not always necessary to identify a specific abuse of a dominant position.[249] The link between Member State measures and the actual or potential abuse of a dominant position by the undertaking need not be as strong as in the more general *effet utile* case law (section 3.2.1).[250]

For co-regulatory schemes, it may be particularly significant that Arts 106/1 and 102 tend to be applied strictly in situations of conflict of interest: granting regulatory authority to a private actor that is active as a competitor in the same area that it should be regulating, such as in *MOTOE*.[251] That judgment follows a more general trend of focusing on procedural and institutional issues in the case law regarding private regulation: by highlighting that the motorcycling association's regulatory authority was not subject to any 'restrictions, obligations and review',[252] the Court makes it clear that the institutional design and governance

[247] Article 106/1 requires Member States, in the case of public undertakings and undertakings to which they granted special or exclusive rights, 'to neither enact nor maintain in force any measure contrary to the rules contained in the Treaties', including the competition provisions. Generally, see Jose Luis Buendia Sierra, *Exclusive Rights and State Monopolies Under EC Law* (Oxford University Press 2000).

[248] See Case C-163/96 *Criminal proceedings against Silvano Raso and Others* [1998] ECR I-00533 paras 27–31, *Merci convenzionali* (n 141) para 17, Case C-323/93 *Société Civile Agricole du Centre d'Insémination de la Crespelle v Coopérative d'Elevage et d'Insémination Artificielle du Département de la Mayenne* [1994] ECR I-5077 para 18 and *MOTOE* (n 143) paras 48–52. Arguably, *OTOC* (n 104) could have been examined under these principles as well.

[249] Still, this does not mean that the combined application of Art 106/1 and Art 102 can be used to challenge any State measure that creates anti-competitive outcomes. Some link with the behaviour of undertakings, even if relatively hypothetical, must be found. At times the Commission and the Court have made this link seem quite tenuous or weak (see, eg Case C-203/96 *Chemische Afvalstoffen Dusseldorp BV and Others v Minister van Volkshuisvesting, Ruimtelijke Ordening en Milieubeheer* [1998] ECR I-4075, para 63), and it is still very much contested just how strong it should be.

[250] A recent illustration of this is the *Greek Lignites* case. In Case C-553/12 P *European Commission v Dimosia Epicheirisi Ilektrismou AE* (*DEI*) (17 July 2014, nyr), the Court sided with the Commission and overturned the General Court's judgment that required a more specific link with a potential abuse. According to the Court, 'all that is necessary is for the Commission to identify a potential or actual anti-competitive consequence liable to result from the State measure at issue ... [such as] where the State measures at issue affect the structure of the market by creating unequal conditions of competition between companies' (para 46).

[251] *MOTOE* (n 143). By analogy with *Silvano Raso* and *OTOC*, this could also apply to situations where only one part of a market is covered by the exclusive right: for example, had the sporting body in *MOTOE* been entitled to regulate (but not compete in) motorcycle competitions of one type, while competing in (but not regulating) the organization of other types of motorcycle competitions, it could conceivably leverage its regulatory prerogative in a way that harms competitors.

[252] Paragraph 52.

criteria of a co-regulatory scheme matter in this context as well. The creation of a dominant position through, for example, delegation of regulatory authority may thus escape scrutiny even if it provides a certain advantage to the private regulator who is also a competitor, if it is subject to effective review by the State or if conflicts of interest are otherwise avoided through appropriate governance mechanisms.

3.2.4 EU-wide co-regulation and competition law

A somewhat neglected question is the application of EU competition law to co-regulatory schemes involving EU institutions and private actors. In principle, nothing excludes the antitrust liability of a private regulator acting within the scope of an EU-sponsored co-regulatory initiative.[253] One would assume, however, that the Commission in particular would show greater deference to the EU institutions than to the Member States if conflicts appear between competition law and the specific regulatory regime, which may also translate to lighter scrutiny for the undertakings or associations that are involved. A similar dynamic can be seen in US law: arguably, a higher level of antitrust immunity is given to federal than to state action.[254]

A dubious question is whether the EU institutions could themselves be found liable under the competition rules. Despite the frequent lip-service in various policy documents and legislation to the need to respect the free movement and competition rules, it is clear that the EU is just as capable of facilitating or creating anti-competitive schemes as the Member States are. Strictly speaking, the '*effet utile*' principle based on the loyalty clause might be said not to apply. Even if that was the case, however, the EU could incur non-contractual liability under Art 340/2 TFEU[255] to individuals such as consumers for its role in facilitating conduct contrary to Art 101 or Art 102.[256]

[253] One example on the EU level is the DPAH (Diet, Physical Activity and Health) platform—a consortium of food industry actors led by the European Commission. Numerous individual commitments and agreements (advertising, promotional campaigns, product reformulation) were agreed within the DPAH, and many of them could be considered to be restrictions of competition. For example, eight major UK retailers agreed within the British Retail Consortium to remove trans-fats from their own-brand food items in 2007. For more details, see <http://ec.europa.eu/health/nutrition_physical_activity/platform/index_en.htm>.

[254] In the latter case, explicit authorization and active supervision are required; for federal regulatory schemes, the fact that a scheme's adoption was merely considered by federal regulators may suffice to immunize its adoption through an agreement. Hovenkamp (n 25) 232–34.

[255] 'In the case of non-contractual liability, the Union shall, in accordance with the general principles common to the laws of the Member States, make good any damage caused by its institutions or by its servants in the performance of their duties.'

[256] On a related issue, Petit and Rato point out that this avenue is difficult to use due to the high barriers to successful claims. Nicolas Petit and Miguel Rato, 'The Commission's Non Contractual Liability in the Field of Merger Control—Don't Use a Hammer When You Need a Screwdriver' (2007) 1 Global Competition Policy.

4. Conclusion

Antitrust lacks a conceptual framework for dealing with private regulation. This chapter has argued that the growing importance of private regulation forces it, at least in some circumstances, to adapt.

This adaptation occurs in the ill-defined area between what is traditionally seen as public and what is traditionally seen as private, and it can lead to two different approaches: a narrow and a broad one. The narrow approach is uncomfortable with a role for competition law in supervising regulatory schemes, especially if that entails taking into account diverse regulatory objectives. Its preferred way of avoiding conflicts with those objectives is by way of judicial or legislative exemptions. The broad approach, on the other hand, would grant competition authorities and courts a broader mandate to review private regulation as well as co-regulatory schemes involving the State, and allow a broader range of arguments and regulatory objectives to be taken into account.

Discussing US antitrust law, Elhauge has argued that:

> [A]ntitrust policy does not stand for the proposition that restraining competition can never serve the public interest. Rather, it stands for the more limited proposition that certain persons—those with financial interests arising out of restraints of trade—cannot be trusted to determine which restraints are in the public interest and which are not.[257]

The point at which EU competition law departs from that suggestion is its readiness to at least entertain the notion that some interested persons—private regulators—can sometimes be trusted to decide on the conditions of competition in their sectors. But this recognition of regulatory autonomy comes at a cost: such regulatory measures remain broadly subject to the competition rules. They may be claimed to be restrictive and violate competition law for reasons that are several steps removed from harm to consumer welfare, such as, for example, the lack of effective appeal against anti-doping decisions. Then again, they may be justified by reasons that do not depend on economic efficiency. The Court has been relatively lax with private regulation in general, as long as it is shown to contain institutional and procedural mechanisms for the prevention of conflicts of interest and rent-seeking. It has also been tolerant towards the measures of the Member State that create co-regulatory schemes, as long as they contain at least minimal supervision mechanisms.

It has moved towards this broader approach, inter alia, by adopting a functional definition of an undertaking, allowing competition law challenges directly against the State either through the 'useful effect' doctrine or through the rules on special and exclusive rights, and introducing a proportionality assessment that enables private regulation to avoid the more stringent Art 101/3 analysis (which has also, however, been interpreted in a somewhat flexible way). The rules on

[257] Elhauge (n 23) 706–07.

services of general economic interest are also evidence of a broader approach in EU law overall.

This shows an overriding set of ideas that, arguably, EU competition law follows, even though this has been obscured by an overlapping multitude of rather formalistically interpreted legal tests. One example is the issue of 'attribution' of conduct to the State or to undertakings in the EU state action doctrine. Categorizing measures into such neat boxes is not helpful. It does, however, reveal the types of issues the Court is concerned with.

In co-regulatory schemes and more broadly, Member States should be able to exclude certain activities from competition. This choice, however, should not favour certain undertakings at the expense of others and the scheme should be designed in a way that prevents capture. These ideas appear time and time again, whether it is in the discussion of scope (economic activity vs. activities of public authorities), Art 101/1 (whether a measure falls within the *Wouters* test), the 'useful effect' doctrine (whether there is improper delegation due to a lack of supervisory mechanisms), services of general economic interest (whether an activity is of 'general economic interest' or not and whether it would be obstructed by competition), and Art 106/1 (whether the grant of a special and exclusive right is illegal in the absence of an actual abuse). A Member State can prohibit dentists from advertising, or require the licensing of motorcycle races. If, however, it allows dentists to freely decide what kind of advertising is permissible, or gives a sporting body the exclusive right to license motorcycle races while also allowing it to organize them on its own for profit, it is likely to violate the competition rules.

As for private regulators, their measures are also deferred to if they can show that they pursue a legitimate regulatory objective while following certain good governance standards. This is not only, or even primarily, an attempt to balance the harm to competition against the benefit to other objectives. EU competition law is rarely used in order to deeply assess the substance of the policies of private regulators. Rather, the question is whether a private regulator has exceeded a permissible margin of discretion. The arguments most frequently raised in that context include conflicts of interest (*MOTOE*, *OTOC*), a lack of procedural safeguards or mechanisms of review (*Meca-Medina*, *FIA*), biased composition of decision-making bodies (*Anonima Petroli Italiana*), or a lack of transparency and openness (the Horizontal Guidelines' section on standard setting).

The increasing reliance on the *Wouters* test is especially important in this sense, because it enables a rather open-ended discussion on the proportionality of regulatory measures. To some extent, this is a welcome development, because it allows a more inclusive analysis of regulatory measures. Future case law will, however, probably need to impose some limits on the types of situations in which *Wouters* can be successfully used. In most cases, a restriction of competition is just that—a restriction of competition, and in the absence of Art 101/3 justification, the 'context' in which it is adopted should not rescue it. Only those private regulators that can show a level of legitimacy in pursuing non-competition objectives should be able to benefit from 'regulatory autonomy' in EU competition law.

IV

The Relationship of Free Movement and Competition Law

1. Introduction

Chapters II and III discussed how the free movement and competition rules apply to cases of private regulation. These cases are also most likely to lead to overlap, that is the application of both sets of rules to the same action or measure. This chapter discusses how these cases could be, and how they have been, dealt with.

It is clear that the two sets of rules are broadly complementary. They are the two basic tools in the creation of the internal market. Past that general point, however, we are far from a consensus on how their relationship should play out. Should one govern instead of the other? Should we reconcile them by inventing new doctrines or blending concepts to give them a common meaning? Has the historical evolution of the two sets of rules (eg the shift of competition law towards economics, or the shift of free movement law towards EU citizenship rights) made it obsolete to think of them as complements?

In this chapter, after explaining why the two sets of rules overlap (section 2) and how this problem is viewed in scholarship (section 3), I will first describe the *status quo* (section 4). The Court, in general terms, has acknowledged the mutually reinforcing role of the two sets of rules while still insisting that they are separate and independent. There is nothing to prevent both of them from being applied at the same time, and principles or legal tests cannot be automatically transposed from one into the other. Still, there are examples of the Court not being entirely true to this 'separation narrative', as I call it.

The Court's approach—both the general possibility of applying both sets of rules, as well as the instances where the Court departs from that—leads to considerable complexity and costs, especially when the institutional set-up is taken into account (section 5). The second step, then, is to discuss the alternatives for dealing with the overlap (section 6), in particular the arguments for convergence between the two sets of rules, and those that try to prevent overlap through selection or conflict rules. I will argue that, while imperfect, the Court's general approach should be maintained, but that the interplay between the two sets of rules should be more readily acknowledged and that the limits to their application, on their own terms, should be clearer (section 7).

2. The Overlap

Overlap between the competition and free movement rules takes place when both, at least potentially, apply to the same facts. In the context of this book, the overlap is unusually common. Private regulation is similar in character and effects to behaviour normally covered by the free movement rules (because it is regulation, and because it is often in some way connected with State action), as well as to behaviour normally covered by the competition rules (because it involves market participants who are often competitors). The weakening of the public–private divide means that overlap happens more frequently. In Waelbroeck's words, 'the distinction between the State—representing the general interest—and economic operators—representing private interests—tends to increasingly soften'.[1]

The way certain legal concepts have been interpreted has also contributed to broadening the area of overlap. Not only the horizontal effect of the free movement rules, but also the broad definition of a restriction of free movement, converging around the market access test, has the effect of catching a wide variety of measures.[2] Under the competition rules, the functional definition of an undertaking and the possibility to apply competition law to the Member State mean that the hybrid status of public–private entities or delegation of certain tasks to private actors cannot always exclude the application of competition law.[3]

Apart from private regulators, overlap can also happen when applying both sets of rules to the Member States. Thus, in numerous judgments of the Court, the same State measure was examined both from the point of view of the free movement rules and of the competition rules under the useful effect doctrine.[4]

[1] Denis Waelbroeck, 'Les rapports entre les règles sur la libre circulation des marchandises et les règles de concurrence applicables aux entreprises dans la CEE' in Francesco Capotorti and Pierre Pescatore (eds), *Du droit international au droit de l'intégration: liber amicorum Pierre Pescatore* (Nomos 1987) 781 (author's translation).

[2] See S Prechal and S de Vries, 'Seamless Web of Judicial Protection in the Internal Market?' (2009) 34 European Law Review 5, 7–8 and the case law cited therein. As Prechal and de Vries note, not just laws but also their actual implementation, guidelines, administrative practices, judicial decisions, decisions of professional organizations, or even comments from officials can constitute restrictions to free movement. The market access criterion, as opposed to a test focused on discrimination or protectionism, also expands the coverage of the free movement rules to a wide variety of actions. See for example the judgment in Case C-415/93 *Union royale belge des sociétés de football association ASBL v Jean-Marc Bosman, Royal club liégeois SA v Jean-Marc Bosman and others and Union des associations européennes de football (UEFA) v Jean-Marc Bosman* [1995] ECR I-4921, para 96, as well as the discussion in the Opinion of AG Lenz in the same case, para 165 et seq. See C Barnard, *The Substantive Law of the EU: The Four Freedoms* (Oxford University Press 2007) 19. For somewhat divergent views, see Julio Baquero Cruz, *Between Competition and Free Movement: The Economic Constitutional Law of the European Community* (Hart 2002) 68 and Gareth Davies, 'Understanding Market Access: Exploring the Economic Rationality of Different Conceptions of Free Movement Law' (2010) 11 German Law Journal 671.

[3] See Chapter III section 3.1.1.

[4] For a discussion, see Kamiel Mortelmans, 'Towards Convergence in the Application of the Rules on Free Movement and on Competition?' (2001) 38 Common Market Law Review 613, 639. Some of the cases where both sets of rules were invoked against a Member State are Case C-18/88 *Régie des télégraphes et des téléphones v GB-Inno-BM SA* [1991] ECR I-5941 and Case 229/83

These cases might be less problematic because, firstly, Member States' measures under the *effet utile* doctrine are not assessed under the same kind of competition law analysis as that applied to undertakings, and because they are nowadays considered to infringe the competition rules almost exclusively in cases when they reinforce existing violations by undertakings.[5] Nevertheless, these cases also pose the question of how the two sets of rules should relate to one another.

A wide variety of decision-makers can be confronted with this overlap. Two main factors contribute to this. One is enlargement: courts and other actors, such as competition agencies, across the twenty-eight Member States can be faced with this type of case. The other is the decentralization of competition law after Regulation 1/2003,[6] enabling national courts and competition agencies to directly apply all of the competition provisions and eliminating the need to notify agreements to the Commission. These developments mean the EU institutions, notably the Court and the Commission, are no longer in the position to effectively control the overlap that they, through the broad interpretations of both sets of rules, have helped create.

3. Competition and Free Movement in the Context of the Internal Market

3.1 The 'seamless web': A mutually reinforcing view

From the very beginning of the Communities, the free movement and competition rules were seen as complementary, tackling both public and private obstacles to cross-border economic activity. This was especially important for those who saw them from an economic constitutionalist perspective.[7] A classic argument for the existence of the competition rules is market integration: private restraints, the theory goes, should not be allowed to erect the same kinds of barriers that are prohibited to States by the free movement rules. This would defeat the purpose

Association des Centres distributeurs Édouard Leclerc and others v SARL 'Au blé vert' and others [1985] ECR 1. More recently, both sets of rules were invoked against Member States in Joined cases C-94/04 and C-202/04 *Federico Cipolla v Rosaria Fazari, née Portolese* (C-94/04); and *Stefano Macrino and Claudia Capoparte v Roberto Meloni* (C-202/04) [2006] ECR I-11421; Case C-531/07 *Fachverband der Buch—und Medienwirtschaft v LIBRO Handelsgesellschaft mbH* [2009] ECR I-3717; and Case C-338/09 *Yellow Cab Verkehrsbetriebs GmbH v Landeshauptmann von Wien* [2010] ECR I-13927. None of those recent judgments, however, found an actual State infringement of competition law, either in addition to (*Yellow Cab, LIBRO*) or instead of (*Cipolla*) a finding of infringement of the free movement rules. A recent exception was the judgment in Joined cases C-184/13 to C-187/13, C-194/13, C-195/13, and C-208/13 *API—Anonima Petroli Italiana SpA v Ministero delle Infrastrutture e dei Trasporti and Ministero dello Sviluppo economico* ECLI:EU:C:2014:2147, where the Court found a violation of Art 101 and dispensed with an analysis of the rules on free movement of services and freedom of establishment.

[5] See Chapter III.

[6] Council Regulation (EC) 1/2003 of 16 December 2002 on the implementation of the rules on competition laid down in Articles 81 and 82 of the Treaty [2003] OJ L1/1.

[7] See the discussion on economic constitutionalism in Chapters I and III.

of the internal market and enable the Member States to circumvent their internal market obligations by privatizing or cartelizing certain areas of the economy, shielding private operators through a public legal form or by claiming immunity for its own actions as a market participant.[8]

The Spaak Report, among others, makes it plain that the initial aim of introducing the competition provisions was market integration.[9] Speaking of restrictions of competition by undertakings, for example, the Report focuses almost exclusively on discrimination by a dominant undertaking or cartel against purchasers from different Member States. Even though much of the mainstream thinking regards it as atavistic,[10] this market integration rationale is still recognized as an important element of EU competition law. For example, a recent Commission decision found that a power exchange abused its dominant position by requiring members of the spot electricity markets to have a national VAT number, thus discriminating on the basis of place of establishment.[11]

This mutually reinforcing quality of the free movement and competition rules gave rise to the idea that the two sets of rules are not just two distinct forms of legal scrutiny with overlapping objectives, but two particular expressions of a more general principle: the creation of an internal market based on a free-market economy and competition.[12] They express, in the words of Koch and Froschmaier,

[8] See Baquero Cruz (n 2) 68, M Waelbroeck, 'Competition, Integration and Economic Efficiency in the EEC from the Point of View of the Private Firm' (1983) 82 Michigan Law Review 1439, 1440 and Miguel Poiares Maduro, 'The Chameleon State: EU Law and the Blurring of the Private/Public Distinction in the Market' <http://ssrn.com/abstract=1575542>.

[9] Rapport des chefs de délégation aux ministres des affaires étrangères, Comité intergouvernemental crée par la conférence de Messine, 21 April 1956 (<http://www.unizar.es/euroconstitucion/library/historic%20documents/Rome/preparation/Spaak%20report%20fr.pdf>): « Le premier fait dont il convient de tenir compte, c'est la dimension atteinte par les entreprises, ou l'usage des ententes entre entreprises et, par suite, les pratiques de monopole, les facultés de discrimination, les possibilités de répartition du marché. Des règles de concurrence qui s'imposent aux entreprises sont donc nécessaires pour éviter que des doubles prix aient le même effet que des droits de douane, qu'un dumping mette en danger des productions économiquement gainés, que la répartition des marches se substitue a leur cloisonnement » (p. 16). This complementary reading of the two sets of rules could also, historically, be linked to the post-war international trade negotiations in which European countries participated. The failed International Trade Association was supposed to include competition as well as trade rules. See Eleanor M Fox, 'Competition Law and the Agenda for the WTO: Forging the Links of Competition and Trade' (1995) 4 Pacific Rim Law & Policy Journal 1, 2–3.

[10] David J Gerber, *Law and Competition in Twentieth Century Europe: Protecting Prometheus* (Oxford University Press 2001) 334 and Giorgio Monti, 'Article 81 EC and Public Policy' (2002) 39 Common Market Law Review 1057, 1062–63. On the other hand, see Rosemary O'Loughlin, 'EC Competition Rules and Free Movement Rules: An Examination of the Parallels and their Furtherance by the ECJ *Wouters* Decision' (2003) 24 European Competition Law Review 62, 64, pointing out that already in the earliest case law it was clear that the protection of competition and the prevention of market-partitioning are separate, if overlapping objectives. For an assessment of the economic effects of policies directed at market integration, see Pinelopi K Goldberg and Frank Verboven, 'Market integration and convergence to the Law of One Price: Evidence From the European Car Market' (2005) 65 Journal of International Economics 49.

[11] Commission Decision of 5 March 2014 in Case AT.39984, *Romanian Power Exchange/ OPCOM* para 298.

[12] Waelbroeck (n 1) 793.

'the fundamental choice of the drafters of the Treaty in favour of an economic system aimed at competition and integrating the economies of the Member States'.[13] The two sets of rules should be read as a 'seamless web' promoting cross-border competition.[14] One of them could be relied on to fill perceived gaps in the other.

This might mean that competition law is applied to various State measures, that the free movement rules also cover individual conduct, or both. Pescatore came close to suggesting a single legality standard for public and private restraints.[15] Waelbroeck has similarly argued that the free movement and competition law rules should apply uniformly to either private or public conduct, since the key issue is always the same: whether or not the effects of the conduct run contrary to the establishment of the internal market.[16] As shown in the previous chapters, both developments—the so-called 'publicisation' of competition law and 'privatisation' of free movement law[17]—have happened, if only to a limited extent.

In addition, in some sectors the two sets of rules were used in a mutually reinforcing, strategic fashion, in order to achieve negative integration and open the way for the development of EU-level policies. It may seem controversial to view the free movement and competition rules as tools used to strategic ends by regulators and courts. This may seem less problematic when it comes to the free movement rules, frequently understood as a way of eliminating existing regulation in order to pave the way for policy outcomes favoured by the EU.[18] Competition law, on the other hand, is not normally seen as a re-regulatory instrument. As shown in Chapter III, however, EU competition law enforcement has leaned in

[13] As cited in Waelbroeck (n 1); author's translation. See also ibid 783–74.

[14] The phrase 'seamless web' has its origin in Luc Gyselen, 'The Emerging Interface Between Competition Policy and Environmental Policy in the European Union' in James Cameron, Paul Demaret, and Damien Geradin (eds), *Trade and the Environment: The Search for Balance* (Cameron May 1996), and was taken up inter alia by Mortelmans (n 4) and Prechal and de Vries (n 2). See also Baquero Cruz (n 2) 87 et seq.

[15] Pierre Pescatore, 'Public and Private Aspects of European Community Competition Law' (1986) 10 Fordham International Law Journal 373. On the opposite end of the debate was G Marenco, 'Competition Between National Economies and Competition Between Businesses—A Response to Judge Pescatore' (1987) 10 Fordham International Law Journal 420.

[16] Waelbroeck (n 1) 798. Waelbroeck criticizes Marenco's suggestion that a holistic interpretation of the two sets of rules would be detrimental for the economic policy competence of the Member States (794). See also, in a similar vein, Jules Stuyck, 'Libre circulation et concurrence: les deux piliers du Marché commun' in Marianne Dony and Aline de Walsche (eds), *Mélanges en hommage à Michel Waelbroeck* (Bruylant 1999) 1486–87. Prechal and de Vries (n 2) 23–24 argue that this could imply either substantive convergence in the scope of application of the rules, or a 'convergence in judicial protection', extending the applicability of the free movement rules to private and the competition rules to public actors through the use of devices such as indirect horizontal effect and the loyalty clause.

[17] Robert Lane, 'The Internal Market and the Individual' in Shuibhne Niamh Nic (ed), *Regulating the Internal Market* (Edward Elgar 2006) 254 et seq.

[18] This can be illustrated by Fritz Scharpf's constitutional asymmetry idea: because the internal market rules preclude certain public policies of the Member States while there are no equivalent positive competences on the EU level, in particular in the area of social policy, the outcome that they in fact lead to is deregulation or liberalization (Fritz W Scharpf, 'The Asymmetry of European Integration, or Why the EU Cannot be a "Social Market Economy"' (2010) 8 Socio-Economic Review 211).

that direction in a number of areas. In network sectors such as energy, it has often been noted that the Commission was using competition law as a tool to promote a way of liberalizing markets that was subsequently transformed into legislation.[19] The area of sports[20] shows how the Commission and the Court have combined their approach under the free movement and competition rules, which was later leveraged by the Commission to plant the seeds of an EU sports policy, partly through negotiations with private regulators.

When dealing with private regulation, the chances of competition and free movement law being jointly used in this way are likely to increase because, firstly, it is the area where these two instruments intersect the most; secondly, because EU law is often the only effective review mechanism over private regulation.[21] In these cases, the free movement and competition rules may be used as part of a single toolkit that provides the EU institutions with flexible choices of controlling or re-regulating certain sectors (sports, the liberal professions, technical standards, and others).

3.2 The separation view

On the opposing side, it has been argued that a unified reading would override all practical limits to the application of EU law on national (or private) regulatory measures, giving the EU institutions complete dominance over economic policy.[22] This side of the debate has insisted on a public–private divide within EU economic law: the free movement rules are there to discipline public, and the competition rules to discipline private actors. A slightly different way of making this point is to rephrase the distinction as being between 'regulatory' and 'market' behaviour.[23]

The practical implications of this view are twofold. First, we are told that the two sets of rules each have their own domain and that not only convergence, but overlap as such should be avoided: some behaviour should fall under one, some under the other. The availability of one is, as such, an argument against applying the other.[24] Second, there is no overarching principle that governs both sets of rules and gives them a common content, or if there is, it should not decide specific cases—if competition law is the 'right' set of rules for a particular restraint, it should be applied on its own terms, regardless of the hybrid public–private nature of the restraint.

Arguably, the separation argument is reinforced by an increasing divergence in the way the two sets of rules are understood. While no one would deny that they

[19] See Chapter III section 2. [20] See Chapter V section 7.

[21] See Chapter I section 6. [22] See Marenco (n 15) 443.

[23] Okeoghene Odudu, *The Boundaries of EC Competition Law: The Scope of Article 81* (Oxford University Press 2006) 30–33.

[24] Jukka Snell, 'Private Parties and the Free Movement of Goods and Services' in Mads Andenas and Wulf-Henning Roth (eds), *Services and Free Movement in EU Law* (Oxford University Press 2002) 229.

are in some sense connected, it seems that the mainstream thinking about free movement and competition law has split off into different directions, especially as competition law has progressed and developed. The more economic approach to the interpretation of the competition rules, the influence of US antitrust scholarship, and the maturity of competition law as a distinct discipline have all shifted the emphasis away from the original ideas of supporting market integration, and towards a more narrowly defined role in securing the efficient operation of markets. On the free movement side, a growing emphasis on non-economic and constitutional aspects and the prominence of EU citizenship rules and the free movement of persons have contributed to a separation in the academic discourse.[25]

Importantly, however, there are two distinct ways of understanding the separation idea. One is to claim that the two sets of rules are conceptually different, because they pursue different aims, apply different tests, or have distinct enforcement mechanisms (doctrinal separation). The other is to claim that the rules are distinct in scope, that is that they apply to entirely different situations (factual separation). These two assumptions are usually packed together in the separation argument. Nevertheless, one does not follow from the other, and they can even be said to contradict each other. If the rules really apply to entirely separate situations, it should not matter if they pursue different aims or not. In other words, arguing for factual separation is not the same as arguing for doctrinal separation. The Court can be said to support doctrinal separation in most cases, albeit with some exceptions. On the other hand, it follows factual separation only in a declaratory manner, if at all (see also section 6.2).

3.3 Objectives: Does the Treaty help?

The case for convergence, that is for a mutually reinforcing vision of competition and free movement law, is based on an *effet utile* argument: competition law is necessary to fill the gaps left by free movement law, and vice versa. An *effet utile* argument, however, implies a clear idea of what the general objective of the gap-filling exercise is. Is it enough to invoke the achievement of an internal market as that objective? Has that objective been complicated or weakened since the heyday of the debates such as those described above?

The common aim of the two sets of rules has often been referred to in policy documents and officials' speeches.[26] It is also based on the text of the Treaties, even though this is not as clear under the Lisbon Treaty as it once was. Among the activities of the Community listed in Art 3 EC (Treaty of Nice), one used to find both 'an internal market characterised by the abolition, as between

[25] See, for example, Alina Tryfonidou, 'Further Steps on the Road to Convergence Among the Market Freedoms' (2010) 35 European Law Review 41.

[26] In the words of former Competition Commissioner Joaquín Almunia: 'As a pillar of the Single Market, competition policy has always been intended as an instrument to build a united Europe.' (SPEECH/12/672, 'Competition Policy as a Pan-European Effort' (2 October 2012) <http://europa.eu/rapid/press-release_SPEECH-12-672_en.htm?locale=en>).

Member States, of obstacles to the free movement of goods, persons, services and capital' and 'a system ensuring that competition in the internal market is not distorted'. In addition, according to Art 4 EC, the tasks of the Community and the Member States included the adoption of an economic policy 'conducted in accordance with the principle of an open market economy with free competition'.

After the Lisbon Treaty,[27] Art 3/3 TEU merely states that 'the Union shall establish an internal market', while the internal market and the competition rules (described as 'necessary for the functioning of the internal market') are listed as EU competences. The general reference to the role of competition in the internal market has been relegated to the Protocol No 27 on the Internal Market and Competition, which repeats the old TEC provision that 'the internal market as set out in Article 3 of the Treaty on European Union includes a system ensuring that competition is not distorted'. Finally, the former Art 4 TEC on economic policy, while still containing the reference to 'an open market economy with free competition', was moved down to the beginning of Title VIII on economic and monetary policy.[28]

Seen together, these textual changes seem to show that free competition, and perhaps the internal market more broadly, has lost some of its constitutional significance. At the very least, it could be argued that the broadening scope of EU law over the last several decades, and especially after the Lisbon Treaty, makes it seem as if the internal market has lost its pride of place, and is now only one of many policies pursued by the EU. There has been quite a debate on this issue.[29] As of yet, however, it does not seem that the reshuffling of policy priorities in the text of the Lisbon Treaty has had any real effect on EU policy and on the adjudication of cases before the EU courts.[30] In any case, looking at the text of the Treaty is unlikely to solve the puzzle of the relationship between the two sets of rules. It is more fruitful to look at the practice, in particular the case law of the Court of Justice.

[27] The exclusion of competition from the provisions on aims was claimed as a major victory at the time of the Lisbon Treaty negotiations by the French President Nicolas Sarkozy. See 'A Less "Anglo-Saxon" EU: Sarkozy Scraps Competition Clause From New Treaty' Spiegel Online International (22 June 2007) <http://www.spiegel.de/international/europe/a-less-anglo-saxon-eu-sarkozy-scraps-competition-clause-from-new-treaty-a-490136.html>.

[28] See L Parret, 'Shouldn't We Know What We Are Protecting? Yes We Should! A Plea for a Solid and Comprehensive Debate about the Objectives of EU Competition Law and Policy' (2010) 6 European Competition Journal 339, 342–43.

[29] See for example Loïc Azoulai, 'The Court of Justice and the Social Market Economy: The Emergence of an Ideal and the Conditions for its Realization' (2008) 45 Common Market Law Review 1335; Constanze Semmelmann, 'The European Union's Economic Constitution Under the Lisbon Treaty: Soul-Searching Shifts the Focus to Procedure' (2010) 35 European Law Review 516.

[30] Ben Van Rompuy, 'The Impact of the Lisbon Treaty on EU Competition Law: A Review of Recent Case Law of the EU Courts' (2011) 1 CPI Antitrust Chronicle and Ioannis Lianos, 'Competition Law in the European Union after the Treaty of Lisbon' in Diamond Ashiagbor, Nicola Countouris, and Ioannis Lianos (eds), *The European Union after the Treaty of Lisbon* (Cambridge University Press 2012).

4. The *Status Quo*: Incomplete Separation

No Treaty provision spells out how to deal with cases where the competition and free movement rules overlap, such as by giving one of them priority.[31] Thus, we have to look to the case law for answers. The Court's judgments broadly conform to the notion that the two sets of rules are closely connected, as the 'normative basis of the EU economic constitution'.[32] This does not, however, mean that the Court has accepted a 'seamless web' reading. While it has found ways of applying competition law to the Member States and the free movement rules to individuals, it has been careful to keep these lines of case law intellectually separate, never going as far as to say that an overarching principle of free market competition binds both the Member States and the individuals in their activities.

4.1 Market integration as the common aim

The overlapping aims of the free movement and competition rules has been pointed out in several distinct lines of the Court's case law. Firstly, competition law cases on vertical restraints have explicitly relied on a market integration rationale, normally associated with free movement law. The classic example is *Consten & Grundig*, where the Court held that 'an agreement … which might tend to restore the national divisions in trade between Member States might … frustrate the most fundamental objectives of the Community. The Treaty … aims at abolishing the barriers between states … and could not allow undertakings to reconstruct such barriers. Article [101(1) TFEU] is designed to pursue this aim […].'[33] This passage has been cited in a number of more recent cases, such as *Sot. Lélos kai Sia and Others* and *GlaxoSmithKline*.[34]

[31] By contrast, the relationship between some other provisions of the Treaties is either explicitly dealt with by the Treaty text (such as the relationship between the free movement of services and the other market freedoms in Art 57/1 TFEU) or settled by case law. For example, in Case C-237/04 *Enirisorse SpA v Sotacarbo SpA* [2006] ECR I-2843, it was held that 'the provisions relating to charges having equivalent effect and those relating to discriminatory internal taxation cannot be applied together, so that the same charge cannot, under the system established by the Treaty, belong to both those categories at the same time' (para 59). Similarly, the scope of today's Art 34 on measures having an equivalent effect to quantitative restrictions 'does not extend to the obstacles to trade covered by other specific provisions of the Treaty', in particular to obstacles of a fiscal nature or equivalent to customs duties covered by today's Arts 23–25 and 110 TFEU. (Case C-17/91 *Lornoy and Others* [1992] ECR I-6523, para 14; see also Case 74/76 *Iannelli & Volpi SpA v Ditta Paolo Meroni* [1977] ECR 557; and Joined cases C-78 to 83/90 *Compagnie Commerciale de l'Ouest and others v Receveur Principal des Douanes de La Pallice Port* [1992] ECR I-1847.)

[32] Erika Szyszczak, 'Competition and the Liberalised Market' in Niamh Nic Shuibhne (ed), *Regulating the Internal Market* (Cheltenham, Edward Elgar 2006) 101–02.

[33] Joined cases 56 and 58–64 *Établissements Consten S.à.R.L. and Grundig-Verkaufs-GmbH v Commission* [1966] ECR 299, 340.

[34] Joined cases C-468/06 to C-478/06 *Sot. Lélos kai Sia EE and Others v GlaxoSmithKline AEVE Farmakeftikon Proïonton, formerly Glaxowellcome AEVE* [2008] ECR I-7139, para 65; Joined cases C-501/06 P, C-513/06 P, C-515/06 P, and C-519/06 P *GlaxoSmithKline Services Unlimited v Commission of the European Communities et al* [2009] ECR I-9291, para 61 and Joined cases

Moreover, some of the language, if not exactly the reasoning, made its way from *Consten & Grundig* into early free movement of goods case law. *Dassonville*'s famous dictum that today's Art 34 TFEU on measures having an equivalent effect to a quantitative restriction covers 'all trading rules enacted by Member States which are capable of hindering, directly or indirectly, actually or potentially, intra-Community trade'[35] is taken almost word for word from *Consten & Grundig* and *Maschinenbau Ulm*,[36] both competition law judgments.[37]

Perhaps the clearest statement of this basic common aim of the free movement and competition rules was made in *Leclerc*, where the Court pointed out that the general Treaty objective of establishing a market characterized by the free movement of goods is 'secured *inter alia* by [Art 34 TFEU] et seq prohibiting restrictions on intra-community trade and by [Art 101 TFEU] et seq on the rules on competition'.[38] In *Eco Swiss*, the Court highlighted the construction of the internal market as the basic aim of the competition rules.[39] In *Laserdisken*, it rejected a claim that the Copyright Directive[40]—an internal market harmonization measure—was contrary to the competition rules, partly because both the Directive and those Treaty rules are meant to 'ensure that competition in the internal market is not distorted', which seemed to exclude even the possibility of conflict.[41]

C-403/08 and C-429/08 *Football Association Premier League Ltd and Others v QC Leisure and Others* (C-403/08) *and Karen Murphy v Media Protection Services Ltd* (C-429/08) [2011] ECR I-90834, para 139. Cf US antitrust law which has, after *Leegin Creative Leather Products, Inc. v PSKS, Inc.* 551 US 877 (2007), been more tolerant of vertical restraints of trade, recognizing their pro-competitive aspects, arguably because the market integration rationale is less salient.

[35] Case 8-74 *Procureur du Roi v Benoît and Gustave Dassonville* [1974] ECR 837, para 5.

[36] Case 56-65 *Société Technique Minière (L.T.M.) v Maschinenbau Ulm GmbH (M.B.U.)* [1966] ECR 235. See also Stuyck (n 16) 1480–82.

[37] This could imply that—at least at the time—the two sets of rules were seen as concerned with the same type of conduct. In *Consten & Grundig* and *Maschinenbau Ulm*, however, the phrase was used not to define a restriction of competition, but to clarify when agreements have an effect on trade between Member States. The phrasing is: 'whether the agreement is capable of constituting a threat, either direct or indirect, actual or potential, to freedom of trade between Member States in a manner which might harm the attainment of the objectives of a single market between States' (para 341), or in the *Maschinenbau Ulm* version, whether 'the agreement in question may have an influence, direct or indirect, actual or potential, on the pattern of trade between Member States'. The purpose of this is to establish whether 'the interference with competition caused by that agreement is caught by the prohibitions in Community law found in article [101], whilst in the converse case it escapes those prohibitions' (para 249).

[38] Case 231/83 *Henri Cullet and Chambre syndicale des réparateurs automobiles et détaillants de produits pétroliers v Centre Leclerc à Toulouse and Centre Leclerc à Saint-Orens-de-Gameville* [1985] ECR 305, para 11. See also Case C-9/99 *Echirolles Distribution SA v Association du Dauphiné and Others* [2000] ECR I-8207, paras 22–24.

[39] The Court stated that Art 101 TFEU 'constitutes a fundamental provision which is essential for the accomplishment of the tasks entrusted to the Community and, in particular, for the functioning of the internal market' (para 36).

[40] Directive 2001/29/EC of 22 May 2001 of the European Parliament and of the Council on the harmonization of certain aspects of copyright and related rights in the information society [2001] OJ L167/10.

[41] Case C-479/04 *Laserdisken ApS v Kulturministeriet* [2006] ECR I-8089, paras 47–49.

The true test of the 'seamless web' reading, however, was to take place in cases where both, or either, competition and free movement rules could be applied. There was no shortage of such occasions. Would the Court follow the seamless web approach, treating them as co-extensive, or would it attempt to draw a line between them?

4.2 Separate legal tests

The limits of the seamless web approach became apparent in *Van de Haar*.[42] A Dutch law fixing cigarette prices, challenged both on the basis of today's Art 34 TFEU and Art 101 TFEU,[43] was claimed not to infringe the free movement rules because it had a relatively small impact on the volume of imports. The defendant was trying to invoke the competition law concept of *de minimis* restrictions as an exemption from the free movement rules. As in the cases on free movement of goods after *Consten & Grundig*, this was an attempt to import concepts from one set of rules into the other—except that here, this would result in exonerating the defendant.

Faced with this prospect, the Court drew a line between the two sets of rules, according to three criteria:

1) Addressees: one is addressed to undertakings and associations of undertakings, the other to the Member States;
2) Aim: one is meant to 'maintain effective competition in the common market', the other to 'ensure free movement of goods' by 'eliminating measures taken by Member States which might in any way impede such free movement';
3) Limits: one is only applied to restraints which 'appreciably affect intra-Community trade', the other 'does not distinguish between measures ... according to the degree to which trade between Member States is affected'.[44]

Thus, while the Court accepts that the two sets of rules are interlinked, it does not endorse a robust 'seamless web' reading. The two sets of rules are presented as independent wholes. All of the Court's distinctions, of course, can be challenged. As for the addressees, other cases have made it quite clear that in some cases the free movement rules can apply to undertakings, and the competition rules to Member States.[45] As to the aim, 'maintaining effective competition' and 'ensuring the free movement of goods' may not have the same meaning but

[42] Joined cases 177 and 178/82 *Criminal proceedings against Jan van de Haar and Kaveka de Meern BV* [1984] ECR 1797.

[43] The Commission argued in the case that 'economic facts' such as those presented in the case could have, in theory, been linked either to the effects of national measures or to the effects of agreements between undertakings, but the 'legal consequences may be different because the provisions at issue have their own internal logic and must be interpreted independently' (para 10).

[44] Paragraphs 11–14.

[45] See Mortelmans (n 4) 634, also pointing out that this point is an oversimplification.

certainly overlap.[46] Finally, the third point is circular: whether the free movement rules apply to cases where trade between Member States is not appreciably affected was supposed to be the conclusion, not one of the premises of the Court's reasoning.

Despite those uncertainties, in subsequent cases the point was made even more clearly. In *Meca-Medina*, the Court of Justice overturned the attempt of the General Court to transpose the notion of economic activity from free movement case law into a competition law case. It insisted that alleged violations have to be assessed in light of the specific and distinct requirements of each set of rules:

> ... even if those rules do not constitute restrictions on freedom of movement because they concern questions of purely sporting interest and, as such, have nothing to do with economic activity ... that fact means neither that the sporting activity in question necessarily falls outside the scope of Articles [101 and 102 TFEU] nor that the rules do not satisfy the specific requirements of those articles ...[47]

True to form, the Court has systematically resisted attempts by defendants in competition cases to invoke free movement case law that would work to their advantage. For example, a professional association of pharmacists, even if its activity was partly regulated by law, could not escape competition law scrutiny on the basis of previous free movement cases where similar schemes were justified by public health aims.[48] In *EPI*, the General Court made the same findings in relation to a patent agents' code of conduct restricting advertising.[49]

The separation narrative was taken a step further in the *Viking Line* and *Laval* judgments.[50] One of the arguments of the defendant trade unions was that collective agreements and collective action as a way of enforcing them are outside the scope of the free movement rules. The claim was based on *Albany*, an earlier judgment where it was held that collective agreements fall outside the scope of

[46] There could be a distinction, depending on one's view of what 'maintaining effective competition' means. With some vertical restraints, for example, it could be argued that promoting the free movement of goods in fact impedes effective competition by reducing economic efficiency. On the other hand, the Court nowadays speaks of market access 'under conditions of normal and effective competition' as the value protected by the free movement rules. See Case C-565/08 *Commission v Italy* [2011] ECR I-2101, para 51.

[47] Case C-519/04 P *David Meca-Medina and Igor Majcen v Commission* [2006] ECR I-6991, paras 31–33.

[48] Case T-23/09 *Conseil national de l'Ordre des pharmaciens (CNOP) and Conseil central de la section G de l'Ordre national des pharmaciens (CCG) v European Commission* [2010] ECR II-5291, para 81.

[49] Case T-144/99 *Institute of Professional Representatives before the European Patent Office v Commission* [2001] ECR II-1087. The fact that rules of certain professional codes of conduct were held to be justified under the free movement rules was 'irrelevant'; 'no conclusion can be drawn from that case-law as concerns the applicability of [Art 101 TFEU] in the present case' (para 66).

[50] C-341/05 *Laval un Partneri Ltd v Svenska Byggnadsarbetareförbundet, Svenska Byggnadsarbetareförbundets avdelning 1, Byggettan and Svenska Elektrikerförbundet* [2007] ECR I-11767 and C-438/05 *International Transport Workers' Federation and Finnish Seamen's Union v Viking Line ABP and OÜ Viking Line Eesti* [2007] ECR I-10779. Azoulai (n 29) 1344–46 and A C L Davies, 'One Step Forward, Two Steps Back? The Viking and Laval Cases in the ECJ' (2008) 37 Industrial Law Journal 126, 135–36. See Chapter II, section 4.1 for more details.

Art 101 due to their social policy objectives.[51] Surely, if social policy objectives save trade unions from the application of the competition rules, the same should be true when they are threatened by the free movement rules?

In *Viking Line*, the Court disagreed. It held that 'the fact that an agreement or an activity are excluded from the scope of the provisions of the Treaty on competition does not mean that that agreement or activity also falls outside the scope of the Treaty provisions on the free movement of persons or services since those two sets of provisions are to be applied in different circumstances'.[52] If *Meca-Medina* excluded the use of free movement law to avoid competition law scrutiny, *Viking Line* was its mirror image: competition law exemptions do not lead to exemptions under the free movement rules or under the directives meant to implement the latter.[53] Moreover, the Court seemed to suggest that, while it is inherent to collective agreements that they result in restrictions of competition, they do not necessarily restrict free movement.

Thus, the Court has consistently followed what I call the separation narrative, treating the two sets of rules as distinct. However, it has not taken it as far as some proponents of the separation view (see sections 3.2 and 6.2) would like, because it did not specify that one excludes the other, that one takes precedence over the other, or that they cannot both be applied simultaneously. It did, however, conflate factual and doctrinal separation when it stated that the rules 'are to be applied in different circumstances'—if that were truly the case, then there would be no issue since there would be no overlap.

This substantive distinction between the two sets of rules can also coincide with a procedural distinction, such as in cases where judicial review is limited to the legality of a Commission decision applying the competition provisions. In *EMC Development*, for example, the General Court refused to take into account whether an undertaking complied with the Construction Products Directive[54] and 'fundamental legal principles of the EC Treaty', since 'judicial review of [the Commission's] decision must necessarily be limited to the competition rules as they result from Articles [101 and 102 TFEU], and consequently

[51] Case C-67/96 *Albany International BV v Stichting Bedrijfspensioenfonds Textielindustrie* [1999] ECR I-5751, paras 59–60. See Chapter III section 3.1.1.

[52] Paragraph 53. See also the Opinion of AG Trstenjak in Case C-271/08 *Commission v Germany* [2010] ECR I-7091, paras 65–66: 'Although both the rules within the field of freedom of establishment and freedom to provides services and the rules in the field of freedom of competition take account of the objective of completing the internal market, the fact that an agreement or activity is excluded from the scope of the competition rules does not necessarily mean that it is excluded also from the scope of the rules on freedom of movement …'

[53] See also the judgment, ibid para 46: '[The Albany exemption from competition law] does not in any way prejudge the separate question, specific to the present case, of compliance … with the European Union rules relating to application of freedom of establishment and the freedom to provide services …'

[54] Council Directive 89/106/EEC of 21 December 1988 on the approximation of laws, regulations and administrative provisions of the Member States relating to construction products [1989] OJ L40/12.

cannot extend to compliance with other provisions of the [TFEU] or of [the] Directive …'[55]

Finally, a different category of cases are those in which the two sets of provisions are applied to two different aspects of a regulatory scheme. For example, a law may be held contrary to free movement while the actions of an undertaking based on that law may be held to infringe competition. In *GB-Inno-BM v RTT*, for example, the competition rules were applied to RTT's authority to pre-approve its competitors' telephones for use, and the free movement rules to the lack of judicial review of those decisions.[56] In *Corsica Ferries*, national measures imposing discriminatory piloting tariffs on cross-border maritime transport were contrary to the free movement of services, while 'inducing' an undertaking to apply those discriminatory rates—by confirming its suggested tariffs—was a violation of today's Art 106/1 on special and exclusive rights.[57] In *Murphy*, UK copyright legislation violated the rules on free movement of services while the conduct of broadcasters violated Art 101.[58] In *OSA*, Czech legislation granting territorial exclusivity to a copyright collecting society was cleared under the free movement rules and under Art 106(1), but the pricing policy of the society was (possibly) an abuse of a dominant position under Art 102 TFEU.[59]

In conclusion, while maintaining the idea that the free movement and competition rules are connected and at least partly pursue the same aim, it seems clear that the Court resists the 'seamless web' approach. The rules are seen as two separate legality standards, and each of them has to be applied in its own right. Criteria (eg the definition of economic activity, the *de minimis* rule, the trade effects criterion, the definition of a restriction) cannot be automatically imported from one into the other as such, even though the result of the analysis might often be the same under analogous elements of the legal tests. None of this prevents the Court from drawing inspiration from one set of rules to develop certain concepts within the other.[60] Legality or illegality under one rule does not, however, in and of itself, imply legality or illegality under the other.

Consequently, it is possible that the same conduct is subject to and infringes both the competition and free movement rules. This was noted, for example, by AG Lenz in *Bosman:* 'No reason can be seen why the rules at issue in this case should not be subject both to [Art 45 TFEU on the free movement of workers] and

[55] Case T-432/05 *EMC Development AB v Commission* [2010] ECR II-1629, para 137.

[56] *RTT v GB-Inno-BM* (n 4). See also Case 90-76 *S.r.l. Ufficio Henry van Ameyde v S.r.l. Ufficio centrale italiano di assistenza assicurativa automobilisti in circolazione internazionale (UCI)* [1977] ECR 1091.

[57] Case C-18/93 *Corsica Ferries Italia Srl v Corpo dei Piloti del Porto di Genova* [1994] ECR I-1783, paras 37 and 45. See also the Opinion of AG Van Gerven in the same case, para 36.

[58] *Murphy* (n 34) para 211, points 3 and 4.

[59] Case C-351/12 *OSA—Ochranný svaz autorský pro práva k dílům hudebním o.s. v Léčebné lázně Mariánské Lázně a.s.* ECLI:EU:C:2014:110.

[60] See n 46 for a recent example of borrowing competition law concepts in free movement law.

to [EU] competition law.[61] In many cases the outcome of a free movement and competition analysis would, of course, be the same. This is especially true in cases of public liability for breaches of competition law, where measures have been held contrary to both the free movement and the competition rules (especially today's Art 106 on special and exclusive rights). In *Merci convenzionali* and *GB-INNO v ATAB* the Court even explicitly said that 'a national measure which has the effect of facilitating the abuse of a dominant position capable of affecting trade between Member States will generally be incompatible with [Art 34 TFEU] ... in so far as such a measure has the effect of ... impeding imports of goods from other Member States'.[62] In other cases such as *ERT*, the Court found the same measure to violate both sets of rules without elaborating on their relationship or on the need to apply them simultaneously.[63]

Conversely, one would assume from the Court's position that it is entirely possible for some conduct to fall through the cracks because it infringes neither set of rules. It seems, however, that the separation narrative was always employed in order to condemn, and not in order to exonerate a measure.

4.3 Shortcuts and hybrids

As we have seen, whenever the Court is confronted on the issue of how the two sets of rules should relate to one another, especially when plaintiffs opportunistically rely on elements of one in order to avoid liability under the other, it emphasizes that they are separate. Still, it does not always stick to its own methodology.

First of all, it sometimes follows one analysis and intentionally skips the other. In *Bosman*, the national court posed questions on the compatibility of the transfer rules and nationality restrictions in football both with the provisions on free movement of workers and with today's Arts 101 and 102. As mentioned *supra*, AG Lenz would have applied both sets of rules to the same conduct and found restrictions under both independently. The Court, however, conducted a detailed analysis under the free movement provisions, but when asked about the competition rules, said only: 'Since both types of rule to which the national court's question refer are contrary to [Art 45 TFEU on the free movement of workers], it is not necessary to rule on the interpretation of Articles [101 and 102 TFEU].'[64]

[61] Paragraph 253 of the Opinion in *Bosman* (n 2). See also the Opinion of AG Capotorti in Case 58/80 *Dansk Supermarked A/S v A/S Imerco* [1981] ECR 181, where the AG found a separate violation of both sets of rules with little fanfare (see the conclusions on pp. 202–03).

[62] Case C-179/90 *Merci convenzionali porto di Genova SpA v Siderurgica Gabrielli SpA* [1991] ECR I-5889, para 21; *RTT v GB-Inno-BM* (n 4) paras 32–36.

[63] Case C-260/89 *Elliniki Radiophonia Tiléorassi AE and Panellinia Omospondia Syllogon Prossopikou v Dimotiki Etairia Pliroforissis and Sotirios Kouvelas and Nicolaos Avdellas and others* [1991] ECR I-2925, paras 28–36.

[64] *Bosman* (n 2) para 138. It should be pointed out that the national court's questions were not alternatively posed, nor did they seem to give greater emphasis on the free movement rules. They also concerned all of the challenged rules of the sporting bodies stated under all of the Treaty provisions together. See also, more recently, AG Cruz Villalon's suggestion in *Yellow Cab* (n 4) para 51 that 'the potential indirect consequences of infringement of freedom of establishment on

A similar approach was taken in *LIBRO*, where national rules fixing book prices were held to infringe the free movement of goods. Again, the Court found it unnecessary to decide whether they also violated today's Art 101 TFEU.[65] More recently, in *Fra.bo*, the Court found the activities of a standard-setting body that effectively regulates entry to a Member State's market to fall under the rules on free movement of goods, but did not answer whether they also fall under the competition rules.[66] In *Wouters* and *Anonima Petroli Italiana*, conversely, the Court applied the competition rules (justifying the former and condemning the latter measure) and then dispensed with the free movement analysis.[67]

Importantly, while the Court considered one set of rules to be superfluous after having applied the other, it did not address the consequences of its position. In *Bosman*, for example: is it unnecessary to answer because free movement liability implies competition liability as well? Or is it the other way round: free movement liability excludes competition liability? Or is it simply that, having already found an illegality under one set of rules, an answer under the other set of rules is not important? The last response is the likeliest. If it is true, however, it may lead to certain problems, as I will address in section 6.

The tendency of the Court to rely more frequently on either the free movement rules (as in *Bosman*), or a type of analysis similar to the free movement rules (as in *Wouters*), has been noticed.[68] Arguably, it can be explained by the relative simplicity and flexibility of those rules. Application of competition law, especially in more complex cases, can require an extensive evidentiary record and the use of economic analysis. In a standard competition case, this work is done by the Commission, a national competition agency, or a national court before it reaches the CJEU. If the case is handled by the Commission, the Court of Justice is acting as the second appeal instance after the General Court. In cases where all the evidentiary and analytical work has not been completed, such as in a reference from a national court unsure whether to apply competition or free movement rules, the Court may therefore be tempted to focus on the free movement rules.

free competition will always be examined in the context of the analysis of that right … in the present case, it is superfluous to assess the requirement … from the point of view of competition also'.

[65] *LIBRO* (n 4) para 37. Both *LIBRO* and *Yellow Cab* can be distinguished from *Bosman* (n 2) insofar as both cases are a challenge to Member State legislation, and not to the practices of private actors.

[66] Case C-171/11 *Fra.bo SpA v Deutsche Vereinigung des Gas—und Wasserfaches eV (DVGW)—Technisch-Wissenschaftlicher Verein* (ECJ, 12 July 2012) paras 32–33. Granted, this case is somewhat specific in that the national courts posed the questions in the alternative: since the answer to the free movement question was affirmative, technically the Court was not required to say anything on the competition provisions. See paras 16, 33, and 34.

[67] Case C-309/99 *J. C. J. Wouters, J. W. Savelbergh and Price Waterhouse Belastingadviseurs BV v Algemene Raad van de Nederlandse Orde van Advocaten, intervener: Raad van de Balies van de Europese Gemeenschap* [2002] ECR I-1577, paras 119–23; *Anonima Petroli Italiana* (n 4). See also O'Loughlin (n 10) 69.

[68] See Mortelmans (n 4) 640–41. Baquero Cruz (n 2) 101 points out that the General Court's specialization in competition law, as opposed to the free movement focus of the Court of Justice, may have an influence.

Those rules are more amenable to application by courts as law interpreters[69] rather than fact-finders. They are based on a relatively straightforward definition of a restriction that does not normally require a detailed effects analysis; in fact, it is generally even less detailed than the analysis of restrictions 'by object' under Art 101.[70] The archetype free movement case is one in which courts are examining legislation or another type of measure[71] which either plainly discriminates against cross-border economic activity, or can be assumed from its meaning alone to produce indirectly discriminatory ('dual burden') or restrictive effects. The free movement rules approach the effects of a measure in a mostly speculative way (ie what kind of consequences is the restraint 'liable' to produce).[72] The proportionality analysis they involve may be especially attractive to judges. It is, as Stone Sweet and Mathews note, the 'doctrinal underpinning for the expansion of judicial power', enabling courts to reinforce their legitimacy while managing conflict over sensitive political issues.[73] It enables a wide variety of arguments to be brought into play, and allows a regulatory scheme to be assessed without making overt value judgments.

Another explanation for the Court's disinclination to apply the competition rules when the free movement rules are also available may have to do with an institutional division of labour. Competition law was always to some extent seen as the Commission's turf.[74] By shifting emphasis to the free movement rules, the Court is preserving the prerogatives of the EU judiciary without trying to impose an agenda on the Commission. Making any kind of deference to the Commission explicit, of course, would be problematic from a constitutional point of view, not to mention the fact that it no longer fully represents the reality of a decentralized competition law. Implicitly, however, the Court's decision to prioritize competition law in certain areas is a signal for the Commission to get involved. Over time, opting for the free movement rules will subtly shift the responsibility over a certain area to generalist courts, and opting for competition law will give more responsibility to competition agencies. This will still, however,

[69] This is reinforced by the status of the free movement rules as 'fundamental' rules of the Treaty. See for example Case C-319/06, *Commission v Luxembourg* [2008] ECR I-4323, paras 30 and 43. AG Lenz has characterized 'the right to freedom of movement as a fundamental right which the Treaty confers individually on each worker in the Community' (Opinion in *Bosman* (n 2) para 203). Neither the Court nor most scholars would fully adhere to AG Lenz's position that the market freedoms as such constitute fundamental rights, but they clearly have a special status in EU law.

[70] This is reflected in judgments where the Court finds the questions dealing with competition law to be inadmissible due to the lack of facts and evidence in the reference, while proceeding to apply the free movement rules—see n 118.

[71] The situation is somewhat complicated if the restraint consists of *de facto* action as opposed to a legal measure (n 2), but this does not seem to radically change the Court's analysis.

[72] Among many other examples, see *Dassonville* (n 35) para 5, Case C-384/93 *Alpine Investments BV v Minister van Financiën* [1995] ECR I-1141, para 27 et seq, para 32 and Case C-55/94 *Reinhard Gebhard v Consiglio dell'Ordine degli Avvocati e Procuratori di Milano* [1995] ECR I-4165, para 37.

[73] Alec Stone Sweet and Jud Mathews, 'Proportionality Balancing and Global Constitutionalism' (2008) 47 Columbia Journal of Transnational Law 68, 87.

[74] Szyszczak (n 32) 102.

preserve the ultimate authority of the Court as long as competition law scrutiny remains an option.[75]

In other cases, the competition law and free movement approaches have merged or influenced one another. At times, the Court imports elements of the analysis under one set of rules into the other. One example is the definition of a restriction to the free movement of goods under *Dassonville*, which was taken from the competition law definition of effects on trade.[76] Mortelmans has similarly noted that, in *Banchero*, the Court essentially relied on the *Keck* exemption from Art 34 TFEU in order to find that a measure restricting the sale of tobacco to outlets approved by the State does not violate the competition rules.[77] More recently, in *Commission v Italy (lawyers' fees)* the test for a restriction of the free movement of services and establishment was whether competitors are 'deprived of the opportunity of gaining access to the market of the host Member State under conditions of normal and effective competition', wording borrowed from competition law.[78] An even more striking example is the *Wouters* 'inherent restriction' test, which introduces a free movement-style proportionality analysis into Art 101.[79] In *Anonima Petroli Italiana*, the Court relied directly on free movement precedent to introduce a requirement of consistency into the *Wouters* test.[80]

Moreover, in some judgments the Court even overrides the referring national court's question and applies the other set of rules, instead of the one mentioned in the reference.[81]

What does this overview of the case law leave us with? To some extent, it is not surprising to observe a range of approaches in individual cases. However, there is a clear tension between the Court's position that, in principle, the two sets of rules are distinct and its actual approach in cases of overlap where the analysis is sometimes abbreviated or combined.

[75] See Howard A. Shelanski, 'The Case for Rebalancing Antitrust and Regulation' (2011) 109 Michigan Law Review 683, 705, claiming that the US Supreme Court's withdrawal of antitrust scrutiny in regulated sectors shifts authority to regulatory agencies.

[76] See section 4.1.

[77] Case C-387/93, *Criminal proceedings against Giorgio Domingo Banchero* [1995] ECR I-4663. See Mortelmans (n 4) 627.

[78] See n 46. In the area of competition law, this phrase is used in Council Regulation (EC) 139/2004 on the control of concentrations between undertakings (the EC Merger Regulation) [2004] OJ L24/1, Arts 7/3 and 8/5. See also Case 27/76 *United Brands Company and United Brands Continentaal BV v Commission* [1978] ECR 207, para 65: '[a] dominant position ... relates to a position of economic strength enjoyed by an undertaking which enables it to prevent effective competition being maintained on the relevant market ...'

[79] See Chapter III section 3.1.3.

[80] Citing Case C-169/07 *Hartlauer Handelsgesellschaft mbH v Wiener Landesregierung and Oberösterreichische Landesregierung* [2009] ECR I-1721 and Case C-384/08 *Attanasio Group Srl v Comune di Carbognano* [2010] ECR I-2055, it found that 'national legislation is appropriate to ensuring attainment of the objective pursued only if it genuinely reflects a concern to attain it in a consistent and systematic manner'. *Anonima Petroli Italiana* (n 4) para 53.

[81] In Case C-22/98 *Criminal proceedings against Jean Claude Becu, Annie Verweire, Smeg NV and Adia Interim NV* [1999] ECR I-5665, for example, the national court's questions dealt only with today's Art 106/1 on special and exclusive rights. Having first established that there was no restriction of the competition rules, and while claiming not to have been 'put in a position to rule' on the

5. The Problems of the *Status Quo*

It is not unusual for the same conduct to potentially fall foul of more than one legal rule. Undertakings in the network sectors fall under general competition law as well as sector-specific regulation with similar, but not identical aims.[82] EU competition law can overlap with national competition rules that may, to some extent, pursue different aims.[83] A serious problem with applying two sets of rules at once would occur if one rule required conduct that the other rule prohibits, so that there was no way of complying with both at the same time. For example, the only way a certain actor can avoid violation of the competition rules is by violating the free movement rules. This scenario does not seem likely. Still, the *status quo* as described above can lead to three kinds of distinct but related problems. It creates uncertainty as actors are not sure under which standard their behaviour will be assessed. It may distort the outcome of the analysis by leading either to under—or over-enforcement. Finally, it complicates the decision-making process.

First, neither the competition rules nor the free movement rules, as far as legal rules go, are particularly clear. They are based on broad prohibitions with relatively abstract justifications, and without an in-depth knowledge of the relevant case law it is difficult to say how they are to be applied to a particular measure. When the same measure is analysed under both of them, the problem is aggravated and compliance costs soar. This is especially relevant for private regulators. They must assess whether their conduct entails a restriction of competition and/or a restriction of free movement, which not only involves answering two different questions, but also means that conduct which might be presumed unproblematic under one set of rules on the basis of a cursory presumption (eg agreements falling under the *de minimis* exception) suddenly needs to be subjected to a more in-depth analysis.

The situation is not helped by the approach of the Court in cases such as *Bosman*, where only one set of rules is actually applied. This creates uncertainty, first, because it leaves open the question whether national courts, the defendants themselves, or third parties should consider there to have been a violation of the rule that was 'skipped' or not. Secondly, it makes the limits of the Court's actual findings unclear. For example, if the football federation in *Bosman* violated only

issue because the question was not asked, the Court still assessed the measure through the lens of the rules on free movement of workers (paras 34–36).

[82] In Case C-457/10 P *AstraZeneca AB and AstraZeneca plc v Commission* ECLI:EU:C:2012:770, para 132, the Court pointed out that 'the illegality of abusive conduct under [Art 102 TFEU] is unrelated to its compliance or non-compliance with other legal rules and, in the majority of cases, abuses of dominant positions consist of behaviour which is otherwise lawful under branches of law other than competition law'.

[83] Case C-238/05 *Asnef-Equifax, Servicios de Información sobre Solvencia y Crédito, SL v Asociación de Usuarios de Servicios Bancarios (Ausbanc)* [2006] ECR I-11125, para 20: 'It is not impossible for the same factual situation to fall within the scope of both Community law and national competition law, even if they consider the practices concerned from different points of view.' See also Case C-7/97 *Bronner* [1998] ECR I-7791, para 19.

the free movement rules, does that violation also extend to rules regarding purely internal transfers?[84]

Predictability and clarity of the law are not absolute values. Increasing complexity, however, may lead to lower compliance with both sets of rules. It may also increase learning and adaptation costs for private actors who have to self-assess their measures up to a dual standard, as well as for courts and agencies that have to apply two different sets of rules. It can even enable infringers to obfuscate suspicious practices with a broader range of legal or quasi-legal arguments.[85]

The second argument against the *status quo* has to do with over—and under-enforcement. Because the resources of courts and agencies are limited, decision-making mechanisms should be developed in a way that minimizes error.[86] In that light, the free movement and competition law rules are each based on a number of trade-offs. There are a number of evidentiary hurdles the decision-makers have to cross, and both instruments have built-in mechanisms of restraint for cases where intervention is less necessary. These may be described as their respective limits, or ways to minimize errors.

Importantly, these limits were developed keeping in mind the standard case: application of only one set of rules at a time, one to States and the other to undertakings. In the case of private regulation, however, a converged or 'hybrid' form of scrutiny that would import elements of one into the other or equate violations of one with violations of the other is problematic since it risks overriding those mechanisms of restraint. In terms of decision theory, this can lead to either over-enforcement (false positives) or under-enforcement (false negatives). This problem does not occur when the two sets of rules are separately and distinctly applied, but could happen in case of hybrid approaches, or even when one of them is skipped.

Moreover, if we were to assume that one of the two sets of rules is 'correct' for a particular restraint, there would be over-enforcement if one set of rules was more demanding than the other in a particular context, by applying the stricter one in addition to the less strict one.[87] Conversely, if we were to assume that the stricter

[84] See Stephen Weatherill, *European Sports Law: Collected Papers* (T.M.C. Asser Press 2007) 107.

[85] See Daniel W Drezner, 'Regime Proliferation and the Tragedy of the Global Institutional Commons' (2009) FILA Discussion Paper No. 1/2009 35. 'The proliferation of international rules, laws, and organizational forms does not necessarily lead to an increase in rule-based outcomes. Institutional thickening weakens the power of pre-existing focal points, raises the costs and complexity of monitoring and compliance, and creates conflicting legal obligations at the global level.' See also Joel P Trachtman, 'Fragmentation, Coherence and Synergy in International Law' (2011) 2 Transnational Legal Theory 505.

[86] Frank H Easterbrook, 'Limits of Antitrust' (1984) 63 Texas Law Review 1. Easterbrook's separate normative point is that false negatives should be preferred to false positives: the game should be rigged against the plaintiff or agency, because of the low ability of courts to absorb economic arguments, difficulties in predicting the future, and a bias against defendants. Similarly, the *Trinko* exemption from antitrust scrutiny in regulated sectors (*Verizon Communications Inc. v Law Offices of Curtis V. Trinko, LLP* 540 US 398 (2004)) was justified by the supposedly higher likelihood of error when cases are dealt with by non-expert judges and juries, rather than regulators. Shelanski (n 75) 708.

[87] This of course begs the question of which rule is 'correct'. As I have argued, this is a rather futile exercise when private regulators are concerned.

rule was the correct one, but the courts chose to rely only on the more lenient one or soften the impact of the stricter one by importing some features of the more lenient standard, the result would be under-enforcement.

Decision costs are the third problem. The possibility of applying both sets of rules increases them in two distinct ways. Firstly, and obviously, courts are required to apply two sets of rules instead of one.[88] Secondly, the procedural possibilities are complicated. For example, the same restraint could be challenged both before a competition agency—relying purely on competition law—and before a court, relying on free movement law. This opens forum-shopping possibilities, and makes it likely that differences and complexities of interpretation increase with the number of decision-makers involved.

6. Possible Solutions: Convergence or Separation?

With these problems in mind, we can ask: is there a better way? Could the cases of overlap be handled in a way which addresses those difficulties?

There are three possibilities. One is convergence: reading the two sets of rules as a single legality standard or at least in a harmonious way. Another is to create a conflict rule: preventing dual application in principle, handling some cases under one and others under the other set of rules. Finally, courts could maintain the existing principle that the rules are separate and that overlap is possible.

6.1 Convergence

The first possibility is convergence: blending the two forms of analysis. This could be done, firstly, by adopting a 'seamless web' reading—claiming that it does not matter which set of rules is applied since these are simply more specific manifestations of a single legal standard. Pescatore, Waelbroeck, and Mortelmans, for example, can be read as arguing for this approach.[89]

More modestly, the rules could be interpreted in a harmonious way—smoothing over some specific differences between them in order to achieve similar outcomes. In *Bosman*, for example, AG Lenz first found a violation of the free movement rules and then suggested that, if an exemption under today's Art 101/3 TFEU was sought, the Commission should aim for a 'uniform result', refusing to justify the conduct under competition law because it violates the free movement rules.[90] Thus, while suggesting that the rules are separate and can apply at the

[88] Snell (n 24) 229 has claimed that applying the free movement to private undertakings when competition law is available would be 'inefficient and unnecessary public intervention'.

[89] See Section 2.

[90] Opinion in *Bosman* (n 2) para 278: 'Since such an exemption would, however, make no difference to the breach of [Art 45 TFEU], it would make sense for the Commission to take that factor into account in the exemption procedure. A uniform result ought to be aimed at in any case ... That would mean that an exemption under [Art 101/3] would also have to be ruled out.'

same time, he advocated a form of convergence when faced with a danger that allegedly restrictive measures could fall through the cracks. Similarly, in *Murphy*, AG Kokott relied on the rules on free movement of services to support her finding of a violation of Art 101 because 'conflicting assessments of the fundamental freedoms and competition law are to be avoided in principle'.[91]

While initially appealing, the convergence scenario is riddled with problems. Firstly, its weaker form overrides the internal limits of both the free movement rules and the competition rules, even after certain adjustments[92] are made to accommodate private regulation as an object of scrutiny. For example, reading the internal situation rule under the free movement rules harmoniously with the effect on trade requirement under the competition rules[93] could mean that factually internal restraints that create cross-border impact on competition would become subject to the free movement rules, or that cases that have some international element without affecting cross-border trade would become subject to the competition rules.[94] While neither development would necessarily be a bad thing, both would be distortive of current legal doctrine, changing it through the back door, only in cases of overlap.[95]

The problem is increased when there is little transparency, so that courts and agencies decide on a case-by-case basis what the 'harmonized' approach should mean. Should it work against or in favour of the defendant? Do we use elements of one analysis to help us condemn a restraint under the other, or instead to exonerate it? The convergence approach gives no obvious answer to those questions.

[91] AG Kokott's Opinion in *Murphy* (n 34) first finds the agreement to be incompatible with Art 101 and then proceeds to also find a restriction of free movement (para 249), citing her own Opinion in Case C-169/08 *Presidente del Consiglio dei Ministri* [2009] ECR I-10821, where she stated: '... the same questions arise with regard to the law of State aid as with regard to the fundamental freedoms, and there is no reason why the reply in relation to the latter should differ from the reply regarding the former. Rather, to avoid conflicting assessments as between the law of State aid and the law of fundamental freedoms, the same criteria must be applied in both cases' (para 134).

[92] See Chapters II and III.

[93] Waelbroeck (n 1) 794 viewed them as being the same requirement. While, arguably, the Court has equated those two requirements in some contexts such as public procurement (see eg Case C-458/03 *Parking Brixen GmbH v Gemeinde Brixen and Stadtwerke Brixen AG* [2005] ECR I-8585, paras 54–55), in general the principle is still that the free movement rules, unlike the EU competition rules, 'cannot be applied to situations ... which are confined in all relevant respects within a single Member State' (see for example Case C-256/11 *Murat Dereci and Others v Bundesministerium für Inneres* ECLI:EU:C:2011:734, para 60 and Case C-434/09 *Shirley McCarthy v Secretary of State for the Home Department* [2011] ECR I-3375, para 45 in the context of free movement of persons).

[94] An agreement between undertakings from two different Member States or with some other cross-border element could only create effects in one Member State, or fail to have an impact on trade within the internal market. Conduct can also fall short of this requirement if the effect on trade is not appreciable, a standard that does not exist in free movement law. See Commission notice—Guidelines on the effect on trade concept contained in Articles 81 and 82 of the Treaty (2004) OJ C 101 sections 2.2 et seq.

[95] As Prechal and de Vries (n 2) 12 point out, 'the Court's broad conception of what constitutes an obstacle must not lead to a situation where the free movement and competition rules become too much intertwined, where no account is taken of their different requirements and modes of application'.

When it is used, such as in the cited Opinions of AG Lenz and AG Kokott, it always seems to make it easier to condemn measures, in order to fill the supposed '*lacuna*' that would occur if a measure was found lawful. If this was ever stated explicitly as the true nature of the convergence argument, it would be obviously problematic—perhaps this is why the debate tends to stay at a rather abstract level.

The second major problem that affects both the stronger and weaker version of the convergence argument is that the two sets of rules are simply different. To be sure, there are important similarities and parallels: their aims overlap to a significant extent and their methodology is broadly similar, first asking whether some conduct falls within their scope, secondly, whether it is restrictive, and thirdly, whether it can be justified.[96] However, they differ on several levels: foundational (the importance of economics, the role of a guiding value vs. balancing a plurality of values), doctrinal (differences in scope, definition of an infringement, method of justification), institutional, and procedural (remedies, jurisdiction, judicial review). This means that full convergence—a single legality standard—is descriptively wrong as a matter of existing law or, if presented in normative terms, would require the architecture of the two sets of rules to change in a rather unclear way.

Crucially, the differences between the two sets of rules cut both ways. It is impossible to generally say that, for example, every violation of free movement by private actors will also be a restriction of competition law, or vice versa. The rules overlap in different, context-specific ways. Because of this, it is also impossible to adopt a general rule such as *lex specialis derogat legi generali*, or to say that because conduct infringes one set of rules, that it also infringes the other.

In the following sections, I will address the differences between the two sets of rules in more detail.

6.1.1 The foundational differences

The first major foundational difference has to do with the role of economics. Both the competition and the free movement rules are in some sense economic in nature. The ways in which economics is embedded[97] in them are, however, significantly different.

A useful distinction here is that made by John Rawls between 'justifying a practice as a system of rules to be applied and enforced' and 'justifying a particular action which falls under those rules'.[98] Rawls's intention in making that

[96] Pernilla Lindh, 'The Influence of Competition Law on Free Movement Rules' in Heikki Kanninen, Nina Korjus, and Allan Rosas (eds), *EU Competition Law in Contest: Essays in Honour of Virpi Tiili* (Hart 2009) 17. On the differences between them, see for example O'Loughlin (n 10) 63. Sometimes the differences are stretched quite far. Gormley has claimed that competition law cannot assist the removal of national barriers to trade through negative integration and that the four freedoms do not involve anything similar to a competition law analysis. Lawrence Gormley, 'Competition and Free Movement: Is the Internal Market the Same as a Common Market?' (2002) European Business Law Review 517, 520.

[97] See David J Gerber, 'Competition Law and the Institutional Embeddedness of Economics' in Daniel Zimmer (ed), *The Goals of Competition Law* (Edward Elgar 2012).

[98] John Rawls, 'Two Concepts of Rules' (1955) 64 The Philosophical Review 3.

distinction was quite different, but the underlying point is that the arguments, assumptions, or reasons on which a certain set of rules is based do not necessarily need to be the same arguments, assumptions, or reasons that come into play each time the set of rules is applied in a particular case. Thus, there is nothing incoherent or contradictory if a set of rules is, in principle, based on economic justifications, but those economic justifications or reasons are not central to adjudicating under that set of rules.[99] A similar distinction is made by Gerber in a context much closer to the one this chapter deals with. Gerber points out that economics should not be seen purely as an abstract set of principles, but that its application depends on the institutional setting in which it is relied on. Thus, economics can be used in a normative way when it shapes the content of legal norms, or in a factual way, when it is used in case assessment.[100]

Arguably, in free movement law economics is used largely in the first, normative, sense. The economic case for free trade and economic integration in the EU context is well known.[101] Through the operation of the free movement rules and other instruments, the EU was able to establish an internal market in which goods, services, workers, and capital circulate freely, achieving economies of scale, enabling specialization etc.

However, the actual analysis under the free movement rules is not 'economic' in any deep sense. It does not enquire into the actual economic effects of a measure—neither the harm nor the benefits of the measure are considered in much detail. Despite occasional exceptions to the rule,[102] it is generally accepted that the creators of restrictive measures, whether Member States or private actors, cannot justify restraints by economic considerations.[103] While, clearly, any number of arguments assessed under the free movement rules could be described in economic terms,[104] economics does not really come into play when actual cases are decided.

[99] Rawls was trying to show how utilitarian arguments can be made with respect to criminal law. In his words: 'One must distinguish between justifying a practice as a system of rules to be applied and enforced, and justifying a particular action which falls under those rules; utilitarian arguments are appropriate with regard to questions about practices, while retributive arguments fit the application of particular rules to particular cases.' ibid 5.

[100] Gerber (n 97) 25.

[101] See for example Willem Molle, *The Economics of European Integration: Theory, Practice, Policy* (5th edn, Ashgate 2006); Jacques Pelkmans, *European Integration: Methods and Economic Analysis* (3rd edn, Financial Times Prentice Hall 2006); and J Pelkmans, 'Mutual Recognition in Goods and Services: An Economic Perspective' (2002) 2 BEEP Briefings. See also Béla A Balassa, *Types of Economic Integration* (International Bank for Reconstruction and Development 1974).

[102] See for example Case 72/83 *Campus Oil Limited and others v Minister for Industry and Energy and others* [1984] ECR 2727, paras 45–51. For the orthodoxy, see Case 7-61 *Commission v Italy* [1961] ECR 317, section D, p. 329.

[103] See for example Case C-446/03 *Marks & Spencer plc v David Halsey (Her Majesty's Inspector of Taxes)* [2005] ECR I-10837, para 44; Opinion of AG Sharpston in Case C-73/08 *Nicolas Bressol and Others and Céline Chaverot and Others v Gouvernement de la Communauté française* [2010] ECR I-2735, para 89 et seq. See Mortelmans (n 4) 637–38.

[104] See Kinga Guzdek, *Binnenmarkt, unverfälschter Wettbewerb und Marktversagen: zur Parallelität der Einschränkungsmöglichkeiten im Rahmen der Grundfreiheiten sowie der Wettbewerbs— und Beihilferegeln des EU-Rechts* (Stämpfli 2012), who frames the definition of a restriction under free movement as a reduction in economic efficiency, and the justifications as ways of addressing market failures.

For example, the free movement rules do not require courts to define a market on which a restraint is supposed to have effects, who the participants in that market are, what the actual state of competition in it is, whether it has been weakened by the measure, and how. This can be explained by the fact that the free movement rules have overwhelmingly been discussed through the lens of the standard case of public, usually legislative measures of general application. For those measures, a restrictive effect can be assumed without an effects analysis.[105]

Following Rawls, this does not mean that the rules are incoherent or insufficiently economic. It merely means that the general assumption can be made that case-to-case practice remains true to the economic content of the rules even if they are not discussed at every instance.[106] The fact that a judge applying the free movement rules is not required to weigh the economically beneficial against the economically harmful consequences of a particular restraint does not mean that the free movement rules in general do not make economic sense.

The application of the competition rules, on the other hand, actively relies on economic reasoning in individual cases. The tools of economic analysis are used in individual cases, not just to inform the interpretation of the rules. The need to analyse the factual and economic context in particular cases means that it is possible to make different conclusions on the legality of formally identical measures, depending on the context in which they take place.[107] As Neven summarizes the more economic approach in EU competition law:

- the analysis of agreements between firms, in particular vertical agreements ... has increasingly focused on effects;
- the assessment of competition has moved away from the formal notion of dominance towards effective competition;
- the analysis of the factors that determine effective competition has become more sophisticated, in particular regarding the definition of the relevant markets, bidding markets, the proximity of competitors' position and buyer power;

[105] See Mortelmans' (n 4) discussion of Keck on 625–27. Going back to the link between *Consten & Grundig* and *Dassonville* (see section 4.1), one could even argue that the trade effects test that competition law uses for purposes of applicability (only the first step in the analysis), is translated by the free movement analysis into a theory of harm, that is into the definition of a restriction.

[106] To demonstrate this on the example of criminal punishment, Rawls (n 98) 6–7 uses the example of the legislator looking to the future and the judge looking to the past, saying that the judge need not (and perhaps should not) rely on utilitarian arguments for every punishment he administers.

[107] See for example Case C-234/89 *Stergios Delimitis v Henninger Bräu AG* [1991] ECR I-935, para 27: '... a beer supply agreement is prohibited by [Art 101/1 TFEU], if two cumulative conditions are met. The first is that, having regard to the economic and legal context of the agreement at issue, it is difficult for competitors who could enter the market or increase their market share to gain access to the national market ... The second condition is that the agreement in question must make a significant contribution to the sealing-off effect brought about by the totality of those agreements in their economic and legal context. The extent of the contribution made by the individual agreement depends on the position of the contracting parties in the relevant market and on the duration of the agreement.'

- the concept of collective dominance has been progressively developed in terms of the theory of collusion in repeated interactions;
- quantitative methods have become more important;
- enforcement procedures, like the leniency programmes, which find some foundation in economic analysis, have been implemented.[108]

The second foundational difference in the way the two sets of rules are interpreted has to do with their aims, or rather, the way in which their aims are conceived. There is a huge literature on what the aims of the EU competition rules are.[109] In order to legitimize the use of public policy arguments, for example, it seems that they need to be somehow recognized as discrete aims of competition law (see Chapter III). In a sense, this shows that the competition rules are consequentialist[110]—their interpretation adapts to the effects the rules create on markets, and having a clear idea of the aims of the rules is supposed to bring a measure of predictability and legal certainty to their application.

There is very little equivalent discussion on the free movement rules. Apart from the uncontroversial notion that the rules are meant to serve market integration, the central questions of free movement law are who gets to regulate and how. It is not itself a regulatory policy, in the sense that it addresses a specific problem in the marketplace and tries to solve it. It is agnostic when it comes to substantive values, such as health or environmental protection, because it is designed to accommodate a number of diverging values and approaches. The debate about the aim of the free movement rules is mostly about the extent of scrutiny: for example, should the rules prevent only protectionist, discriminatory measures, or all measures that can impede economic activity?[111] The real issue here is the impact of the free movement rules on the regulatory autonomy of the Member States (and, as we have seen, some private actors), including whether market aims are appropriately balanced with an open-ended set of regulatory objectives.[112] The central feature of the free movement rules is thus their relatively open-ended proportionality analysis.[113] The debates on these issues are not concerned with finding a set of guiding aims for the free movement rules in the same sense as with the competition rules.

[108] Damien Neven, 'Competition Economics and Antitrust in Europe' (2006) 21 Economic Policy 741, 746.

[109] See Chapter III section 2.1.

[110] See for example Brian Z Tamanaha, *Law as a Means to an End: Threat to the Rule of Law* (Cambridge University Press 2006) and Ioannis Lianos, '"Lost in Translation": Towards a Theory of Economic Transplants' Jean Monnet Working Paper 08/09 <http://ssrn.com/abstract=1485378> at 43.

[111] See for example the discussion in René Joliet, 'The Free Circulation of Goods: The Keck and Mithouard Decision and the New Directions in the Case Law' (1994) 1 Columbia Journal of European Law 436, 446 et seq.

[112] Moreover, the available justifications are not restricted to the ones listed in the Treaty, due to the Court's introduction of mandatory requirements or overriding reasons related to the public interest. See Case 120/78 *Rewe-Zentral AG v Bundesmonopolverwaltung für Branntwein* [1979] ECR 649 and *Gebhard* (n 72).

[113] See Stone Sweet, and Mathews (n 73).

A third basic difference between the competition and free movement approaches is their level of precision. When compared to the legal rules and institutional apparatus underpinning competition law, free movement law seems like a somewhat blunt instrument. This can have its advantages. In particular, it is much easier for generalist judges to apply. It also enables the swift removal of egregious obstacles to free movement, such as Member State legislation, without the need for lengthy procedures and detailed market analysis.

The competition law analysis, however, is suited to dealing with factually difficult cases where the risk of false negatives is more of a concern. Thus, the free movement rules are better at removing barriers, and the competition approach is better employed as a tool for maintaining the efficient operation of markets[114]—although, of course, the line between the two is not watertight. Hancher and Larouche make a similar observation in the context of network industries and services of general economic interest, where the law has evolved from the simple removal of barriers to the construction of the internal market towards an inclusive, more detailed, and economically substantiated approach. Once a certain level of market integration is achieved, attention shifts to competition law as the primary way of resolving economic conflicts.[115] Growing legal and economic complexity seems to shift the emphasis from the free movement rules in favour of more detailed regulation and/or competition law.[116]

6.1.2 The doctrinal differences

The second group of important differences between the competition and free movement rules lies in the nitty-gritty of legal doctrine. The discussion in the following paragraphs will focus on the legal issues that are relevant to applying the free movement and/or competition rules directly to private actors, rather than on the overlap between free movement and competition law that happens in

[114] D O'Keefe and A F Bavasso, 'Four Freedoms, One Market and National Competence: In Search of a Dividing Line' in David O'Keefe and Antonio F Bavasso (eds), *Judicial Review in European Union Law—Liber Amicorum in Honour of Lord Slynn of Hadley*, vol 1 (2000) 543–45 conceptualize the protection against market partitioning and the maintenance of competition as distinct aims, describing the competition rules as an 'endo-integrated, positive set of rules' and the free movement rules as a 'negative set of rules' based on prohibitions.

[115] Leigh Hancher and Pierre Larouche, 'The Coming of Age of EU Regulation of Network Industries and Services of General Economic Interest' in Peter Craig and Grainne de Búrca (eds), *The Evolution of EU Law* (2nd edn, Oxford University Press 2011). They distinguish a formalist/legalistic method based on removing barriers and a 'managed competition' way of regulating, based on economic analysis and a case-by-case approach. They point out that the growing sophistication of regulation in network industries leads to a gradual abandonment of the fixation with market access and the removal of barriers as the sole regulatory aim. Perhaps the contrast between the free movement and the competition approach can be seen in a similar way. See also Szyszczak (n 32).

[116] Similarly, the example of sports shows that an initial wave of market opening achieved through the free movement rules gives way to the competition rules (see Chapter V). See also Azoulai (n 29) 1336–37, discussing a growing plurality of values in EU constitutionalism that may push the free movement rules down on the list of priorities.

relation to State actors. The reason for this is that applying competition law to the measures of the Member States under the *effet utile* doctrine is a rather specific form of scrutiny: State measures are analysed largely as facilitating a separate violation. This means that, in relation to these measures, the convergence argument is stronger—it seems likely that, by violating competition law, a Member State would also be violating the free movement rules.[117]

(i) Admissibility

The first practical difference is that the same factual record may not suffice for an informed finding under both the free movement and the competition rules. In *Lehtonen* and *Deliège*, the Court applied the free movement rules but held the national courts' questions on the conformity of the very same measures with competition law to be inadmissible, because the information provided did not enable it to form 'sufficient knowledge of the factual and legal context'. In order to apply the competition rules, the Court lacked information on market definition, character, and number of undertakings operating in that market, existence and volume of trade between Member States, and effect on trade.[118] These evidentiary requirements are, in themselves, an argument against convergence, at least insofar as a convergent reading could lead to a thin factual background compiled under the free movement standard being used to find a violation of the competition rules.

(ii) Scope

The convergence argument need not mean that the scope of the two sets of rules needs to be the same in all circumstances. It could, however, be claimed that certain specific questions should be answered similarly; for example, that the notion of economic activity or the cross-border requirement should be read uniformly across two sets of rules.

The case law, however, makes it clear that the scope of the free movement and competition rules, while often overlapping, is not the same. The notion of economic activity, central to the question of scope of the two sets of rules, differs.[119]

[117] See the discussion of *GB-Inno-BM* and *Merci convenzionali* in section 4.2. See also R Joliet, 'Das Recht des unlauteren Wettbewerbs und der freie Warenverkehr' [1994] GRUR Int 1, suggesting that if a contract breaches today's Art 101, and is reinforced by public law, then that public law is also contrary to today's Art 34 TFEU.

[118] Case C-176/96 *Jyri Lehtonen and Castors Canada Dry Namur-Braine ASBL v Fédération royale belge des sociétés de basket-ball ASBL* (*FRBSB*) [2000] ECR I-2681, para 27 et seq and Joined cases C-51/96 and C-191/97 *Christelle Deliège v Ligue francophone de judo et disciplines associées ASBL, Ligue belge de judo ASBL, Union européenne de judo* (C-51/96) *and François Pacquée* (C-191/97) [2000] ECR I-02549, paras 36–37.

[119] In free movement law, economic activity is discussed explicitly in the area of free movement of services, while in competition law it is the key element of the definition of an undertaking. See also Okeoghene Odudu, 'Economic Activity as a Limit to Community Law' in Catherine Barnard and Okeoghene Odudu (eds), *The Outer Limits of European Union Law* (Hart 2009) and Vassilis Hatzopoulos, 'The Concept of "Economic Activity" in the EU Treaty: From Ideological Dead-ends to Workable Judicial Concepts' College of Europe Research Paper in Law 06/2011 <http://www.coleurope.eu/sites/default/files/research-paper/researchpaper_6_2011_hatzopoulos.pdf>, as well as the Opinion of AG Maduro in Case C-205/03 P *Federación Española de Empresas de Tecnología Sanitaria (FENIN) v Commission* [2006] ECR I-6295, para 51 and that of AG Kokott in Case

This is rather uncontroversial, especially after the clear statements in *Meca-Medina* and *Viking Line* among others (see section 4.2).

A more detailed comparison of the scope of the two sets of rules shows that there are numerous specific differences that can cut both ways—for some specific issues, one set of rules is broader, for other issues, the other. This means, first, that hastily adopted convergent readings could distort the legal analysis and, second, that a general rule such as *lex specialis derogat legi generali* would be inaccurate.[120]

It is true that, more often than not, the scope of the free movement rules is broader. Firstly, activities that are based on the principle of solidarity and essential public functions are in general excluded from the competition rules as they do not constitute economic activity. Thus, in *FENIN* AG Maduro argued that Member States should be free to withdraw activities such as the purchasing activity of health funds from the scope of competition law by organizing them in a way that emphasizes solidarity. Nevertheless, those activities would be subject to the free movement rules.[121] In addition, the judgment in *FENIN* seems to say that purchasing as such is not subject to competition law at all as it does not concern an offer of goods or services on the market.[122] At the same time, purchasing activities are not exempt from the free movement rules, regardless of their purpose. For example, had the health fund in *FENIN* discriminated against foreign suppliers in its procurement activities, the free movement rules would certainly have applied.

A separate line of cases creates a *de facto* exemption from competition law for collective agreements that result from bargaining between workers and employers.[123] As established by *Viking Line*, however, this does not mean that movement scrutiny is excluded as well (see section 4.2). In this area, the free movement rules also seem to have a wider scope.

Finally, a reason why free movement rules are frequently broader in scope is the absence of a *de minimis* test. As already mentioned, the Court has refused to set this sort of threshold for the application of the free movement rules.[124] Instead, the mechanism for the exclusion of relatively insignificant free movement cases is the so-called remoteness test, asking the question whether cases are 'too uncertain and indirect' for the application of the free movement provisions.[125]

Importantly, however, on some points the free movement rules could have a narrower scope. Odudu has claimed that, whereas the rules on free movement (in particular of services) require actual supply of a service for remuneration, the

C-284/04 *T-Mobile Austria GmbH and Others v Republik Österreich* [2007] ECR I-5189, arguing that the conceptions of economic activity across different parts of EU law are not the same.

[120] See, in that sense, Opinion of AG Trstenjak in *LIBRO* (n 4) para 192.

[121] Opinion of AG Maduro in *FENIN* (n 119) para 51.

[122] Paragraphs 25–28.

[123] See Prechal and de Vries (n 2) 12.

[124] See, for example, *Van de Haar* (n 42) para 13. A *de minimis* test was famously proposed by AG Jacobs in Case C-412/93 *Société d'Importation Edouard Leclerc-Siplec v TF1 Publicité SA and M6 Publicité SA* [1995] ECR I-179, para 42 et seq.

[125] E Spaventa, 'The Outer Limit of the Treaty Free Movement Provisions: Some Reflections on the Significance of Keck, Remoteness and Deliege' in Catherine Barnard and Okeoghene Odudu (eds), *The Outer Limits of European Union Law* (Hart Publishing 2009) 245.

competition rules require only the possibility that an activity can be carried out for profit.[126] To complicate matters further, the scope of the free movement rules is idiosyncratic, depending on which of the market freedoms is at issue: goods, services, establishment, capital, or workers. This may mean, for example, that an activity may fall under the competition rules but escape the rules on free movement of capital because it does not concern capital movements as described in the Annex to Directive 88/361/EEC.[127]

Another peculiarity of free movement law is the 'internal situation' test, which excludes situations that are enclosed within a single Member State in all their factual aspects, and therefore seen as unrelated to the internal market. This rule has often been criticized because it is can depend on random facts, not asking what impact a measure may create for trade.[128] In competition law, the closest equivalent would be the trade effects test, under which the relevant issue is whether an agreement (under Art 101 TFEU) or abuse of a dominant position (under Art 102 TFEU) may affect trade between Member States. Under the trade effects test, it is possible that a restraint which is in all its factual elements contained within one Member State affects cross-border trade. In such a situation, the scope of the competition rules would seem to be broader. On the other hand, a measure that has some factual cross-border characteristics may still be held not to affect trade under competition law.[129]

(iii) Restriction

Defining a restriction is the central question of both free movement and competition law, and is rather unsettled under both. As with matters falling under scope, the differences in the definitions can cut both ways.

In answering the question of which set of rules defines harmful conduct more broadly, the text is of little use. The general notion of an 'agreement having as its object or effect the restriction of competition' from Art 101 seems equally broad as that of 'rules capable of impeding free movement'.[130] The way the rules are applied in practice, however, yields more clues. Under competition law, especially when conduct is analysed as a restriction of competition by effect under Art 101, the existence of a restriction can depend on a variety of contextual factors, requiring a full market analysis.[131] Finding an abuse of dominance under Art 102, moreover, is more difficult than finding a restriction of free movement at least insofar as

[126] See n 119.

[127] Council Directive 88/361/EEC for the implementation of Art 67 of the Treaty (1988) OJ L 178 is used *de facto* as a list of measures falling under the free movement of capital.

[128] Alina Tryfonidou, *Reverse Discrimination in EC Law* (Kluwer Law International 2009); Miguel Poiares Maduro, 'The Scope of European Remedies: The Case of Purely Internal Situations and Reverse Discrimination', in Claire Kilpatrick, Tonia Novitz, and Paul Skidmore (eds), *The Future of European Remedies* (Hart 2000) and Mislav Mataija, 'Internal Situations in Community Law: An Uncertain Safeguard of Competences within the Internal Market' (2009) 5 Croatian Yearbook of European Law & Policy 31.

[129] See n 94.

[130] *Bosman* (n 2) para 103.

[131] See for example *Delimitis* (n 107).

it requires market definition (in what market is an undertaking supposed to be dominant?) and market power (dominance). Thus, in the abstract, even though the two sets of rules will frequently point in the same direction,[132] one could more easily imagine a case of a free movement restriction not being a restriction of competition than vice versa.[133]

In addition to these doctrinal and evidentiary hurdles, certain restraints are more easily perceived as restrictions of free movement than of competition because of their character and market effects. Prechal and de Vries place quality standards and product requirements in that category.[134] Finally, cases like *Angonese* show that the rules on free movement of persons, especially when restrictions by private actors are concerned, sometimes transcend the economic paradigm. The discrimination that Mr Angonese suffered restricted his free movement rights, but it is difficult to imagine how a bank's rule on language testing for potential employees could violate Art 102, or even Art 101 in case of an agreement.[135]

The other option, however, is also open: in some circumstances, measures that could be held to restrict competition law would not restrict the free movement rules. One example is price-setting: agreements on prices can hardly ever be justified under Art 101 TFEU, but not all price-fixing legislation restricts free movement.[136] Some measures that concern 'selling arrangements' and thus do not constitute restrictions of the free movement of goods under the rule laid down in *Keck*[137] could still be a restriction of competition: an agreement among supermarkets to ban selling below cost would almost certainly violate Art 101 TFEU. The Court has also made clear that simple contracts between individuals—unlike for example agreements that collectively regulate work conditions—do not violate

[132] Mortelmans (n 4) 632 et seq, for example, claims that under both sets of rules, there are ways to account for manifest and less manifest restrictions in different ways. In addition, the way the notion of market access, now commonly seen as the central criterion under the free movement rules, is understood, draws parallels with competition law concepts. For example, Case C-169/07 *Hartlauer Handelsgesellschaft mbH v Wiener Landesregierung and Oberösterreichische Landesregierung* [2009] ECR I-1721, paras 33–39 and Joined cases C-570/07 and C-571/07 *José Manuel Blanco Pérez and María del Pilar Chao Gómez v Consejería de Salud y Servicios Sanitarios* (C-570/07) and *Principado de Asturias* (C-571/07) [2010] ECR I-4629, para 55 show that potential limitations of output in a certain sector constitute limitations of market access.

[133] One example is supplied in AG Lenz's Opinion in *Bosman* (n 2). According to him, a rule is not a restriction of competition simply because it creates a barrier to access to market, if that barrier is only financial in nature. In free movement law, even such a barrier would suffice to find a restriction.

[134] Prechal and de Vries (n 2) 11.

[135] Case C-281/98 *Roman Angonese v Cassa di Risparmio di Bolzano SpA* [2000] ECR I-4139.

[136] See for example Joined cases 80 and 159/85 *Nederlandse Bakkerij Stichting and others v Edah BV* [1986] ECR 3359, paras 14–15; Case C-249/88 *Commission v Belgium* [1991] ECR I-1275, paras 15–16. On the other hand, national price control measures have frequently been found to be restrictive, if not necessarily unjustified. See for example Case 188/86 *Ministère public v Régis Lefèvre* [1987] ECR 2963, paras 10–18 and *LIBRO* (n 4) pp 21–29 as well as Case C-58/08 *The Queen, on the Application of Vodafone Ltd and Others v Secretary of State for Business, Enterprise and Regulatory Reform* [2010] ECR I-4999 (regarding EU-level price-fixing). See Prechal and de Vries (n 2) 11.

[137] Joined cases C-267/91 and C-268/91 *Criminal proceedings against Bernard Keck and Daniel Mithouard* [1993] ECR I-6097.

the rules on free movement of goods, whereas there is no such general exclusion from Art 101.[138]

All of these points, however, are somewhat incomplete, as they focus only on the nature of the measure, disregarding who adopts them. Prechal and de Vries suggest that the definition of a restrictive measure and the addressees of the rules are two separate questions.[139] This is not realistic. Of course, it is the starting point of this book that the line between the addressees of the two sets of rules is not clear or simple: both private and public actors (however one defines either) can be held liable under both sets of rules. Nevertheless, that does not mean that the source of the measure is irrelevant. For example, a small retailer may adopt a certain product requirement, such as that it will only sell *halal* meat. If a national retailer association or a public body adopts the same policy, is this the same kind of restriction? Only in a very formal sense. The identity of the measure's author is relevant, not because it allows us to categorize measures into neat public–private boxes, but because it helps us understand whether a measure is truly capable of restricting market access or competitive conditions. For example, an ordinary undertaking without significant market or regulatory power may not be able to restrict the free movement rights of others (putting discrimination against persons to one side), but may violate the competition rules by participating in a hard-core cartel.

(iv) Justification

Despite the numerous differences in terms of evidentiary requirements, scope, and the definition of a restriction, the question of justifications presents perhaps the starkest contrast between the competition and free movement rules.

As was explored at length in the chapters *supra*, the free movement justifications (those contained in the Treaty as well as the Court-developed, open-ended 'mandatory requirements')[140] are generally broader than the competition law justifications (Art 101/3 and objective justification under Art 102), inasmuch as they allow for a variety of non-economic considerations to be taken into account. To be sure, the difference between economic and non-economic is not always clear, and the free movement justifications can often be read in an economic light.[141] Often the two types of justification will consider similar arguments, such as the aim of the measure and its proportionality. In the context of private regulation, this similarity may increase, as both tests will likely look into certain features of the private regulator's governance and decision making process. It seems clear, however, that the free movement rules, compared in particular to Art 101/3 and 'objective

[138] Case C-159/00 *Sapod Audic v Eco-Emballages SA* [2002] ECR I-5031.

[139] See for example Prechal and de Vries (n 2) 10.

[140] It is usually thought that discriminatory restrictions may only be justified by invoking the Treaty provisions, but there are examples where mandatory requirements were also used to justify discriminatory rules. See Mortelmans (n 4) 636 for some examples; *LIBRO* (n 4) can also be added to that list.

[141] See Guzdek (n 104). For the broader discussion, see Chapter III sections 2.1, 3.1.4 and 3.1.5.

justification' under Art 102, offer broader and more flexible opportunities of justification through their open-ended proportionality test.[142] This seems to reflect the (usually) broader scope of the free movement rules: since relatively little conduct is filtered out at the scope or restriction stage, the justification stage needs to be more flexible in its filtering function. The increasing reliance on the *Wouters* 'inherent restriction' test in competition law may have bridged the gap between competition and free movement justifications to some extent, but that doctrine is still much less developed than proportionality under the free movement rules.

Nevertheless, here we can also find instances where the free movement justifications could be narrower. Notably, the free movement rules normally do not allow economic justifications: the mere fact that a measure is economically beneficial for a particular Member State or its industry cannot justify it.[143] In contrast, a restriction of competition under Art 101 can be justified if it 'contributes to improving the production or distribution of goods ... while allowing consumers a fair share of the resulting benefit' (Art 101/3).

6.1.3 Differences in institutions and remedies

An analysis of the functioning of free movement and competition law should not stop at the substantive law. It should also take into account which institutions apply the rules and how. Diversity in terms of the plaintiffs that can challenge certain practices, the institutions that can apply the rules, and the remedies that follow makes the convergence argument less convincing.

Firstly, whether the competition rules, free movement rules, or both can be applied in a given case depends on the procedural setting. Secondly, the decentralization of competition enforcement to national agencies and courts after Regulation 1/2003 makes it harder to implement convergent solutions because of the large number of institutions involved. Thirdly, the differences in remedies mean that it matters which rules are applied.

While free movement law is reserved for national and European courts, competition law is dominated by specialized agencies, starting with the Commission's DG Competition. Since the 2003 modernization package, national competition authorities and courts have had a larger role in applying Arts 101 and 102 TFEU, including the direct applicability of Art 101/3. Joining the NCAs and the Commission into the European Competition Network has stabilized a circle of practitioners specialized in competition law and economics, enabling them to build up expertise and develop common approaches to problems.[144] Judicial

[142] For two very clear examples where competition law justification did not go as far as free movement justification would have, see the discussion of *EPI* and *CNOP* in section 4.2.

[143] See the text accompanying n 103.

[144] Antonio Manganelli, Antonio Nicita, and Maria Alessandra Rossi, 'The Institutional Design of European Competition Policy' (2010) EUI RSCAS WP 2010/79; Stephen Wilks, 'Agency Escape: Decentralization or Dominance of the European Commission in the Modernization of Competition Policy?' (2005) 18 Governance 431–52; Lee McGowan, 'Theorising European Integration: Revisiting Neo-functionalism and Testing its Suitability for Explaining the

review of the agencies' decisions is provided by national and European courts.[145] The General Court provides judicial review of Commission decisions, and the Court of Justice acts on appeal against the General Court's judgments. While the administrative model dominates competition enforcement in Europe, there is still the possibility for national courts to apply competition law directly in adjudicating private disputes, in particular damages claims.[146]

The free movement rules, conversely, are not enforced by a dedicated institutional apparatus. The Commission can challenge practices as contrary to the free movement rules, but only in an infringement action against a Member State, which is of limited relevance to cases of private regulation because private actors cannot be defendants (of course, this procedure could also be used to apply the competition rules against the Member States if they are complicit in anticompetitive arrangements). Thus, the majority of free movement cases related to this book are likely to come from national courts that deal with private disputes, with the possibility of a preliminary reference to the Court of Justice.

This institutional design is summarized in the following Table:

Table 1 The Institutional Design of Competition and Free Movement Enforcement

	Free movement law	Competition law
Public enforcement	Commission vs. Member States (not directly against private regulators) before the Court of Justice	Commission / NCA vs. private actor infringing Arts 101/102; judicial review possible by the General Court with appeal to the Court of Justice, or by national courts in case of NCAs; Commission vs. Member State (possible for co-regulatory schemes in which Member States are complicit in anticompetitive private action) before the CJEU
Private enforcement	Private actor vs. private actor before national courts; Possible reference for a preliminary ruling to the CJEU	

Development of EC Competition Policy?' (2007) 11 European Integration Online Papers; Firat Cengiz, 'Regulation 1/2003 Revisited' (Tilburg Law and Economics Center Discussion Paper, 2009); Mislav Mataija, 'The European Competition Network and the Shaping of EU Competition Policy' (2011) 6 Croatian Yearbook of European Law and Policy 75.

145 See for example Laura Parret, 'Judicial Protection after Modernisation of Competition Law' (2005) 32(4) Legal Issues of Economic Integration 339.

146 This possibility remains difficult, as there is still no framework for the effective private enforcement of competition law in most of the Member States, due to problems of evidence, inability to obtain satisfactory damages, problems with relying on agency/Commission decisions, etc. See *The Judicial Application of Competition Law: Proceedings of the FIDE XXIV Congress Madrid 2010 Vol. 2* (Gil Carlos Rodriguez Iglesias and Luis Ortiz Blanco (eds), Facultad de Derecho Universidad Complutense 2010). The Directive 2014/104/EU of the European Parliament and of the Council on certain rules governing actions for damages under national law for infringements of the competition law provisions of the Member States and of the European Union (2014) OJ L349 has been adopted to make private enforcement more effective. See also Communication of the Commission on quantifying harm in actions for damages based on breaches of Arts 101 or 102 of the Treaty on the Functioning of the European Union C (2013) 3440.

This simple overview presents several problems for a convergent reading which would equate the two sets of rules or explicitly require the outcomes to be reconciled—although it does not necessarily speak against using certain elements of one of them as inspiration when interpreting the other. Firstly, competition agencies do not have the power to apply the free movement rules, and competition cases before the Court of Justice on appeal have their roots in a Commission decision based on Regulation 1/2003, under which the Commission is not authorized to apply the free movement rules.[147] This means that the free movement and competition rules might be applied together only before a national court, and before the Court of Justice in case of reference for a preliminary ruling.[148] This may lead to different interpretations of the competition rules by agencies—not presented with the overlap issue—and national and European courts which, in the adjudication of private disputes, might pursue a convergent reading.

Secondly, the decentralized competition law enforcement mechanism makes a convergent reading especially difficult. Under the rules in force prior to the adoption of Regulation 1/2003, convergence between the free movement and competition rules could have to some extent been managed by the Commission, as the only body authorized to directly apply all of the Treaty competition provisions. Article 101/3 is particularly relevant here, as it could have allowed the Commission to consider arguments related to the free movement rules, by, for example, refusing justification of schemes that also restrict free movement.[149] The relationship of the free movement and competition rules today is a matter that can be decided on by a variety of national courts. The risk that the convergent reading will distort the interpretation of various elements of the two legal tests therefore increases.

Thirdly, remedies are an important reason to keep the two sets of rules distinct.[150] Infringements of free movement law are sanctioned only with a duty of the court adjudicating the dispute (a national court, possibly assisted by a reference to the CJEU) to disapply the offending measure, according to the *Simmenthal* mandate.[151] Of course, in a standard case where a Member State is

[147] In *Meca-Medina* (n 47) paras 57–59, the Court made it clear that appeals to Commission competition decisions—as well as, presumably, the decisions themselves—cannot consider infringements of the free movement rules.

[148] But see Mortelmans (n 4) 632, who draws the opposite conclusion, citing Joined cases C-147/97 and C-148/97 *Deutsche Post AG v Gesellschaft für Zahlungssysteme mbH GZS* (C-147/97) and *Citicorp Kartenservice GmbH* (C-148/97) [2000] ECR I-825 and Case C-379/98 *PreussenElektra AG v Schhleswag AG, in the presence of Windpark Reußenköge III GmbH and Land Schleswig-Holstein* [2001] ECR I-2099 as types of cases where, presumably, national competition authorities should also apply the free movement rules. Mortelmans's claim seems to be focused on the substantive, rather than on the procedural aspect.

[149] See n 90.

[150] Shelanski (n 75) 696 discusses the US doctrine, after *Trinko* (n 86), 540 US 398 (2004) and *Credit Suisse v Billing* 551 US 264 (2007), of excluding antitrust scrutiny in regulated sectors. One reason for doing so is to avoid the situation where finding a violation of antitrust would also mean finding a violation of the sector-specific regulation, leading to more intrusive remedies being applied.

[151] Case 70/77 *Simmenthal SpA v Amministrazione delle finanze* [1978] ECR 1453, p 21.

found to infringe the free movement rules, the court's decision is likely to have an impact beyond the four corners of the dispute: even if there is no direct mechanism under EU law to render these offending measures invalid, the Member State would have to eliminate or adapt the measure in order to avoid further litigation, in particular by the Commission. But how does this relate to private actors who violate the free movement rules? There is no equivalent opportunity for the Commission to follow up on a court judgment in order to ensure that the private actor does not infringe the free movement rules in the future. There are no specific remedies for infringing conduct that can be imposed at the EU level. Thus, even if the private regulator's practices or measures are found to be infringing, it is largely up to the national legal system to ensure that they are accountable. Whether a private regulator's measure found by a national court to violate the free movement rules has to be declared null and void, and whether damages can be sought, is a matter for national procedural rules, provided that these are sufficiently effective and that they provide remedies equivalent to those available for breaches of domestic law.[152]

The competition rules, on the other hand, may provide more extensive and more detailed remedies. Firstly, Art 101/2 provides that 'any agreements or decisions prohibited pursuant to this Article shall be automatically void'. This provision has to be applied by all national courts. The Court's case law, moreover, has established that nullity on the basis of Art 101/2 is *erga omnes*, having effect in relation to third parties as well, and that it applies *ex tunc*, rendering the agreement void of all legal effects from the moment of its conclusion.[153]

Moreover, the *Courage* judgment requires that it be 'open to any individual to claim damages for loss caused to him by a contract or by conduct liable to restrict or distort competition' in violation of Art 101.[154] While it could be argued that the useful effect of EU law (as well as an analogy with *Francovich*)[155] requires

[152] See, recently, Case C-240/09 *Lesoochranárske zoskupenie VLK v Ministerstvo životného prostredia Slovenskej republiky* [2011] ECR I-1255, para 48: '... the detailed procedural rules governing actions for safeguarding an individual's rights under EU law must be no less favourable than those governing similar domestic actions (principle of equivalence) and must not make it in practice impossible or excessively difficult to exercise rights conferred by EU law (principle of effectiveness).' See, among others, also: Case 45-76 *Comet BV v Produktschap voor Siergewassen* [1976] ECR 2043, para 13; Case C-312/93 *Peterbroeck, Van Campenhout & Cie SCS v Belgian State* [1995] ECR I-4599, para 12; Case C-432/05 *Unibet (London) Ltd and Unibet (International) Ltd v Justitiekanslern* [2007] ECR I-2271, para 43; and Case C-268/06 *Impact v Minister for Agriculture and Food and Others* [2008] ECR I-2483, para 46.

[153] See Case C-453/99 *Courage Ltd v Bernard Crehan and Bernard Crehan v Courage Ltd and Others* [2001] ECR I-6297, para 22 and Case 22-71 *Béguelin Import Co. v S.A.G.L. Import Export* [1971] ECR 949, para 29. See also Alfonso Lamadrid de Pablo and Luis Ortiz Blanco, 'Nullity/Voidness: An Overview of EU and National Case Law' 49199 e-Competitions.

[154] *Courage* (n 153) para 26. See also Szyszczak (n 32) 100–02.

[155] Joined cases C-6/90 and C-9/90 *Andrea Francovich and Danila Bonifaci and others v Italian Republic* [1991] ECR I-5357, paras 31–37 first established the principle whereby 'the Member States are obliged to make good loss and damage caused to individuals by breaches of [EU] law for which they can be held responsible'. By analogy, if an individual is capable of breaching the rules of primary EU law, the effective application of EU law would imply that other individuals harmed by that conduct can seek redress and obtain damages.

the same in the free movement context, the CJEU has so far never stated that national courts should provide compensation to victims of private infringements of free movement. This difference will be further increased by the recent Directive on antitrust damages actions, which requires Member States to facilitate private damages actions through, among others, rules on evidence disclosure, passing-on defences, time limits, settlements, and the recognition of competition authorities' decisions in private litigation.[156]

Because of all this, it makes a difference whether a particular measure is found to violate the free movement provisions, the competition provisions, or both. A convergent reading could obfuscate this fundamental point. Skipping the competition rules because a violation of free movement was already found may deprive the plaintiff of the more effective remedy. Equating a violation of free movement law with a violation of competition law where, perhaps, an independent competition law analysis on its own would not find an infringement, would impose overly strict remedies.

In addition, the Commission has an entirely separate and quite powerful toolbox when applying the competition rules. It can, for example, adopt a decision accepting commitments by undertakings.[157] When an infringement decision is made, the Commission is able to order the termination of an infringement directly,[158] order the undertakings not to engage in further behaviour of 'like effect',[159] and even impose a wide variety of behavioural or structural remedies.[160] Finally, the Commission is authorized to impose substantial fines on undertakings,[161] the level of which has grown over the years. Similar competences are also conferred on national competition authorities. As mentioned *supra*, NCAs and the Commission as a competition enforcer are not authorized to apply the free movement rules together with the competition rules. Nevertheless, in the long term, a convergent reading could induce both courts and competition agencies in the Member States to equate free movement violations with competition violations, imposing a highly powerful and intrusive set of remedies instead of the more limited possibilities provided by the free movement rules.

It may be understandable for the Court of Justice to gloss over the differences in remedies when, as in *Bosman* or *Fra.bo*, it finds a violation of the free movement rules and then skips the analysis under the competition rules. After all, the Court does not decide on remedies in preliminary rulings. The national courts, however, do, and they are likely to follow the analysis of the Court. By skipping one of the two legal tests, then, the Court of Justice may inadvertently distort the outcome of the case.

156 See n 146.

157 Article 9 of Regulation 1/2003 (n 6) See also Bellamy & Child, *European Community Law of Competition* (Peter Roth and Vivien Rose (eds) (6th edn, Oxford University Press 2008) section 13.113 et seq.

158 Article 7/1 of Regulation 1/2003 (n 6).

159 Bellamy & Child (n 157) section 13.127.

160 ibid section 13.128.

161 Article 23/2 of Regulation 1/2003 (n 6).

6.2 Selection or conflict rules

A second major strategy that is often proposed as a response to the overlap of the free movement and competition rules is to impose conflict or selection rules. This approach, too, could have different forms.

Firstly, it could draw a line between the two sets of rules depending on certain features of the cases that they should apply to. Conduct could be categorized into the free movement box or the competition box according to the relevant facts. For example, 'market behaviour' would fall under competition law and 'regulatory behaviour' under free movement law; autonomous conduct would fall under competition law, and State-influenced conduct under free movement law. Semmelmann has suggested, for example, that the key is to identify 'whether the parties at issue represent their own interests (which would suggest that competition law would be the more appropriate set of rules) or whether there is a link to the public interest which would lead to the application of the free movement provisions'.[162]

Alternatively, a selection rule could acknowledge the possibility of simultaneous application to the same conduct, but impose some selection principles that relate to the rules themselves. For example, it could consider one of them to be *lex specialis* that should govern in cases of overlap. It could apply the one that is more favourable to the defendant (*in dubio pro reo*). Finally, it could consider one of them, most likely the free movement rules, to be more fundamental, so that only a small set of more serious violations (whatever the benchmark may be in that respect) rise to a level where they also fall under the more serious set of rules.

As I have pointed out in section 3.2, arguments in favour of separating the two sets of rules or preventing overlap sometimes confuse these two ways in which they could be separated. Paradoxically, however, the argument for conceptual separation or doctrinal separation (including the second kind of selection rule that I have just described) is premised on the possibility of factual overlap, thus making a conflict rule based on facts (the first kind of selection rule) superfluous. In other words, if the rules were actually applied to completely distinct sets of facts, there would be no need to distinguish between their aims or define their relationship one way or the other.

One especially frequent version of the conflict or selection argument assumes that competition law is the 'normal' way of dealing with private actors, therefore viewing free movement scrutiny as an aberration that should be restricted as much as possible. This is usually justified on broad private autonomy grounds which may or may not be convincing on their own terms, but shed little light on the relationship between free movement and competition: if anything, competition law with its dedicated enforcement apparatus and intrusive remedies is more of an intrusion into liberty than free movement law.

162 Semmelmann (n 29) 529.

Prechal and de Vries, for example, make this point almost in passing, claiming that extending the horizontal effect of the free movement rules to all situations would be 'a disproportionate interference with and permanent risk for the exercise of contractual freedom of private parties' (a claim that is difficult to disagree with, when posed this broadly), whereas competition law should rather define the 'outer limits' of scrutiny.[163] Similarly, Snell claims that 'competition rules are much more suitable for dealing with private parties than the free movement provisions', concluding that the rules on free movement of goods and services should not apply if today's Arts 101 and 102 TFEU are available. According to him, competition law is *lex specialis* when private actors are concerned.[164]

The argument is sometimes made in a narrower way, explaining how the ability of one set of rules to adequately address certain restraints has justified or would justify limiting scrutiny under the other set of rules. Oliver and Roth, for example, claim that the limited horizontal effect of the rules on free movement of goods can be explained by the high capability of the competition rules to deal with private restraints dealing with goods.[165]

In an ideal world, a conflict rule would be desirable. It would address many of the problems associated with the *status quo* (see section 5), notably by making the decisions simpler, reducing the likelihood and gravity of errors, respecting the structural limits of both sets of rules, and making the legal position of potential defendants more predictable. The problem with this strategy, however, is that the bright lines a conflict rule might try to follow are not as bright as it seems.

Firstly, the distinctions between public and private or regulation and market are not the answer—they are the question.[166] Thus basing a conflict rule on those distinctions is bound to raise further difficulties. Even rephrasing the public–private distinction in terms of public and private interest,[167] so that for example a private actor could be seen to pursue a public interest, leads to similar problems: what makes the aim of an activity inherently public or inherently private? These arguments usually collapse into a tautology: interests are defined as public because they are usually pursued by public actors, and then their public nature is used to argue that those pursuing the interests should be treated as public actors.

The cases that this book deals with are precisely the ones where overlap between free movement and competition is most likely, and they make the limited value of these distinctions clear. When a sports association restricts the sponsorship opportunities of a professional athlete, or when a bar association restricts the entry of new professionals, is this public or private, regulation or market conduct? The

[163] Prechal and de Vries (n 2) 18.

[164] This is based on systemic arguments (competition law is subsidiary and meant to prevent the circumvention of the internal market rules), but also on its ability to deal with many private restraints, on the possibilities of conflict between the two sets of rules (in particular differences in justifications) and broader procedural powers of the Commission under competition law. Snell (n 24) 232.

[165] Peter Oliver and Wulf-Henning Roth, 'The Internal Market and the Four Freedoms' (2004) 41 Common Market Law Review 407, 423–24.

[166] See, in particular Chapter II section 2.

[167] See n 162.

answer we give to that question is not a neutral description of the case, nor is it distinct from the question of whether those activities violate EU law. It is a part of the conclusion of the legal assessment, whether we apply the competition or the free movement rules.

Odudu, for example, has argued in favour of a public–private distinction in this context.[168] Mentioning inter alia the difficulty of complying with both sets of rules at the same time, he has suggested that the different definitions of economic activity under free movement and competition law are the 'outcome of a deliberation over which mutually exclusive Treaty provisions ought to apply to a particular measure'.[169] In a later paper, however, he seems to nuance this by pointing out that the interpretation of the free movement/competition distinction has moved towards 'a functional distinction *within* Treaty provisions—how a particular Treaty provision applies depends on whether it is being applied to public or private functions'.[170]

This analysis itself shows that 'public' and 'private' are loaded words, because they inevitably underlie our determination of a case (whether the measure is restrictive, how it can be justified). As Odudu also acknowledges, this happens under either set of rules.

The second kind of selection principle that I have outlined above—relating to the rules themselves, for example *lex specialis/lex generalis*—is unworkable for different reasons. Notably, as I have tried to show when discussing the convergence argument, the relationship between the free movement and competition rules as they are currently interpreted cannot be unequivocally described at either step of the analysis. It cannot be said that one of them has a broader or a more narrow scope, that one of them covers more or fewer restrictions, nor that one of them allows for more or less generous justifications. In many cases, admittedly, the two sets of rules will point in the same direction,[171] but in others they will differ in unpredictable ways. It is impossible to say which of the rules is more or less strict—this can depend on many features of a given case. Therefore, any broad, single conflict rule that we adopt is likely to be highly imprecise and lead to unsatisfactory outcomes.

As I have argued in section 5, in some circumstances it can be desirable to limit the application of two sets of similar rules to the same type of conduct. Whether doing so by broad conflict rules is a good idea, however, is a different question. For example, in *Trinko* the US Supreme Court established a rule against the application of antitrust law in regulated sectors: where there is 'a regulatory structure

[168] See n 23.

[169] Odudu, 'Economic Activity as a Limit to Community Law' (n 119) 236 et seq. He thus took issue with AG Lenz's position in *Bosman* that there is nothing in principle to prevent overlap.

[170] Sophie Robin-Olivier, Okeoghene Odudu, and Loïc Azoulai, 'The Public/Private Divide in European Union Law' [2010] CEJEC-WP 2010/7, 4–5.

[171] See Vassilis Hatzopoulos, *Regulating Services in the European Union* (Oxford University Press, 2012) 305: 'More often than not, a measure in breach of competition rules, when it is the result of private action, will also be incompatible with the internal market rules as soon as it is reclassified as public action.'

designed to deter and remedy anticompetitive harm', antitrust law should be modestly enforced because 'the additional benefit to competition provided by antitrust enforcement will tend to be small, and it will be less plausible that the antitrust laws contemplate such additional scrutiny'.[172]

It would be tempting to apply a similar solution to the problem of this chapter, for example by limiting the application of free movement law when competition law is applicable. Again, however, this approach would run into problems. Firstly, the *Trinko* rule is based on a previously well-established presumption under US law that sectorial regulation should have precedence over antitrust in cases of conflict. There is little basis for such an argument in our context, either in favour of competition or in favour of free movement. Secondly, the *Trinko* judgment assumes that sectorial regulation imposes a more demanding standard of conduct than antitrust—something that cannot easily be stated for the free movement rules since, as outlined already, the differences between free movement and competition law cut both ways. Thirdly, as Shelanski has argued, a presumption against the application of antitrust is fully convincing only in cases where there is a possibility of outright conflict between the two disciplines (which is difficult to imagine in the context of free movement and competition), or when there is a danger of confusion of different legal requirements. Shelanski calls this the anti-bootstrapping principle:[173] one type of liability should not be represented as the other. As long as there is clarity in this respect, dual application should not be an issue as such.[174]

7. Conclusion—Maintaining Separation

As I have pointed out, the overlapping application of free movement and competition law is not without costs. Nevertheless, the two broad solutions that are sometimes put forward—convergence and conflict rules—present more problems than advantages. How can the difficulties associated with the *status quo* be addressed, then?

The answer I propose here is relatively modest. Instead of converging or strictly separating the two sets of rules, it is to allow the overlap to continue, but to limit the number of cases where it happens, be explicit about its costs and benefits, and to apply both sets of rules fully, avoiding shortcuts.

[172] See Shelanski (n 75) 699. [173] ibid 692–99.

[174] This is why muddling the differences between free movement and competition law is particularly problematic: it may lead to certain elements of the two tests being confused, changing the standards of liability under either. As a side note, it does not seem as if *Trinko* has found fertile ground in EU law, even in the narrower context of the relationship between competition law and sector-specific regulation, having been rejected in judgments such as Case C-280/08 P *Deutsche Telekom AG v European Commission* [2010] ECR I-09555, para 92 and Case T-398/07 *Spain v Commission* ECLI:EU:T:2012:173, paras 55–56. In the context of the relationship between EU and national competition law, the Court has similarly made it clear that overlap is not problematic in itself (see n 83).

The first element of this approach is to acknowledge the possibility of dual application and treat the two tests as separate. This means that a case of overlap can, in principle, have any of the following outcomes:

1) Violation of both competition law and free movement;
2) Violation of competition law, but not of free movement;
3) Violation of free movement, but not of competition law; and
4) No violation of either.

The second element is to avoid hybrid forms of analysis and shortcuts. The two legal tests should be treated as distinct. The fact that, for example a violation of free movement law is found should neither automatically mean that there is also a violation of competition law, nor that the competition law analysis is superfluous. In fact, skipping competition law analysis after a violation of free movement is found, a common practice of the Court of Justice, can be particularly problematic.[175] If certain elements of the legal assessment under one set of rules can be helpful under the other, they can be used, but it should be made clear that this was done for reasons of judicial economy, not because the law requires an identical response. For example, if a private regulator's conduct is justified by a legitimate interest under the *Wouters* test, the same arguments could serve to justify it under the free movement proportionality test. This, however, should not imply that convergence between the two justification tests is legally required. Broadly speaking, arguments that are relevant under one analysis can often be used under the other as well—in itself, this is not problematic.[176]

Viewing the two sets of rules as distinct may have the perfectly acceptable consequence that a particular measure escapes liability altogether. The fact that certain measures might escape both forms of scrutiny does not mean that there is a *lacuna* in the law, as is sometimes claimed.[177] There is only a *lacuna* if formalistic arguments enable measures that have a serious impact on the internal market to circumvent both sets of rules, for example if a hybrid public–private actor can claim to be exempt from the free movement rules because of its private features as well as from the competition rules because of its public features.[178] A functional interpretation of both sets of rules on a case-by-case basis can prevent this from happening, but responding to their overlap with sweeping distinctions (such as the one between public and private interest) can make such a *lacuna* more likely.

[175] The opposite may be less troublesome, at least insofar as competition law remedies go far beyond the free movement remedies. In practical terms, little is gained for the plaintiff by finding a violation of free movement on top of a violation of competition law. There may, however, be other reasons for applying the free movement rules, for example some particular aspects of an undertaking's conduct may not fall under the competition rules.

[176] As has been discussed *supra*, cases as diverse as *Consten & Grundig* (n 33), *Dassonville* (n 35), *Wouters* (n 67), *Commission v Italy* (2011) (n 46), and *Murphy* (see n 58 and n 91) clearly show that arguments and concepts have been copied from one set of rules into the other.

[177] See for example Snell (n 24), claiming that a lacuna takes place if the free movement rules are not applied to non-undertakings.

[178] See Maduro (n 8).

All this should not, however, mean that overlap should be encouraged. As I argued, it should be avoided. The best way to do that, however, is to clarify the outer limits of the rules, on their own terms. It should be made clear, for example, that even though there is no broad principle preventing the application of the free movement rules to private action, only a fraction of private behaviour will actually be found to restrict free movement. This, as I have argued in Chapter II, could be translated into a special free movement *de minimis* rule for private actors, or simply into a clearer definition of a restriction based on the actual ability to impede the access to the market of a Member State.[179] On the competition law side, making it clear that certain activities, such as those that reflect a democratic choice of a Member State to organize a public service on a non-market basis, fall out of the scope of competition law can be helpful in eliminating the fear that all forms of co-regulation will be subjected to an economic efficiency benchmark imposed by the 'standard' competition law analysis.

Ultimately, the ability of free movement law to deal with a certain class of measures effectively can be used as a supporting argument to limit competition law scrutiny, or vice versa. On its own, such an argument means relatively little: the mere existence of one rule does not mean that the other rule should not be applied. However, if there are good reasons to limit the applicability of, for example, competition law in a particular narrowly defined context, the fact that free movement scrutiny remains an option can alleviate the possible concerns for the preservation of the internal market. Again, this argument should be made explicitly.[180] A good example is the area of social policy and the activities of trade unions: as described *supra*, collective agreements are removed from the scope of the competition rules because they could constitute restrictions in an inordinate number of cases, without much possibility of justification on public policy grounds in that type of analysis. They are not, however, removed from the scope of the free movement rules, arguably because in that area restrictions are not as likely[181] and because the free movement rules allow for a broad set of justifications.

Broadly put, the relative costs and benefits of allowing the overlap, compared to the costs and benefits of restricting the applicability of one set of rules, can vary across contexts. Costs of error, for example, can increase when applying both in a very complex or technical area. This argument, however, should be made in a context-specific way and dealt with explicitly, instead of either separating the two sets of rules across a broad, formalistic divide or converging them into an unpredictable, hybrid form of analysis which disregards their outer limits.

179 See Lindh (n 96).
180 See, for example, Snell (n 24) 232 et seq.
181 *Viking Line* (n 50) para 52.

V

Conditional Autonomy

EU Internal Market Law and the Private Regulation of Sport

1. Introduction

Sport is one of the paradigmatic examples of private regulation. Sporting rules, which cover much more than just the 'rules of the game', are overwhelmingly developed and enforced by a network of private organizations, in manifold and ever-changing relationships to each other. National sporting organizations are responsible for the organization and structure of a particular sport in a certain EU Member State. These rules may be reinforced or limited by legislation of that Member State.[1] In addition, there are international sporting bodies, whose standards and procedures are at least *de facto* binding for national federations and athletes. These international bodies may be set up either on a global or regional scale or both, such as in football (UEFA and FIFA).[2] Outside the confines of a particular sporting discipline, there are some rules of public international law as well as private or hybrid public–private regulation that relate to sports in general, most notably the Olympic Movement whose rules apply to all Olympic sports.

In addition to rule-setting, dispute settlement and enforcement in the sporting realm are often privately handled, as sporting bodies endeavour to exclude or circumvent the intervention of States.[3] The best-known example of this is the Court of Arbitration for Sports (CAS), an arbitral tribunal with its seat in Switzerland. CAS decisions are subject to limited review by the Swiss Federal Tribunal. Due to its primary location in Switzerland, with additional chambers

[1] See Robert Siekmann and Janwillem Soek, 'Models of Sport Governance within the European Union' in James A R Nafziger and Stephen F Ross (eds), *Handbook on International Sports Law* (Edward Elgar 2011), discussing the various more or less interventionist models of Member State involvement in regulating sport (115 et seq).

[2] On the international governance of sports, see James A R Nafziger, 'International Sports Law' in Nafziger and Ross (n 1). The more influential organizations tend to be those in charge of commercially attractive sports, such as football. See Stephen Weatherill, *European Sports Law: Collected Papers* (T.M.C. Asser Press 2007) 81.

[3] See, for example, the speech of Michel Platini, President of UEFA, at the 12th Council of Europe Conference of Ministers responsible for Sport in Belgrade (15 March 2012) <http://hub.coe.int/20120315-platini-belgrade>: 'Let us not allow purely sporting disputes to be taken before state courts. Ask yourselves, what would happen if the rules were interpreted differently in Madrid, Rome and Brussels?'

in Sydney and New York, CAS decision-making is to a significant extent isolated from the supervision of the CJEU.[4]

The relationship between sport and law has always been tense, and a number of national and international legal mechanisms fit awkwardly in the sport context. For example, the general rules of labour law can be at odds with the activity of professional football or basketball players, especially when it comes to issues like the duration and cancellation of contracts. The segregation of competitions according to gender, nationality, and disability raises concerns of discrimination under national, EU, or international law. National law may also have quite extensive regulations on various issues of interest to sport, such as the status of professional athletes, legal structures, financing, transparency, etc. Nevertheless, the majority of the decisions of crucial importance for the structure and organization of sports writ large are made on the transnational level by sporting bodies themselves.

The fact that EU law is itself supranational has, at least partly, increased the likelihood of high-profile clashes with the sporting world. The central issue for EU law has always been to what extent sport should be regulated autonomously by its own governing bodies. In other words, should sport be left alone because it is 'special'?[5] Despite this lingering question, EU law has had a significant impact on the world of sports, leading to a number of changes to the organization of competitions, the course of athletes' careers, and commercial activities such as sponsorship and media rights.

Various practices of these bodies have given rise to controversy. They have been accused of low governance standards, a lack of transparency, and outright corruption.[6] Well-known athletes have spent years embroiled in legal battles

[4] On this, see the Opinion of AG Lenz in Case C-415/93 *Union royale belge des sociétés de football association ASBL v Jean-Marc Bosman, Royal club liégeois SA v Jean-Marc Bosman and others and Union des associations européennes de football (UEFA) v Jean-Marc Bosman* [1995] ECR I-4921, para 109, rejecting the argument that Belgian courts had no jurisdiction in the main action: 'It is beyond doubt … that the rules of UEFA apply *inter alia* in all the Member States of the Community … *Finally, it should be observed that that question could not be discussed at all in the Swiss courts or referred to the Court of Justice under [Art 267 TFEU]*.' (emphasis added). See also M Wathelet, 'Sport Governance and EU Legal Order: Present and Future' in Simon Gardiner, Richard Parrish, and Robert Siekmann (eds), *EU, Sport, Law and Policy: Regulation, Re-Regulation and Representation* (T.M.C. Asser Press 2009) 71. Switzerland being an EFTA member, however, it is to an extent bound by the rules of EU internal market law. For example, EU competition law has been found by Swiss courts to be relevant, as a public policy ground, for the adjudication of disputes in the area of sport. See Commercial Court of Zurich ZR 104 (2005) 97 No 27. For a different view, however, see the judgment of the Swiss Federal Tribunal in *Tensacciai S.P.A v Freyssinet Terra Armata S.R.L* 4P 278/2005.

[5] 'Should the "law" of international sporting bodies be treated as an autonomous system worthy of protection from disruption by state law or the law of transnational entities such as the EC? The intellectual case could be made that this is an internally coherent system, which responds to the special interests of sport, and which should not be invaded by differently motivated, alien systems.' Weatherill (n 2) 141–42. Weatherill also points out a debate with which this chapter is only marginally concerned: to what extent should the private regulation of sports be treated as law. On this, see Antoine Duval, 'Lex Sportiva: A Playground for Transnational Law' (2013) 19 European Law Journal 822.

[6] A recent example is the controversy over the so-called Garcia Report on corruption in world football, which FIFA commissioned but then refused to publish its integral version. See the Statement

against anti-doping sanctions.[7] Commercially successful clubs have argued for a bigger share of the financial pie.[8] Ticket-selling arrangements and joint selling of media rights have been disputed (see section 4).

While these issues are of much broader political and legal significance, EU law has translated them largely into issues of free movement and competition. These two sets of rules have provided by far the most powerful framework through which the private regulation of sport has been challenged and reformed. This has occasionally led EU economic law into uncharted territory and forced it to adapt, as I have argued in more general terms in Chapters II and III. The use of competition law against anti-doping decisions is a good example. The German speed-skater Claudia Pechstein has recently relied on competition law to successfully challenge the way in which anti-doping decisions taken against her were reviewed by the Court for Arbitration for Sport and the Swiss courts. The Oberlandesgericht of Munich found a violation of the German equivalent of Art 102 TFEU (relying heavily on CJEU case law) and thus a reason to refuse the enforcement of the arbitral award against Ms Pechstein, essentially, because of the biased procedure for appointing CAS arbitrators.[9] As discussed in Chapter III, this in effect turns competition law into a sort of administrative law for sporting bodies, instead of a narrow mechanism for the promotion of effective competition in the marketplace. As I will show, a similar dynamic can be seen in a number of free movement and competition cases.

In this chapter, I will briefly describe the characteristics of sports regulation (sections 1.1. and 1.2), and the way it has been approached under EU policy (section 2), the free movement (section 3) and competition rules (section 4). I will then assess the relationship between those two forms of legal scrutiny. The two sets of rules have, I argue, converged to an unusual extent in this area, and have been used in a re-regulatory fashion, based on the notion of 'regulatory autonomy' described in Chapter II. Under both sets of rules, however, EU law can be expected to defer to the measures of sporting bodies that are non-discriminatory and based on good governance principles (sections 5 and 6). Finally, I will argue that institutional choices and strategies, rather than legal doctrine as such, have been decisive in how the two sets of rules were interpreted and applied to sports (section 7).

of the Chairman of the Adjudicatory Chamber of the FIFA Ethics Committee on the Report on the Inquiry into the 2018/2022 FIFA World Cup Bidding Process (13 November 2014) <http://www.fifa.com/mm/document/affederation/footballgovernance/02/47/41/75/statementchairmanadjcheckert_neutral.pdf>.

[7] See, generally, Stephen Weatherill, 'Anti-doping Revisited—The Demise of the Rule of "Purely Sporting Interest"' (2006) 27 European Competition Law Review 645; Richard W Pound and Kerwin Clarke, 'Doping in Sport' in Nafziger and Ross (n 1).

[8] See Ben Van Rompuy, *Economic Efficiency: The Sole Concern of Modern Antitrust Policy?* (Kluwer Law International 2012) 294.

[9] Antoine Duval, 'The *Pechstein* Ruling of the OLG München (English Translation)' (6 February 2015) <http://ssrn.com/abstract=2561297>. See also David McArdle, 'CAS 2009/A/1912–1913 *Pechstein v International Skating Union*' in Jack Anderson (ed), *Leading Cases in Sports Law* (Springer 2013).

1.1 The specificity of sport and the European sport model

Faced with legal and political challenges, the strategy of the sporting world has been to assert immunity, or at least argue that the law should take into account the 'special nature' of sport. Over time, this argument has become more refined. While some aspects of sport regulation such as ticket selling or media rights can easily be described as economic activity subject to the free movement and competition rules, even decades of case law of the CJEU have not clarified how far the argument for specificity holds with regard to other issues.

The reason for this is that certain factors distinguish sport from other economic activities. Firstly, sport is based on interdependence between competitors. Credible competition or 'competitive balance' between clubs and athletes needs to exist in order to keep leagues and tournaments uncertain in outcome and attractive to spectators. This requires some sort of co-operation between clubs, which may entail restrictions of competition or even outright re-distribution.[10] Moreover, certain means of competing that would be perfectly acceptable in other markets could damage the integrity of a sport. For example, in professional football and basketball, players may normally be transferred from one club to another only within predefined periods.[11]

Another point of specificity is the close link between professional and amateur sports. While professional sport receives most of the media attention and is obviously of great economic significance, the vast majority of athletes are amateurs. Professional and amateur sports depend on each other, which may involve redistribution of resources.

Lastly, sport can be considered specific because of its connection to a variety of public interest objectives, such as education, health, tolerance, solidarity, and culture.[12] These objectives are in some sense reflected at all levels of sport regulation and are sometimes relied upon to justify restrictive measures. They are also increasingly accepted by the European institutions as policy goals which the EU should be actively pursuing. At the opposite end of the spectrum, sport is often associated with undesirable activities such as hooliganism, racism, doping, match-fixing, and other forms of corruption. The fight against these has also been prominent in EU policy documents.

All these to some extent cause the most important specificity of them all: the way in which sport is regulated. One aspect of this is the dominance of private

[10] Weatherill (n 2) 103. Budzinski, however, points out: 'The reluctance of the Commission to embrace the competitive balance defense as a justification for antitrust exemptions ... corresponds to a growing skepticism in the sports-economics literature.' Oliver Budzinski, 'The Institutional Framework for Doing Sports Business: Principles of EU Competition Policy in Sports Markets' (2012) 11 International Journal of Sport Management and Marketing 44, 60.

[11] More precisely, players may only be re-registered at a different club if their transfer was effected during the 'transfer window'. On this, see for example Case C-176/96 *Jyri Lehtonen and Castors Canada Dry Namur-Braine ASBL v Fédération royale belge des sociétés de basket-ball ASBL (FRBSB)* [2000] ECR I-2681.

[12] This is highlighted by the Commission, 'White Paper on Sport' COM (2007) 391 final, section 2.

regulation. The other, especially important in professional sports, is the so-called 'European sport model'[13] with features such as monopolistic 'pyramid' structures,[14] promotion, and relegation.[15] The best teams are usually part of a professional league, whose interests do not always converge with those of amateur teams or those of the federation that governs both groups. In the US, on the contrary, leagues within a sport tend to compete with each other and are not typically governed by a single national federation. There is also no promotion or relegation. This, however, leads to stronger redistribution mechanisms within the leagues in order to preserve competitive balance, such as drafts (under which the less successful teams get the first pick among incoming players) and salary caps.

All of these specificities have affected the way EU law, notably free movement and competition law, approaches sport. From the outset, the central issue has been the scope of the so-called 'sporting exception'—the extent to which the EU institutions grant sporting bodies a degree of autonomy due to the specific nature of sport. The early distinction between measures that relate to economic activities and so-called 'purely sporting rules' has been continuously refined. The current position, which seems to be common to both free movement and competition law, is that, while a level of autonomy for sports organizations clearly exists, it is impossible to draw an *ex ante* dividing line between 'sporting' and 'economic rules'. This case-by-case approach is important not so much in terms of substance, but in terms of who decides. By defining the limits of EU law in such a way, the EU institutions and other institutions applying EU law, notably the Commission as a competition enforcer, the Court of Justice, as well as national competition agencies and courts, have a broad mandate to scrutinize the measures of sport regulators. As was described in general terms in Chapter II, however, this openness to scrutiny in principle usually tends to be compensated by a light touch in reviewing the substance of the measures of sport bodies.

[13] ibid 12 et seq. For an economic angle, see Wladimir Andreff, 'Some Comparative Economics of the Organization of Sports: Competition and Regulation in North American vs. European Professional Team Sports Leagues' (2011) 8 European Journal of Comparative Economics 3.

[14] This means that, for a particular sport, there is a single national body, usually a member of or at least governed by the rules of a single European body that in turn belongs to a worldwide body. Budzinski (n 10) 47–48, citing Philip Kienapfel and Andreas Stein, 'The Application of Articles 81 and 82 EC in the Sport Sector' (2007) 3 Competition Policy Newsletter 6. For English football, for example, the chain would be: FA (Football Association), UEFA (Union of European Football Associations), and FIFA (Fédération Internationale de Football Association). The picture is more complex, of course. The FA is a member of both UEFA and FIFA; the Premier League is only partly disciplined by the FA, and the lower leagues even less so. In some sports, national associations are members of a worldwide body, and there are only European competitions, not dedicated associations. British Rowing is thus a member of FISA (International Federation of Rowing Associations), as well as of the British Olympic Association.

[15] Both professional and amateur clubs usually belong to a league, and leagues are based on a promotion and relegation system—the best teams from lower leagues advance and the worst teams from higher leagues are relegated.

1.2 Measures that can raise EU law concerns

EU law does not dispute that only eleven people per team can play in a football match, or that the hitting surface of a tennis racket may not exceed 39.4 cm in length. These would be viewed as purely sporting rules that do not call for legal scrutiny. However, a surprisingly broad array of rules and practices of sporting organizations have been disputed under EU law. This includes, among others:

- rules that are related to the actual practice of sport but may have economic consequences, for example limits on the number of participants in a tournament or the 'home and away' rules for matches;
- rules restricting the transfer of players between clubs;
- rules restricting the access of clubs or athletes to competitions, for example those on club licensing (the controversial UEFA Financial Fair Play Regulations,[16] prohibiting clubs from operating at a loss, would also fall in this category);
- rules restricting the pursuit of professions such as coaches or players' agents;
- rules restricting the legal form, ownership, and partnerships of clubs;
- nationality-based limits on the participation of athletes in competitions, including indirectly discriminatory measures (eg the 'home grown' rules in football, requiring clubs to field a minimum number of players that were trained in that club as youths);
- rules on the distribution of gains from economic activities;
- co-ordination of purchasing or selling (eg joint selling of media rights);
- closed internal jurisdictions, waivers of judicial review, mandatory arbitration;
- rules on procedures and sanctions for unwanted practices, for example in doping;
- conflicts of interest (eg if a market participant is allowed to license new entrants).

Some of these rules were examined by the Commission and the EU Courts and were found to infringe EU law, while others were exonerated. In various policy documents of the Commission in particular, one can find indicative lists of sporting practices that almost always violate, potentially violate, or normally do not violate EU free movement and competition law.[17]

In the sections that follow, I will provide an overview of how these two sets of rules were applied. Before that, however, I will describe how sports have been

[16] The rules can be found at <http://www.uefa.org/MultimediaFiles/Download/Tech/uefaorg/General/01/80/54/10/1805410_DOWNLOAD.pdf>.

[17] For example, the Commission, 'The EU and Sport: Background and Context', Accompanying document to the White Paper on Sport (Staff Working Document) COM(2007) 391, 70 et seq distinguishes, regarding the competition provisions, between rules that are 'unlikely to infringe' (rules on the participation of athletes in competitions, 'home and away' rules, rules on multiple club ownership, nationality clauses for national teams, anti-doping rules, rules on transfer periods,

addressed by the EU Treaties and to what extent the EU can be described as having a sports policy. The application of free movement and competition law to sports regulators should be seen in that context.

2. Sport and the EU Political Process

Because of the lack of a clear legislative competence in the area, EU legislation has dealt with sport only incidentally. The Audiovisual Media Services Directive allows the Member States to require public access to certain broadcasts of major interest, including sporting events.[18] Also of relevance for sports professionals are the Diploma Directive, the Annex to which refers inter alia to recreational services,[19] and the general Services Directive.[20] Broadly speaking, however, even the strictly economic aspects of sport have not been the subject of comprehensive EU legislation.

The Lisbon Treaty may lead to some limited changes in the EU's engagement with this area, given that for the first time it includes a specific provision on sport, Art 165 TFEU:[21]

> The Union shall contribute to the promotion of European sporting issues, while taking account of the specific nature of sport, its structures based on voluntary activity and its social and educational function.
>
> ... Union action shall be aimed at ...
>
> —developing the European dimension in sport, by promoting fairness and openness in sporting competitions and cooperation between bodies responsible for sports, and by protecting the physical and moral integrity of sportsmen and sportswomen, especially the youngest sportsmen and sportswomen.[22]

and club licensing rules) and rules which 'may infringe' (rules shielding commercial activities from competition, rules on exclusive internal judiciaries, other nationality clauses, transfer rules, rules on sports agent licensing).

[18] Directive 2010/13/EU of the European Parliament and of the Council on the co-ordination of certain provisions laid down by law, regulation, or administrative action in Member States concerning the provision of audiovisual media services [2010] OJ L95/1 Art 15. Case C-204/11 P *FIFA v Commission* (1) ECLI:EU:C:2013:477 and Case C-205/11 P *FIFA v Commission* (2) ECLI:EU:C:2013:478; and Case C-201/11 P *UEFA v Commission* ECLI:EU:C:2013:519 concerned a challenge by FIFA and UEFA against their competitions' being placed on this list.

[19] Directive 2005/36/EC of the European Parliament and of the Council on the recognition of professional qualifications [2005] OJ L255/22 Annex IV List III part 4.

[20] Directive 2006/123/EC of the European Parliament and of the Council on services in the internal market [2006] OJ L376. See in particular recitals 33 and 35. On both the Directives, see Samuli Miettinen, 'Regulating Sports Services in Community Law' in Richard Parrish, Simon Gardiner, and Robert C R Siekmann (eds), *EU, Sport, Law and Policy: Regulation, Re-regulation and Representation* (T.M.C. Asser Press 2009).

[21] The provision appears in Title XII of the TFEU (Education, vocational training, youth, and sport). For an analysis, see Stephen Weatherill, 'EU Sports Law: The Effect of the Lisbon Treaty' in Andrea Biondi, Piet Eeckhout, and Stefanie Ripley (eds), *EU Law After Lisbon* (OUP 2012).

[22] The article goes on to provide that the Union and the Member States shall 'foster cooperation with third countries and the competent international organisations' in sports, including the Council of Europe.

Importantly, for the achievement of these goals, the EU legislator is only allowed to adopt incentive measures, excluding any harmonization of laws.

By all accounts, the impact of this provision has so far been modest. Even though sporting bodies have lobbied aggressively for its inclusion (especially for the reference to the 'specific nature of sport'),[23] it may even be the case that Art 165 encourages rather than limits the interventions of EU law in the sporting world.

It would be wrong, however, to only look at legislation or lack thereof as evidence of an EU sport policy. The Council and the Parliament in particular have occasionally adopted various soft law measures, some of which have been quite important in setting the context in which the Commission and Court, as enforcers of EU law, and the sporting bodies themselves operate. The political process has frequently pursued a relatively conservative direction, arguing for more deference to the sporting organizations. The Commission, reacting to these political statements, has attempted to reconcile the application of EU internal market law with the broader ideas of an EU sport policy, making small steps towards their recognition as policy concerns while claiming not to be a fully fledged sports regulator. In doing so, it has frequently sought partnerships with sporting bodies with occasional forays into competition law enforcement.

This back-and-forth has been particularly visible since the 1990s. The Treaty of Amsterdam included a brief Declaration on Sport, highlighting the social significance of sport and the need for dialogue with sporting organizations.[24] Following that, the Helsinki European Council of 1999 asked the Commission to draft its first significant policy document on sports: the Helsinki Report. While the instructions given to the Commission ('a report with a view to safeguarding current sports structures and maintaining the social function of sport within the Community framework') seemed to push the idea of deference to the sporting bodies, the actual Report was more nuanced, insisting on the application of the free movement and competition rules while encouraging a 'partnership' between the European institutions, the Member States, and the sports organizations in achieving the 'social goals' of sport.[25]

The 'specificity of sport' argument can be traced in the Nice Declaration adopted by the European Council in 2000, emphasizing the 'specific characteristics' of

[23] Borja García and Stephen Weatherill, 'Engaging with the EU in Order to Minimize its Impact: Sport and the Negotiation of the Treaty of Lisbon' (2012) 19 Journal of European Public Policy 238.

[24] This was Declaration 29: 'The Conference emphasises the social significance of sport ... [It] therefore calls on the bodies of the European Union to listen to sports associations when important questions affecting sport are at issue ...' Richard Parrish, 'The Politics of Sports Regulation in the European Union' (2003) 10 Journal of European Public Policy 246, 253–54.

[25] As Parrish notes, the Helsinki Report was 'the EU's first attempt to co-ordinate the Single Market and socio-cultural policy strands of its involvement in sport' (ibid 254). See Commission, 'Report from the Commission to the European Council with a view to safeguarding current sports structures and maintaining the social function of sport within the Community framework—The Helsinki Report on Sport' COM(1999) 644 final.

sport,[26] as well as in a study on professional football commissioned by the UK Council presidency, the 'Arnaut report'.[27] The Arnaut report strongly argued in favour of the autonomy of sports governing bodies[28] in order to preserve the European sport model,[29] provided a list of practices that should be automatically exempt from EU law, and recommended an explicit recognition of the principle of subsidiarity in favour of football federations. In exchange, the sports federations should adopt certain reforms to improve their governance, open up to consultations, and co-operate with the European institutions on the basis of a formal agreement.[30]

Simultaneously, other voices in the political discourse were pleading for the development of positive European policy interests in sports, going beyond the internal market. For example, the 1994 Larive Report and the 1997 Pack Report both highlighted the relative poverty of EU sports policy and the need for the EU to focus more on issues such as the cultural and educational aspects of sports, fighting violence and xenophobia, and financing sports projects.[31]

The attempt to complement the internal market approach to sport with more substantive policies defines the modern EU approach to sport, as outlined in particular by the Commission's 2007 White Paper on Sport.[32] The White Paper highlighted the primary role of the sporting bodies in achieving the social and cultural aims of sports and points out that 'most challenges can be addressed through self-regulation respectful of good governance principles, provided that EU law is respected'. It further developed various substantive policy aspects recognized in previous documents (public health, the fight against doping, sports in education, promoting volunteering, social inclusion, fight against racism and violence, and development). Nevertheless, it also discussed the future application of the competition and free movement rules,[33] insisting that there should be no strict separation between 'purely sporting rules' and those subject to the internal market rules, and that each case will have to be assessed on its own merits.

In another display of differences with the Commission, this final aspect was immediately criticized in a European Parliament Declaration of 2008 which, highlighting

[26] European Council 'Declaration on the specific characteristics of sport and its social function in Europe, of which account should be taken in implementing common policies' [2000] 13948/00.

[27] José Luis Arnaut, *Independent European Sport Review* (2006). See also José Luis Arnaut, *The Need to Preserve the European Sport Model* (Parliamentary Assembly of the Council of Europe Committee on Culture, Science and Education 2007) respectively. The IESR focused on football but could be read as applying to professional sport in general.

[28] IESR (n 27) 3.

[29] The example of professional basketball with its breakaway ULEB cup is therefore cited by the CoE report (section B para 3) as something to avoid, as it departs from the pyramid structure.

[30] IESR (n 27) 10.

[31] Jessica Larive, *Report of the Committee on Culture, Youth, Education and the Media on the European Community and Sport* (European Parliament, 1994) and Doris Pack, *Report on the Role of the European Union in the Field of Sport* (European Parliament Committee on Culture, Youth, Education and the Media, 1997). Parrish (n 24) 253.

[32] White Paper on Sport (n 12).

[33] On this, the accompanying document 'The EU and Sport: Background and Context' (n 17) gave a wealth of information.

the autonomy of sporting bodies and the national organization of sport, made a point of asking the Commission 'to have due respect for the specificity of sports, by not taking a case-by-case approach and to provide more legal certainty by creating clear guidelines on the applicability of European law to sports in Europe'.[34]

The latest significant document produced by the Commission was a 2011 Communication.[35] It made use of the Lisbon Treaty's new provision on sport to announce several incentive and co-ordinating measures and to propose a negotiating mandate for the EU's accession to the Council of Europe Anti-doping Convention. Interestingly, it also relied on Art 165 TFEU, in combination with Arts 18 and 21 TFEU on EU citizenship, to broaden the scope of the prohibition of discrimination to 'all EU citizens who have used their right to free movement, including those exercising an amateur sport activity'.[36] From this example, it seems that the Commission does not view the new Art 165 TFEU as limiting, but rather as expanding the EU's role in sport.[37]

Most recently, the EU has engaged with sport in two different ways. Firstly, the Lisbon Treaty has given rise to the development of certain substantive sport policies, such as the link between education and sport.[38] At the same time, the EU institutions have continued to engage sporting bodies in policy dialogue. One example of this is the controversial 2014 Arrangement for Cooperation between the European Commission and UEFA,[39] which seems to be quite supportive of existing football governance structures. Secondly, the long-debated issue of state aid to sport has finally been opened up, with several Commission and national decisions in the pipeline.[40]

Few of these policy developments, however, would likely have occurred had it not been for the case-by-case engagement of EU law with sporting rules. While the policy debate has provided the context, it was itself largely spurred on by developments in the legal area. I will address the free movement and competition rules in turn.

[34] European Parliament resolution on the White Paper on Sport [8 May 2008] 2007/2261(INI) para 4.

[35] Commission 'Developing the European Dimension in Sport' (Communication) COM(2011) 12 final.

[36] ibid 11. This reading of the provisions on EU citizenship goes beyond the notion, recognized in Joined cases C-51/96 and C-191/97 *Christelle Deliège v Ligue francophone de judo et disciplines associées ASBL, Ligue belge de judo ASBL, Union européenne de judo* (C-51/96) *and François Pacquée* (C-191/97) [2000] ECR I-02549, that amateur sport is subject to EU law insofar as it is an economic activity. See also Commission 'Sport and Free Movement: Accompanying Document to the Communication "Developing the European Dimension in Sport"' (Staff Working Document) SEC(2011) 66 final.

[37] Commission, 'Sport and Free Movement' (n 36) 9.

[38] One example of this is the Erasmus + programme for Education, Training, Youth, and Sport for 2014–20.

[39] Commission Decision C(2014)7378 of 14 October 2014 adopting the Arrangement for Co-operation between the European Commission and the Union of European Football Associations (UEFA).

[40] See, for example, Richard Craven, 'Football and State Aid: Too Important to Fail?' (2014) 14 International Sports Law Journal 205.

3. Free Movement and the Regulation of Sport

The history of the engagement of EU law with sports is well-known, and to some extent touched upon in Chapters II and III. For the purposes of this chapter, it will suffice to give a broad sketch.

The free movement rules were where the first encounters of the sporting world and EU law took place. They were first applied to the rules of sporting organizations in the 1970s, in *Walrave* and *Dona v Mantero*.[41] In these judgments, the ECJ confirmed that the rules on free movement of persons and services apply to the rules of non-State sporting bodies that discriminate on the basis of nationality, because they are 'aimed at regulating in a collective manner gainful employment and the provision of services'.[42] From there on, the horizontal application of the free movement rules was no longer going to be an issue for the Court when it came to regulation by sporting bodies. Nevertheless, the judgments formulated a 'sporting exception': the free movement rules do not prohibit discrimination in matters of purely sporting interest that do not involve economic activity[43] such as the composition of national teams.[44] The dividing line between these two categories of measures would become, and to some extent it still is, the main battleground between the sporting organizations, the Commission, and other stakeholders.

The next wave of judgments concerning sporting rules did not arrive until the mid-1990s with the watershed judgment in *Bosman*, in which nationality caps[45] and transfer rules[46] in professional football were held to violate the free movement

[41] Case 36-74 *B.N.O. Walrave and L.J.N. Koch v Association Union cycliste internationale, Koninklijke Nederlandsche Wielren Unie and Federación Española Ciclismo* [1974] ECR 1405 and Case 13-76 *Gaetano Donà v Mario Mantero* [1976] ECR 1333.

[42] *Walrave* (n 41) para 17. As Weatherill (n 2) 24 notes, while the early cases made it seem as if all employers in the sports sector, such as clubs, were subject to the free movement rules (see also the Opinion of AG Warner in *Walrave*), the Court was more likely to have meant to include only 'collective action by non-governmental bodies which in practice control individual employers'. See, however, Art 7/4 of both Regulation (EU) 492/2011 of the European Parliament and of the Council on freedom of movement for workers within the Union [2011] OJ L141/1 and its predecessor Regulation (EEC) 1612/68 of the Council on freedom of movement for workers within the Community (1968) OJ L257: 'Any clause of a collective or individual agreement or of any other collective regulation concerning eligibility for employment, remuneration and other conditions of work or dismissal shall be null and void in so far as it lays down or authorises discriminatory conditions in respect of workers who are nationals of the other Member States.'

[43] *Donà* (n 41) para 12.

[44] After the somewhat vague reference to 'rules on the composition of sport teams' in *Walrave*, the Court clarified this exception in *Donà* (n 41): '... those provisions do not prevent the adoption of rules or of a practice excluding foreign players from participation in certain matches for reasons which are not of an economic nature, which relate to the particular nature and context of such matches and are thus of sporting interest only, such as, for example, matches between national teams from different countries' (para 14). See also the Opinion of AG Lenz in *Bosman* (n 4) paras 137–40.

[45] Rules limiting the number of foreigners, including nationals of other EU Member States, that may be fielded in a game.

[46] Rules requiring, in order for a player to be re-registered after changing clubs, a transfer fee from a player's new club even when his previous contract had expired.

rules. Apart from its tremendous impact on the football world, the *Bosman* judgment presented some significant legal innovations.

Firstly, it made it clear that not only discriminatory rules, but any rules impeding the free movement of workers are restrictions covered by today's Art 45 TFEU.[47] Secondly, it put flesh on the notion of 'purely sporting' rules. Invoking the principles of free association, subsidiarity, cultural concerns, and the significant potential impact on the organization of football did not manage to remove the rules into the 'purely sporting' box.[48] Thirdly, it showed that private defendants can in principle invoke any type of public interest or Treaty justification that would be available in cases of public restrictions to free movement.[49] Finally, the Opinion of AG Lenz, if not the judgment itself, opened the door to competition law enforcement in sports by finding a parallel violation of Art 101 TFEU.

The principles underlying *Bosman* were confirmed in *Lehtonen*,[50] dealing with player transfer deadlines, and *Deliège*,[51] concerning caps on the number of participants in international judo competitions. Of the two, *Deliège* is especially significant as it makes clear that the free movement rules can be applied even to a largely amateur sport.[52]

The idea that Arts 45 and 56 TFEU apply to both professional and semi-professional athletes was more recently explicitly confirmed in *Bernard*.[53] The case concerned a provision of a collective agreement for French football according to which a young player is required to sign a contract with the club that trained him or compensate the club's losses. The Court confirmed *Bosman* in that provisions which deter or make the use of free movement less attractive[54] constitute restrictions under Art 45 TFEU.[55] Relying, however, on the same objective as the one cited in *Bosman*—encouraging the recruitment and training of young players—the Court found that a measure that links compensation to the actual

[47] *Bosman* (n 4) para 97.

[48] ibid paras 79–87. AG Lenz, in his Opinion, considered that subsidiarity is not applicable because the internal market is an exclusive competence of the EU (para 130). The Court did not go that far, simply saying that the argument could not affect the outcome (para 81).

[49] *Bosman* (n 4) para 86.

[50] *Lehtonen* (n 11).

[51] *Deliège* (n 36).

[52] Even amateur competitions, according to the Court, can involve 'the provision of a number of separate, but closely related, services which may fall within the scope of [Art 59] of the Treaty even if some of those services are not paid for by those for whom they are performed', such as grant contracts for the athlete, ticketing, broadcasting, advertising, sponsorships, etc. (para 56). See n 36.

[53] Case C-325/08 *Olympique Lyonnais SASP v Olivier Bernard and Newcastle UFC* [2010] ECR I-2177, para 28.

[54] ibid paras 33–37.

[55] A separate line of cases examined the issue of nationality-based discrimination against players from third countries that have concluded a stabilization and association agreement (or similar) with the EU and its Member States. Based on *Bosman*, it was held that sporting rules which treat players from those countries (Slovakia and Russia respectively) as foreigners and thus restrict their opportunity to take part in official matches are contrary to EU law. See Case C-438/00 *Deutscher Handballbund eV v Maros Kolpak* [2003] ECR I-4135 and Case C-265/03 *Igor Simutenkov v Ministerio de Educación y Cultura and Real Federación Española de Fútbol* [2005] ECR I-02579.

costs of training can be justified (this seemed, however, not to be the case with the French rules at issue).

Bernard was also the first judgment to cite Art 165/1 TFEU, the first specific Treaty provision on sport. The Court made clear that the reference to the social and educational character of sport in that provision should be reflected in the analysis of proportionality of sporting rules:

> In considering whether a system which restricts the freedom of movement of such players is suitable to ensure that the said objective is attained and does not go beyond what is necessary to attain it, account must be taken ... of the specific characteristics of sport in general, and football in particular, and of their social and educational function.[56]

National courts have also applied the free movement rules to the practices of sporting bodies. An important recent example is the *Wilhelmshaven* dispute, in which a German court found, contrary to the CAS, that FIFA's rules on training compensation—reformed after *Bosman* and indirectly touched upon by *Bernard*—should be applied to a player transferring from Argentina to Germany.[57] This dispute may lead to a broader examination of the current rules on player transfers which have so far received the blessing of the European Commission.[58]

4. Competition Law and Sport

Vigorous antitrust enforcement by the Commission started in the mid-1990s, coinciding with the *Bosman* judgment. After that period, as Budzinski points out, 'virtually all areas of sports business have become directly subject to competition rules, including apparently genuine sporting activities like defining, developing and enforcing the regulatory framework of a sports discipline's major championships, leagues and tournaments'.[59] Rather than with the issues of discrimination and the free movement of athletes, competition law was more frequently concerned with the structural and organizational rules of sporting bodies, as well as their buying and selling activities.[60]

[56] Paragraph 40.

[57] See Antoine Duval, 'SV Wilhelmshaven: A Rebel with a Cause! Challenging the Compatibility of FIFA's Training Compensation System with EU Law' (Asser International Sports Law Blog, 24 February 2015) <http://www.asser.nl/SportsLaw/Blog/post/sv-wilhelmshaven-a-rebel-with-a-cause-challenging-the-compatibility-of-fifa-s-training-compensation-system-with-eu-law>.

[58] The current rules on player transfers are largely a result of *Bosman*. Many have argued that they still violate the free movement and competition rules. See, most recently, Geoff Pearson, 'Sporting Justifications under EU Free Movement and Competition Law: The Case of the Football "Transfer System"' (2015) 21 European Law Journal 220. Pearson argues that 'the Commission-endorsed system has arguably *reduced* the ability of players to exercise their right to free movement in the EU and *further restricted* the ability of clubs to enter into the market for elite players' (226).

[59] Budzinski (n 10) 46 et seq.

[60] As Parrish summarizes: 'These investigations have included examinations into football's restructured transfer system, competition between sporting federations, rules preventing the multiple ownership of sporting clubs, rules preventing club relocation, the operation of Formula One motor-racing, ticketing arrangements for major sporting events and restrictive practices in the sale and purchase of broadcasting rights and the transmission of sporting events.' Parrish (n 24) 252.

The analysis of sporting rules under competition law has several broad steps. The first relevant question is the applicability of the Treaty competition provisions—Art 101 or (less frequently) Art 102. This includes, most importantly, asking whether the challenged entity is an undertaking or an association of undertakings, which means asking whether the particular activity is economic (see Chapter III section 3.1.1).[61] A 'sporting exception' can be at work here, and may not always turn out in the same way as it does under the free movement rules.[62] The Court has, however, interpreted the notion of undertaking rather broadly in the sports context. *Piau*, a judgment on licensing rules for players' agents, showed that FIFA, the global governing body of football, is not just an association of undertakings under Art 101[63] but also an undertaking under Art 102. The Court found:

> The fact that FIFA is not itself an economic operator that buys players' agents' services on the market and that its involvement stems from rule-making activity, which it has assumed the power to exercise in respect of the economic activity of players' agents, is irrelevant ... since FIFA is the emanation of the national associations and the clubs ... and it therefore operates on this market through its members.[64]

This broad reading of 'undertaking' could, perhaps, be linked to the specific context of sports. As I have described in Chapter III, the space that was carved out of competition law by describing certain activities as, for example, 'public authority functions', reflects deference to the political choice of a Member State to withdraw a certain activity from the market. In the sports context, arguably, the Member States do not have such a role. It is the sporting world itself that has traditionally decided where commercial competition should take place. Without the reference point of traditional Member State functions in this field,[65] therefore, the Court may be tempted to retain the power of review over the activities

[61] In the context of sport, see 'The EU and Sport: Background and Context' (n 17) 66–67 (explicitly arguing, among others, that amateur athletes can be undertakings when they perform an economic activity, on the basis of the free movement precedent in *Deliège*; implicitly, the same would apply to amateur clubs as well), as well as Case C-171/05 P *Laurent Piau v Commission* [2006] ECR I-37, para 69.

[62] See section 4.2.1 on the *Meca-Medina* judgment below. In Case C-519/04 P *David Meca-Medina and Igor Majcen v Commission* [2006] ECR I-6991, paras 31–34 and 38, the Court did not enter into a specific analysis of whether the International Olympic Committee was an undertaking. Still, it overruled the General Court's finding that anti-doping rules were not of an economic nature.

[63] This is because it groups national football associations, which themselves are associations of undertakings (even though many of their members are amateur clubs; the Court found that amateur clubs can also be undertakings for the purposes of competition law) or even undertakings, such as when they engage in selling media rights (paras 71–72).

[64] *Piau* (n 61) para 116. Both Arts 101 and 102, thus, seem relevant for sporting regulators. Cf. the vexing issue, under US law, of whether professional sports leagues, when jointly selling media rights, are acting as a single enterprize. See, most recently, *American Needle Inc. v National Football League* (2010) 560 US 183.

[65] Indeed, the General Court in *Piau* points out the absence of Member State legislation ('there is at present no organisation of the occupation of players' agent and no generalised national rules'), as an argument in favour of the legitimacy of FIFA's rules (para 100).

of private regulators that, in another context, may not be described as economic at all.

Secondly, the question is whether there is a *prima facie* restriction of competition or abuse of a dominant position. Even if competition is restricted, however, sporting rules or practices will survive scrutiny under Art 101/1 if they satisfy the *Wouters* and *Meca-Medina* test, that is if the restriction, seen in context, is inherent to a justified, necessary, and proportionate regulatory measure.[66] Finally, even if the *Wouters* exception does not apply, there is still the possibility of justification under Art 101/3 or 'objective justification' under Art 102.

The sports cases dealt with under competition law are rather diverse. To facilitate the discussion—rather than highlight any deep differences—I will follow the Commission's distinction between two broad groups: first, 'revenue-generating activities connected to sport' and, second, 'the organisation of sport'.[67]

4.1 'Business as usual'

The first group relates to 'revenue-generating activities connected with sport' or 'normal buying and selling behaviour'.[68] These cases do not straddle difficult dividing lines between 'purely sporting rules' and economic activity. Of course, this does not mean that they are less important or less of a concern for the sporting organizations. To the contrary, competition enforcement in this area can have enormous financial implications and deeply affect the organization of sports markets. Nor does it mean that these cases are easy or obvious from a competition law perspective. Sports media cases, for example, are characterized by difficult market definition problems due to changing technologies.[69] It only means that the applicability of competition law is not questioned.

These cases mostly concern ticket-selling arrangements sports media rights. The first category has included ticket-selling schemes for various competitions that, among other restrictions, imposed distributor exclusivity,[70] discriminated

[66] See Chapter III section 3.1.3. As examples of possible justifications in this context, the Commission, as summarized by Budzinski, uses: fair competitions with equal chances for all athletes, ensuring the uncertainty of results by eliminating match-fixing, the protection of athletes' health or spectator safety, encouraging the training of young athletes, financial stability of clubs, the rules of the game, etc. See 'The EU and Sport: Background and Context' (n 17) 68 and Budzinski (n 10) 50.

[67] 'The EU and Sport: Background and Context' (n 17) Annex I sections 2 and 3. Budzinski (n 10) 66 et seq classifies competition cases in sport into: (I) the internal regulation of sport (genuine sporting rules or the rules of the game), (II) business practices (buying and selling behaviour of sports enterprises, like ticketing arrangements, exclusivity contracts, etc.), and (III) the sale of broadcasting rights.

[68] Budzinski (n 10) 51 et seq.

[69] 'The EU and Sport: Background and Context' (n 17) section 3.1.1. On this and other complexities of cases on media rights, see Ben Van Rompuy and Caroline Pauwels, 'The Recognition of the Specificity of Sport in the European Commission's Article 81 EC Decisional Practice Related to Sports Media Rights' in Parrish, Gardiner, and Siekmann (n 20).

[70] In *Distribution of package tours during the 1990 World Cup* (Cases IV/33.384 and IV/33.378) Commission Decision 92/521/EEC (1992) OJ L326/31, the Commission found an infringement of Art 101 in a scheme which granted a single travel agency exclusive ticket-selling rights for package tours.

between buyers from different Member States,[71] and allowed credit card payments through one company only.[72] The Commission's concern was to enable non-discriminatory access to international events of interest to consumers.

The second category has constituted the bulk of competition enforcement related to sports. Usually, what is at stake is an arrangement whereby a sporting body or a league acts as the joint seller, instead of individual clubs, for the audio-visual rights to all events within a league or competition (eg the English FA Premier League, the UEFA football Champions League, or Formula 1 races).[73] Because of access foreclosure and output reduction, options for consumers to access sports media in different packages or on different media can be restricted and prices remain high.[74] Yet joint selling can be seen as economically efficient, and it is claimed to be indispensable for redistributing a part of total revenues to smaller clubs and the sporting bodies themselves.

The Commission has not condemned these kinds of arrangements outright. In decisions such as *UEFA Champions League*,[75] it acknowledged the pro-competitive aspects of joint selling, such as common branding and the creation of a league product as well as lower transaction costs because of a single point of sale.[76] Just as in the ticketing cases, the Commission has favoured an approach that mixes justification under Art 101/3 with targeted behavioural or structural remedies,

[71] In the scheme condemned in *1998 Football World Cup* (Case IV/36.888) Commission Decision 2000/12/EC OJ L5/55, it was necessary to have a mailing address in France or a mailed order for non-French residents to buy tickets.

[72] See the Commission press releases IP/03/738 of 23 May 2003 (Case 38703 *Athens Olympics 2004*) and IP/05/519 of 2 May 2005 (Case 39177 *World Cup 2006*).

[73] Another group of cases has dealt with restrictions imposed by buyers, either unilaterally by powerful broadcasters or by a broadcaster buying consortium. In both situations, anticompetitive effects can occur. The sporting body, for example, may offer league games only in an all-inclusive bundle or fix prices per game; it may sell all media rights (free TV, pay-TV, Internet, mobile etc.) in one package only; it may grant exclusive licenses on a territorial basis or with discriminatory conditions. On the other end, a purchasing broadcaster such as a pay-TV provider may not be interested in the rights for a particular medium, but would still acquire them simply to stave off competition from alternative media.

[74] As Budzinski summarizes, joint marketing 'prevents the individual clubs from competing for television deals, often sets a uniform price (price-fixing), often reduces the number of available rights in order to increase the price (artificial output reduction), leads to market foreclosure in media markets, and can hamper the development of certain sub-markets (eg new media markets in order to protect pay-TV revenues)'. Budzinski (n 10) 52.

[75] *Joint selling of the commercial rights of the UEFA Champions League* (Case COMP/C.2-37.398) Commission Decision 2003/778/EC [2003] OJ L291/25. See also *Joint selling of the media rights to the German Bundesliga* (Case COMP/C-2/37.214) Commission Decision of 19 January 2005 and *Joint selling of the media rights to the FA Premier League* (Case COMP/C-2/38.173) Commission Decision of 22 March 2006.

[76] See 'The EU and Sport: Background and Context' (n 17) 81. With individual selling, transaction costs increase because of the number of negotiating parties, but also because of the uncertainty of sports competitions. Not knowing in advance which clubs would advance to a certain stage in a competition would make negotiation and programming decisions difficult. As Budzinski points out, however, 'having a monopoly supplier reduces transaction costs in the sense that costs of searching and selecting disappear. It would be a mistake in economic reasoning, however, to confuse "minimum transaction costs" with "efficiency". Competition involves necessary transaction costs since it creates product and service diversity.' Budzinski (n 10) 59.

either imposed through decisions or by closing the investigation on the acceptance of certain commitments.

These remedies have addressed selling methods, requiring rights unbundling (offering several different packages of rights depending on the downstream markets and/or number of rights) and transparent competitive tendering according to objective criteria, or banning the practice of tying tender offers for different rights.[77] They have also imposed limits on buyers, for example restricting the duration of exclusivity or imposing the 'no single buyer' rule (preventing a single buyer from acquiring all rights).[78] At times, they were directly targeted at governance deficiencies of sporting bodies, such as when they required a trustee to be appointed in order to supervise the tendering process.[79]

It is not just the Commission that has objected to the practices of sporting bodies on media rights. In the preliminary reference in *Murphy*, the Court has effectively made it illegal to prohibit the use of TV decoders enabling access to sports content in a country for which they were not sold. This applied both to legislation (a restriction of Art 56 TFEU on free movement of services) and to contracts between IP holders and broadcasters (a restriction of Art 101).[80] Another stumbling block for, in particular, UEFA and FIFA, is EU legislation allowing the Member States to prevent exclusivity in broadcasting 'events of major importance to society'. The Commission has confirmed, with ultimate agreement by both the General Court and the Court of Justice,[81] the United Kingdom's decision to put the entire World Cup and the entire Euro on the list of 'events of major importance'. Both the Commission and the EU courts exercised relatively lax reviews, highlighting the discretion of Member States in making the choice according to their own circumstances.

4.2 Regulatory and organizational aspects

The second group of competition cases concerns the rules of sporting bodies on, broadly, the organization of sports:[82] how, by whom, where and when certain competitions can be organized, the licensing of clubs, players, coaches, and agents, sanctions for violations of various rules, etc. These cases frequently concern the governance design, mechanisms for preventing conflict of interest, and the procedures followed by sporting bodies in making decisions. From the point of view of private regulation and the extent to which regulatory autonomy is recognized in the area of sports, this group is therefore more significant.

[77] See for example *Bundesliga Decision* (n 75) paras 27 et seq and *FA Premier League Decision* (n 75) paras 32–42.

[78] See *UEFA Champions League* (n 75) para 117.

[79] See 'The EU and Sport: Background and Context' (n 17) 84.

[80] Joined cases C-403/08 and C-429/08 *Football Association Premier League Ltd and Others v QC Leisure and Others* (C-403/08) and *Karen Murphy v Media Protection Services Ltd* (C-429/08) [2011] ECR I-90834.

[81] See n 18.

[82] 'The EU and Sport: Background and Context' (n 17) Annex I section 2.

Moreover, in this group overlap with the free movement rules is more likely, as the Commission itself recognizes, arguing that issues that have been treated under the free movement rules such as transfer rules or nationality caps could equally fall under Arts 101 or 102.[83]

In general terms, the same type of analysis is applicable to these cases as to the first group. The key difference lies in one additional step: the 'inherent restriction' test, as applied to sporting cases by the Commission in *ENIC* and by the Court in *Meca-Medina* (see section 4.2.1). Neither the Commission nor the Court have deeply challenged the legitimacy of sporting bodies as sport regulators. The way in which their measures are formulated or applied, however, can raise suspicion. This comes down to a proportionality analysis, focused more frequently on the governance and procedure employed by sporting bodies than on the substance of their measures. This dynamic, insisting on good governance as 'a condition for the autonomy and self-regulation of sport organisations'[84] is recognized by the various policy documents described in section 2, but can also be traced in the application of both free movement and competition rules.

Thus, competition law has been used to prevent conflicts of interest in decision-making. A good example is *MOTOE*, where the Greek automotive association ELPA was exclusively authorized by law to license motorcycling events, but at the same time organized many of those events itself, profiting from sponsoring, advertising, and insurance contracts. While the idea that sporting bodies should be allowed to regulate and license the organization of events was not questioned, the danger of ELPA's abusing its regulatory power to further its economic interests, while not being subject to any 'restrictions, obligations and review', led the Court to conclude that ELPA's exclusive right is precluded by Arts 102 and 106 TFEU.[85] Similar governance and capture issues were implicit in the *FIA* case, where the Commission criticized the lack of transparency in internal decision making and the lack of separation between regulatory and commercial activities

[83] ibid section 2.2.

[84] Commission 'Developing the European Dimension in Sport' (n 35) 10. More broadly, see Jens Alm (ed), *Action for Good Governance in International Sports Organisations* (Play the Game/Danish Institute for Sports Studies Report 2013). Interestingly, the same trade-off is recognized by sports organizations as well, if perhaps with a difference in emphasis. See, for example, the speech of Thomas Bach, vice-president of the International Olympic Committee, 'European Union, Sport and Athletes—Quo Vadis' at the 'European Evening of Sport' Brussels (27 February 2013) <http://www.dosb.de/fileadmin/fm-dosb/arbeitsfelder/Internationales/Rede_Bach_Europa_Bruessel_engl_270213BXL_final_pdf.pdf> '... "autonomy" is indispensable for the existence of sport and is necessary for the dissemination of sporting values ... On the other hand, sport should ensure a decision-making process characterised by the rules of good governance' (4).

[85] Case C-49/07 *Motosykletistiki Omospondia Ellados NPID (MOTOE) v Elliniko Dimosio* [2008] ECR I-4863, para 48. Analysing whether this made ELPA an undertaking in the sense of Art 102 TFEU, the Court distinguished ELPA's economic and non-economic activities: 'the fact that, for the exercise of part of its activities, an entity is vested with public powers does not, in itself, prevent it from being classified as an undertaking ... in respect of the remainder of its economic activities' (para 25). For an analysis, see Samuli Miettinen, 'Policing the Boundaries Between Regulation and Commercial Exploitation: Lessons From the *MOTOE* Case' in Parrish, Gardiner, and Siekmann (n 20).

of Fédération Internationale de l'Automobile (FIA), the governing body of Formula 1 racing.[86]

Competition law has also addressed dispute settlement mechanisms. Sports organizations frequently require contractual waivers of judicial review, for example from athletes or clubs participating in competitions. While internal dispute-settlement is not problematic as such, the Commission has at times objected to their exclusivity or the way they are organized. For example, it insisted that FIFA change its rules on player transfers so that 'arbitration would be voluntary and would not prevent recourse to national courts',[87] and that FIA adopts an explicit rule opening its decisions to challenge before national courts, and not just within the private dispute-settlement bodies of the organization.[88] In the more recent *Pechstein* case, the composition of arbitration tribunals has been framed as a competition issue, which could lead to significant reforms of the procedures of CAS, the most important sport dispute settlement venue.[89]

Finally, perhaps the broadest response to the question of legitimacy of sporting bodies as regulators was given in *Piau*, a challenge to FIFA's rules on football players' agents that, among other limitations, required mandatory licensing, uniform testing, and professional indemnity insurance, imposed sanctions for violations and banned clubs and players from dealing with non-licensed agents or legal entities as agents. The General Court used vocabulary that would not normally belong in a competition law analysis, noting that the rule-making power over economic activities claimed by FIFA, not formally delegated to it by a Member State, is 'open to question', as a possible violation of 'civil and economic liberties'.[90] This did not lead the Court to find any of FIFA's measures illegal. It was, however, a clear message: EU competition law can be applied to broadly discipline the proportionality and fairness of the rules of private regulators. Interestingly, this is placed in the broader context of the absence of either Member State rules or self-regulation of players' agents as a profession: because FIFA is the sole regulator, there is a need for EU law to provide a measure of review.

[86] Notice published pursuant to Article 19(3) of Council Regulation 17 concerning Cases COMP/35.163—Notification of FIA Regulations, COMP/36.638—Notification by FIA/FOA of agreements relating to the FIA Formula One World Championship, COMP/36.776—GTR/FIA [2001] OJ C169/5. See the press releases IP/01/1523 'Commission closes its investigation into Formula One and other four-wheel motor sports' (30 October 2001) and IP/03/1491 'Commission ends monitoring of FIA/Formula One compliance with 2001 settlement' (31 October 2003), claiming that FIA fulfilled the terms of the settlement to 'limit its role to that of a sports regulator, to guarantee access to motor sport to any racing organization meeting the requisite safety criteria and to no longer prevent teams and circuit owners not to participate in other races'.

[87] See the press release IP/02/824 'Commission closes investigations into FIFA regulations on international football transfers' (5 June 2002). FIFA also changed its rules in order to create 'an effective, quick and objective arbitration body with members chosen in equal numbers by players and clubs and with an independent chairman ... FIFPro [the main players' union] will also nominate representatives for the new Arbitration Tribunal for Football, to which decisions of the Dispute Resolution Chamber can be appealed.'

[88] See n 86 and 'The EU and Sport: Background and Context' (n 17) 74.

[89] See n 9.

[90] *Piau* (n 61) paras 76–78.

The very same argument, however, helped to find all of FIFA's rules acceptable within Arts 101/3 and 102: because nobody else is effectively regulating the conduct of players' agents, the Court largely defers to FIFA's rules. While the Court did not apply the *Wouters* exception,[91] it followed a similar logic, finding, for example, that mandatory licensing is 'appropriate for the attainment of the objective of raising professional standards for the occupation of players' agent'. It also implicitly approved the Commission's finding of a justification under Art 101/3 that used the *Wouters* wording ('the restriction inherent in the licence system is proportionate and essential').[92]

4.2.1 The Meca-Medina *test*

As discussed in Chapter III, in *Wouters* the Court decided that certain agreements, decisions, or concerted practices that restrict competition nevertheless fall outside the scope of Art 101 altogether if, seen in context, their restrictive consequences are inherent and proportionate to the pursuit of a legitimate regulatory objective.

The *Wouters* test was first explicitly applied in the sporting sector in Commission decisions. *Mouscron* (*Lille v UEFA*) actually predates the *Wouters* judgment. There, the Commission did not consider the complaint against UEFA's 'home and away from home' rule (preventing a Belgian club from playing European matches at a stadium in France) to raise a sufficient Community interest, relying on arguments similar to those that will later be used in *Wouters* and *Meca-Medina*. The decision shows how, at the time, the Commission seemed to advocate a clear separation between regulatory and economic aspects of sports, or at least a presumptive exclusion from the scope of the Treaty competition rules for rules that are necessary for legitimate sporting purposes.[93] The later *ENIC v UEFA* decision, concerning a UEFA rule prohibiting the same entity from owning multiple football clubs, was closer to the *Wouters* approach. It concluded that there was no restriction of Art 81(1) EC because the rule was necessary to achieve the legitimate objective of ensuring the integrity of sporting competitions and uncertainty of results.[94]

The most important precedent for the application of competition law to the regulation of sporting activities without obvious commercial aspects was,

[91] Indeed, the General Court seemed to read the *Wouters* test as only applying to cases where rule-making powers are 'conferred by a public authority in connection with a recognised task in the general interest' (para 74). *Meca-Medina* (n 62) goes significantly beyond that.

[92] *Piau* (n 61) para 103 and para 100 respectively.

[93] '(1) la Commission reconnaît le pouvoir réglementaire des organisations sportives pour les aspects non-économiques qui se rattachent à la nature spécifique du sport; (2) les réglementations des organisations sportives nécessaires pour assurer l'égalité de chances entre clubs, l'incertitude des résultats, l'intégrité et le bon déroulement des compétitions échappent, en principe, aux règles de concurrence du Traité …' Commission, 'La Commission émet un signal clair quant aux limites de l'application des règles de concurrence du Traité au secteur du sport' (Press release) IP/99/965.

[94] See Commission, 'Commission closes investigation into UEFA rule on multiple ownership of football clubs' (Press release) IP/02/942.

however, set by the Court in *Meca-Medina*,[95] where two swimmers suspended for using forbidden substances challenged the anti-doping rules and practices of the International Olympic Committee (IOC). They claimed that the illegal substance in their bodies could have been naturally produced. When that did not work, they asked the European Commission to find that the anti-doping rules were contrary to the Treaty rules on competition and free movement of services.

Clearly, anti-doping rules are far from what most people would consider to be the domain of competition law. In principle, however, there is nothing to prevent the application of the competition rules. The IOC can be described as an association of undertakings, or an 'association of associations of undertakings', when regulating—and occasionally restricting—the ability of athletes to take part in competitions. The way in which this regulation is implemented could have the object or effect of restricting competition, for example in the sponsorship market for individual athletes.

Thus, the appellants claimed that, even though the anti-doping rules have a legitimate objective ('healthy rivalry between athletes'), the sanctions for violating them were excessive and 'intended to protect the IOC's own economic interests'.[96] There was no clear explanation of what the IOC's 'economic interests' were when it came to anti-doping. Nevertheless, the Court acknowledged the danger of overly restrictive practices and agreed that they could amount to a violation of the competition rules. Thus, 'in order not to be covered by the prohibition laid down in [Art 101/1 TFEU], the restrictions thus imposed by those rules must be limited to what is necessary to ensure the proper conduct of competitive sport'.[97] Analysing the threshold of prohibition and the available scientific knowledge, the Court found that this requirement is fulfilled.[98] In terms of substance, *Meca-Medina* makes it clear that competition law takes broad regulatory objectives into account when dealing with sporting bodies.[99]

While the Commission did not support such an outcome before the Court, it has since placed great emphasis on the *Meca-Medina* test. An Annex to the White Paper on Sport, for example, claims:

> ... the application of [Arts 101 and 102 TFEU] provides sufficient flexibility to take account of the specificity of sport and does not impede sporting rules that pursue a legitimate objective (such as the organisation and proper conduct of sport), are indispensable (inherent) to achieve the objective and proportionate in light of the objective pursued ... the ECJ's *Meca Medina* judgment strongly confirms that it is not possible to pre-determine

95 *Meca-Medina* (n 62). 96 ibid para 46. 97 ibid para 47.

98 The Court points out that the level of penalties could be an issue, but does not address it since it was not pleaded by the appellants (para 55).

99 Arguably, this is not unique to EU law. See, for example, the US Supreme Court's recognition, in *NCAA v Board of Regents of the University of Oklahoma* (1984) 468 US 85, that the aim of competitive balance can be invoked in antitrust analysis. The question is whether that requires a special 'regulatory' exception such as the one in *Wouters* and *Meca-Medina*. Chapter III has argued that there are valid reasons for it. For a contrary perspective, see Pablo Ibáñez Colomo, 'Rules of Purely Sporting Interest and EU Competition Law: Why the *Wouters* Exception is Not Necessary' (2012) 8 Competition Law International 54.

an exhaustive list of sporting rules which breach [Art 101] and/or [Art 102 TFEU] (or of those which do not) ... it is necessary to examine [their] specific requirements in each individual case.[100]

This paragraph illustrates the central features of the approach of EU free movement and competition law to private regulators: first, the desire to maintain a flexible mechanism of review over a broad range of practices and, second, the willingness to use that review mechanism in order to defer to the legitimate decisions of private regulators.

Meca-Medina was crucial in enabling this flexibility. The Commission thus linked the Court's proportionality test to a 'case by case' approach, rejecting the sporting world's preference for clear *ex ante* exemptions for certain categories of measures. The General Court's first instance review decision had decided, relying on precedents from free movement law, that anti-doping rules were of a purely sporting nature and did not relate to economic activity. The Court reversed this finding, first, because it conflated free movement and competition law and, second, because it interpreted the specificity of sport as a bright-line rule. Instead, the Court said, even rules which are purely sporting in nature are subject to the free movement and competition provisions of the Treaty as long as they govern an economic activity.[101]

The *Wouters* test also seems to influence national courts deciding on competition law issues in sport. For example, the International Handball Federation's rules on the mandatory uncompensated release of players from their clubs to national teams have been condemned by a German court as an abuse of dominance. The court, however, analysed whether such rules could be 'objectively justified' and whether they are the least restrictive alternative to achieve a legitimate objective.[102]

5. The Specificity of Sport as Regulatory Autonomy

Several points emerge from the preceding discussion. Even today, the EU does not and cannot regulate sport in a systematic manner. Sporting bodies are likely to keep a leading role in that respect. On the other hand, the free movement and competition rules have, in effect, defined the limits and conditions of the autonomy of sport regulators.

It is important to note the nature of the autonomy argument in sports. What is at stake is rarely pure private autonomy. Few actors in the conversation are arguing for example that clubs must be free to circumvent the national organization of sports by organizing breakaway leagues, or that there should be no rules on corruption, player's agents, and club licensing. The question is, rather, who should decide on these issues: the EU, the Member States, or the governing bodies of

[100] 'The EU and Sport: Background and Context' (n 17) 69.

[101] Paragraphs 27–28.

[102] LG Dortmund (14 May 2014) Az 8 O46/13.

sports? The autonomy of sports is thus more aptly described as regulatory autonomy, rather than private autonomy in the strict sense. The 'shopkeeper argument' against applying EU law (see Chapter II) holds no sway here.

This is why the arguments for blanket exclusion of free movement or competition scrutiny over the measures of sports organizations have tended to fail. If they still survive, it is in a narrower form, focused on certain very specific types of measures.[103] The Commission sometimes accepts such arguments, such as with regard to nationality restrictions in national teams or straightforward 'rules of the game', but always with the proviso that each case should be assessed on its own merits and that comprehensive *ex ante* exemptions are not possible.

With the case-by-case approach, the analysis of measures taken by private regulators thus tends to move to the stage of justification. Instead of disputing the applicability of EU free movement or competition law to sports, the private autonomy argument in this stage tries to balance the measure's restrictive effects against values such as the right of association or the right of assembly (autonomy-based balancing). These kinds of arguments have been present in some free movement cases on sports, but—as seems to be the case with private regulation in general—to little effect.[104]

This can be explained by a trade-off that seems to be at work between private autonomy in the strict sense and what I have called 'regulatory autonomy'. If an organization is seen as a fully fledged regulator with legitimacy derived either from the Member States through a form of co-regulation, or even directly from the social context in which it operates, its private autonomy loses value while its regulatory autonomy gains value.

The regulatory autonomy argument is reflected in the analysis of the measures of sporting bodies. It can be seen in their ability to invoke a wide set of substantive justifications, such as the need for competitive balance between clubs or the need to compensate clubs for training costs. This is a central finding of the *Bosman* case. Before the Court, Germany claimed that, in general, public authorities' intervention in private affairs should be limited, whereas UEFA argued that the free movement rules should not apply to private parties because of their inability to raise Treaty or case-law based public policy justifications. These pure private autonomy arguments were rejected by the Court, finding that even private sports organizations can invoke substantive public policy justifications.[105]

This was more than just a technical issue of the applicability of a Treaty provision or of equality of arms in litigation. On the one hand, in a move reminiscent

[103] See n 27.

[104] For one example, see the Opinion of AG Lenz in *Bosman* (n 4) para 216, dismissing the idea that the restrictive effects of UEFA's rules should be balanced against the freedom of association. The freedom of association argument was also a dead end in *Deliège* (n 36; see the Opinion of AG Cosmas para 27) and *Kolpak* (n 55; see the Opinion of AG Stix-Hackl para 29). See however the Opinion of AG Alber in *Lehtonen* (n 11) para 69.

[105] *Bosman* (n 4) paras 85–86. The transfer rules, for example, were thus claimed to be justified by the 'need to maintain a financial and competitive balance between clubs and to support the search for talent and the training of young players' (para 105).

of *Cassis de Dijon*, the broader scope for justification was used to offset the broader reach of the free movement rules.[106] On the other hand, the justification debate was moved to a new playing field. Instead of UEFA's right to govern itself as it sees fit, as reflected in private autonomy justifications such as freedom of expression, contract, or assembly, the Court dealt with the specific decision-making processes and the policy behind its measure. This move is important, therefore, because it shifts the discussion to regulatory autonomy: sporting bodies are broadly recognized as legitimate, but in exchange they remain subject to the disciplines of EU law.

Apart from their substantive policies, sporting bodies can claim deference to the ways in which sport is organized. The 'specificity of sporting structure'[107] can be recognized as a value in itself, potentially capable of justifying restrictions of competition or free movement. For example, the need to maintain a pyramid structure of sport by preventing breakaway leagues (as the well-known 'G-14' group of major European football clubs once mooted) might be such a concern. This is what the General Court may have been referring to in *Piau* when it spoke of a special category of measures that fall under the 'freedom of internal organisation enjoyed by sports associations'.[108]

To see how the shift from pure private autonomy to regulatory autonomy happens, an example is useful. Let us imagine a small group of mid-level football clubs that breaks away from all the competitions in which they currently take part, national and European, starting a new 'breakaway league', completely unmoored from existing regulatory structures (FIFA, UEFA, national federations). Let us further assume that the new league adopts a restrictive rule, for example one that completely prohibits a certain type of sponsorship or imposes a very short transfer window. In principle it seems clear that both the free movement and competition rules could apply to those measures. But it may be the case, if such a league is relatively small and economically insignificant, that it could get away with this measure even when FIFA or UEFA could not. Under the free movement rules, a court could conceivably find that the league's rules are a purely private contractual arrangement that does not rise to the level of a restriction to free movement; under the competition rules, it could find that there is no market power. In other words, market discipline could be said to suffice. The reach of the free movement or competition law prohibitions would be narrower and private autonomy would be preserved.

On the other hand, such a league may not be able to defend its actions by public policy aims.[109] Of course, it is clear from *Bosman* that, *formally* speaking, private organizations can do so. Yet, in *Bosman*, the public policies were invoked

106 On this analogy, see Weatherill (n 2) 99.

107 White Paper on Sport (n 12) 13.

108 *Piau* (n 61) para 74.

109 Weatherill (n 2) 152–53 notes a similar dynamic in relation to the cases on joint selling of media rights: 'The Commission ... seems ready to override normal assumptions of competition in the market for broadcasting rights provided the proceeds accruing to the cartel are shared throughout the sport for the sake of its general health. This could be taken as a hint that collective selling is impermissible if used merely as a tool of wealth maximisation, which might lead one to suppose

by organizations that could legitimately claim to follow them. In the case of the small breakaway league, however, if scrutiny has been narrowed in order to protect private autonomy, a corresponding reduction in its ability of justification would inevitably follow.[110] For example, FIFA or UEFA could invoke the policy of redistribution between professional and amateur sport to justify certain measures, because this is an area in which they are actually active.[111] The small breakaway league, while legally (in the abstract) able to invoke that justification, cannot do so in practice if it is not actually engaged in pursuing that aim. Thus the private autonomy argument comes at the expense of the regulatory autonomy argument; conversely, the price to be paid for deference and recognition is opening up to legal control.

6. The Relationship Between Free Movement and Competition

It is beyond dispute that both the competition rules and the free movement rules apply to the rules and practices of sports organizations. In many cases, as AG Lenz noted in his Opinion in *Bosman*, they can apply simultaneously.[112]

In fact, the overlap between the free movement rules and competition rules in the sports area is almost complete. Basic ideas such as the specificity of sport and the regulatory autonomy of sporting bodies are equally relevant to both contexts. The foundational free movement judgments such as *Bosman* and *Deliège* are often cited in competition cases. Finally, in cases such as *Bosman* the same sporting rules were challenged both under the free movement and the competition rules.[113] This has been internalized by all the stakeholders. There are no truly separate discussions on the application of free movement law and competition law to the sports area. Rather, the debate revolves around the limits of the

that a newly formed league that breaks away from traditional organisational structures in search of an increased slice of the financial cake would be denied an exemption for arrangements involving collective selling.'

[110] As broader justifications tend to follow broader definitions of a restriction (see eg Wolf Sauter and Harm Schepel, *State and Market in European Union Law: The Public and Private Spheres of the Internal Market Before the EU Courts* (Cambridge University Press 2009) 39), the converse should also be true.

[111] See for example *UEFA Champions League* (n 75) para 165, where the Commission, in an *obiter dictum*, in principle accepted the redistribution objective under Art 101/3: 'The Commission understands that it is desirable to maintain a certain balance among the football clubs playing in a league because it creates better and more exciting football matches ... The same applies to the education and supply of new players ... The Commission recognises that a cross-subsidisation of funds from richer to poorer may help achieve this.' More recently, the Commission—UEFA Arrangement (n 39) even stated that 'redistribution mechanisms concerning, for example, audiovisual media revenues and training compensation fees should be recommended, in accordance with the EU *acquis*' (para 2.6).

[112] See para 253 of the Opinion, noting that the Commission had argued that only competition law should cover the rules on transfers, but then recanted its view.

[113] In *Murphy* (n 80), different aspects of a licensing scheme were challenged under the free movement and competition rules respectively. See Chapter IV section 4.2.

autonomy of sports regulators imposed by EU law, citing competition law and free movement law precedent simultaneously. Even the Commission, for example, justifies its approach in competition enforcement by relying heavily on free movement case law.[114]

The possibility of overlap has been clear from the outset,[115] even if the earliest judgments like *Walrave* did not address the issue. The tension resurfaced years later in *Meca-Medina*. There, as already mentioned, the Court refused to follow the reasoning of the General Court, which relied on free movement precedent to exclude a case it viewed as 'purely sporting' from competition law.[116] This approach, according to the Court, was an error of law, since the rules constitute two separate legal tests that can, for any number of reasons, lead to different outcomes. For example, the notion of economic activity which is required under both sets of rules could be interpreted in a different way. The free movement rules could be considered inapplicable to a case which is internal in nature, whereas the competition rules could cover even internal cases as long as there is an effect on trade.[117] The two sets of rules may differ on their definitions of a restriction.[118] Justifications may be more flexible under the free movement rules, even though the 'inherent restriction' test on top of either Art 101/3 or the objective justification test under Art 102 can be equally broad in practice.[119]

In practice, however, the notion that the competition and free movement rules are independent and separate tests is not always fully followed. For example, *Bosman* was a clear opportunity to apply both sets of rules, yet the Court stopped after finding a restriction of the free movement rules, unlike the Advocate General who applied (and found a violation of) both.[120] As argued in Chapter IV, while understandable for reasons of judicial economy, such 'shortcuts' can be problematic. Moreover, sometimes hybrid forms of scrutiny are put forward. For example, AG Lenz in *Bosman* suggested that Art 101/3 should be applied in a way that internalizes the free movement provisions.[121] In *Piau*, the General Court spoke, somewhat opaquely, of the possibility that a violation of the free movement of services could, as such, constitute a 'concomitant infringement of the rules on competition'.[122]

[114] See 'The EU and Sport: Background and Context' (n 17), in particular Annex I section 2.

[115] See in particular Weatherill (n 2) 25.

[116] Paragraphs 31–33.

[117] Weatherill (n 2) 107–08, for example, has argued that the *Bosman* judgment could not apply to transfers between two clubs in the same Member State (and that, therefore, transfer fees could still be demanded in those cases even after a player's contract had expired), but that competition law could still prohibit such rules.

[118] See ibid 139.

[119] In theory, one could even argue that there is a broader possibility of justification for regulatory sports measures under competition law, because both Art 101/3 and the 'inherent restriction' test are available. In practice, for the Commission, the Court, or a Member State authority to find that a measure fails either the Art 101/1 proportionality analysis (because, for example, it exceeds what is necessary to protect the legitimate aim at stake) or the free movement justification stage, while nevertheless being justified under Art 101/3, seems rather unlikely.

[120] See paras 253 et seq.

[121] Paragraph 278.

[122] *Piau* (n 61) para 106.

At the same time, the choices of the Commission and various litigants—not necessarily supported by the legal tests themselves—have differentiated the free movement and competition approach. As Weatherill predicted after *Bosman*: 'The use of the law of free movement … in *Bosman*, is a blip … The Commission has now picked up the baton, and it seems plain that, *Bosman* notwithstanding, it is competition policy that will be the major battleground …'[123] This was, for the most part, fulfilled. While the free movement provisions were initially more important,[124] the majority of the sports cases after *Bosman* were based on competition law.

Thus, free movement law seems to have become somewhat side-lined, perhaps because of the difficulties in accessing the CJEU. For individual athletes, judicial review as such is a poor remedy due to the brevity of their careers, making an additional reference to the European Court even less likely to help. Competition law may provide a more flexible choice of *fora*: plaintiffs can file simple complaints with the Commission or a national competition authority, and can also start actions before national courts on the basis of European or national competition rules. After Regulation 1/2003, national competition authorities have a clear authority over the measures of sporting bodies on the basis of EU law, and may apply both Art 101/1 and Art 101/3.[125] There also seems to be an established practice of alleging competition law infringements as a public policy ground for refusing to execute CAS arbitral awards in EU Member States.[126] Coupled with the huge commercial significance of cases on media rights, this means that competition law is likely to remain the centre of attention. Free movement scrutiny may be reserved for impediments to individual cross-border movement of athletes, especially direct discrimination on the basis of nationality,[127] rather than structural and organizational aspects of sports regulation.

[123] Weatherill (n 2) 138.

[124] Budzinski (n 10) 46 et seq.

[125] See, for some examples of national competition law enforcement in sports, *Sweden: Market Court's Decision in Automobile Sports Federation Case* (ECN Brief 1/2013, 2013); *BAGS v AMRAC* (UK Court of Appeal 2009); Bundeskartellamt, 'Bundeskartellamt gives green light for DFL's marketing plans: DFL obliged to award media rights in a fair, non-discriminatory and transparent manner and offer a number of different packages' (press release) <http://www.bundeskartellamt.de/SharedDocs/Meldung/EN/Pressemitteilungen/2012/13_01_2012_DFL.html>; Italian Competition Authority, 'Equestrian sports: antitrust authority puts a stop to FISE's exclusive over recreational activities: members may participate in competitions arranged by other entities' (press release) <http://www.agcm.it/en/newsroom/press-releases/1135-federitaliafederazione-italiana-sport-equestri-fise-italian-equestrian-sports-federation.html>; Autorité de la concurrence, 'The Autorité de la concurrence fines the French Football Federation and the company Sportfive €6.9 million for having colluded in order to eliminate all competition in the awarding of the Federation's marketing rights' (press release) <http://www.autoritedelaconcurrence.fr/user/standard.php?id_rub=316&id_article=1221>.

[126] One example is *Pechstein* (n 9). The *Wilhelmshaven* case shows, however, that the same can equally be true of the free movement rules (n 57).

[127] In Commission 'Developing the European Dimension in Sport' (n 35), the Commission discusses the free movement rules almost exclusively through the lens of discrimination based on nationality. Most other issues are discussed in the framework of the competition rules. A notable recent case where the free movement rules applied in a different sport-related context is *Murphy* (n 80).

7. Institutional Strategies: Interactions Between the Court, the Commission and the Political Process

The EU has no clear legislative competence in the area of sport, and the European Parliament and the Council have generally been less supportive of strong EU action in the area. These difficulties associated with putting the EU political process to work in the sports field may be a reason why the judicial route and the Commission as the competition enforcer have become so prominent. EU law has affected the governance of sports mainly through free movement and competition law. This 'creeping juridification'[128] did not happen because of a sudden decision to start regulating sports on the EU level, but incrementally.

The Commission and the Court, however, have not followed exactly the same dynamic. Broadly speaking, the Court has laid down the basic principles and developed the main concepts in several pivotal judgments. The 'horizontal effect' of the free movement rules on sporting regulators, the idea of the specificity of sport and of 'purely sporting rules' (*Walrave*), the broad definition of a restriction to free movement (*Bosman*), the possibility for sports organizations to invoke broad public interest justifications (*Bosman*, *Meca-Medina*), the intellectual separation between free movement and competition law (*Meca-Medina*)—all these are the building blocks of any analysis of a sporting rule under EU law. The Commission has taken up the opportunities created by the Court and developed its own sports policy on that basis, but the big steps forward have mostly come from the Court.

One might suppose that the Commission, being the 'guardian of the Treaties', would fight restrictive practices of the sporting federations with the same or even greater zeal than when it came to Member State measures. In fact, however, the history of EU sports regulation shows a constant interplay between the Commission and sporting bodies, avoiding confrontation while negotiating certain reforms.[129]

In *Bosman*, an intervention by the Court, contrary to the Commission's agreement with UEFA, was necessary in order to kick-start the scrutiny of sports regulators.[130] A similar dynamic could be seen in *Meca-Medina*: while the Commission and the General Court were unwilling to see anti-doping rules as a restriction of competition, the Court of Justice was ready, in principle at least, to entertain the claim that a restriction of competition took place. The future of the

[128] Parrish (n 24) 249.

[129] 'Despite condemning restrictions on player mobility, the Commission's negotiated settlement approach with the sports world initially resulted in sport and competition law operating in separate realms. The Commission appeared keen to avoid confrontation with sport.' ibid 252.

[130] As Weatherill (n 2) 110 points out, before *Bosman* the Commission 'has been reticent ... to take on the football authorities and its image as guardian of the Treaties is tarnished by its agreement to practices exposed in *Bosman* as unlawful'. For a description of this agreement, see the Opinion of AG Lenz in *Bosman* (n 4) paras 39 and 148.

Commission's latest agreement with football regulators, promoting the highly controversial Financial Fair Play regulations,[131] is also uncertain. The same might even be said for the 'home-grown rule' that received the Commission's blessing in 2008.[132]

In a sense, the Commission's approach is understandable. As the sporting regime is to a great extent unmoored from traditional legal structures, no public regulator (the EU, a state, an international organization) can single-handedly count on being able to regulate it. The possibility for actors outside the sporting hierarchy to assert their influence will therefore depend on their ability to engage the sporting bodies directly. The Commission can do so, with the help of the free movement and competition rules. By requiring narrowly tailored remedies and changes to various regulatory schemes, while retaining the possibility of rejecting complaints when there is little 'Community interest',[133] as well as occasionally publishing indicative lists of acceptable and unacceptable practices,[134] it was possible to enact the Commission's favoured reforms while avoiding direct judicial conflicts. The Court has, on the one hand, empowered the Commission in this strategy by opening up the sporting bodies to legal scrutiny. On the other hand, the Court's approach has at times been at odds with the bargains between the Commission and the sports world.[135]

Bosman is a very good example of the agenda-setting approach of the Court itself. With surprising candour, AG Lenz urged the Court to find the reference admissible for what can only be described as reasons of institutional politics. The scarcity of references on issues of the organization of sports, according to the AG, shows that 'those affected are either unwilling or unable to have the matter clarified by the courts';[136] he concluded that 'it is extremely unlikely that a reference will ever again reach the Court which raises the question of the compatibility

[131] See, inter alia, Jean-Christophe Roda, 'Sport et droit de la concurrence: L'exemple du football professionnel' (2012) 3 Concurrences 71 section B. See the Joint Statement by Vice-President Joaquín Almunia and President Michel Platini of 21 March 2012 <http://ec.europa.eu/competition/sectors/sports/joint_statement_en.pdf>. While the statement concerns only the state aid rules, finding that they share the same objectives as the FFP rules, they undoubtedly lend strong political support to the scheme. In the meantime, legal challenges are already underway. UEFA won the first one, by the sanctioned Spanish club Malaga, at the CAS (see the press release at <http://www.tas-cas.org/fileadmin/user_upload/2013.06.1120Media20Release20rev.pdf>). The Commission refused to investigate a complaint by the Belgian players' agent Daniel Striani and the case is currently pending in Belgian courts.

[132] See the press release IP/08/807 'UEFA rule on "home-grown players": Compatibility with the principle of free movement of persons' (28 May 2008). Simon Gardiner and Roger Welch, '*Bosman*—There and Back Again: The Legitimacy of Playing Quotas under European Union Sports Policy' (2011) 17 European Law Journal 828 discuss the legality of two alternative solutions to pre-*Bosman* regulations proposed by the sporting bodies: FIFA's '6+5' proposal and UEFA's home-grown rules.

[133] See *Certain joueur de tennis professionnel/Agence mondiale antidopage + ATP + CIAS* (Case COMP/39.471) Commission Decision of 12 October 2009 as an example of a discretionary rejection decision.

[134] See n 17. [135] Weatherill (n 2) 135.

[136] Opinion of AG Lenz in *Bosman* (n 4) para 112.

with Community law of the rules on foreign players'.[137] An additional argument in favour of responding was the fact that the Commission was unlikely to start infringement proceedings in sports cases for procedural reasons: sporting organizations are private and a link with Member State conduct would be difficult to find.[138] The AG's conclusion was: 'If… the Court declines to answer the question, regulation of this field will continue to be left to the whim of the sporting associations. I regard that as scarcely tolerable.'[139]

8. Conclusion

This overview of how the free movement and competition rules were applied to private regulation in sport leads to several conclusions that, by and large, support the general points made in Chapters II–IV.

Firstly, free movement and competition law are both broadly applicable to a wide range of measures of sporting bodies, while allowing them a rather wide margin to justify their measures. The rules have, in this sense, adapted to the context of private regulation by recognizing the regulatory autonomy of sporting bodies. They can no longer invoke arguments such as private autonomy or the freedom of contract to fully escape scrutiny, but can justify their measures by a range of public interest objectives on a case-by-case basis.

Secondly, this case-by-case scrutiny is often focused less on the substance of the measures, but rather on the governance and procedures employed by the sporting world. Competition law, for example, is unlikely to deeply question the substantive criteria for licensing competitions or second-guess whether a particular substance should be considered doping, but it can be used to challenge conflicts of interest, dispute settlement procedures, or the composition of decision-making bodies.

Thirdly, the case-by-case approach allows enforcers, and especially the Commission, to maintain a flexible strategy: in principle, most measures of sporting bodies are open to scrutiny, but there is a large scope of manoeuvre for forgoing actual case-work and pursuing negotiated solutions. Because of this, the application of competition law in sport is not just about attacking anti-competitive practices for the benefit of consumers, but also about supporting the development of a more general EU sports policy. This is especially important in view of the fact that the EU has limited legislative competence and that private bodies are the ones that set the main rules in the sport context. EU economic law is thus leveraged in order to build a reform-oriented dialogue with the sporting world, in line with the general idea of 'conditional autonomy' of sporting bodies.[140] This may not in practice involve aggressive competition or free movement scrutiny. Indeed, recent events such as the statements in favour of Financial Fair Play or the 2014

[137] ibid para 117. [138] ibid para 112. [139] ibid para 117.
[140] García and Weatherill (n 23) 241.

Arrangement with UEFA show that the Commission seems to be more interested in partnerships with sporting bodies than in legal confrontation. Yet it is not hard to see that negotiation happens against the background of possible legal enforcement. The Court's active approach has likely bolstered the Commission's bargaining power.

Overall, therefore, the case study of sport regulation aligns with the main conclusions of this book. It is a good example of what I have called a trade-off between private and regulatory autonomy, especially in free movement law. It is precisely in *Bosman* that it first became clear that arguments linked to regulatory autonomy (ie various substantive policy justifications, whether contained in the Treaties or not) are available to private actors. Sporting bodies have extensively relied on such arguments, and have been treated by the Court as legitimate regulators, along with the recognition of a margin of discretion. In some respects, that margin of discretion is indeed broader than is habitually granted to Member States' bodies (eg the recognition of structural arguments such as 'the nature, the organisation and the financing of the sport concerned' in *Deliège*). This means, however, that sporting bodies can no longer rely on pure private autonomy arguments, such as a strong version of the 'sporting exception', or even values like freedom of contract or association, to defend their measures.

This case study also conforms to the general picture portrayed in Chapter IV. The competition and free movement rules largely overlap when applied to the measures of sporting bodies. Similar arguments are used under either of the two sets of rules to attack or defend various measures. The Court has decided that the competition and free movement rules should be applied distinctly, but has at times employed a blended approach or dispensed with one form of analysis after completing the other.

On the other hand, the case study of sport does depart from the overall argument in some respects. Most importantly, it shows in two distinct ways the limited relevance of legal doctrine when it comes to the overlap of free movement and competition law. Firstly, the two sets of rules have empirically *diverged* not because of legal doctrine, but because enforcement practice—perhaps due to more extensive procedural possibilities and more flexible remedies, but to some extent probably simply because of path dependencies—tends to lean heavily in favour of the competition rules for all issues except for the free movement of individual athletes and discrimination on grounds of nationality. This divergence is not required by doctrine at all. Secondly, in some instances, the rules are strategically blended, like in various policy documents of the Commission, perhaps because that allows for a more compelling narrative in favour of the desired reforms. Again, the niceties of legal doctrine are not decisive.

Finally, certain specificities of the sporting sector should be kept in mind, even if they do not contradict the overall conclusions. Firstly, this is a sector where private regulation is exceptionally widespread and developed, and has been for a long time. In a sense, the CJEU started its attempts to accommodate private regulators in the analysis under the free movement rules precisely to respond to the specificities of sporting bodies (eg *Walrave*). This, of course, shows the importance of this case study to the overall topic, but it may make it somewhat *sui generis*, in terms of scale and depth rather than principle: there are very many actual and possible cases under both sets of rules to analyse. Secondly, the absence of EU legislative competences makes the overall picture rather neat: the only effective ways for EU law to intervene are the two sets of rules analysed by this book. While this supports the overall conclusions, the argument that internal market law is used in order to induce private regulators to reform may be stronger in this sector than elsewhere. The following two case studies, however, will not present this problem.

VI

The Learned Art

Regulating the Legal Profession

1. Introduction

'Pursuing a learned art as a common calling in the spirit of a public service' is how Roscoe Pound described the legal profession.[1] Many others have a more cynical view, along with Dickens, who dryly noted that 'the one great principle of the English law is to make business for itself'.[2]

The profession to which they both refer is one of the so-called 'liberal professions', including, among others architects, engineers, medical doctors, pharmacists, attorneys, notaries, and real estate agents.[3] These professions require specialized knowledge and training, impose strict entry requirements, enforce quality standards and codes of ethical conduct, and are characterized by a high level of both public and private regulation frequently performed by powerful associations with a special legal status or even a legal monopoly. From the point of view of competition and free movement law, the practices of these governing bodies are challenged on similar grounds and justified by similar arguments. Most frequently, regulation is claimed to be necessary to compensate for asymmetries of information between providers and clients (see section 2.1).

The legal profession, however, is specific on two counts. Firstly, it provides a relatively high number of pertinent cases, especially judgments of the CJEU, to study. In addition, several important EU directives specifically deal with the free movement of lawyers (section 4). Therefore, within the broader area of the liberal professions, it makes sense to focus on the legal profession as a good case study of the interaction of free movement, competition, and internal market legislation, which have all been used for similar ends, but at different times and by different actors. This also provides an interesting contrast with the area of sports, where

[1] Roscoe Pound, *Lawyer from Antiquity to Modern Times* (West Publishing 1953) 5–6. See also Stephen Breyer 'The Legal Profession and Public Service' Gauer Distinguished Lecture in Law and Public Policy (12 September 2000) <http://www.supremecourt.gov/publicinfo/speeches/sp_10-10-00.pdf> 2.

[2] Charles Dickens, *Bleak House* (Bradbury and Evans 1853) 385–86.

[3] Commission 'Report on Competition in Professional Services' (Communication) COM/2004/0083 final 3 defines them simply as 'occupations requiring special training in the liberal arts or sciences'.

there is little directly relevant legislation and the focus has been almost exclusively on the Treaty provisions.

Briefly, this chapter will claim the following. The legal profession[4] is characterized by co-regulation, and not simply self-regulation. This means that the public and private aspects of regulation are intertwined (section 2). As with sports, competition and free movement scrutiny tend not only to overlap, but also to rely on similar arguments. Structural justifications such as the need for the profession to self-regulate as a safeguard of independence have an important role to play. In this area, however, the pervasiveness of co-regulation means that full autonomy from either discipline is unlikely.

The application of EU economic law to the legal profession has, over the years, moved in different directions. Firstly, it has moved from free movement law (section 3) to competition law (section 5). Secondly, it has moved from focusing on rules of entry to rules of conduct, even though the latter category is still scrutinized much less forcefully. Thirdly, it has shifted from the EU level to the national level. Fourthly, it has moved from direct enforcement to soft forms of re-regulation through influencing and convincing national policy-makers and the professional bodies themselves (section 6).

2. The Context of Legal Services Regulation

The history of regulation in the legal profession is as long as that of the profession itself.[5] Traditionally, lawyers are organized into national and regional bar associations or similar professional bodies. Entry into the profession and professional conduct are heavily regulated, partly through rules adopted by those bodies and partly through legislation. While the details vary from one jurisdiction to the next, this general description applies to all of the EU Member States.

At this stage, one could ask whether the regulation of legal services truly falls within the scope of this book. Is this really private regulation? It could be argued

[4] A word of clarification: while using the term 'lawyer', this chapter will focus largely on attorneys, rather than lawyers in general. Other legal or quasi-legal professions found in some EU jurisdictions that can be said to provide services, such as notaries, conveyancers, patent agents, or bailiffs, will be addressed only insofar as that helps broader conclusions to be drawn.

[5] Rostain links the evolution of the modern legal profession in the United Kingdom and the United States with the industrial revolution, after which the authority of lawyers was no longer linked to class and social standing but to an ideology of professionalism. 'In claiming self-regulatory authority, professions sought to create an occupational realm shielded from both the market and the state … They contended that regulation of practice was necessary to protect professional judgement from the potentially distorting effects of competitive forces. They also asserted that they were better suited than government authorities, by virtue of expertise, to determine the institutional arrangements …' Tanina Rostain, 'Self-regulatory Authority, Markets, and the Ideology of Professionalism' in Robert Baldwin, Martin Cave, and Martin Lodge (eds), *The Oxford Handbook of Regulation* (Oxford University Press 2010) 170. See also Michael Burrage, *Revolution and the Making of the Contemporary Legal Profession: England, France, and the United States* (Oxford University Press 2006) and Jonathan Rose, 'The Legal Profession in Medieval England: A History of Regulation' (1998) 48 Syracuse Law Review 1.

that bar associations are public law bodies because, in many cases, they are created by law or have comprehensive, legally defined rights and obligations. Secondly, even if bar associations themselves were seen as private, their measures tend to be heavily linked to legislation. Indeed, one would be hard pressed to find a single CJEU judgment that addresses purely private self-regulation by a professional body of lawyers. A public element is almost always present.

These objections are, of course, true. The intention of this book, however, is not to draw lines in the sand between public and private; in fact, I have tried to criticize such formalistic distinctions as unhelpful. While bar associations have important public features, they are self-governing professional bodies that independently develop rules affecting not only the members of the profession but other stakeholders, most importantly their clients. The fact that the State also has an important regulatory role to play is not exclusive to professional regulation. Even in sport, which may be the most private of all areas of private regulation, Member States play an important regulatory role. This is not to say that these distinctions are irrelevant. The different involvement of the State and professional bodies will be reflected in what follows.

2.1 Restrictive measures and their justifications

What do these co-regulatory schemes regulate? A useful distinction can be made between rules that govern entry to the profession, such as educational requirements, and those that govern the conduct of professionals, such as ethical rules, tariffs, or advertising restrictions.[6] Table 1 presents a non-exhaustive list of these rules, and in particular those that could be said to restrict market access or competition.

The list is long, and one might be forgiven for thinking that regulating a professional activity so extensively is disproportionate at best and self-serving at worst. Some rules, of course, are justifiable. Especially in earlier case law, a frequent reaction of the professional bodies to challenges under competition law, free movement rules, or secondary legislation has been to invoke the 'dignity' of the profession or its public service aspect—somewhat akin to the 'sport is special' argument we have seen in the previous chapter. This has had limited success. One need not, however, resort to nebulous arguments to explain the need for *some* level of regulation. To a certain extent, conventional economic theory supports regulatory intervention in the markets for legal services[7] in order to respond to market failures.

[6] See Tinne Heremans, *Professional Services in the EU Internal Market: Quality Regulation and Self-regulation* (Hart 2012) 11–12. See also Iain Paterson, Marcel Fink, and Anthony Ogus, *Economic Impact of Regulation in the Field of Liberal Professions in Different Member States* (IHS Research Report—Study for the European Commission, DG Competition, 2003) sections 3.2.1 and 3.2.2.

[7] See Frank H Stephen, 'The Market Failure Justification for the Regulation of Professional Service Markets and the Characteristics of Consumers' in Claus-Dieter Ehlermann and Isabela Atanasiu (eds), *European Competition Law Annual 2004: The Relationship Between Competition Law and the (Liberal) Professions* (Hart 2006) 143, arguing that it is misleading to speak of a single market for legal services because the sector can be distinguished in a number of distinct markets.

Table 1 Examples of entry and conduct rules in the legal profession

Entry rules	Conduct rules
– Nationality and residence requirements; – Qualification rules: rules on education, vocational training and diplomas necessary for admission into professional practice; – Aptitude tests; – Rules on the use of professional titles; – Registration requirements, eg mandatory registration with the professional body; – Mandatory membership in professional bodies; – Reserved tasks: rules allowing only qualified attorneys to eg represent parties in some or all judicial proceedings, or even to provide out-of-court services.	– Rules on professional ethics, attorney-client privilege, and confidentiality; – Business structure rules: bans or restrictions on multidisciplinary partnerships, restrictions on international partnerships, limits on corporate form; – Limits on the ability of lawyers to work as salaried employees; – Limits on other professional activities a lawyer may pursue; – Advertising restrictions—complete or partial bans on advertising and other forms of publicity; – Price restrictions: mandatory or recommended, minimum or maximum prices (perhaps reinforced by legislative rules on the recovery of fees in judicial and other proceedings); limits or bans on particular types of fees, eg contingency fees; – Rules on professional liability and mandatory insurance; – Disciplinary rules (both the substance of disciplinary violations and the procedure, eg rules on decision-making, sanctions, remedies, judicial review etc.).

In this context, the classic market failure is the asymmetry of information between the lawyer and the client. Legal services have been described as experience goods[8] (consumers can judge their quality only *ex post*—eg if their lawyer 'wins') or even credence goods[9] (consumers cannot judge their quality even upon consumption, unless they have considerable experience or are able to rely on external information such as the reports of a rating agency). These information asymmetries, depending on the context, can lead to two distinct problems: adverse selection and moral hazard. Adverse selection means that, because of the inability of consumers to distinguish between high and low-quality services, providers in an unregulated market would have an incentive to compete only on price.[10] This would lead to a situation of undersupply of high-quality legal services. Moral hazard, on the other hand, may happen when service providers are insufficiently disciplined by consumers in deciding which services they will actually render. An uninformed consumer may be persuaded to buy more legal services than he

[8] Phillip Nelson, 'Information and Consumer Behavior' (1970) 78 Journal of Political Economy 311.

[9] Winand Emons, 'Credence Goods and Fraudulent Experts' (1997) 28 RAND Journal of Economics 107.

[10] George A Akerlof, 'The Market for "Lemons": Quality Uncertainty and the Market Mechanism' (1970) 84 The Quarterly Journal of Economics 488.

actually needs, leading to an oversupply in comparison with what an efficient market might require.[11]

Externalities are another possible market failure in this context. This refers to the imposition of costs (negative externality) or benefits (positive externality) on third parties that have not been considered in the lawyer–client transaction and are thus not reflected in the price. Positive externalities would lead to an undersupply and negative externalities to an oversupply of particular legal services. A standard example of externalities as grounds for regulation[12] in the liberal professions is that of an unskilled architect designing (cheaply) a building that later collapses, harming many more people than just the building's owner. In the context of legal services, the externalities argument is less obvious, but can still be made. Skilled attorneys create positive externalities by improving the overall administration of justice: the work of judges, for example, is made easier by well-drafted briefs and well-argued pleadings. By contrast, unskilled attorneys can create negative externalities or social costs by making the administration of justice less efficient.[13]

Finally, it is sometimes claimed that professional services have a public good character. A public good, in the economic sense, is a good access to which cannot be easily restricted and the use of which by one individual does not prevent use by another. Clean air, street lighting, and national defence are examples. The reason why a public good leads to market failure is the 'free rider' problem: because everyone benefits from street lights, whether or not they have paid for them, and because there is no practical way to restrict their use to those who pay, a free market would generally undersupply street lights. Legal services are unlikely to fit that bill. A well-functioning legal system is a public good because the society as a whole benefits from it, but a particular legal service is not likely to be a public good as such. A high quality legal service largely benefits the consumer; whatever additional value it has for the legal system in general is likely to be too diffuse and unnoticeable to lead to free-riding.[14]

Market failures are staples of the so-called public interest theory of regulation, which implies a well-meaning, rational regulator that aims to increase social welfare.[15] Another way of analysing regulation in economic terms are so-called private interest theories,[16] which claim that regulation happens not because of a genuine concern for social welfare, but because of the interests of the regulators

[11] For a more detailed discussion of the application of economic theories of regulation to liberal professions, see Heremans (n 6) ch 2 section B.

[12] Of course, the existence of externalities is not necessarily grounds for regulation if there are effective alternatives for dealing with the social cost, as famously shown by Ronald H Coase, 'The Problem of Social Cost' (1960) 3 Journal of Law and Economics 1.

[13] One could even go further. For example, inadequate lawyers could cause courts to develop a harmful line of precedent preventing future litigants (even those with good attorneys) from obtaining redress.

[14] Heremans (n 6) 42.

[15] Cento Veljanovski, 'Economic Approaches to Regulation' in Baldwin, Cave, and Lodge (n 5) 19–22.

[16] ibid 24–27.

and those able to influence them. A profession that regulates various aspects of its activity with governmental blessing can be very effective in restricting competition to the benefit of its members, since it is able to prevent events that would normally tend to destabilize a cartel, in particular the entry of new competitors and defection. The legal profession is well equipped to influence or even capture public regulators.[17] Genuine and self-serving motives can, of course, be intertwined or difficult to tell apart.[18]

On the other hand, the economic literature also recognizes the advantages of self-regulation, such as superior knowledge, lower costs, flexibility, and speed.[19] Some reform proposals have sought to retain these benefits while simultaneously addressing the risks of anticompetitive behaviour and the lack of democratic legitimacy of professional bodies. One possibility is to create independent regulatory bodies to supervise or meta-regulate[20] the activities of professional bodies.[21] Another option is competitive self-regulation: instead of a single professional body controlling the market access and conduct of lawyers, it would be possible to license several bodies which would then compete in the market, in theory meaning that none of them would be able to secure supra-competitive rents for their members or otherwise unnecessarily restrict competition.[22]

There are arguments for some level of regulation of legal services, just as there are reasons to worry about anticompetitive and self-serving behaviour of professional bodies as regulators. All sides of the debate seem to recognize both points.

[17] One should also not disregard the 'revolving door' between the high levels of politics and administration and the legal profession. See Gregory C Shaffer, 'How Business Shapes Law: A Socio-Legal Framework' (2009) 42 Connecticut Law Review 147, 156–57.

[18] In Van den Bergh's words: 'The legal professions satisfy all criteria to be qualified as powerful interest groups: they are small, well organized and able to cope with the free riding problem through compulsory membership of the professional bodies ... When there are sound public interest arguments in favour of regulation, the scope for regulatory capture increases since it is difficult to identify the rent-seeking behaviour and private interest restrictions may be more easily enacted.' Roger Van den Bergh, 'Towards Better Regulation of the Legal Professions in the European Union' Rotterdam Institute of Law and Economics (RILE) Working Paper No 2008/07 <http://ssrn.com/abstract=1113310>, 7.

[19] ibid 7–8. See also Heremans (n 6) ch 3 and Roger Van den Bergh, 'Towards Efficient Self-regulation in Markets for Professional Services' in Claus-Dieter Ehlermann and Isabela Atanasiu (eds), *European Competition Law Annual 2004* (n 7) section II.

[20] This may not only eliminate rent-seeking but improve compliance as well. Cary Coglianese and Evan Mendelson, 'Meta-regulation and Self-regulation' in Baldwin, Cave, and Lodge (n 5) 161.

[21] This has in fact been implemented in England and Wales. Frank H Stephen, 'Regulation of the Legal Professions or Regulation of Markets for Legal Services: Potential Implications of the Legal Services Act 2007' (2008) 19 European Business Law Review 1129.

[22] See Ségolène Barbou des Places, 'Self-Regulation and the Professions: A Perspective from Regulatory Competition Theory' in Fabrizio Cafaggi (ed), *Reframing Self-Regulation in European Private Law* (Kluwer Law International 2006). In the US context, Simon has suggested that the many beneficial activities of bar associations could be preserved without granting them a monopoly in regulating the provision of legal services. William H Simon, 'Who Needs the Bar: Professionalism without Monopoly' (2002) 30 Florida State University Law Review 639.

What is not clear is how much regulation there should be, and who gets to decide on that question. In the following section, I will address how EU law has tackled that problem, first looking at free movement, then at sector-specific EU legislation, and finally at competition law.

3. Free Movement of Lawyers

The early application of EU law to the legal profession largely dealt with State measures that impeded the free movement of lawyers providing services or seeking establishment. *Reyners* opened Pandora's box by ruling that reserving access to the profession of lawyer to a State's own nationals, even when nationals of other Member States have the necessary qualifications, violates the freedom of establishment.[23] The argument that the profession of *avocat* as a whole is 'connected with the exercise of official authority' and that it should therefore be exempt from the free movement rules failed.[24] Soon afterwards, the *Van Binsbergen* judgment applied the rules on free movement of services to a Dutch law requiring attorneys appearing before courts to reside in the Netherlands. While finding the residence requirement to be disproportionate and thus contrary to the Treaty,[25] the Court made it clear that the imposition of 'professional rules justified by the general good', in particular rules on 'organization, qualifications, professional ethics, supervision and liability' and those connected with the administration of justice is, in general, legitimate.[26]

[23] With this historic precedent in mind, it is troubling that the Court has more recently allowed a trainee lawyer of Bulgarian nationality, holding an Austrian law degree, residence, and work permit and lawfully employed by a Viennese law office, to be refused registration with the Bar as a trainee lawyer simply because of his nationality. Even though the Bulgarian Association Agreement at the time required the removal of discrimination in working conditions, and even though there seemed to have been solid precedent for removing discriminatory rules on access to work for legally resident nationals of association countries, as well as for the fact that trainee lawyers can be considered workers (Case C-109/04 *Karl Robert Kranemann v Land Nordrhein-Westfalen* [2005] ECR I-2421, paras 12–18 and Case C-313/01 *Christine Morgenbesser v Consiglio dell'Ordine degli avvocati di Genova* [2003] ECR I-13467, paras 59–61), the Court found that access to a regulated profession does not fall under the scope of the SAA provisions on employment. Case C-101/10, *Gentcho Pavlov and Gregor Famira v Ausschuss der Rechtsanwaltskammer Wien* [2011] ECR I-5951, paras 27–28.

[24] Case 2-74 *Jean Reyners v Belgian State* [1974] ECR 631, paras 43–53. The Court did, however, accept in principle that some more narrowly defined activities of attorneys could be defined as 'in themselves involving a direct and specific connexion with the exercise of official authority' (para 54). See also Case 38/87 *Commission v Greece* [1988] ECR 4415, paras 14–17. More recently, the Court found that the activities of notaries cannot be reserved to a Member State's own nationals, but that 'guaranteeing the lawfulness and legal certainty of documents entered into by individuals' could justify proportionate rules on appointments, caps on the number of providers, territorial jurisdiction, remuneration, independence, disqualification from other offices, etc. See Case C-47/08 *Commission v Belgium* [2011] ECR I-4105, paras 97 and 123. There are equivalent judgments against Luxembourg, Germany, and Austria, among others.

[25] Case 33-74 *Johannes Henricus Maria van Binsbergen v Bestuur van de Bedrijfsvereniging voor de Metaalnijverheid* [1974] ECR 1299, paras 15–17.

[26] Paragraphs 12 and 14.

In *Thieffry*, the Court was faced with the first free movement claim against a decision of a bar association. It found a violation of the freedom of establishment in the Paris Bar's refusal to register a lawyer with a Belgian degree, even though his degree was recognized as equivalent to the French one and even though he had passed the French bar exam.[27] The Court found that the free movement provisions have to be respected not only by States but also by professional bodies, at least those that are 'recognized by law'.[28] Some years later, in *Klopp*, the Paris Bar was similarly held to have violated the freedom of establishment by refusing the title of *avocat* to a fully qualified lawyer on the sole basis that he also maintained chambers in Germany.[29]

Much like *Walrave* and *Donà v Mantero* in the area of sports, these early judgments set the tone for what followed. By bringing professional rules on lawyers within the scope of the fundamental freedoms, rejecting the claim of full autonomy of the profession from EU law (*Reyners*) but at the same time leaving the door open to broad substantive justifications of various professional rules (*Van Binsbergen*) the Court opened up a dialogue with the Member States and professional bodies (*Thieffry*) on how the profession should be regulated.

As in sports, the crucial cases based on the free movement rules came in the 1990s. These judgments set a broad market access standard for defining restrictions of free movement, catching not only discriminatory rules, but all rules capable of hindering the establishment or free provision of services by lawyers from other Member States.[30] They also imposed further-reaching specific requirements on the Member States and professional bodies.[31]

Vlassopoulou—with facts just predating the entry into force of the first general directive on the recognition of qualifications[32]—insisted that a request for admission into the profession by recognition of a law degree from another Member State

[27] Case 71-76 *Jean Thieffry v Conseil de l'ordre des avocats à la cour de Paris* [1977] ECR 765. See also the later judgment in Case C-19/92 *Dieter Kraus v Land Baden-Württemberg* [1993] ECR I-1663, on the need for individuals to obtain official authorization for the use of an academic degree obtained in another Member State. The Court insisted that such requirements be simple, subject to judicial review and fundamental rights guarantees, and limited to the question whether the degree was properly awarded by a competent academic institution (paras 33–41).

[28] See paras 17 and 18: 'Since the practical enjoyment of freedom of establishment can ... in certain circumstances depend upon national practice or legislation, it is incumbent upon the competent public authorities—including legally recognized professional bodies—to ensure that such practice or legislation is applied in accordance with the objective defined by the provisions of the Treaty relating to freedom of establishment.'

[29] Case 107/83 *Ordre des avocats au Barreau de Paris v Onno Klopp* [1984] ECR 2971.

[30] Case C-340/89 *Irène Vlassopoulou v Ministerium für Justiz, Bundes- und Europaangelegenheiten Baden-Württemberg* [1991] ECR I-2357, para 15; Case C-76/90 *Manfred Säger v Dennemeyer & Co. Ltd* [1991] ECR I-4221, para 12; Case C-55/94 *Reinhard Gebhard v Consiglio dell'Ordine degli Avvocati e Procuratori di Milano* [1995] ECR I-4165, para 37; and *Kraus* (n 27) para 32.

[31] Of the cases cited in n 30, only *Gebhard* was specifically about a bar association's decision. Still, by analogy with *Thieffry*, it seems clear that the same findings would apply to bar associations.

[32] Council Directive 89/48/EEC of 21 December 1988 on a general system for the recognition of higher-education diplomas awarded on completion of professional education and training of at least three years' duration [1989] OJ L19/16.

should not be automatically rejected, but that the authorities should take into account the 'diplomas, certificates and other evidence of qualifications which the person concerned has acquired', as well as additional courses of study or practical experience in the host Member State.[33]

Gebhard dealt with an Italian bar's refusal to grant the title of *avvocato* to a German qualified lawyer. According to the Court, while access to a profession and the use of a professional title may be restricted to 'holders of a diploma, certificate or other evidence of formal qualifications ... persons belonging to a professional body or to persons subject to particular rules or supervision',[34] those rules impede free movement and must be applied in a non-discriminatory way, pursue imperative requirements in the general interest, be suitable for the attainment of those goals, and not go beyond what is necessary.[35] These four requirements codified the legal test for the analysis of professional regulation under the free movement rules.

The case law has also extended to the qualification of trainee lawyers. In *Morgenbesser*, the Court found that admission to practical training cannot be excluded solely because the applicant has a law degree from another Member State, but that a *Vlassopoulou*-like comparison of all their relevant knowledge and experience needs to be done by the relevant authority.[36]

While qualification rules made the bulk of litigation under the free movement rules, other types of measures were challenged as well. Firstly, in *Säger*, *Broede*, and most recently in *Commission v Austria*, the Court addressed legislation imposing a reserved task: the need to hire a local lawyer or patent agent in certain legal proceedings. While such rules were condemned in *Säger* and *Commission v Austria*,[37] in *Broede* the Court justified a rule preventing debt-collecting agencies from representing clients before courts except through an attorney, even though the parties were free to represent themselves or appoint a non-professional representative.[38]

[33] *Vlassopoulou* (n 30) paras 16–21.

[34] *Gebhard* (n 30) para 35. These factors should not justify restrictive rules in areas where the market failure justifications for regulation are not relevant. *Säger* (n 30) paras 16–20, for example, rejected restrictive rules on the practice of patent agents insofar as the plaintiff was merely providing a patent renewal service without actually advising clients.

[35] Paragraphs 37–38. In practice, the Bar had to follow the *Vlassopoulou* requirement of comparing the acquired qualifications before deciding on the use of the title.

[36] Case C-313/01 *Christine Morgenbesser v Consiglio dell'Ordine degli avvocati di Genova* [2003] ECR I-13467, paras 57–72. All this, even though Ms Morgenbesser could rely neither on the Qualifications Directive nor on the Lawyers' Establishment Directive (see section 4).

[37] See *Säger* (n 30) para 21 and Case C-564/07 *Commission v Austria* [2009] ECR I-100 (operative part). In the latter case, Austria breached EU law by requiring patent agents from other Member States who temporarily provide a service in Austria to appoint a locally resident agent.

[38] Case C-3/95 *Reisebüro Broede v Gerd Sandker* [1996] ECR I-6511. Putting to one side the need to protect the parties' interests by requiring knowledgeable and independent representation (which is moot since the parties are free to appoint an incompetent non-professional agent anyway), another claim was that the rule excluding professional representatives is aimed at reducing costs—yet the legislator seemed not to object to the situation where both a debt collection agency and an attorney would have to be paid. See para 35.

Secondly, the Court applied the free movement rules in two cases dealing with fee tariffs fixed by the Italian bar association and confirmed by Italian legislation: *Cipolla* and *Commission v Italy*.[39] In *Cipolla*, the Court found these tariffs to be a justified and proportionate restriction of the freedom of establishment and of the freedom to provide services, based partly on the fact that they are relatively flexible and can be changed by courts when deciding on costs. In *Commission v Italy*, a reformed scheme under which only maximum fees were imposed, however, was held not to be a restriction at all. I will address these cases in greater detail in the segment on the relationship between free movement and competition, as they overlap with competition law claims.

We can draw several conclusions from the development of the free movement case law. Firstly, it has overwhelmingly been used to discipline entry rules, in particular rules on qualifications and establishment. More recent cases have made some inroads into challenging conduct rules, in particular those on reserved tasks and prices. The Court, however, seems to have been less demanding in this category, largely deferring to the regulatory choices of the State or professional bodies. *Broede* is an example of that, as are *Cipolla* and (especially) *Commission v Italy*. Professional bodies are in principle required to open access to professionals from other Member States. Once initial market access is ensured, however, there is a rather large margin of discretion in setting and enforcing rules of conduct.[40]

Discussing only the free movement rules would be incomplete without taking into account the internal market legislation governing the free movement of lawyers. I will examine this in the following section.

4. Internal Market Legislation

A characteristic feature of the free movement of services and establishment in this area is the existence of two directives specifically addressed to the legal profession, as well as the relevance of other major pieces of legislation—in particular the Services Directive[41] and the Diploma Directive.[42] It is beyond the scope of this chapter to discuss any of these, much less the accompanying case law, in detail. Apart from a very brief explanation of what these directives are about, I will restrict myself to discussing the extent to which they address professional bodies.[43]

[39] Joined cases C-94/04 and C-202/04 *Federico Cipolla v Rosaria Fazari, née Portolese* (C-94/04) and *Stefano Macrino and Claudia Capoparte v Roberto Meloni* (C-202/04) [2006] ECR I-11421 and Case C-565/08 *Commission v Italy* [2011] ECR I-2101.

[40] See for example Case 292/86 *Claude Gullung v Conseil de l'ordre des avocats du barreau de Colmar et de Saverne* [1988] ECR 111, para 31.

[41] Directive 2006/123/EC of the European Parliament and of the Council on services in the internal market [2006] OJ L376.

[42] Directive 2005/36/EC of the European Parliament and of the Council on the recognition of professional qualifications [2005] OJ L255/22, as amended by Directive 2013/55/EU of the European Parliament and of the Council [2013] OJ L354.

[43] For more extensive discussions, see Heremans (n 6) ch 6 and Sjoerd Claessens, *Free Movement of Lawyers in the European Union* (Wolf Legal Publishers 2008) 24–76. For an earlier,

4.1 The Lawyers' Services Directive

The Lawyers' Services Directive[44] was adopted in 1977. It loosely requires mutual recognition: Member States ('host states') must allow attorneys from other Member States to provide services, without imposing a duty to register, as long as they only use their home title.[45] In principle, these lawyers only remain subject to the professional rules of their home State. This would seem to be a rather powerful set of negative harmonization rules; however, it is dampened by several exceptions.

Firstly, when it comes to the representation of parties in legal proceedings, the Member States can require the lawyer to work in conjunction with a host state lawyer and to be 'introduced' to the presiding judge and president of the Bar.[46] In addition, host state rules of professional conduct apply to those proceedings, 'without prejudice' to home state rules, imposing a sort of 'double deontology'.[47]

Secondly, in all other activities, home state deontological rules are overlaid by a set of mandatory host state rules of professional conduct (in particular, those on conflicts of interest, secrecy, relations with other lawyers, and publicity) that are 'capable of being observed' by the foreign lawyer and justified for reasons of the 'proper exercise of a lawyer's activities, the standing of the profession and respect for the rules concerning incompatibility'.[48] In brief, the Directive leaves the Member States, and presumably professional bodies, a rather wide margin of discretion in deciding which of their own rules of professional conduct to apply to service providers from other Member States.

While the Directive is addressed to the Member States, its Art 7 allows the 'competent authority of the host Member State'—normally, the local bar association—to request proof of the service provider's qualification as a lawyer. It also makes these 'competent authorities' the gatekeepers of the host state's rules of conduct, allowing them to determine the consequences of non-compliance and authorizing them to obtain information from the home state competent authority.

extensive overview, see Roger J Goebel, 'Lawyers in the European Community: Progress Towards Community-Wide Rights of Practice' (1991) 15 Fordham International Law Journal 556.

44 Council Directive 77/249/EEC of 22 March 1977 to facilitate the effective exercise by lawyers of freedom to provide services (1977) OJ L78/17.

45 Articles 1–3.

46 Article 5. This cannot include registration or residence requirements (Art 4/1). In Case 427/85 *Commission v Germany* [1988] ECR 1123, the Court found that the Treaty rules on free movement of services still apply in addition to the Directive, leading to the conclusion that joint representation cannot be required in proceedings where representation by a lawyer is not mandatory (para 14). In addition, this requirement should not be applied too strictly, so that for example the domestic lawyer has to be present at all hearings (paras 22–28; see also Case C-294/89 *Commission v France* [1991] ECR I-3591).

47 Article 4/2. For more on this problem, see Heremans (n 6) 192–94 and Claessens (n 43) 27. Another exception from the general rule is that the Member States can exclude in-house lawyers, as long as they do so in a non-discriminatory way (Art 6).

48 Article 4/4. In *Gullung* (n 40), the Court concluded from a joint reading of Arts 4/1, 4/2, and 4/4 simply that 'it follows from those provisions that members of the legal profession, when providing services, are required to comply with the rules relating to professional ethics in force in the host Member State' (para 18).

Indeed, in *Gullung*, Art 7/2 of the Directive was used in favour of two French bar councils against a German lawyer and ex-French notary who was previously condemned by French notaries' authorities of violating rules of good conduct. The bar councils prohibited their members from assisting Mr Gullung. The Court found that Mr Gullung, having once violated the host State rules of professional conduct, could not rely on the Directive at all.[49] Thus, the bar councils were able to exercise their gatekeeper function in order to completely prevent a lawyer, lawfully registered in another Member State, not only from representing clients (in which case he would need the partnership of a host state lawyer and Bar member) but *de facto* from providing any other kind of legal service. The Court did not impose any conditions on the exercise of this gatekeeper function—for example whether a specific delegating act is needed for a professional body to be a 'competent authority' or whether specific domestic rules on the use of the authority granted under Art 7 need to exist (presumably, a bar council could not directly invoke the Directive against an individual).[50]

The *Gullung* judgment shows a tendency similar to what I already noted in relation to the free movement rules: conduct rules are seen as the domain of professional bodies. While the Directive seems to provide robust market access guarantees, this can to a large extent be compensated by the strict enforcement of conduct rules that the Court is not always eager to question.[51]

4.2 Qualifications and establishment: The general framework under the Diploma Directive

Like all regulated professions,[52] lawyers are subject to the general rules on the mutual recognition of qualifications, which are today contained in the Diploma Directive of 2005, as amended in 2013.[53] The Directive covers both the free provision of services and freedom of establishment.

According to its preamble, the Lawyers' Services Directive and the Lawyers' Establishment Directive (to which I will return later) are 'not affected' by the

[49] ibid para 22.

[50] Relying directly on Art 7 would be problematic regardless of whether the bar councils are seen as private bodies (because directives do not have horizontal effect) or as 'emanations of state' (because Member States cannot invoke a directive against an individual). The point was not discussed in *Gullung*. We do not know on what basis the bar councils were held to be 'competent authorities' in the sense of Art 7 (eg whether there needs to be a specific legal provision delegating that task to them), if there actually were any French rules specifically implementing Art 7, or even if any specific rules were pleaded by the Bar council against Mr Gullung at all.

[51] The Directive remains largely unchanged since 1997. However, a recent study financed by the Commission has suggested some changes and simplification, most importantly the elimination of double deontology for the provision of services. See SJFJ Claessens, MCC van Haeften, NJ Philipsen, BJ Buiskool, HEGS Schneider, SLT Schoenmaekers, DH Grijpstra, and HJ Hellwig, 'Evaluation of the Legal Framework for the Free Movement of Lawyers: Final Report' (2013) <http://ec.europa.eu/internal_market/qualifications/docs/studies/2013-lawyers/report_en.pdf>.

[52] See Art 1(a) of the Diploma Directive (n 42).

[53] This section cannot do justice to the complexity of the Directive, much less to the history of the EU qualifications regime, which has developed from the initial stage of painstakingly harmonizing educational requirements for specific professions, through the first General Systems'

Diploma Directive.[54] This does not necessarily mean that they are *lex specialis* and therefore exclude the application of the Diploma Directive.[55] With regard to services, the Diploma Directive does defer to any 'specific rules' of EU law, which would include the Lawyers' Services Directive. This is important because the Diploma Directive seems to be more liberal in terms of the host State professional rules that can be imposed on the service provider, limiting this to rules that are 'directly linked to professional qualifications', and in terms of the rules on notification of the local professional body.[56] As far as establishment is concerned, however, it was made clear in *Ebert* that diploma recognition under the Diploma Directive and establishment under the Lawyers' Establishment Directive are two separate routes to access the legal profession—neither of them excludes the other.[57]

In a nutshell, the Directive requires the Member States to grant access to professionals fully qualified in another Member State under the same conditions as to its own nationals, as long as their qualifications are at least equivalent to one level below that required in the host State. In some cases, however, including when the applicant's training concerned substantially different matters[58]—like in the legal profession—the host State can impose 'compensation measures'. These can take the form of an aptitude test or of an adaptation period. Normally, the applicant can choose between the two, but in the legal profession[59] the host State can impose its choice. In practice, almost all Member States have chosen to impose an aptitude test.[60] Importantly, however, when imposing the aptitude test or adaptation period, the host State has to take into account the knowledge acquired by the applicant through professional experience and assess whether this can at least partially compensate for the differences in training.[61]

Directive 89/48 (n 32) which moved to a system of mutual recognition, until today's Directive 2005/36 which consolidates all the relevant rules and the 2013 changes which introduce, among others, the 'European professional card' for certain professions. For an overview, see Claessens (n 43) 30–35. Case law on Directive 89/48 may still, of course, be relevant for the interpretation of the new Directive.

[54] Recital 42.

[55] For a different interpretation, see for example the German Bar Association, 'Position Paper on the Proposal for a Directive of the European Parliament and of the Council mending Directive 2005/36/EC on the recognition of professional qualifications and Regulation on administrative cooperation through the Internal Market Information System (COM(2011) 883 final)' (2012) Position Paper No 77/2012 <http://anwaltverein.de/de/newsroom/id-2012-77?file=files/anwaltverein.de/downloads/newsroom/stellungnahmen/2012/DAV-Stellungnahme-77-2012-Berufsqualifikationsrichtlinie.pdf>, 4 and 6.

[56] Articles 5/3 and 7.

[57] Case C-359/09 *Donat Cornelius Ebert v Budapesti Ügyvédi Kamara* [2011] ECR I-269, paras 33–34.

[58] Article 14/1.

[59] As well as other professions 'whose pursuit requires precise knowledge of national law and in respect of which the provision of advice and/or assistance concerning national law is an essential and constant aspect of the professional activity' (Art 14/3).

[60] Heremans (n 6) 226 and Claessens (n 43) 326.

[61] Article 14/5. See also Case C-118/09 *Robert Koller* [2010] ECR I-13627, paras 38–39 and *Ebert* (n 57) para 33.

Thus, one way for a lawyer to become established in a Member State other than the one where he is fully[62] qualified, under host State title, is to take an aptitude test. These tests have to be proportionate and based on transparent rules: they should not be more demanding than for domestic candidates,[63] and the authorities have to conduct a case-by-case comparison of the candidate's training and experience before deciding on its precise content.[64]

Professional bodies are required to admit those who pass the aptitude test under the same conditions as lawyers with domestic qualifications. As the Court clarified in *Ebert*, they are bound by EU law disciplines, especially the principle of non-discrimination.[65] Presumably, apart from the requirements of the Directive, this would also involve rules of free movement and competition law, regardless of the exact public or private law status of the professional body and its place in the domestic co-regulatory scheme.

Finally, the Diploma Directive relies on professional bodies as partners in implementation. Much like the codes of conduct foreseen by the Services Directive (see section 4.4), the Diploma Directive enables national or European professional organizations to propose 'common training frameworks' or 'common training tests' enabling more or less automatic access to the profession (Arts 49a and 49b), that could then be adopted by the Commission. Like the other rules imposed by professional bodies, these would, as recital 16 of the Directive confirms, have to respect EU law, including competition law. To date, the legal profession has not shown interest in proposing common training frameworks.

4.3 The Lawyers' Establishment Directive

The Establishment Directive, adopted in 1998 after difficult negotiations and with some controversy,[66] provides two additional paths for fully qualified lawyers to access the profession in another Member State: first, under their own (home State) title and second, under host State title.

[62] *Morgenbesser* (n 36) probed the applicability of the old Qualifications Directive as well as the Lawyers' Establishment Directive to the case of a French citizen applying for a traineeship with a lawyer in Italy. While the Directives were held to be inapplicable, the case was dealt with under the Treaty rules on establishment and workers. The latest changes to the Diploma Directive (Art 55) require at least partial recognition of professional traineeships taken in other Member States.

[63] As Claessens (n 43) 33–34 points out, the Court did not rule on this specific point in Case C-145/99 Commission v Italy (2002) ECR I-2235, but it can be deduced from the proportionality requirement that 'the outermost border of an aptitude test lies with the test national lawyers must take'.

[64] Case C-145/99 Commission v Italy (2002) ECR I-2235, 51–53.

[65] In *Ebert* (n 57) paras 40–41, the Court found mandatory registration with the Bar as a precondition for entering the profession (after taking an aptitude test) not to be problematic, as it is one of the rules 'relating to organisation, qualifications, professional ethics, supervision and liability' that can be imposed to the legal profession, but pointed out that the Bar has to apply those professional rules in accordance with EU law and, in particular, non-discrimination.

[66] Directive 98/5/EC of the European Parliament and of the Council of 16 February 1998 to facilitate practice of the profession of lawyer on a permanent basis in a Member State other than that in which the qualification was obtained [1998] OJ L77/36. See the account of Luxembourg's attempt to overturn the Directive in Claessens (n 43) 56–59.

For establishment under home state title, it suffices to register with the host State's competent authority, normally the local Bar, by presenting a certificate attesting registration in the home Member State.[67] After this, the lawyer can work in all areas as his host State colleagues, including advising on host State law, but without using a host State title. He or she also has the right to be represented in the relevant professional body.[68] Much like under the Lawyers' Services Directive, however, the host States can (and in practice do) impose additional requirements, including the requirement to work in conjunction with a host State lawyer when representing parties in legal proceedings.[69]

Being established in the host State, these lawyers are fully subject to its rules of professional conduct.[70] The Directive requires the competent authorities (including professional bodies) of the home and host State to inform each other of disciplinary proceedings against a lawyer and co-operate in conducting them. In addition, withdrawal of authorization to practise in the home State leads to automatic exclusion from practice in the host State.[71] Finally, decisions to refuse registration or to impose disciplinary measures have to be reasoned and subject to judicial review (Art 9).

Full establishment under host state title (without an aptitude test, which is a separate qualification track under the Diploma Directive)[72] is possible after three years of practising under home State title, if that involved 'effectively and regularly' dealing with host state law, including EU law.[73] Crucially, the candidate has to prove that this was the case to the competent authority (ie the professional body) on the basis of the number and nature of cases he or she dealt with. All of the candidate's pertinent knowledge and experience has to be taken into account, and negative decisions must be reasoned and subject to appeal.[74]

[67] The Directive's rule on registration amounts to complete harmonization, meaning that Member States cannot impose additional requirements such as language skills or periodic re-registration, nor can they restrict the ability of lawyers established under home State title to practise beyond the limitations outlined in Arts 5/2 and 5/3 (representing parties in legal proceedings in conjunction with a local lawyer and exclusion from 'deeds for obtaining title to administer estates of deceased persons and for creating or transferring interests in land' if this is reserved to special categories of lawyers in the host State). See Case C-193/05 *Commission v Luxembourg* [2006] ECR I-8673, para 73 and Case C-506/04 *Graham J. Wilson v Ordre des avocats du barreau de Luxembourg* [2006] ECR I-8613, paras 64–67. Moreover, recent case law shows that bar associations cannot prevent domestic lawyers from obtaining qualification in another Member State with the sole purpose of practising in their own State as 'European lawyers'—while it is clearly a way of circumventing national rules, it is not an abuse of rights. Joined Cases C-58/13 and C-59/13 *Angelo Alberto Torresi and Pierfrancesco Torresi v Consiglio dell'Ordine degli Avvocati di Macerata* ECLI:EU:C:2014:2088.

[68] See Art 6/2. This includes at least the right to vote in elections to those associations' governing bodies. Naturally, if these lawyers later manage to establish themselves under host State title they should be accorded full representation rights.

[69] What the Court had to clarify in relation to the Lawyers' Services Directive (see n 46), here is explicit: this can only apply 'insofar as the law of the host Member State reserves such activities to lawyers practising under the professional title of that State'.

[70] See Heremans (n 6) 198–99.

[71] Article 7.

[72] See section 4.2. See also Art 10/2.

[73] Article 10/1.

[74] Articles 10/1 and 10/3. Negative decisions can in principle be based only on the absence of proof of the fulfilment of the conditions. There is, however, the possibility to refuse the use of the

The latter is an especially important point for professional bodies, which frequently have a special internal mechanism for deciding on appeals against decisions on registration. The design of such mechanisms was examined in *Wilson*, where a barrister was refused registration under home State title by the Luxembourg Bar. One of his arguments was that the quasi-judicial bodies deciding his case were biased, consisting exclusively or mainly of Luxembourg lawyers who are members of the Bar. The Court responded by translating its usual standard of what is a 'court or tribunal' for the purpose of accepting preliminary references, read in light of the fundamental right to effective judicial protection, into a substantive requirement of independence and impartiality for the bar association bodies deciding on appeals.[75]

Several conclusions from the Lawyers' Establishment Directive and the accompanying case law are relevant for professional bodies. Firstly, while it is for the Member States to transpose the Directive, its actual implementation, including both rule-making and enforcement, is likely to be delegated to professional bodies, that is bar associations.[76] Unlike the Lawyers' Services Directive, the Lawyers' Establishment Directive even requires Member States to designate the 'competent authorities' empowered to receive and decide on applications and notify them to the Commission and the other Member States (Art 14). The Court does not place any emphasis on the distinction between the role of the Member State and the role of the professional body in the co-regulatory schemes through which the Directive is implemented.

Secondly, in line with the general trend already noted when discussing the free movement rules and the Lawyers' Services Directive, professional bodies are granted a rather wide margin of discretion when it comes to the rules of conduct, unlike the rules on entry and practice authorization which are fully harmonized by the Directive.[77] The host State professional body is authorized, for example, to ensure that a 'European lawyer' does not act in matters for which he or she does not have adequate knowledge,[78] and can freely, although on a non-discriminatory basis, subject them to a system of disciplinary rules and professional liability. While the Member States are not allowed to impose barriers

host State title if the authority 'considers that this would be against public policy, in a particular because of disciplinary proceedings, complaints or incidents of any kind' (Art 10/4).

[75] *Wilson* (n 67) paras 43–62. See also *Torresi* (n 67) paras 15–33.

[76] On this point, see Case 246/80 *C. Broekmeulen v Huisarts Registratie Commissie* [1981] ECR 2311 para 16, making it clear that while 'it is incumbent upon Member States to take the necessary steps to ensure that within their own territory the provisions adopted by the Community institutions are implemented in their entirety', they are free to assign the task of implementing those provisions to 'a professional body acting under a degree of governmental supervision'.

[77] Thus, the Court has described the Directive as bringing together 'a plan of action combining consumer information, restrictions on the extent to which or the detailed rules under which certain activities of the profession may be practiced, a number of applicable rules of professional conduct, compulsory insurance, as well as a system of discipline involving both the competent authorities of the home Member State and the host State.' Case C-168/98 *Luxembourg v European Parliament and Council* [2000] ECR I-9131, para 43.

[78] ibid.

to entry, the concerns of expertise and consumer protection which may have led them to do so can be to a large extent substituted by the rules of professional conduct and discipline, the traditional domain of bar associations. In a sense, the application of the Directive, ostensibly meant to achieve an internal market in legal services, leads in practice to a shift in regulatory power from the Member States, more frequently in charge of setting entry rules *ex ante*, to the professional bodies, more frequently in charge of the rules of professional conduct.

An even clearer example of that shift is the Court's explicit reliance on professional conduct rules as an argument against strict Member State regulation of the profession. For example, the Court has repeatedly referred to a rule of the CCBE (Council of Bars and Law Societies of Europe) Code of Conduct, a non-binding document developed by what is in essence an international NGO with no powers over national professional bodies, that requires lawyers to refrain from handling matters in which they know they are incompetent.[79] Without specifying at any point whether the lawyers concerned were actually subjected to such an obligation and on what basis, but simply using this as an example of 'rules of professional conduct applicable to lawyers', 'breach of which may lead to disciplinary sanctions',[80] the Court made the argument that the imposition of barriers to entry by the Member States is unnecessary. Implicitly, it also signalled a rather open-ended mandate to the profession and its bodies, official or unofficial, to develop its own norms of conduct, especially if this is done on a transnational level.[81] Indeed, the CCBE is promoting the adoption of its Code of Conduct by national bar associations.[82]

This wide margin of discretion is partly counterbalanced by the need to respect the requirements of free movement and competition law, as well as the principle of proportionality in rule-making and enforcement. Thus, in *Ebert* the bar council was required to follow the principle of non-discrimination[83] and in *Jakubowska* the Court found that rules of professional conduct must be proportionate ('provided that those restrictions do not go beyond what is necessary in order to attain the objective of preventing conflicts of interest and apply to all the lawyers registered

[79] ibid para 42; *Commission v Luxembourg* (2006) (n 67) para 44 and *Wilson* (n 67) para 74. Charter of core principles of the European legal profession and Code of conduct for European lawyers [2008] CCBE Art 3.1.3.

[80] For what could be read as a critique of that sort of impressionistic recognition of professional rules, see the Opinion of AG Maduro in Case C-305/05 *Ordre des barreaux francophones et germanophone and Others v Conseil des ministres* [2007] ECR I-5305, paras 36–38. Speaking of whether there exists a general principle of lawyers' professional secrecy that EU law has to respect, he pointed out: 'In order to accept the requirement of Community protection, the Court's case-law cannot content itself either with a social axiom or with a professional rule. Existing and having to exist are two very different things ... it does not follow from the fact that a rule appears to have a higher value in certain social or private orders that it must be enshrined as a general principle of Community law.'

[81] See Panagiotis Delimatsis, '"Thou Shall Not ... (Dis) Trust": Codes of Conduct and Harmonization of Professional Standards in the EU' (2010) 47 Common Market Law Review 1049 section 2.5.

[82] See 'Status of the CCBE Code of Conduct at a national level' <http://www.ccbe.eu/index.php?id=32>.

[83] See n 65.

in that Member State'), even though no such specific requirement exists in the Lawyers' Establishment Directive.[84]

4.4 The Services Directive

The general Services Directive[85] may also apply to the legal profession. Like the other Directives referenced above, it is indirectly addressed to professional bodies. Thus, it applies to 'any obligation, prohibition, condition or limit provided for in the laws, regulations or administrative provisions of the Member States or in consequence of case law, administrative practice, the rules of professional bodies, or the collective rules of professional associations or other professional organisations, adopted in the exercise of their legal autonomy'.[86]

In substantive terms, Art 17 of the Directive states that its rules on free provision of services do not apply to areas covered either by the Lawyers' Services Directive, or by the Diploma Directive.[87] As for the provisions of the Services Directive dealing with establishment, the situation is slightly more complex. By virtue of Art 3 of the Services Directive, in case of conflict with any specific legal acts dealing with specific professions, the more specific act will prevail. This explicitly includes the Diploma Directive, and implicitly the Lawyers' Establishment Directive as well. Still, the Services Directive may add to those directives without creating a conflict.

In practice, this could mean that certain rules of professional bodies could be prohibited, if not already under the Treaty free movement rules or by other directives, then under Art 14 of the Services Directive (eg residence requirements for lawyers, prohibitions on establishment or registration in more than one Member State, reciprocity conditions, economic needs tests).[88] Others, including some that are common in the legal profession, should be subject to evaluation under Art 15. For example, quantitative or territorial restrictions, obligation to take a specific legal form, bans on having more than one establishment in the same State, a minimum number of employees, fixed minimum or maximum tariffs[89] should be checked by the Member States (including, presumably, bodies such as bar

[84] Case C-225/09 *Edyta Joanna Jakubowska v Alessandro Maneggia* [2010] ECR I-12329, para 64.

[85] Services Directive (n 41).

[86] Again, while this probably could not be used as an argument to directly invoke the Directive against a fully private body (which is less relevant for the legal profession since bar associations are generally not treated as such), it binds those bodies indirectly. Delimatsis (n 81) 1072 sees the Services Directive as an example of 'alternative methods of regulation' through which the EU 'recognizes the reality of self-regulation'.

[87] This might leave room for application to non-lawyers authorized in their home State to provide a service which, in the host State, is regulated as a legal service. See Claessens (n 43) 128–29 and Heremans (n 6) 237.

[88] Some of the prohibited requirements are expressly allowed for regulated professions. Thus, despite the Services Directive, members of bar associations can continue to decide on matters concerning the lawyer seeking establishment even though they are his competitors, and insurance or financial guarantees can be imposed. See Art 14/6 and 14/7.

[89] Article 15/2.

associations) for non-discrimination, proportionality, and necessity, and notified to the Commission and other Member States.[90]

In the context of this chapter, there is still one other particularly interesting aspect of the Services Directive: namely, its rules on codes of conduct. As many other EU legislative acts, in particular since the 1990s, the Services Directive relies in part on private regulation, notably on the European level, as an implementing tool.[91] It encourages the adoption of European codes of conduct for regulated professions, with the aim of facilitating free movement.[92] These codes of conduct are not binding EU law; indeed, the Directive itself notes in particular that their compatibility with the competition rules should be ensured and that the Member States remain free to adopt more demanding rules in accordance with EU law.[93]

In the legal profession, the best-known example is the CCBE Code of Conduct,[94] introduced not as a response to the Services Directive but in order to remedy the 'double deontology' problem posed by the lawyers' directives: by identifying what the CCBE calls consensual professional rules across EU jurisdictions, the standards of professional conduct should be harmonized, rendering the national differences less relevant.[95] While this code is not legally binding,[96] it is far from irrelevant in the interpretation of EU law, as was already mentioned. Finally, as with all codes of conduct, there is the theoretical possibility that they will be replaced with binding law: as the Inter-institutional Agreement on Better Lawmaking foresees, the Commission is charged with scrutinizing the conformity of self-regulatory schemes with EU law (presumably, including competition and free movement law), as well as the criteria of transparency, representativeness and added value for the public interest. In case of a failure to observe those requirements it can put forward a legislative proposal.[97]

Like the free movement rules, EU legislation dealing with the regulated professions in general and the legal profession in particular consistently recognizes the role of professional bodies in laying down and enforcing rules of professional

[90] New requirements have to be notified and checked by the Commission (Art 15/7) and ones that existed at the end of 2009 should have been notified in the 'mutual evaluation' report dealt with under Art 39 of the Directive.

[91] Paul Verbruggen, 'Does Co-Regulation Strengthen EU Legitimacy?' (2009) 15 European Law Journal 425, 427.

[92] Recital 114. See the Report 'Enhancing the quality of services: The role of European codes of conduct' <http://ec.europa.eu/internal_market/services/docs/services-dir/codeconduct/the_role_of_european_codes_of_conduct_en.pdf> (2007). See also the EESC database of codes of conduct at <www.eesc.europa.eu/self-and-coregulation>.

[93] Recitals 113 and 115.

[94] See n 79 and n 82.

[95] Article 1.3.1 of the Code.

[96] See however the CCBE's description of the code in the EESC database (<http://www.eesc.europa.eu/self-and-coregulation/full.asp?ID=72>): 'The organisations representing the legal profession through the CCBE propose that the rules codified in the following articles ... be recognised at the present time as the expression of a consensus of all the Bars and Law Societies of the European Union and European Economic Area; be adopted as enforceable rules as soon as possible in accordance with national or EEA procedures in relation to the cross-border activities of the lawyer in the European Union and European Economic Area ...'

[97] Interinstitutional agreement on better law-making [2003] OJ C321/1 paras 17, 22, and 23. See also Delimatsis (n 81) 1066.

conduct. It grants them a wide margin of discretion as well as a measure of trust as partners in the implementation of EU law. This trust, however, comes at a price: professional bodies cannot claim to be immune from primary or secondary law, and they have to assess many of their measures under a form of proportionality analysis. The latter requirement has, so far at least, perhaps not had a major influence on the behaviour of professional bodies as far as conduct rules are concerned. Greater potential for that sort of reform may lie in the third set of EU rules that discipline professional regulators: competition law. This will be examined in the following section.

5. Competition Law and the Legal Profession

The most recent incursion of EU law into the regulation of the legal profession took place in the 2000s by way of competition law, through a combination of casework and policy initiatives. After a wave of initial market-opening judgments under the free movement rules and the adoption of sector-specific legislation, the basic legal elements for access to the legal professions of different Member States were in place. The structure and organization of the profession itself, however, including professional rules on advertising, fees, multidisciplinary partnerships, or more broadly the way in which professional bodies were controlled in exercising the powers delegated to them by the Member States, were yet to receive serious scrutiny under EU law. This is where the competition rules entered the frame.

5.1 EU case law

The regulation of the legal profession[98] was challenged under competition law quite late in the game with *Arduino* and *Wouters*, two important judgments delivered on the same day in 2002. These cases respectively dealt with tariffs and multidisciplinary partnerships. It is useful to juxtapose them, as they deal with the two distinct ways in which competition law appears in co-regulated markets: *Arduino* is about the application of competition law to a Member State, and *Wouters* about direct application of Art 101 TFEU to the rules of a professional body.

In *Arduino*, the Court examined a price-fixing scheme in which the Italian Bar, CNF, proposed minimum and maximum prices for particular legal services, both in-court and out of court, which became binding law on approval by the Minister of Justice, upon consulting an inter-ministerial committee on prices and the Council of State. It was claimed, and the Court agreed, that the CNF is a body composed exclusively of Bar members (ie competitors), and that the scheme

[98] See Ioannis Lianos, 'Competition Law in the European Union After the Treaty of Lisbon' in Diamond Ashiagbor, Nicola Countouris, and Ioannis Lianos (eds), *The European Union after the Treaty of Lisbon* (Cambridge University Press 2012) n 58 on price-fixing in the liberal professions generally.

does not include any substantive or procedural mechanisms guaranteeing that the 'public interest' would be taken into account by the CNF in producing its draft tariff.[99] Nevertheless, the scheme was held not to restrict competition, for two specific reasons.

Firstly, the Minister retained decision-making power in the last instance, he was required to consult other bodies, and there was evidence that, in the previous round of amendments, he requested price increases to be implemented more slowly. Secondly, courts could be flexible in awarding fees in specific proceedings, for example by setting the exact fee between the minimum and maximum depending on the seriousness and number of issues dealt with, or even by going below the minimum or over the maximum in exceptional cases.[100] The broader and more important reason, however, was that, despite the national court's question quite clearly addressing the decision of the CNF and not its legislative context, the Court chose to conceptualize the case as a State restriction of competition. This put the case in a straitjacket since, as discussed in Chapter III, actual findings of a Member State violation of competition law are rare.[101]

Wouters[102] seemed to hold more promise, as it addressed the restraint—a ban on multidisciplinary partnerships between lawyers and accountants imposed by the Dutch Bar—directly as a decision of an association of undertakings. This case was discussed already at several points. It suffices to point out the ways in which it addresses the position of the legal profession under competition law.

Firstly, bar associations are treated as associations of undertakings that are engaged in economic activity, meaning that they fall under Art 101.[103] Thus, what *Reyners* was for the free movement rules, *Wouters* was for competition law: a rejection of the profession's claim for complete autonomy. The Dutch Bar neither fulfils a social function on the basis of solidarity, nor does it exercise powers that are typically those of a public authority. Rather, it 'acts as the regulatory body of a profession, the practice of which constitutes an economic activity'.[104]

[99] Such mechanisms would exist, for example, where the members of the professional organization can be characterized as independent experts who are legally required to take the public interest into account when setting tariffs. Case C-35/99 *Criminal proceedings against Manuele Arduino, third parties: Diego Dessi, Giovanni Bertolotto and Compagnia Assicuratrice RAS SpA* [2002] ECR I-1529, para 37.

[100] Paragraphs 41–42. See also the Order in Case C-386/07 *Hospital Consulting Srl and Others v Esaote SpA and Others* [2008] ECR I-67 where the Court repeated its findings in relation to the Italian system.

[101] See however the well-known Opinion of AG Léger in that case, paras 85–91, where he argued for the application of a proportionality test, including an element of 'effective control' over the behaviour of undertakings, to Member State measures challenged under the competition rules.

[102] Case C-309/99 *J. C. J. Wouters, J. W. Savelbergh and Price Waterhouse Belastingadviseurs BV v Algemene Raad van de Nederlandse Orde van Advocaten, intervener: Raad van de Balies van de Europese Gemeenschap* [2002] ECR I-1577.

[103] Cf the US Supreme Court judgment in *Goldfarb v Virginia State Bar* 421 US 773 (1975), the first to hold that attorneys are engaged in commerce and thus covered by the Sherman Act, condemning bar association price-fixing as long as it is not directly 'compelled' by the state.

[104] Paragraph 58. See Laurel S Terry, 'The European Commission Project Regarding Competition in Professional Services' (2009) 29 Northwestern Journal of International Law & Business 1, 20–21.

Its rules are 'attributable to it alone' and thus subject to competition law. This would not be the case where a Member State delegates regulatory authority to a professional body but defines the 'public-interest criteria and the essential principles with which its rules must comply and also retains its power to adopt decisions in the last resort'.[105]

Secondly, the measures of bar associations will as a rule affect trade between Member States, as they apply to the entire market of a Member State.[106]

Thirdly, it was clear from the Court's analysis that the rules at stake created anticompetitive effects. Despite that, the ban on partnerships was exonerated already under Art 101/1 because its anticompetitive effects were held to be 'inherent' in the regulation of the legal profession: taking into account its context and objectives,[107] the rule was necessary for the proper pursuit of the legal profession. As described in Chapter III, this jurisprudential invention was notable because it introduced[108] a proportionality test, similar to the one in free movement law, into competition law analysis. This test allows a relatively broad margin of discretion to professional bodies, but it does not create a free-for-all. As discussed in Chapter III, recent cases such as *OTOC*, on the regulation of accountants' training, show when professional bodies will fail this proportionality test.

After *Wouters*, the only notable judgment in which the Court of Justice applied competition law to the legal profession was the Order in *Mauri*,[109] a seemingly far-fetched challenge by a failed bar exam candidate to Italian legislation laying down the composition of the examining committee. Interestingly, while this was not borne out by the facts, the Court accepted the idea that, if members of the profession dominated the committee and if there was no active supervision by the State, it would be possible to speak of a restriction of competition. *Mauri* could be interpreted as laying down a more stringent test for Member State restrictions of competition than *Arduino*, inquiring into the Ministry's actual possibilities of review over the decisions of the professional body and the existence of judicial

[105] Paragraphs 68–69. This could be read as saying that, if the Member State does not violate competition law because it fulfils the *Arduino* criteria, the professional body is also beyond reproach—which would be difficult to reconcile with the idea, based on the *Fiammiferi* and *Ladbroke* case law, that Member State and undertaking in co-regulatory schemes can be liable independently (see Chapter III section 3.2.2).

[106] *Arduino* (n 99) para 33 and *Wouters* (n 102) para 95. See also Commission 'Report on Competition in Professional Services' (Communication) COM/2004/0083 final para 73.

[107] These were 'the need to make rules relating to organisation, qualifications, professional ethics, supervision and liability, in order to ensure that the ultimate consumers of legal services and the sound administration of justice are provided with the necessary guarantees in relation to integrity and experience' (para 97).

[108] See Ian S Forrester, 'Where Law Meets Competition: Is Wouters Like a Cassis de Dijon or a Platypus?' in Claus-Dieter Ehlermann and Isabela Atanasiu (eds), *Competition Law Annual 2004: The Relationship Between Competition Law and the (Liberal) Professions* (Hart 2006) on the question whether this case is so context-specific that it is unlikely to be repeated in other areas. As discussed in Chapter III, subsequent case law shows otherwise.

[109] Case C-250/03 *Giorgio Emanuele Mauri v Ministero della Giustizia and Commissione per gli esami di avvocato presso la Corte d'appello di Milano* [2005] ECR I-1267.

review as arguments that Italy had not 'given up the exercise of its powers in favour of private economic operators'.[110]

The notion that competition law could apply to the facts of *Mauri* is somewhat reminiscent of *Meca-Medina*.[111] In both cases, it seems counter-intuitive that applying professional rules to a single person would have anticompetitive ends or effects. Still, the Court's case law shows that liability is not inconceivable, turning competition law into a rather open-ended review of the professional body's decision making: if it fails to respect certain principles of good governance (representation, transparency, fair hearing, judicial review, etc.) it could be found to infringe.

5.1.1 Public or private restrictions of competition?

Regulation of the legal profession is, as explained, best described as co-regulation.[112] Drawing a line between the public and private aspects is difficult; indeed, both professional bodies and the Member States have been subject to both the competition and free movement rules. An unfortunate consequence of this is that, in individual cases, it becomes difficult to know the nature of the legal test that will be applied to the Member State and/or to the professional body.

As described in Chapter III, several distinct lines of case law need to be brought together in order to understand the relationship between Member State liability and the liability of the professional body. In principle, both could be liable independently of each other.[113] As was found in *CNSD* and *Wouters*, while its formal public-law status is irrelevant, the decisions of a professional body may fall out of the scope of the competition rules if they are adopted by independent experts bound to take into account broader interests than those of the profession itself and subject to review by State bodies, or if they are composed by a majority of representatives of public authorities.[114] If that is the case, the Member State will also probably avoid competition law scrutiny under the *Arduino* approach.

If that is not the case, however, both the State and the association could be found to infringe. The association might avoid scrutiny only if it shows that it had no scope for action and was completely bound to act in an anticompetitive fashion. If the association had some scope for action, on the other hand, it could be held to infringe, and the Member State as well if it condoned or supported that infringement.[115] The

[110] See paras 32–37. [111] See Chapter III section 3.1.3.

[112] Fred C Zacharias, 'The Myth of Self-Regulation' (2009) 93 Minnesota Law Review 1147.

[113] See, similarly, Hans Gilliams, 'Competition Law and Public Interest: Do We Need to Change the Law for the (Liberal) Professions?' in Claus-Dieter Ehlermann and Isabela Atanasiu (eds), *European Competition Law Annual 2004* (n 7) 303–04.

[114] See Case T-513/93 *Consiglio Nazionale degli Spedizionieri Doganali v Commission* [2000] ECR II-1807, paras 39 and 54–56 and Wouters (n 102) paras 68–69.

[115] See Case C-35/96 *Commission v Italy* [1998] ECR I-3851, on the liability of Italy for the scheme condemned in *CNSD II* (n 114).

Member State will, however, not be held liable under competition law merely because it legislates in an anticompetitive fashion.[116]

Despite these complexities, what the case law clearly suggests is that the way in which a co-regulatory scheme is designed matters. A scheme with several layers of truly independent review by public bodies, explicitly formulated public-interest aims, and judicial review is much more likely to survive scrutiny than one that lacks those features, whether the Member State or the professional body is challenged. This could be described as a sort of structural or organizational justification: institutional safeguards take the place of deep, substantive review of the profession's practices.[117]

In addition to this, *Wouters* broadened the possibilities of substantive, policy-based justification of the measures of a professional body. What is especially important for the profession is the way in which this proportionality test was performed. In comparison to the standard free movement case against a Member State, the Court was more lenient: even though less restrictive means may have existed, such as simply applying the professional rules of conduct that are meant to ensure lawyers' independence, the overall conclusion was that the Bar was entitled to consider this particular measure to be necessary—and the least restrictive—in the Dutch context.[118] In US terminology, this would be called a rational basis or minimum rationality test, the least intrusive method of questioning regulatory choices.

The deference granted to bar associations, allowing regulators to integrate non-efficiency concerns as well as to pursue different levels of protection, can be read as a compensatory mechanism for the broad reach of competition law.[119] Indeed, on the face of it almost any rule of conduct in the legal profession—given that they are largely prescribed by measures of professional bodies—could be subject to competition law scrutiny. The same is true of transnational codes of conduct, such as the CCBE's. So far, however, there seems to have been only one case dealing with international codes of conduct: in *EPI*,[120] the General Court confirmed the Commission's finding that rules of the Code of Conduct of the Institute of Professional Representatives before the European Patent Office prohibiting

[116] Case C-446/05 *Criminal proceedings against Ioannis Doulamis* [2008] ECR I-1377 paras 18–24. As discussed in Chapter III section 3.2.1, the application of competition law to the State has not been a very successful route for plaintiffs. See also Gilliams (n 113) 315, claiming that the 'added value [of this case law] seems extremely limited'. Advertising rules may, on the other hand, violate free movement law, especially if they are discriminatory or inconsistent, as was the case in Case C-500/06 *Corporación Dermoestética SA v To Me Group Advertising Media* [2008] ECR I-5785.

[117] See the Opinion of AG Maduro in *Cipolla* (n 39) paras 32–37, concluding that the only way to reconcile the rules on the liability of undertakings under *Wouters* and those on the liability of Member States in *Arduino* is to 'adopt a criterion requiring effective supervision of the State, including examination of the decision-making process leading to adoption of the rule in question'.

[118] Paragraphs 105–09.

[119] This is not necessarily the only reason for the *Wouters* judgment. There is some force in the argument that the *Wouters* exception was motivated by the procedural concern that the national court, at the time, could not apply Art 101/3. See Gilliams (n 113) 319. This does not, however, explain the frequent reliance on the *Wouters* jurisprudence in recent years.

[120] Case T-144/99 *Institute of Professional Representatives before the European Patent Office v Commission* [2001] ECR II-1087.

comparative advertising were a restriction under Art 101/1. The Commission, however, found those rules to be temporarily exempt under Art 101/3.[121]

5.2 The Commission's Report on Competition in Professional Services

After the Court's largely deferent approach in *Arduino* and *Wouters*, one might think that competition law has little potential for re-regulating the legal profession. Nevertheless, the Commission quickly took up the cause of reform. It started discussions with the national competition authorities, commissioned studies,[122] invited comments and held a conference on the issue of opening professional services to competition.[123] This process resulted in the 2004 Report on Competition in Professional Services.[124] The Report pointed out that many of the rules regulating the professions, which it divided into price fixing, recommended prices, advertising regulations, entry requirements, and rules on business structure and multi-disciplinary practices, may be 'excessive or out-dated', eliminating competition between providers, limiting choice, stifling innovation, and keeping prices high.[125] It also, however, acknowledged the market failure explanations for maintaining some level of regulation.[126]

With this in mind, the Report went on to discuss the pros and cons of various categories of measures. While some of them are, according to the Commission, more easily justified than others,[127] the overall buzzword was proportionality: the

[121] See para 78 of the judgment, where the General Court seems to apply a necessity test to the EPI's Code of Conduct (asking whether the absolute prohibition of comparative advertising is 'objectively necessary in order to preserve the dignity and rules of conduct of the profession concerned' as a condition for escaping Art 101 altogether).

[122] Paterson, Fink, and Ogus (n 6). The study indexed the level of regulation in fifteen Member States and found that there is no evidence that lighter regulation increases complaints or creates other problems, while finding some evidence that it increases the number of market participants and turnover. For criticisms of the study, see Terry (n 104) section IV and Mario Siragusa, 'Critical Remarks on the Commission's Legal Analysis in its Report on Competition in Professional Services' in Claus-Dieter Ehlermann and Isabela Atanasiu (eds), *European Competition Law Annual 2004* (n 7).

[123] On the history of this process, see Terry (n 104) section II. The process was based on a clear reform agenda. See, for example, the speech of Mario Monti, 'Competition in Professional Services: New Light and New Challenges' (21 March 2003) SPEECH/03/149: 'The present level of rules and regulation of liberal professions owe some debt to historical convention. How many are still needed in the modern world? Do they hinder or favour the development of the sector? Let me be provocative: Do they protect the consumers or the professionals?'

[124] Commission 'Report on Competition in Professional Services' (Communication) COM/2004/0083 final.

[125] The Report refers to Paterson, Fink, and Ogus (n 6), mentioning that 'the data seems to indicate that light regulation is not a hindrance but rather a spur to overall wealth creation' (7).

[126] Paragraph 28.

[127] While price fixing, for example, is generally held to have no redeeming qualities (except for maximum prices in markets with low levels of effective competition and high entry barriers which, however, the Commission did not see as a realistic scenario in the liberal professions), rules on multidisciplinary practices or business structures were considered as having some merit in markets where independence is an important concern, such as the legal services market. In most cases, the Commission's recommendation was to pursue the least restrictive strategy: entry restrictions based

Commission 'wanted to see' the regulators, including professional bodies, conduct a thorough review of all the existing restrictive rules, leading either to their removal or replacement with less restrictive measures.

The Report was pushing the envelope. The analysis of the various measures was not based on legal precedent but directly on citations of economic theory and empirical studies. Moreover, the legal strategy outlined in the second section of the Report was stretching the existing law. For example, it read the *Wouters* proportionality test in a quite intrusive way, even implying a proportionality *stricto sensu*.[128] It also portrayed the relationship between the application of competition law to the States and to professional bodies in a more intrusive way than *Arduino* and *Wouters* seemed to suggest. Firstly, it made it clear that in the Commission's view both the State and the professional body can infringe competition law; secondly, it emphasized the *Fiammiferi* holding that legislation requiring anti-competitive conduct such as price-fixing has to be set aside by national competition agencies;[129] thirdly, it argued that rubberstamp approvals or the inability of Member States to amend the proposals of a professional body would, as such, violate competition law. It even went so far as to suggest that, for Member State liability, 'a proportionality test would seem appropriate to assess to what extent an anti-competitive professional regulation truly serves the public interest'—which was previously suggested, notably by the Advocates General in *Pavlov* and *Arduino*, but was never accepted by the Court.[130]

One might think that the Commission presented the law in this way to prepare for an enforcement offensive, but this was not the plan at all. The Report primarily advocated voluntary re-regulation: either the Member States or professional bodies should 'carry out a thorough analysis of the need for reform in the respective professions and of the compatibility of existing rules with competition law principles'.[131] This proportionality review should be narrowly focused, asking not if it is justified for the profession as a whole to be regulated, but whether each particular rule should be maintained in light of its market context. Of course, this analysis would have to take into account that the justifications for regulation

on qualifications or experience should be lowered if they are disproportionate to the professional's tasks, and reserved tasks should be narrowed, for example in the case of an overall exclusive right of lawyers to provide legal advice.

[128] Paragraph 75. The Commission considers that there are two separate questions: first, 'whether the consequential effects restrictive of competition are inherent in the pursuit of those objectives and if they are therefore necessary in order to ensure the proper practice of the profession' and second, whether the effects restrictive of competition 'go beyond what is necessary in order to ensure the proper practice of the profession'. Separating the second question could be interpreted as a form of cost-benefit analysis or proportionality *stricto sensu*. See J P Trachtman, 'Trade and ... Problems, Cost-Benefit Analysis and Subsidiarity' (1998) 9 European Journal of International Law 32, 35–36.

[129] Case C-198/01 *Consorzio Industrie Fiammiferi (CIF) v Autorità Garante della Concorrenza e del Mercato* [2003] ECR I-8055, paras 50–51.

[130] See the Opinion of AG Jacobs in Joined cases C-180/98 to C-184/98 *Pavel Pavlov and Others v Stichting Pensioenfonds Medische Specialisten* [2000] ECR I-6451, para 163 and the Opinion of AG Léger in *Arduino* (n 99) para 91.

[131] Paragraph 92. See also Gilliams (n 113) 328.

may carry more weight in different market segments. Advising sophisticated business users on international tax issues and representing private parties in criminal proceedings call for different regulatory approaches.

Alternatively, the Commission continued, enforcement is possible. That enforcement, however, should mainly be the task of national competition authorities.[132] Indeed, the Report was published just before the entry into force of Regulation 1/2003 which decentralized the application of competition law and allowed NCAs to fully apply EU competition rules. As for the Commission itself, it viewed its future role as monitoring progress, ensuring a coherent approach, and discussing potential changes with national regulators. Infringement proceedings were only briefly mentioned as a distant possibility.[133]

6. National Case Law and Reforms

The Report and its surrounding documents were one of the hot topics of EU competition law at the time. Nevertheless, after 2005 or 2006 the liberal professions seem to largely disappear from the radar. There has been virtually no competition law enforcement on the EU level as far as the legal profession is concerned. The website of the Commission's DG Competition dedicated to professional services shows a relative lack of activity post-2006.

In this regard, the Commission's Report proved to be prophetic. Centralized enforcement did not happen. What did happen, however, were significant if still slow reforms at the national level as well as a measure of enforcement by national competition agencies and courts.

6.1 National reforms

The most important events in the regulation of legal services following the Commission's report took place on the national level. This chapter cannot present these developments in detail, but even a cursory overview shows that the changes have been quite important.

The most far-reaching were probably those in England and Wales, where, on the basis of the so-called Clementi Report and in response both to the Commission's Report and a previous report by the UK Office of Fair Trading, the regulatory function was removed from professional bodies and entrusted to independent regulators, the Legal Services Board, and the Office for Legal Complaints, with a majority of non-lawyer members.[134]

[132] Paragraph 100.

[133] Paragraphs 100–02. The other EU institutions have also participated in the discourse led by the Commission's Report, in some cases taking the opposite line. See for example the European Parliament Resolution of 23 March 2006 on the legal professions and the general interest in the functioning of legal systems (2006) OJ C 292E/105. See also Terry (n 104) 69.

[134] See n 21. David Clementi, *Review of the Regulatory Framework for Legal Services in England and Wales: Final Report* (December 2004) <http://www.legal-services-review.org.uk/content/report/index.htm>.

Other important reforms were discussed or brought about in Scotland (alternative business structures), Denmark (removal of representative functions from the bar association), Poland (reform of the disciplinary rules), the Netherlands (outside investment in law firms), Spain (multidisciplinary services, employment of attorneys), and Ireland.[135] In Italy, the so-called Bersani decree loosened the rules on minimum and maximum fees and advertising.[136] There have been discussions in Slovenia on removing mandatory Bar membership and forming independent regulators,[137] and the Dutch Ministry of Justice has launched consultations on forming an independent regulatory body staffed by non-lawyers that would supervise local bar associations.[138] Several Member States have relaxed the restrictions on multidisciplinary practices, or non-lawyer ownership of law firms.[139]

Some of the more recent changes have been partly spurred on by the economic crisis. Reforms in Ireland, for example, would introduce a central regulatory body for the legal profession with all of its members appointed by the Ministry of Justice.[140] Italy has adopted a law allowing up to a third of non-lawyer partnership as well as the use of any kind of corporate structure for law firms.[141] Additional reforms took place in Greece, where some rules on reserved tasks and minimum fees were repealed[142] and the competition agency has reportedly reviewed the activities of a number of liberal professions and issued several opinions.[143] Portugal is putting in place horizontal legislation for regulated professions which would reform the qualification rules, remove advertising restrictions, and eliminate certain reserved tasks,[144] and legal aid provision has been centralized

For more details about the reform, see <http://www.legalservicesboard.org.uk/about_us/history_reforms>.

135 See Terry (n 104) 63–65.

136 Bruno Nascimbene and Elisabetta Bergamini, *The Legal Profession in the European Union* (Kluwer Law International 2009) 144.

137 See CCBE Info No 31 (November 2012) 11 <http://www.ccbe.eu/fileadmin/user_upload/NTCdocument/newsletter_31_enpdf1_1352876731.pdf>.

138 See CCBE Info No 29 (January 2012) 3–4 <http://www.ccbe.eu/fileadmin/user_upload/NTCdocument/newsletter_29_enpdf1_1327503311.pdf>.

139 Evaluation of the Legal Framework for the Free Movement of Lawyers: Final Report (n 51) 10.

140 The text of the proposed Legal Services Regulation Bill (2011), along with amendments resulting from its lengthy review process, can be found at <http://www.oireachtas.ie/viewdoc.asp?DocID=19208>.

141 CCBE Info No 29 (n 138) 4.

142 See International Monetary Fund, 'First and Second Reviews Under the Extended Arrangement Under the Extended Fund Facility, Request for Waiver of Applicability, Modification of Performance Criteria, and Rephasing of Access' (2013) IMF Country Report 13/20, 137 and International Monetary Fund, 'Fifth Review Under the Extended Arrangement Under the Extended Fund Facility, and Request for Waiver of Nonobservance of Performance Criterion and Rephasing of Access' IMF Country Report (2014) 14/151, 19.

143 See 'Greece: The Hellenic Competition Commission exercises its Advocacy Powers and issues formal Opinions on Liberal Professions and other regulatory Restrictions' (2012) ECN Brief 4/2012.

144 International Monetary Fund, 'Portugal: Fourth Review Under the Extended Arrangement and Request for a Waiver of Applicability of End-June Performance Criteria' (2012) IMF Country Report 12/179, 33.

under governmental supervision and payment. These measures seem to have been adopted largely as a result of Troika (Commission, ECB, and IMF) de-regulatory initiatives.[145]

6.2 National enforcement

Since 2006, there have been a number of cases where national courts or competition agencies applied competition law to the legal profession. Their efforts can be linked to the Commission's initiative and the 2004 Report. NCAs, in particular, collaborate in the context of the European Competition Network (ECN), which has a subgroup dedicated to the liberal professions.[146] Due to the highly opaque and informal nature of the ECN, we do not have systematic data on national enforcement, nor access to the conclusions of any debates of the liberal professions subgroup. Therefore, I can only offer an anecdotal description of some of the cases launched by national authorities.

The one relatively comprehensive report only covers the period between February 2004 and the spring of 2006, showing that twenty-two cases were opened and twelve closed across all areas of professional services. The most frequent restrictions analysed were rules on fixed or recommended prices (both of which were generally found by NCAs to violate competition law), followed by those on advertising.[147]

There are other, more sporadic reports on various national cases. In 2005, the Hungarian NCA found a local bar council's schedule of recommended prices to be contrary to Hungarian competition law, relying on the Commission's Report. In 2006, the same NCA found rules prohibiting certain kinds of advertising (highlighting lower prices in comparison to competitors, the use of slogans, or website advertising, etc.) to violate Art 101 TFEU, and in 2009 it adopted a commitment decision in relation to high and potentially discriminatory registration fees of a local bar council.[148] In 2005, the Slovakian NCA condemned a ban on law firms using the name of other law firms (normally, large multinationals with which they partner), as well as detailed regulation on the manner and content of advertising.[149] The Spanish Supreme Court held in 2008 that a ban on using contingency fees (*pactum de quota litis*) was contrary to competition law as a form

[145] CCBE Info No 30 (May 2012) 9 <http://www.ccbe.eu/fileadmin/user_upload/NTCdocument/newsletter_30_enpdf1_1347517429.pdf>

[146] For more on the ECN, see Firat Cengiz, 'Multi-level Governance in Competition Policy: The European Competition Network' (2010) 35 European Law Review 660.

[147] Commission, 'Overview of national competition authorities' advocacy and enforcement activities in the area of professional services (February 2004–Spring 2006)' <http://ec.europa.eu/competition/sectors/professional_services/national_enforcement_advocacy.pdf>. See in particular 4–5.

[148] See the press releases at <http://www.gvh.hu/domain2/files/modules/module25/115103032956DE521.pdf> and <http://www.gvh.hu/domain2/files/modules/module25/86477EF5F187307F.pdf>.

[149] Lipka Jurav and François Veit, 'The Slovak Antimonopoly Office holds that several provisions of the lawyers' rules of professional conduct breach both Slovak and EU competition provisions (Slovak Bar Association)' (2005) 452 e-Competitions.

of price-fixing.[150] In 2012, the Romanian NCA adopted an infringement decision against an association of judicial executors for imposing excessive and discriminatory entry fees and for fixing prices.[151] The Polish NCA found the Polish notaries association's rules prohibiting price undercutting (2002) and opening an office in the same building where there is another notary (2012) to violate competition law.[152] Finally, the Italian NCA recently found the measures of local bar associations imposing additional conditions on the entry of 'European lawyers' to violate the competition rules.[153] It has also, however, exonerated a bar association that applied disciplinary rules on 'hoarding clients' to a law firm calling itself 'Legal assistance for all'.[154]

7. Relationship Between Free Movement and Competition

As in sports, there seems to be an unspoken division of tasks between free movement and competition law, with some areas of overlap. Free movement law deals largely with free movement of individual lawyers, that is the market access of lawyers either as service providers, workers, or self-employed persons. Competition law enters the picture when it comes to structural and organizational rules, such as the rule against multidisciplinary partnerships. This division is not dictated by the law. For example, restrictions on the free establishment of individual lawyers imposed by bar associations are treated almost exclusively as a free movement issue, either under the Treaty or under the relevant directives, even though they could be seen as an agreement among competitors to restrict new entry under Art 101.

So far, overlap has taken place in the area of tariffs (*Arduino*, *Cipolla*, *Commission v Italy*)[155] and, to a lesser extent, multidisciplinary partnerships (*Wouters*). This is a very limited set of cases, but the conclusions from the general chapter on the relationship of free movement and competition seem to hold. The Court pursues an incomplete convergence strategy. Firstly, it avoids making clear statements separating the two legal tests. Indeed, this may be even more difficult in the

[150] Aitor Montesa Lloreda and Angel Givaja Sanz, 'The Spanish Supreme Court firmly protects price competition in the liberal professions and gives a controversial view on the interaction between EC and national competition Law (Ricardo)' (2008) 23835 e-Competitions.

[151] See 'Romania: The Competition Council decides to impose Fines on the National Association of Judicial Executors' 4 ECN Brief (2012).

[152] See the press release at <http://www.uokik.gov.pl/news.php?news_id=2011>. This list would seem to suggest that the 'new' Member States' NCAs are more active in this area. This may be because of a high number of restrictive rules that survived EU accession. In any case, however, this list is too short and non-representative for such conclusions.

[153] OECD, 'Annual report on competition policy developments in Italy' (2014) DAF/COMP/AR(2014)26 para 32.

[154] See the press release at <http://www.agcm.it/en/newsroom/press-releases/1622-i719-order-of-lawyers-of-brescia-to-be-investigated.html>; as for the ultimate resolution of the case, see AGCM, 'Bollettino Settimanale Anno XXIII - n. 43'<www.agcm.it>, 5 et seq.

[155] *Commission v Italy* (2011) (n 39).

regulated professions sector as a public–private distinction that usually motivates such attempts is difficult to draw: many bar associations are linked to the State, and many of their measures fall within a broader co-regulatory context. Hardly anyone would argue that bar associations are exempt from the free movement rules. *Wouters* and other judgments have also made it clear that there are no broad exemptions from competition law for professional regulation. As a result, almost any restrictive entry or conduct rule adopted by a professional body could be subject to both the free movement and the competition rules.

Secondly, the case law shows a preference for handling cases under a free-movement style proportionality analysis. In *Cipolla*, the Court dismissed the case under competition law for the same reasons as in *Arduino*, but then applied the free movement rules, finding a restriction but justifying the measure.[156] In *Wouters*, on the other hand, the case was handled under the competition rules but by way of a free movement-like proportionality analysis.

Finally, a tacit, but potentially far-reaching move towards convergence can be seen in the judgment *Commission v Italy*, an infringement case based purely on the free movement rules challenging the reformed Italian rules on lawyers' fees (which, after the Bersani decree, mandated only maximum fees). The Court could have dealt with the case similarly as in *Cipolla*: find the measures to restrict free movement, but to be justifiable for purposes of consumer protection and sound administration of justice, depending on the national market conditions which have to be assessed by the national court. After all, maximum fees are more easily justified than minimum fees which were at stake in *Cipolla*.[157] The Court, however, went one step further and held that the rules on fees were not a restriction of free movement at all.

Arguably, maximum fees are also restrictive: after all, they could easily be said to 'render access to the Italian legal services market more difficult' for law firms from other Member States.[158] The test in *Commission v Italy*, however, was significantly reformulated: the question, according to the Court, was whether the rules have the 'object of effect' of depriving lawyers of 'the opportunity of gaining access to the market of the host Member State under conditions of normal and effective competition'.[159] Under this standard, the relatively flexible rules on maximum fees were not considered to restrict market access.

The wording of the test is important, since it is taken almost word for word from competition law precedent. The criterion of 'restrictive object or effect' is taken from the text of Art 101, under which it is used to distinguish between restrictions that do and those that do not require an extensive effects analysis in

[156] *Cipolla* (n 39) paras 49–53 and 55–70.

[157] See Commission 'Report on Competition in Professional Services' (Communication) COM/2004/0083 final para 35 and the Opinion AG Maduro in *Cipolla* (n 39) para 94 distinguishing between minimum and maximum fees in terms of their justification under the free movement rules.

[158] *Cipolla* (n 39) para 58. In *Commission v Italy* (2011), the Commission argued that the rules on maximum fees were restrictive as they imposed 'additional costs resulting from the application of the Italian system of fees' and created 'a reduction in profit margins' (para 48).

[159] Paragraphs 51–52.

light of actual market conditions. Under the free movement rules, measures are normally considered to be restrictive if they are liable to impede market access, which does not entail a detailed analysis of effects. Potentially, this could lead to an introduction of such an analysis into free movement case law. Secondly, the phrase 'conditions of normal and effective competition' is taken from *United Brands*, an Art 102 judgment.[160] In *United Brands*, it meant that a dominant undertaking charging excessive prices that it could not obtain under normal and effective competition was committing an abuse. In the free movement context, this threshold might be read as making it more difficult to presume the existence of a restriction: a barrier to entry will not be deemed restrictive unless the market is characterized by abnormal or ineffective competitive conditions.[161]

So far, it is not clear whether this wording will have any consequences, either for cases dealing with the legal profession or more generally. Potentially, it could make it more difficult to scrutinize the organizational and conduct rules of the profession under free movement law, therefore moving the emphasis of reform even more towards competition law or national-level re-regulation. It may, in addition, lead to some of the problems outlined in Chapter IV. Since the overlap between competition and free movement in this area is practically complete, excessive mixing and blending of the two legal tests may create uncertainty and lead to adverse procedural consequences: for example, if free movement law steps in for competition law, the remedies that can be obtained are not as effective.

While the legal tests do largely overlap, however, when it comes to the definition of a restriction the Court has not proposed any automatic conclusions—such as a restriction of one implying a restriction of the other rule. As for justifications, the *Wouters* case enabled the use of broad public policy justifications under the competition rules. While this may be seen as excessively converging the two legal tests, the *Wouters* exception has certain advantages, even for advocates of reform. By subjecting the rules of professional bodies to a single and relatively simple overarching proportionality test, this limited convergence may be beneficial both for the regulators and for competition law enforcers. As argued in Chapter IV, however, the Court should make it clear that the two tests are separate, even if they revolve mostly around the same arguments and questions.

8. Conclusion

In this chapter, I have outlined the developments under free movement law, competition law, and internal market legislation relating to the legal profession. Like

[160] Case 27/76 *United Brands Company and United Brands Continentaal BV v Commission* [1978] ECR 207, paras 248–50.

[161] Marc Fallon and Damien Gerard, 'Trailing the trailers in search for a typology of barriers: Sketching a scale of relative gravity and exploring its implications' Cahiers du CeDIE Working Paper No 2012/6 10 pick up on *Commission v Italy* (2011), suggesting a distinction between free movement restrictions by object or effect.

with the previous case study, this analysis broadly supports the conclusions of the general chapters, while also showing certain sectoral specificities.

Like sport, the legal profession is a good example of the fact that the recognition of private regulatory autonomy means that the arguments for full autonomy from scrutiny lose value. Most challenges under EU law boil down to substantive justifications like professional independence, rather than 'private autonomy' arguments such as the protection of freedom of association. The upshot is that bar associations of all sorts—whatever their precise legal status on the national level—are recognized as legitimate regulators, along with a measure of deference to their choices (*Wouters*), in particular as far as conduct rules are concerned (*Gullung*).

In line with the general conclusions, the broad scope of both competition and free movement law is offset by case-by-case deference. This is particularly true with regard to rules on professional conduct. Measures which make the registration of lawyers from other Member States and their entry into the legal market difficult, such as nationality quotas, local residence requirements, and overly strict qualification rules have been successfully challenged both under the free movement rules and under the Directives. Rules on fees, advertising, multidisciplinary practices, and disciplinary violations, on the other hand, were overwhelmingly not held to violate EU law when presented to the Court. There may be good institutional and economic reasons for this. In particular, the professional bodies as regulators are likely to disfavour the interests of new entrants who are not represented in the organization, as well as those of consumers whose individual costs of participation are often too high to get involved. These biases are addressed by the free movement rules as well as the Directives' lists of exhaustive requirements for lawyers seeking to establish or provide services in a Member State other than their own.

When it comes to conduct and disciplinary rules, however, the case is more ambiguous. Once lawyers from other Member States have gained establishment, at least they have the right to be represented in the professional body, making it less likely that those rules will act against their interests. An approach that is strict on entry rules but lax on conduct rules is also less likely to meet resistance: the CCBE, for example, broadly supports the free movement of lawyers, but is at times quite defensive when it comes to structural reforms.[162]

The legal profession also shows how competition law attempts to accommodate regulatory measures in the analysis, rather than refrain from scrutinizing them altogether. The best example of this is *Wouters*—a case which now serves as the template for the competition law scrutiny of professional bodies, as more recent judgments like *OTOC* and *Consiglio nazionale dei geologi* show. Like the challenges to anti-doping rules described in the previous chapter, this may at

[162] Compare, for example, *CCBE response to the Commission's consultation on the Professional Qualifications Directive* (CCBE Position Paper) 2 with the press release 'European and US lawyers alert IMF against Troika-imposed reforms affecting the independence of the profession in 'bail-out' countries' (5 January 2012) <http://www.ccbe.eu/fileadmin/user_upload/NTCdocument/PR_on_CCBEABA_lettel_1325761475.pdf>.

times mean that competition authorities are faced with challenges to measures far removed from traditional antitrust (*Mauri*).

This chapter also shows how the approach to the legal profession has been shaped by sector-specific considerations.

First, while the precise legal status of bar associations differs depending on national law, it is clear that both national and EU law sees them, at least, as bodies with important public responsibilities. The lawyers' directives on services and establishment, for example, are explicitly addressed to them. Free movement scrutiny has not been nearly as controversial as, for example, in the area of sport. Therefore, the fact that EU law is broadly applicable may be less surprising than in other areas.

Second, the margin of discretion given to professional bodies could at least partly be explained by the fact that the EU political process has shown itself to be relatively capable in this area. The lawyers' directives, in addition to the Services Directive and the Diploma Directive, provide a solid if limited framework for dealing with the free movement of lawyers.

The overlap of free movement and competition has also played out somewhat differently than the general analysis in Chapter IV may suggest. For example, I have suggested that free movement and competition law are generally drifting apart and are now (rightly) seen as two distinct sets of rules. However, the *Commission v Italy* judgment on attorneys' fees seemed to converge the two sets of rules in a way that potentially significantly reduces the likelihood of legal challenges under EU law.

A final interesting development is the relative lack of competition law enforcement on the EU level. The Commission's reluctance to pursue an active enforcement strategy against bar associations can be partly explained by limited resources: one enforcer cannot effectively supervise regulatory developments across all of the Member States. The second explanation is that, as the legal profession is heavily regulated almost everywhere and is likely to remain so, simply imposing free competition by removing restrictive rules may not create results without a subsequent, positive programme of reform that would formulate effective and less restrictive rules.[163] Finally, in contrast to the strength of transnational regulation in sports, almost all of the significant regulation (and thus, potential threats to free movement or competition) is on the national level, making it more difficult for the Commission to enforce reforms through a centralized, European-level dialogue with professional bodies.

National competition authorities and legislators can do a better job on all of these counts. Firstly, in terms of knowledge and capacity they are better equipped to deal with the national liberal professions. Secondly, they can use competition advocacy to push for reform. The Commission's Report is rather useful in this context. Even though, arguably, it goes further than the actual enforcement of

[163] Frédéric Jenny, 'Regulation, Competition and the Professions' in Claus-Dieter Ehlermann and Isabela Atanasiu (eds), *European Competition Law Annual 2004* (n 7) 140–41.

competition law ever went, it can be effectively used by the NCAs in their advocacy efforts as a document that presents EU law as it stands. This may be quite convincing to the legislators and even national bar associations, and can push reform processes forward. While being reluctant about inviting too many cases that challenge the rules of bar associations, the Court may also be said to have followed the Commission's strategy of empowering the national competition authorities: in *Fiammiferi*, it made clear that the NCAs are authorized and required to disapply national legislation that violates the competition rules.[164]

Indeed, national policymakers have pushed reform beyond what is required by EU law, leading to some of the most far-reaching competition-oriented reforms of professional regulation in recent years. This was not an entirely predictable development. With a long tradition of co-regulatory regimes and powerful professional bodies, the normal expectation would be that highly interested and well-organized professionals would influence the political process to their advantage.[165] Nevertheless, national competition authorities as well as political processes, bolstered by the agenda set by the Commission in 2004, have taken up the task of pushing reforms at the national level. In some cases, this has even led to the creation of new institutions providing independent scrutiny over professional bodies.[166]

[164] See n 129.

[165] See n 16, as well as Neil K Komesar, *Imperfect Alternatives: Choosing Institutions in Law, Economics, and Public Policy* (University of Chicago Press 1994) ch 3.

[166] See Van den Bergh, 'Towards Efficient Self-regulation in Markets for Professional Services' (n 19) for a discussion of the potential benefits and risks of such solutions.

VII

Standard Setting, Competition, and Trade

1. Introduction

Standards are ubiquitous in daily life. They determine the size, interoperability, composition, safety, and other features of a multitude of products and, increasingly, services.[1] The size of the thread of a screw, the way in which data is transmitted over the Internet, how computer components should be made in order to work together, how food should be handled in a restaurant, and when fish is caught in an environmentally sustainable way are all (very diverse) examples of standards. In more abstract terms, the EU defines them as 'voluntary technical or quality specifications with which current or future products, production processes or services may comply'.[2]

Standards can have different purposes, such as guaranteeing a certain level of safety, quality, or compatibility between different products, or reducing variety in order to achieve economies of scale.[3] They can achieve those purposes in different ways: some refer to the end-product while others deal with the process of production; some are based on *ex ante* and others on *ex post* certification, etc.[4]

[1] Services standards have recently been placed higher on the EU agenda, even though product standards still dominate. On the other hand, the very distinction between product and service standards is not clear-cut, as acknowledged by Regulation (EU) No 1025/2012 of the European Parliament and of the Council of 25 October 2012 on European standardisation [2012] OJ L316/12 recital 10: 'In practice, it is not always possible to clearly distinguish standards for products from standards for services. Many standards for products have a service component while standards for services often also partly relate to products.'

[2] European Standardization Regulation (n 1) recital 1. See, similarly, Commission, 'Guidelines on the applicability of Article 101 of the Treaty on the Functioning of the European Union to horizontal co-operation agreements' (Communication) (2011) OJ C 11 para 257.

[3] See Knut Blind, *The Economics of Standards: Theory, Evidence, Policy* (Edward Elgar 2004) 14–23.

[4] For a discussion of various groups of standards, see Alan O Sykes, *Product Standards for Internationally Integrated Goods Markets* (Brookings Institution Press 1995) 2–8 and ABA Section on Antitrust Law, *Handbook on the Antitrust Aspects of Standards Setting* (American Bar Association 2004) ch 1. Depending on the context, economic theory points to various benefits of standardization. As summarized by Blind, 'standards help to reduce costs of transactions between the different actors and therefore the emergence and organization of markets [...] [S]tandards can also be used as instruments to solve market failures, as in the case of obligatory environmental, safety or health standards. They are able to correct both negative externalities and information asymmetries.' Blind (n 3) 4.

Standards are produced by firms or by various private, public, or hybrid standard-setting organizations ('SSOs'). Even in the case of official, publicly recognized SSOs, however, standard setting is almost always heavily dependent on industry input. It is the quintessential example of private regulation justified by technical expertise. It first developed precisely in areas where command-and-control regulation by the legislator would have been too costly in light of the technical knowledge involved, and where frequent changes in technology required flexible and fast decision-making.

This explains the images most of us have in mind when standards are mentioned: building codes, power sockets, nuts, and bolts, etc. Indeed, standard setting is particularly important in areas such as construction products and electrical engineering. More recently, however, it has become prominent even in areas where the classic justification of technical expertise is not the main driver, such as corporate social responsibility and sustainability standards like GlobalGAP, Forest Stewardship Council (FSC), Marine Stewardship Council (MSC), or the Fair Labor Association Workplace Code of Conduct.[5]

Sometimes the word 'standard' is used to describe all sorts of rules, even laws. The legal perspective, however, tends to distinguish (voluntary) standards from (mandatory) 'technical regulations'.[6] This chapter only addresses the latter category insofar as private regulators are involved in their development. Even if we take technical regulations out of the equation, however, voluntary standards run the gamut in terms of who makes them and what their effects are. Some of them are created by a single actor, but they still affect the entire supply chain due to that actor's market power. By developing the Windows operating system, for example, Microsoft can be said to have created a number of standards that have to be followed by any developer of applications for that platform.[7] A large retailer's requirement to comply with a unilaterally developed food safety standard quickly reverberates up the supply chain to food processors and farmers.[8] More frequently, however, standards are set collectively through associations that gather industry actors and, possibly, other stakeholders including public bodies, academics, consumers, and NGOs. In this category, further distinctions could be

[5] See Axel Marx, 'Global Governance and the Certification Revolution: Types, Trends and Challenges' in David Levi-Faur (ed), *Handbook on the Politics of Regulation* (Edward Elgar 2011); Axel Marx and Dieter Cuypers, 'Halting deforestation and forest certification: What is the macro-impact of the Forest Stewardship Council?' (2010) Leuven Centre for Global Governance Studies Working Paper No 56; Janelle M Diller, 'Private Standardization in Public International Lawmaking' (2012) 33 Michigan Journal of International Law 481; and David Vogel, 'Private Global Business Regulation' (2008) 11 Annual Review of Political Science 261.

[6] Apart from EU law (see section 2.1), WTO law also distinguishes between these two categories. See the WTO Agreement on Technical Barriers to Trade (TBT) Annex 1 paras 1–2.

[7] See for example Case T-201/04 *Microsoft Corp. v Commission* [2007] ECR II-3601, paras 386–92.

[8] See Bernd van der Meulen (ed), *Private Food Law: Governing Food Chains Through Contract Law, Self-Regulation, Private Standards, Audits and Certification Schemes* (Wageningen Academic Publishers 2011); Tetty Havinga, 'Private Regulation of Food Safety by Supermarkets' (2006) 28 Law & Policy 515; Fabrizio Cafaggi, 'Private regulation, supply chain and contractual networks: The case of food safety' EUI RSCAS WP 2010/10.

made between purely market-based standards and standardization through more formal channels, notably the 'recognized' national (eg the French AFNOR or the German DIN), European (CEN, CENELEC and ETSI)[9] and international (eg ISO and IEC)[10] standard setting bodies. While they are usually not State bodies in the strict sense, some of the recognized SSOs have a particular legal status, are granted with some level of formal recognition, or other special powers.[11] This is where the European approach tends to differ from the one in the US, where standardization is to a large extent informal and market-based.[12]

In the narrow sense, standard setting refers just to the process of enacting standards (which is, in itself, quite complex and may involve a number of stages with different decision-makers).[13] There is more to standardization than that, however. It normally also involves conformity assessment, verifying whether a product or service actually satisfies the provisions of a standard, as well as certification: attesting conformity with a certificate or mark. These stages can be performed by a single actor or different actors, each of whom could be public, private, or a mix of the two.[14]

The legal controversy over standard setting largely follows two mutually intertwined lines. The first one questions the democratic accountability and legitimacy of taking important decisions in a relatively opaque environment dominated by private and self-interested actors. These problems could be either alleviated or worsened by the use of co-regulation (eg adoption of private standards by legislation, relying on them in public procurement, or using them as a basis for judicial decision-making), depending on the extent to which the governance and decision-making process of SSOs is reviewed by State bodies.[15]

[9] European Committee for Standardization, European Committee for Electrotechnical Standardization and the European Telecommunications Standards Institute.

[10] International Organization for Standardization and the International Electrotechnical Commission.

[11] See Harm Schepel and Josef Falke, *Legal Aspects of Standardisation in the Member States of the EC and EFTA: Comparative Report*, vol 1 (Luxembourg: Office for Official Publications of the European Communities 2000).

[12] See Tim Büthe and Walter Mattli, *The New Global Rulers: The Privatization of Regulation in the World Economy* (Princeton University Press 2011) on this distinction and its effects.

[13] See, for the example of European standards, Commission, 'Vademecum on European standardisation' <http://ec.europa.eu/growth/single-market/european-standards/vademecum/index_en.htm> section 2.

[14] For example, a group of food producers could formulate a standard for healthy food accompanied by a 'healthy choices' label, and subsequently test and certify products, whether their own or made by others. Alternatively, an NGO could set the standard, the companies could implement it, a laboratory (itself certified by an NGO) could assess conformity, and the NGO could certify products. This type of practice may also be linked to State regulation if, for example, instead of the standard there was binding legislation that laid down more abstract health requirements which the standard and the label would describe in more detail (similarly, for instance, to the Electronic Cigarette Industry Trade Association (ECITA) audits for e-cigarettes which verify compliance with legal requirements), or if the producers' commitments on healthy food were merely encouraged, approved, or adopted at the initiative of a public body (such as DPAH, the EU Platform for Action on Diet, Physical Activity, and Health).

[15] Christian Joerges, Harm Schepel, and Ellen Vos, 'The law's problems with the involvement of non-governmental actors in Europe's legislative processes: the case of standardisation under the "New Approach"' (1999) EUI Working Paper LAW No 99/9; Doris Fuchs, Agni Kalfagianni,

The second line of criticism has to do with standards' economic impact. The economic effects depend on the context, but it is clear that there is a trade-off between the benefits arising from economies of scale, interoperability (positive network effects), and the reduced likelihood of negative externalities on the one hand and the costs of increased concentration, reduced variety, and lock-in (using a standard where a non-standard solution might be preferable because of network effects) on the other. In addition, the regulatory diversity created by different standards prevailing in different states or regions—even when they are not turned into mandatory rules—can harm trade. The need for certification and conformity assessment is among the most serious non-tariff barriers in practice.[16]

These basic tensions are reflected in EU law as well. Over the years, it has dealt with standard setting in a variety of ways, the most famous of which has been the use of product standards as an alternative to legislative harmonization through the so-called 'New Approach'. More recently, however, standard setting has emerged as an important topic in competition law, especially in connection with the use and abuse of intellectual property rights. In addition, the judgment in *Fra.bo*[17] shed light on the somewhat neglected problem of the horizontal effect of the Treaty rules on the free movement of goods, precisely in relation to an SSO. This poses the question of how EU economic law disciplines are applied to standard setting, whether and how they overlap.

This chapter will follow the structure of the previous two case studies on sports and the legal profession, addressing the application of competition law, free movement law, and secondary legislation to standard setting. I will, however, proceed in a different order, starting with secondary legislation, which is helpful to discuss first in order to understand the rather complex European standard-setting system.

2. Standard Setting in EU Law: The New Approach and Product Legislation

The main element of the EU's standard-setting strategy has been the so-called New Approach to harmonization, an important element of the 'completion' of the internal market at the end of the 1980s.[18] Under the New Approach, the EU

and Tetty Havinga, 'Actors in Private Food Governance: The Legitimacy of Retail Standards and Multistakeholder Initiatives With Civil Society Participation' (2009) 28 Agriculture and Human Values 353; Caroline Bradley, 'Consultation and Legitimacy in Transnational Standard-Setting' (2011) 20 Minnesota Journal of International Law 480.

16 See for example Sykes (n 4) 133 et seq. For an in-depth look at the trade impact of non-tariff measures like standards and conformity assessment, see World Trade Organization, 'World Trade Report 2012' <https://www.wto.org/english/res_e/reser_e/wtr12_brochure_e.pdf>.

17 Case C-171/11 *Fra.bo SpA v Deutsche Vereinigung des Gas- und Wasserfaches eV (DVGW)—Technisch-Wissenschaftlicher Verein* (ECJ, 12 July 2012).

18 See n 33.

legislator was to stop painstakingly legislating on product rules. Instead, it would set the broad, essential requirements of product quality and safety and delegate the task of setting detailed rules to SSOs.

EU legislation relevant to SSOs can be divided in two groups. The first group concerns rules dealing with the application of technical regulations. The second group deals with voluntary standards.

The first group, as explained, is not the main concern of this chapter. It may be useful, however, to address the rules on national technical regulations insofar as they impact SSOs.

2.1 SSOs and technical regulations

Technical regulations, that is legally binding 'standards', can be subject to a wide range of EU law disciplines. This is equally true when private regulators take part in their adoption. As already explained, binding technical regulations should be distinguished from standards in the proper sense of the world which are, both in EU law and in the law of the WTO, voluntary.[19] This is not to say that the line is always perfectly clear: in *US-Tuna II*,[20] for example, the WTO Appellate Body found a law laying down conditions for the use of a voluntary 'dolphin friendly' label on tuna products to be a technical regulation under the TBT Agreement.

As they are binding measures, technical regulations can clearly be subject to any of the relevant free movement rules. Secondary law, such as regulations establishing common market organizations would also be applicable, notably by limiting the possibility of industry bodies to participate in enacting binding rules on the quality, safety, or other features of a particular product.[21]

Private regulators that participate in adopting or implementing technical regulations would also be subject to EU regulations that deal in detail with the application of national technical rules to products lawfully marketed in other Member States (Regulation 764/2008),[22] the accreditation of conformity assessment bodies and market surveillance (Regulation 765/2008),[23] as well as to the Decision 768/2008 on a common framework for the marketing of products which regulates conformity assessment.[24]

[19] See n 6. [20] *US—Tuna II (Mexico)* WT/DS381/AB/R.

[21] See for example Joined cases 47/83 and 48/83 *Administrative appeal proceedings against a disciplinary measure brought by Pluimveeslachterij Midden-Nederland BV* [1984] ECR 1721.

[22] Regulation (EC) 764/2008 of the European Parliament and of the Council of 9 July 2008 laying down procedures relating to the application of certain national technical rules to products lawfully marketed in another Member State and repealing Decision No 3052/95/EC [2008] OJ L218. See in particular Art 2/1 under a) to c).

[23] Regulation (EC) 765/2008 of the European Parliament and of the Council of 9 July 2008 setting out the requirements for accreditation and market surveillance relating to the marketing of products and repealing Regulation (EEC) No 339/93 [2008] OJ L218.

[24] Decision No 768/2008/EC of the European Parliament and of the Council of 9 July 2008 on a common framework for the marketing of products, and repealing Council Decision 93/465/EEC [2008] OJ L218. The Decision may be relevant for private or hybrid standard-setting bodies, because conformity assessment schemes may be carried not only by public authorities but also by manufacturers or notified bodies (Art 6). On all these acts, see also Karsten Engsig Sørensen,

In addition, the Notification Directive,[25] which requires the Member States to notify technical regulations[26] to the Commission, may apply to co-regulatory schemes as well as to straightforward State measures. In particular, this will be the case with so-called *de facto* technical regulations under the Directive (Art 1/11), which include:

a) References to technical specifications in the laws, regulations, or administrative provisions of a Member State[27] which confer a presumption of conformity with legal obligations. Thus, legislation that refers to a private standard would be considered a technical regulation under the Directive.
b) Voluntary agreements between a public authority and, for example, industry representatives that include compliance with technical specifications in the public interest. The term 'technical specification' would also cover private, market-based standards that are not developed by recognized standards bodies.[28]
c) Fiscal or financial measures that encourage the consumption of products that satisfy certain technical specifications or other requirements.

The Directive requires the Member States to notify the drafts of technical regulations to the Commission, which notifies the other Member States. Both the Commission and the Member States may then make comments. For three months after notification (four in the case of voluntary agreements), the technical regulation may not be adopted.[29]

In addition to these procedural duties for the Member States, the case law has ascribed more far-reaching consequences to the Directive. Notably, in *CIA Security* and *Unilever Italia* the Court held that technical regulations that were not duly notified to the Commission or were adopted during the standstill period may not be invoked in disputes between individuals.[30] This has been referred to

'Non-Harmonized Technical Regulations and the Free Movement of Goods' (2012) 23 European Business Law Review 163, 200 et seq.

[25] Directive 98/34/EC of the European Parliament and of the Council of 22 June 1998 laying down a procedure for the provision of information in the field of technical standards and regulations and of rules on Information Society services [1998] OJ L 204/37 (Notification Directive), as amended in particular by Directive 98/48 [1998] OJ L217/18 and by the European Standardisation Regulation (n 1).

[26] For the detailed definition of 'technical regulation' for purposes of the Notification Directive, see Joined cases C-213/11, C-214/11, and C-217/11 *Fortuna sp. z o.o.* (C-213/11), *Grand sp. z o.o.* (C-214/11), and *Forta sp. z o.o.* (C-217/11) *v Dyrektor Izby Celnej w Gdyni* ECLI:EU:C:2012:495, paras 27, 31–32, and 35.

[27] Professional codes or codes of practice which in turn refer to technical specifications are covered as well.

[28] This excludes public procurement tender specifications.

[29] If the Commission or a Member State delivers a detailed opinion claiming that the proposed technical regulation may create obstacles to the free movement of goods, it may not be adopted for six months. The standstill period may be extended in some circumstances (Art 9) and excluded in others (Art 9/7).

[30] Case C-194/94 *CIA Security International SA v Signalson SA and Securitel SPRL* [1996] ECR I-2201, para 54 and Case C-443/98 *Unilever Italia SpA v Central Food SpA* [2000] ECR I-7535,

as the 'incidental horizontal effect' of the Notification Directive.[31] In practice, it means that co-regulatory schemes between private SSOs and Member States that involve referring to private standards by way of legislative or administrative measures, voluntary agreements, or fiscal measures should also be notified or else risk becoming a dead letter. This is true even of technical regulations that would impede free movement of goods, or those that pursue legitimate policy objectives.[32]

2.2 The EU standardization system

Standards in the true sense of the word—voluntary technical specifications—have been central to internal market regulation since the advent of the so-called 'New Approach' in the mid-1980s.[33] The idea behind this was to replace outright harmonization of detailed product requirements with simpler legislation that only specifies the essential requirements, leaving it to the European standardization bodies to translate those into 'harmonised standards'. While these standards remain voluntary, certification of compliance with them grants a presumption of conformity with EU legislation. In principle, this prohibits the Member States from hindering their access to the market or imposing any additional conformity assessment.

The project has been successful. There are over thirty directives and regulations based on the 'new approach', regulating construction products, machinery, medical devices, toys, cosmetics, explosives, etc. In addition, standardization through the European bodies (CEN, CENELEC, and ETSI)[34] has affected many areas beyond the New Approach directives.

The main features of EU standardization policy are outlined in Regulation 1025/2012 on European standardization.[35] The system is based on co-operation between the Commission, the European standardization organizations (ESOs), and national standardization bodies (NSBs). The latter are central national clearing houses for standards, notified to the EU by the Member States.[36] They are

paras 49–52. This is only relevant to the reliance on such standards as technical regulations, that is on their binding effect. It would probably not affect the functioning of the standard as such. For example, if complying with a standard is a contractual term, the argument that the party did not fulfill its obligations by not complying with the standard could still be made. See also Case C-226/97 *Criminal proceedings against Johannes Martinus Lemmens* [1998] ECR I-3711, paras 35–36, clarifying that a violation of the Notification Directive only prevents the Member States from applying technical regulations in a way that impedes trade, and not for example from using the products based on those regulations (in that case, breathalysers).

[31] Sørensen (n 24) 189.

[32] Case C-13/96 *Bic Benelux SA v Belgian State* [1997] ECR I-1753, para 20. See also Sørensen (n 24) 183–84.

[33] Commission, 'White Paper on Completing the Internal Market' (1985) COM(85)310 final, 19–22. For an early commentary, see Jacques Pelkmans, 'The New Approach to Technical Harmonization and Standardization' (1987) 25 Journal of Common Market Studies 249; more recently, see Harm Schepel, *The Constitution of Private Governance: Product Standards in the Regulation of Integrating Markets* (Hart 2005) 63–75.

[34] See Annex I of the European Standardization Regulation (n 1).

[35] European Standardization Regulation (n 1)

[36] The Commission periodically publishes a list of those bodies in the Official Journal.

normally not a part of the State administration, but their composition, powers, and functioning are a mix between public and private.[37]

The centrepiece of the system is the development of European standards by the three ESOs: CEN, CENELEC, and ETSI, each in their respective fields. Most important of the European standards are harmonized standards, made upon the Commission's request or 'mandate'. These standards grant a presumption of conformity with the requirements of the relevant Directive after a reference to them is published in the Official Journal by the Commission.[38] They are created with the participation of NSBs, who also implement them, that is translate them and make them accessible to producers, normally for a fee.

The system does not prevent the NSBs from developing their own standards. Indeed, the more prominent NSBs in particular continue to adopt many standards that often serve as the only practical way of entering their Member State's market. Unlike, for example, the United States, the European system is almost completely focused on the recognized European and national bodies. EU legislation has relatively little to say on market-based standardization which is, of course, common in a variety of sectors in the EU as well.

The reliance of EU institutions on the standardization system seems to have grown over the years. Standardization is not seen simply as a way of eliminating barriers to free movement in the Member States. Rather, the development of European standards has become a fully-fledged European industrial policy instrument, claiming to benefit EU industry and enable the production of higher quality, safer, and interoperable products. It is also seen as a tool of trade policy, pushing for international standards that conform as closely as possible to the European ones and thus giving EU producers an edge over their international competition.[39] Importantly, it is a policy largely managed by the Commission with relatively little interference from the Parliament, Council, and Member State institutions (being seen as a technical, rather than political issue)[40] and with an

[37] See n 11. The Regulation provides that the Member States should encourage the participation of public authorities such as those dealing with market surveillance in national standardization activities (Art 7).

[38] This makes them a part of EU law and susceptible to interpretation by the Court of Justice. Without publication, they will be seen as private standards. The CE marking, indicating compliance with harmonized standards, cannot be used for such products. See Case C-185/08 *Latchways plc and Eurosafe Solutions BV v Kedge Safety Systems BV and Consolidated Nederland BV* [2010] ECR I-9983, paras 31–35.

[39] See Commission, 'A strategic vision for European standards: Moving forward to enhance and accelerate the sustainable growth of the European economy by 2020' (Communication) COM(2011) 311 final, in particular 17–19. The Communication argues, for example, that 'standardisation bodies based in the EU should ... continue to put forward proposals for international standards in those areas where Europe is a global leader to maximise European competitive advantage' (18). Büthe and Mattli (n 12) discuss the incentives of US and EU policy-makers to influence the international standard-setting process and put forward a theory of 'institutional complementarity' explaining why the EU has been more successful in influencing international product standards.

[40] See however Art 11 the European Standardization Regulation, enabling the Member States or the European Parliament to object to harmonized standards, forcing the Commission to reconsider their publication.

air of legitimacy (being based on technical expertise and with decisions made on a sort of consensus).[41]

With these broad aims in mind, it is perhaps understandable that the EU approach to standardization is less about challenging the behaviour of SSOs and more about reinforcing the system, making it more effective and increasing its output. This may have broader institutional and legal implications. In particular, the application of EU competition or free movement rules is likely to be relatively lax, at least when it comes to recognized Europan or national SSOs. The case law has so far, arguably, fulfilled that expectation (see sections 3 and 4).

The EU standardization system does, however, require SSOs to follow certain good governance standards in their work. The European Standardization Regulation, in particular, addresses transparency, openness, and participation. The WTO's Technical Barriers to Trade (TBT) Code of Good Practice for the Preparation, Adoption, and Application of Standards,[42] to which both the ESOs and NSBs have signed up, pursues similar aims. The Code imposes good governance requirements (publishing work programmes, allowing standstill periods for comments, consultation, etc.), along with a duty to abstain from interfering with international trade or discriminating, as well as to use international standards as a basis for SSOs' work.

Under the Regulation, both ESOs and NSBs are required to publish detailed work programmes at least once per year. Their draft standards have to be made accessible to other ESOs and NSBs as well as the Commission. They are required to respond to comments made by their peers and consult with the ESOs and the Commission if any of the comments suggest a negative impact on the internal market. The Regulation also requires the ESOs (but not the NSBs) to broaden the participation of all relevant stakeholders, even those outside of the industry—SMEs, consumer organizations, environmental and social stakeholders, universities, and research centres—in the standardization process.[43] Finally, the Regulation requires NSBs to facilitate access to both standards as final products and the standardization process by small and medium enterprises.[44]

The European Standardization Regulation could be applied in a dispute between individuals, if one of its provisions was held to have direct effect. In

[41] In this context, consensus is not quite the same as unanimity. For instance, CEN defines it as 'general agreement, characterised by the absence of sustained opposition to substantial issues by any important part of the concerned interests and by a process that involves seeking to take into account the views of all parties concerned and to reconcile any conflicting arguments'. See also Büthe and Mattli (n 12) 11 et seq, criticizing the view that standardization is about objective, apolitical scientific truths.

[42] Annex III of the TBT Agreement (n 6).

[43] Articles 3–5. See also Art 12, requiring the Commission to set up a notification system for all relevant stakeholders enabling them to participate at various stages, from the adoption of its Union work programme to taking a decision on formal objections etc.

[44] This obligation, however, is relatively weak: Art 6 of the Regulation merely lists a number of examples of practices that could be implemented, such as enabling non-member SMEs to participate in standard setting, providing special rates, or free access to draft standards.

practical terms, what is likely to be more important, however, is the applicability of the substantive legislation related to products, such as New Approach regulations. The difference between regulations and directives is relevant here: New Approach directives cannot be directly applied in a dispute between two individuals,[45] and can be invoked directly against an NSB only insofar as it is as an 'emanation of State'.[46]

3. Standard Setting and Competition Law

While official as well as market-based standard setting have clear competitive benefits,[47] distortions of the standard-setting process may occur and competition law has a role to play in preventing them.[48] This is true even when, as is usually the case, a standard is voluntary and alternative routes to the market exist.[49] Agreeing on how products should be made or how they should interoperate could in itself have anticompetitive aims or effects, or at least provide a convenient setting for collusion.

Article 101 TFEU has thus been applied to standardization agreements and SSOs, and Art 102 to dominant undertakings that abuse the standard-setting process. In either case, similar criteria have been used. For example, the Horizontal Guidelines which directly concern only Art 101 have been routinely cited in Art 102 cases.

As Schweitzer concluded in her overview of this area, EU competition law shows a 'strong concern with open, transparent standard-setting procedures' and 'fair and non-discriminatory access of all competitors to a standard once agreed'.[50] Moreover, it promotes[51] standard setting by formally established standard-setting organizations with open and transparent rules and procedures, with a particular

[45] In Case C-80/06 *Carp Snc di L. Moleri e V. Corsi v Ecorad Srl* [2007] ECR I-4473, paras 20–22, it was confirmed that there is no direct horizontal effect either of a New Approach directive or of a decision implementing its conformity assessment requirements addressed to a Member State.

[46] Case C-188/89 *A. Foster and others v British Gas plc* [1990] ECR I-3313, para 20.

[47] The Horizontal Cooperation Guidelines (n 2) 263 mention 'promoting economic interpenetration on the internal market and encouraging the development of new and improved products or markets and improved supply conditions'. 'Standards thus normally increase competition and lower output and sales costs, benefiting economies as a whole. Standards may maintain and enhance quality, provide information and ensure interoperability and compatibility (thus increasing value for consumers).'

[48] Schweitzer has pointed out that markets may not guarantee a 'rational procedure for selecting optimal standards'. Heike Schweitzer, 'European Standard-Setting Policy and the Role of Competition Law' in Carl Baudenbacher (ed), *Current Developments in European and International Competition Law 15th St Gallen International Competition Law Forum (ICF) 2008* (Helbing & Lichtenhahn 2009) 30–31.

[49] See Joined cases 96-102, 104, 105, 108, and 110/82 *NV IAZ International Belgium and others v Commission* [1983] ECR 3369, para 20, holding that non-binding recommendations fall under Art 101/1 if they have an appreciable influence on the relevant market.

[50] Schweitzer (n 48) 62.

[51] The Commission's Horizontal Cooperation Guidelines (n 2) para 258 exempt 'preparation and production of technical standards as part of the execution of public powers'.

emphasis on the EU-sanctioned system of NSBs and ESOs.[52] Competition law scrutiny over standard setting is, thus, very much based on procedural criteria and good governance.[53] In that vein, Schepel has argued that a 'procedural public interest' test should be applied to standardization, highlighting the 'potential competition law has for subjecting private transnational governance to a more or less coherent set of procedural requirements that are cut loose from hierarchical conceptions of legitimacy'.[54]

The scope of competition law in relation to standard setting can be a difficult issue, in particular as regards standardization through recognized bodies. This is not only due to the fact that NSBs and ESOs would be expected, more than market-based bodies, to have detailed and well-formulated procedures in place, but also because they could be claimed not to be undertakings or associations of undertakings at all. The current Guidelines do not go this far, merely pointing out that 'the European standardisation bodies recognised under Directive 98/34 ... are subject to competition law to the extent that they can be considered to be an undertaking or an association of undertakings'.[55] In the *EMC* decision, however, the Commission found that the European standardization organization CEN is not an association of undertakings, given that its members are national standardization bodies and that it 'has to be considered a body entrusted with the general economic interest'.[56] National bodies are less likely to be exempt, not only because they are less removed from industry then ESOs are, but also because they act as undertakings in their own right to the extent that they sell access to their standards.[57]

Standard setting directly performed by Member State bodies or international organizations, especially if it eventually leads to the adoption of technical regulations, will also frequently avoid competition law scrutiny. In *SELEX*, for example, the activities of the European Organization for the Safety of Air Navigation (Eurocontrol), an international organization charged with developing and adopting technical standards related to air space management,[58] fell completely outside

[52] Paragraph 308 of the Guidelines highlights that 'Union wide standards may facilitate market integration and allow companies to market their goods and services in all Member States, leading to increased consumer choice and decreasing prices.'

[53] '... competition law in both the European Union and the United States demands procedural guarantees to satisfy antitrust requirements ... This procedural turn is a bid to solve two dilemmas. The first is to disentangle market aspects of standards from their regulatory aspects; the second is how to fit in "public interest" criteria of health and safety into the economic analysis to which competition law confines reasoning.' Schepel (n 33) 287.

[54] ibid 338. [55] See n 51.

[56] EN 197-1 Standard EMC/European Cement Producers (Case COMP/F-2/38.401) Commission Decision SG-Greffe (2005) D/205249 paras 73–74. The Decision, and the Horizontal Co-operation Guidelines that were in force at the time, seem to immunize recognized (European and national) bodies from the scope of EU competition law. Arguably, at least the wording that is in place today (see n 51) could not support such a broad exemption.

[57] Rob Van Gestel and Hans-W Micklitz, 'European Integration Through Standardization: How Judicial Review is Breaking Down the Club House of Private Standardization Bodies' (2013) 50 Common Market Law Review 145, 147.

[58] See the General Court's decision in Case T-155/04 *SELEX Sistemi Integrati SpA v Commission* [2006] ECR II-4797 and the Court's decision on appeal, Case C-113/07 P *SELEX Sistemi Integrati SpA v Commission of the European Communities and Organisation européenne pour la sécurité de la navigation aérienne* (*Eurocontrol*) [2009] ECR I-2207.

the scope of Art 102 as they were not considered to be economic. Of course, some conceptually distinct activities of such bodies may be viewed as economic. This was also at issue in *SELEX*. The General Court considered that, when Eurocontrol formally adopts 'standards', making them binding on its member states, it is performing a 'legislative activity' which is 'directly connected with the exercise of public authority' and thus outside the scope of competition law. The same was not true, however, of the distinct process of developing those standards, which could be an economic activity.[59] In its judgment on appeal, however, the Court disagreed, finding the two to be inseparable.[60]

When the competition rules do apply, it is useful to distinguish between two groups of cases.

The first group is where most of the discussions on standard setting and competition law today take place: unilateral conduct that abuses the standard-setting process so that its benefits are lost or diminished, in particular through practices related to the inclusion of IP into a standard. While these restrictions of competition may not be at the heart of the private regulatory project itself,[61] this line of cases has certainly affected the practices of SSOs.

The second group is concerned with standard setting as such: whether the behaviour of standard-setting organizations or other actors in standardization schemes, such as certification bodies, is anticompetitive. A subgroup relates to more straightforward cases of anticompetitive behaviour such as price-fixing that piggybacks onto the standard-setting process, essentially using an SSO as a forum for a cartel.

I will address these two groups in turn, focusing on what lessons we can draw from them on the EU's approach to private regulation.

3.1 Anticompetitive abuse of standard setting

Standard setting has been a central aspect of the so-called 'patent wars' fought between the world's leading high-technology companies in recent years. EU competition law has thus been applied in a number of high-profile cases on the abuse of intellectual property in standard setting, starting with *Rambus* and *Qualcomm*.[62] These cases concern IP (primarily patents) that is included in a standard and that cannot be effectively designed around.[63] Users thus must obtain a licence from the IP holder in order to comply with the standard; hence the term 'standard essential patents' (SEPs).

[59] *SELEX* (2009) (n 58) para 90.

[60] ibid paras 91–93.

[61] cf the 'business as usual' restrictions in the area of sports, discussed in Chapter V section 4.1.

[62] *Rambus* (Case COMP/C-3/38 636) Commission Decision SG-Greffe(2010)D/275 C(2010) 150; press release 'Antitrust: Commission closes formal proceedings against Qualcomm' (24 November 2009) MEMO/09/516.

[63] *Google/Motorola Mobility* (Case No COMP/M.6381) Commission Decision C(2012)1068 paras 54 et seq. It is clear from this Decision that, for the Commission, 'each SEP can be considered as a separate market in itself as it is necessary to comply with a standard and thus cannot be designed around' (para 61).

So far, these issues have mostly been analysed under Art 102 and the Merger Regulation.[64] The main potential competition concerns are hold-up (the SEP holder is able to extract higher rents than under competitive, pre-inclusion conditions),[65] patent ambush (the SEP holder intentionally fails to disclose the existence of a patent during the negotiation of the standard),[66] and abusive injunctions (the SEP holder refuses to genuinely negotiate a licence and/or attempts to exhort high payments under the threat of an injunction).[67] These can happen not only in the context of market-based standardization but also in recognized European and national bodies. In the *Google-Motorola* decision, for example, the Commission discussed the issue of Motorola's patents essential for ETSI standards.

The threat to competition in these cases is not standard setting as such. Quite to the contrary, standard setting in the high-tech sector, aimed at inter-operability, lower research and development costs, and launching innovative products, is indispensable. These anticompetitive uses of intellectual property are problematic precisely because they endanger the standard-setting process for the benefit of the IP holder.[68]

It is not, however, only SEP holders that have been affected. The need to comply with competition law has led to changes of the intellectual property policies of SSOs, relied upon as gatekeepers of the standard development process.[69] Even though the cases in this group have not been analysed as agreements under Art 101, the Horizontal Cooperation Guidelines require SSOs to impose, by way of specific IP policies based on good faith,[70] disclosure of existing IP, and the obligation of FRAND (fair, reasonable, and non-discriminatory) licensing on any entity whose IP is included in the standard.[71] This means that those entities have to make the patent available to third parties, that they cannot discriminate, and that the terms of the licence must be fair and reasonable. Within those limits, however, the SEP holder is free to negotiate the terms of the licence and can, in principle, sue

64 Council Regulation (EC) 139/2004 of 20 January 2004 on the control of concentrations between undertakings (the EC Merger Regulation) [2004] OJ L 24/1.

65 Qualcomm (n 62). See also Mario Mariniello, 'European antitrust control and standard setting' Bruegel Working Paper 2013/01 7–8.

66 *Rambus* (n 62).

67 See press releases 'Antitrust: Commission welcomes IPCom's public FRAND declaration' (10 December 2009) MEMO/09/549 and 'Antitrust: Commission accepts legally binding commitments by Samsung Electronics on standard essential patent injunctions' (29 April 2014) IP/14/490; *Google/Motorola Mobility* (n 63) para 109, and *Motorola—Enforcement of GPRS Standard Essential Patents* (Case COMP AT.39985) Commission decision C(2014)2892.

68 This assumption is sometimes made explicit. The Commission, for example, found Rambus's patent ambush anticompetitive because it 'undermines confidence in the standard-setting process'. *Rambus* (n 62) paras 28–29.

69 See, for example Knut Blind et al., 'Study on the Interplay between Standards and Intellectual Property Rights (IPRs): Final Report' <http://ec.europa.eu/enterprise/policies/european-standards/files/standards_policy/ipr-workshop/ipr_study_final_report_en.pdf> 23; Mark A Lemley, 'Intellectual Property Rights and Standard-Setting Organizations' (2002) 90 California Law Review online.

70 See *Rambus* (n 62) para 31.

71 Horizontal Cooperation Guidelines (n 2) para 285; see also *Google/Motorola Mobility* (n 63) para 57.

and seek injunctions against infringing uses of its IP, at least as long as the potential licensee is not willing to purchase the licence under FRAND terms.[72]

3.2 Anticompetitive standard setting

Standard setting can also give rise to other kinds of anticompetitive behaviour, and in particular to agreements, decisions, or concerted practices contrary to Art 101. Either the process (the composition of the SSO, the procedure used to formulate a standard, its openness and transparency, etc.), the substance of a standard (eg if the formulation of the standard makes it impossible for certain competitors to enter the market), or both give cause for concern. The Horizontal Cooperation Guidelines outline three main ways in which standardization can restrict competition: facilitating collusion, limiting technical development and innovation by creating barriers to entry for technologies that are not included, and preventing effective access to the standard or the IP included in it.[73]

Overall, both the Commission and the Court have been broadly supportive of standardization as such and have respected the regulatory autonomy of SSOs. In particular, the Commission has been supportive of recognized standardization processes in the framework of national or European bodies, especially when other departments of the Commission were involved in the adoption of the standard. That said, it should be made clear that a measure of discipline has been imposed on both the procedural and substantive aspects of standard setting.

According to the Horizontal Guidelines, using a standard as a part of a broader restrictive agreement aimed at excluding competitors is a restriction of Art 101 by object.[74] Most other standardization agreements, however, would be analysed as restrictions by effect, meaning that a more detailed analysis would be required. This would, firstly, involve asking whether there is market power, or in other words, whether there is 'effective competition between a number of voluntary standards'.[75] Even if there is market power, however, standardization agreements are exempt from scrutiny if they satisfy four conditions based on the Court's case law,[76] which can be described as good governance criteria: first, unrestricted participation in the standard-setting process for all affected competitors, objective

[72] See the cases cited in n 67. On the other hand, even with FRAND commitments in place a restriction of competition remains possible, and an actual breach of an SSO's IP policy would not be strictly necessarily for a violation of the competition rules (*Google/Motorola Mobility* (n 63) 113). The precise extent of the IP holder's ability to seek and enforce injunctions is still somewhat uncertain, which explains the Commission's decision not to impose a fine in *Motorola—GPRS* (n 67). At the time of writing, the best statement of the law seems to be the judgment in Case C-170/13 *Huawei Technologies* ECLI:EU:C:2015:477. See also Michela Angeli, 'Willing to Define Willingness: The (Almost) Final Word on SEP-Based Injunctions In Light of Samsung and Motorola' (2015) 6 Journal of European Competition Law & Practice 221.

[73] Paragraphs 265–68. [74] Paragraphs 273–74. [75] Paragraph 277.

[76] See Richard Whish and David Bailey, *Competition Law* (7th edn, Oxford University Press 2012) 609, linking the Guidelines with Case T-432/05 *EMC Development AB v Commission* [2010] ECR II-1629, paras 79–104 (discussing openness, transparency, and non-discrimination of the standard's adoption procedure).

and non-discriminatory voting rights and criteria for technology selection; second, transparent development and adoption process; third, no obligation to comply with the standard; and fourth, the ability for others to access the standard on FRAND terms.[77] The latter point is particularly relevant if the standard involves issues of IP licensing, but could be applied more broadly to examine the accessibility of a standard to potential users.

If a standard-setting scheme fails to fall within this safe harbour, it will be subject to a full effects-based analysis. At this stage, scrutiny is similarly dominated by process concerns: whether an SSO's members remain free to develop non-complying products or alternative standards, how accessible the standard is, how broad its coverage is, whether the procedure for its adoption allows competitors and other stakeholders to participate on an open and non-discriminatory basis, whether there are several competing standards, etc.[78]

These principles can be loosely tracked through the case law. In some cases, the SSO is used simply as a forum for price-fixing, market-sharing, or preventing new products from reaching the market. In the *Pre-insulated pipes* decision,[79] for example, cartel members set up an SSO that was, in theory, meant to develop product standards and share technical information but was in practice mostly a 'handmaiden to [a] cartel'[80] which 'us[ed] norms and standards in order to prevent or delay the introduction of new technology which would result in price reductions'.[81] In particular, the fact that the cartel prohibited its members from marketing non-compliant products was seen as a red flag.

In *Belasco*, a Belgian 'cooperative society' of roofing felt manufacturers agreed on prices, quotas, penalties for breaches, joint advertising, as well as standard setting and certification. Firstly, Belasco certified products covered by IBN (Belgian Standards Institution) standards with a common mark called 'Benor'; secondly, it also started laying down specifications for so-called 'new products' not yet covered by IBN standards. According to the Commission's decision, these activities went beyond facilitating other restrictions of competition. Standardization itself restricted Art 101/1 because, by maintaining a common product range and setting down specifications for new products, it was 'at least partly intended to restrict members' freedom to differentiate their products'.[82]

Thus, restricting product differentiation is seen as a competition evil as such. Would this not condemn standardization in general? Arguably, the decision was

[77] Paragraphs 280–86. See, however, para 279, pointing out that because 'there exist different models for standard-setting and competition within and between those models is a positive aspect of a market economy', SSOs are free to put in place different procedures as long as they do not violate the competition rules. This will, of course, make it harder for them to defend themselves against an Art 101 challenge, as the safe harbour described in the Guidelines will not apply.

[78] See paras 292 et seq.

[79] *Pre-Insulated Pipe Cartel* (Case No IV/35.691/E-4) Commission Decision 1999/60/EC [1999] OJ L24/1.

[80] Paragraph 116.

[81] Paragraph 147.

[82] *Roofing felt* (Case IV/31.371) Commission Decision 86/399/EEC (1986) OJ L232/15 (*Belasco*) para 73.

not meant to apply so broadly. It was the context of a binding agreement that imposes a common product range and sanctions violations that made standardization problematic:[83] according to the judgment on appeal, it intensified the overall restrictive agreement and had an anticompetitive intent.[84]

Similarly, requiring the exclusive use of a standard—making it mandatory for the parties—will usually be considered a red flag. Such agreements are unlikely to either avoid the finding of a restriction under Art 101/1 or be justified under Art 101/3. In *Philips/VCR*, for example, a seemingly beneficial agreement committing the participants to use the VCR standard for videocassettes and recorders violated Art 101 largely because it prevented them from making equipment on the basis of any other standard, unless they were willing to risk forfeiting the licences on the IP of the other parties to the agreement.[85]

This shows the importance of context. Standard-setting that does not form part of a broader scheme that restricts competition will, in principle, be seen favourably. If the participants are free to offer non-conforming products, advertise and enter into agreements with customers or suppliers independently, and if the standard is openly accessible (though not necessarily free of charge) after development, it will be much more likely to pass scrutiny—under Art 101/3 if not under Art 101/1. In those circumstances, even if an SSO has strict membership criteria or if the development of the standard is closed, normal competition in the market can be an effective remedy for any of the difficulties created by the standard.[86]

Another potential 'red flag' is market-partitioning. Thus, in *IAZ* an infringement of Art 101 was found in an agreement between washing machine manufacturers and importers on one side and a group of Belgian water suppliers on the other, introducing a conformity label related to drinking water quality. The effect of the agreement was that only washing machines sold by manufacturers and exclusive distributors could obtain the label, effectively blocking parallel imports because the water supply companies required households to use labelled washing machines only.[87]

[83] ibid para 74. The Commission also notes: 'It is true that new products were developed independently by each producer ... Nevertheless, as new products gained in importance, the members intended to progressively extend the price arrangements provided for in the Agreement to them, as far as this was possible for new products that were not covered by official standards, hence the need to agree basic specifications.'

[84] Case 246/86 *SC Belasco and others v Commission* [1989] ECR 2117, para 30.

[85] *Video cassette recorders* (Case IV/29.151) Commission Decision 78/156/EEC (1978) OJ L46/42 (*Philips/VCR*).

[86] *X/Open Group* (Case IV/31.458) Commission Decision 87/69/EEC (1987) OJ L35/36, while eventually finding a restriction of Art 101/1, in principle supports restrictive membership of an SSO: 'The aims of the Group could not be achieved if any company willing to commit itself to the Group objectives had a right to become a member' (para 45). See also *Ship classification* (Case 39416) Commission Decision (2009) C(2009) 7796 final, para 36: '... the Commitments strike an appropriate balance between maintaining demanding criteria for membership of IACS on the one hand, and removing unnecessary barriers to membership of IACS on the other hand. The new criteria will ensure that only technically competent CSs are eligible to become member of IACS, thus preventing that the efficiency and quality of IACS' work is unduly impaired ...'

[87] *IAZ* (n 49). The Court found that the agreement had both the object (para 23) and effect (para 27) of restricting competition.

3.2.1 Substance and procedure in the competition law analysis of standard setting

So far, I have discussed cases where a restriction of competition was found either because standards reinforced other anticompetitive behaviour or because of other 'red flags' such as exclusivity. For less obvious cases, one general conclusion can be made: the analysis primarily looks at the procedural aspect of standardization, not at the substance of standards.

A good example is *EMC Development*,[88] a case scrutinizing official standardization through ESOs and NSBs. The maker of a novel type of reinforced cement claimed that its more established competitors, along with the industry association Cembureau and the European standards organization CEN, violated Art 101 by formulating a harmonized European standard that excludes its product. EMC attacked, firstly, the substance of the standard—claiming that it should have been based on product performance rather than prescribe cement composition, and that it is inherently exclusionary by only covering 'traditional and well tried' cements. Secondly, they claimed that its adoption procedure was biased because the relevant CEN technical committee was chaired by an employee of one of the members of Cembureau.[89]

Several conclusions can be drawn from the Commission's decision,[90] which found no violation of Art 101, and the General Court judgment confirming it.

Firstly, there is reluctance to question the substance of a standard through competition law, for example by addressing the exclusionary effect of formulating the standard in prescriptive rather than performance-based terms. According to both the Commission and the General Court, that claim does not relate to competition law but perhaps to the Construction Products Directive, which specifically provides that European standards should be formulated in terms of product performance.[91] Thus, the Court rejected an attempt at converging competition law with the requirements of an internal market directive.

Secondly, while it is taken as a given that standards are voluntary, there is some space for the argument that some standards can be seen as *de facto* mandatory (and therefore suspect) when there are no commercially viable alternatives. Yet, neither the Commission nor the GC had much patience with that argument in the case at hand. The large market share held by products complying with the standard was, rightly, held not to be problematic as such.[92] The apparently

[88] *EMC Development* (n 76).

[89] Overall, EMC claimed that the standard did not pass the bar set by the version of the Horizontal Guidelines that was in force at the time, according to which non-mandatory standards adopted by the recognized standards bodies and based on non-discriminatory, open, and transparent procedures do not fall under Art 101/1.

[90] EMC Decision (n 56).

[91] Council Directive 89/106/EEC of 21 December 1988 on the approximation of laws, regulations, and administrative provisions of the Member States relating to construction products [1988] OJ L40/12, Art 7/2. In the meantime, the CPD was replaced by Regulation (EU) 305/2011 of the European Parliament and of the Council of 9 March 2011 laying down harmonised conditions for the marketing of construction products and repealing Council Directive 89/106/EEC [2011] OJ L88/5.

[92] *EMC Development* (n 76) para 117.

exclusive reliance on the standard in Member State public procurement was also not considered problematic. Finally, the GC agreed with the Commission's claim that an alternative way of entering the market, through a 'European technical approval' was 'working adequately', dismissing arguments that this route was excessively difficult and costly.[93]

Thirdly, recognized and especially European standards bodies are granted a measure of deference in competition law analysis.[94] They are assumed to follow 'non-discriminatory, open and transparent procedures', unless it is shown that those principles were not respected in the case of a specific standard.

The GC, for example, notes that CEN is a recognized body under the Notification Directive and that its rules foresee the inclusion of industry experts in technical committees. It then rejects the argument that the Commission should have scrutinized the standard more thoroughly, stating that 'the applicant does not ... indicate in what respect the situation in the present case represented a special case with regard to CEN's operating rules'.[95] The Commission's decision, similarly, defers to the opinion of its own department dealing with standardization, which criticized but ultimately endorsed the standard and published a reference to it in the Official Journal.[96]

This light review over formalized schemes that involve EU or Member State institutions reflects the Commission's general view of standard-setting. The Guidelines, for example, discuss an example of 'government encouraged standardisation' in which a group of manufacturers, on the basis of a government report on unhealthy foods, set maximum recommended fat levels in processed food, and find this not to restrict competition at all, despite reducing consumer choice.[97]

Finally, *EMC Development* recognizes industry expertise as the central justification for standard-setting. Thus, the Commission found that Cembureau members did not exceed the limits of normal lobbying activity, and that it is usual and justifiable for technical committees to include industry representatives who are 'normally the experts' in the field.[98]

3.2.2 Can EU law impose mutual recognition on SSOs?

Competition law, as we have seen, tends not to discipline the substance of a standard. It may, however, affect the substance of a standard-setting scheme through

93 ibid para 127.

94 See also *Belasco* (*decision*) (n 82) para 73 (vi), making a point of not addressing Belasco's participation in setting IBN standards.

95 Paragraph 92.

96 'If the Commission services observed that the adoption process of EN-197-1 Standard had been not open, discriminatory and non-transparent they would neither have published in the Official Journal the references of this Standard nor expressed publicly the view that the Standard is compatible with CPD' (para 104).

97 Paragraph 330. Government involvement is not specifically mentioned as the reason for exonerating such a cartel, however.

98 EMC Decision (n 56) para 101.

the back door by imposing mutual recognition requirements. This would mean that products or services that are not certified under a standard, but can show that they fulfil 'equivalent guarantees', have to be either certified or otherwise accepted by those who require compliance with the scheme (eg a Member State, through public procurement).

This was contemplated in *SCK*. The Commission[99] and the General Court imposed a set of structural requirements, namely openness, independence, transparency, and the 'acceptance of equivalent guarantees from other systems' on a scheme that certified firms hiring out construction cranes for compliance with a range of legal requirements, prohibiting them from outsourcing work to non-certified firms.

In the words of the General Court, the ban on subcontracting with non-certified firms 'cannot be objectively justified by an interest in maintaining the quality of the products and services ensured by the certification system'. The General Court thus endorsed the Commission's 'acceptance of equivalent guarantees' criterion.[100]

While insisting on such a requirement would be almost second-nature in free movement law where it is routinely imposed on the Member States, it does not translate easily to the standardization context. It seems to defeat the purpose of a certification scheme, which is precisely to reduce the transaction costs of verifying firms for compliance with certain requirements on a case-by-case basis.[101] Indeed, if read broadly, it would impose a mutual recognition requirement on standard-setting in general.[102]

3.2.3 Justification under Article 101/3 and beyond

Even when standard-setting schemes violate Art 101/1, Art 101/3 provides an avenue for justification. In that context, the Guidelines acknowledge the efficiencies of standardization: reducing transaction costs and time to market, while increasing choice, quality, interoperability, and innovation. The criteria that are used to find whether such efficiencies offset restrictions of competition, however, are largely similar to the criteria used within Art 101/1 itself. For indispensability, for example, it matters whether participation in standard setting is open to all competitors, whether the standard is of a broad scope, whether it is binding, and whether the power to test for compliance is reserved or open

[99] *Stichting Certificatie Kraanverhuurbedrijf and the Federatie van Nederlandse Kraanverhuurbedrijven/Dutch Cranes* (Cases IV/34.179, 34.202, 216) Commission Decision 95/551/EC (1995) OJ L 312.

[100] Joined cases T-213/95 and T-18/96 *Stichting Certificatie Kraanverhuurbedrijf (SCK) and Federatie van Nederlandse Kraanbedrijven (FNK) v Commission* [1997] ECR II-1739, para 137.

[101] See Schepel (n 33) 290–93.

[102] This broad reading is probably not pursued by the Commission, at least not any more. See the Horizontal Cooperation Guidelines (n 2) para 319, where *SCK* is cited only to the effect that 'standardisation agreements that entrust certain bodies with the exclusive right to test compliance … may restrict competition'.

to competition.[103] For pass-on to consumers, it matters 'which procedures are used to guarantee that the interests of the users of standards and end consumers are protected'.[104] Whether competition has been substantially eliminated will depend on the sources and levels of competitive constraint in the marketplace, and on whether third parties have effective access to the standard.[105]

Unlike in the previous two case studies, competition law in this context has not gone beyond an efficiency analysis by introducing a proportionality test based on public policy justifications (environmental protection, health and safety, etc.), in the *Wouters* or *Meca-Medina* fashion. One failed attempt was *IAZ*, where the fact that the washing machine certification scheme was pursuing the aims of public health did not change the finding that it restricted competition by object.[106] On the other hand, in *CECED*, another agreement setting standards for washing machines was justified under Art 101/3 even though it prevented the manufacturers from producing less environmentally efficient machines and thus reduced choice and increased prices.[107] While the type of analysis used in *CECED*, as discussed in Chapter III section 3.1.4, is largely focused on efficiencies, it does show how public policy arguments can play a role in the analysis of standardization. Similar arguments may carry even more weight if the scheme is encouraged or supported by State policy aimed at protecting the environment or achieving other legitimate aims.[108]

This brings us to another avenue for justification that has so far not been addressed by the case law: whether or not standard setting could benefit from the Art 106/2 exception as a service of general economic interest. As for the recognized European and national standards bodies, at least insofar as they are acting within the remit of the official standardization system, it seems that the answer could be positive.[109] Of course, this does not mean that the behaviour of undertakings in the context of, for example, a CEN technical committee would thus also be exempt from scrutiny.

3.3 Standards and the application of competition law to the State

Competition law has also been applied to Member State measures granting undertakings special and exclusive rights, such as the right to set binding 'standards',

[103] ibid para 315 et seq. [104] ibid para 321. [105] ibid para 324.

[106] *IAZ* (n 49) para 25: '[T]he purpose of the agreement ... is appreciably to restrict competition ... notwithstanding the fact that it also pursues the objective of protecting public health and reducing the cost of conformity checks.' It should be noted, however, that the agreement was not notified to the Commission as was necessary at the time; therefore, Art 101/3 was never applied.

[107] *CECED* (Case IV.F.1/36.718) Commission Decision 2000/475/EC [1999] OJ L187/47. The *CECED* situation is used as an example of an agreement that would pass Art 101/3 scrutiny in the Guidelines (n 2) para 329.

[108] ibid; see also the example in para 330 (n 97).

[109] Whether this is the case will depend on the circumstances of a particular SSO: for example whether its task of adopting standards in a particular area is actually of general economic interest and whether it has been entrusted with it by an act of official authority (see Chapter III section 3.1.5). See, however, Schepel (n 33) 316–17, expressing the general view that 'national standards bodies operating under standards laws, like [the French] AFNOR' could 'easily avail themselves' of the Art 106/2 exception.

that is technical regulations for a particular sector, perform conformity assessment, and certify products for entering the national market.

GB-Inno-BM was such a case. The Belgian telecom RTT, at the time still a public monopoly, both produced telephones and was, by law, in charge of certifying telephones produced by other companies. The Court considered this to violate today's Arts 102 and 106/1 on special and exclusive rights, read in conjunction, because RTT was given the power to regulate the same market in which it was itself competing. This led it, if not to specific abusive conduct, at least to a situation where it could extend its monopoly (in certifying telephones) to a neighbouring market (the market for telephones).[110] The Court explained that type-approval of telephones, for safety and consumer protection reasons, would not be problematic if it was performed by an independent undertaking.[111] This restates a lesson that comes up time and again for co-regulatory regimes: while the substance of product certification rules will not be easily challenged, if the regulatory scheme shows signs of bias, conflict of interest, or is free of effective control by the public party in the co-regulatory scheme, the scheme could violate competition and/or free movement law.

One could imagine even non-binding standards that violate Arts 101 or 102 as such leading to Member State liability if the State has somehow reinforced their effects (under the '*effet utile*' case law) or led a dominant undertaking into a situation of abuse connected to that standard.[112] Conceivably, this kind of legal construct could apply to the situation in *Fra.bo* (see section 4). It is hard to predict the outcome of such a test. There are clear differences from the situation just described which could argue against imposing Art 102 and Art 106/1. Firstly, a standard such as that in *Fra.bo* was not binding; the fact that it seemed to be the only realistic way to enter the market may or may not suffice. Secondly, the SSO challenged in that case did not itself compete in the market that it regulates. On the other hand, it may have been largely composed of those that do.

4. Standard Setting and Free Movement

In terms of the substance of what they regulate, standards are classic examples of restrictions to the free movement of goods: product rules capable of hindering trade. At least, that is true of binding technical regulations such as those dealt with in *Cassis de Dijon* or the *Beer Purity* case,[113] to give just two examples. Unless there are EU rules harmonizing the characteristics a product must satisfy, the basic discipline imposed by EU law is mutual recognition: allowing into

[110] Case C-18/88 *Régie des télégraphes et des téléphones v GB-Inno-BM SA* [1991] ECR I-5941, para 20.

[111] ibid para 26.

[112] See Chapter III section 3.2.

[113] Case 120/78 *Rewe-Zentral AG v Bundesmonopolverwaltung für Branntwein* (1979) ECR 649 and Case 178/84 *Commission v Germany* [1987] ECR 1227 respectively. For more details, see Sørensen (n 24) section 2.

the market products lawfully produced in other Member States that ensure an equivalent level of protection.[114] It is disproportionate for such rules to insist on national specifications alone. The extent to which the idea of mutual recognition is relevant in the context of non-binding and private standards remains an open question, as already discussed. It is clear, however, that it has influenced the legal treatment of SSOs both under free movement and competition law.[115]

Regardless of that difficult issue, however, more than just outright legislative product requirements like the ones in *Cassis de Dijon* can constitute restrictions to free movement. As described in section 2.1, private regulators such as SSOs can participate in the process of adopting *de facto* technical regulations, for example through agreements with public actors or through references in legislation. These kinds of measures will, as a rule, be subject to free movement scrutiny. In *Dundalk*, for example, conditioning a public tender on a national standard that only one (local) producer was certified for, without allowing for equivalent guarantees, amounted to an unjustified restriction of free movement.[116]

Moreover, co-regulatory arrangements between a State and an SSO have been subject to the free movement rules even when the measures they produced were not binding.[117] The rules on free movement of goods have been applied to the measures of hybrid public–private bodies such as the Apple & Pear Development Council, the industry association in *Buy Irish*, and the agricultural products' development and marketing fund in *Commission v Germany*.[118] The latter case is interesting in this context as it concerns non-binding product certification that discriminated against imports by highlighting 'German quality'. The defendant's quality label, despite being optional, was viewed as 'ascribable to the State' and restrictive of trade.[119] This shows that, if a standard or a certification scheme is placed in the box of 'public measures', it would tend to fall under the scope of the free movement rules even if it is not binding.

Another judgment that could be relevant for SSOs or certification bodies whose activities are 'ascribable' to the State is *A.G.M.-COS.MET*, where a Finnish official's public statement that Italian vehicle lifts shirk safety requirements (even though they carry a CE marking) violated the free movement of goods. The

[114] In Case 188/84 *Commission v France* [1986] ECR 419 (*Woodworking machines*), the Court found that Member State measures cannot 'require imported products to comply strictly and exactly with the provisions or technical requirements laid down for products manufactured in the Member State in question when those imported products afford users the same level of protection' (para 16). They are, on the other hand, entitled to pursue a higher level of protection (para 17).

[115] See section 3.2.3 in relation to competition law.

[116] Case 45/87 *Commission v Ireland* [1988] ECR 4929, paras 20 and 22.

[117] See Schepel and Falke (n 11) 57–59.

[118] Case 222/82 *Apple and Pear Development Council v K.J. Lewis Ltd and others* (1983) ECR 4083; Case 249/81 *Commission v Ireland* [1982] ECR 4005; and Case C-325/00 *Commission v Germany* [2002] ECR I-9977 respectively. See also Case 29/82 *F. van Luipen en Zn BV against a disciplinary measure adopted against it* [1983] ECR 151, where mandatory membership of exporters of agricultural products in a private-law body whose task was to control quality standards was held to violate the free movement of goods.

[119] Paragraphs 20–25.

benchmark for 'attributing' that statement to the State was whether 'the persons to whom those statements are addressed can reasonably suppose ... that they are positions taken by the official with the authority of his office'.[120]

Interestingly, the judgment shows that the justification of such measures also depends on whether they are attributed to the State, with different justifications being available as a scheme moves along the continuum between purely private and purely public—thus highlighting once more the trade-off between regulatory and private autonomy. If the statements are seen as public measures, they could in principle be justified on the basis of public health (which, based on the facts, they were not); had they been seen as private speech, they could be justified under freedom of expression.[121]

The lesson of these cases for SSOs whose activities are closely connected to State measures is that their non-binding standards, labels, or even informal statements could be subject to the free movement rules.

4.1 Standard Setting beyond functional definitions of the State: The implications of the *Fra.bo* judgment

A more difficult question, however, is whether the free movement rules apply to standard setting in the strict meaning of the term: the development of non-binding product specifications that is not attributable to a Member State, not referenced in EU or Member State legislation, or turned into quasi-legislation through, for example, references in the official journal. The difficulty here is that the bulk of standard setting activity concerns products, and as the usual view holds, the rules on free movement of goods should not normally be applicable to private actors.[122] There is case law to that effect even in the context of standardization. In *Sapod Audic*, a contract between two companies on certification for a waste management scheme (and the accompanying duty to affix a 'Green Dot' logo on the products of the client) was held not to fall under the free movement rules 'since it was not imposed by a Member State but agreed between individuals'.[123] *Sapod Audic* seems to stand for the proposition that there is no horizontal effect of the rules on free movement of goods. This may have, however, always been an overstatement, as discussed in Chapter II section 2.5.

The view that the rules on free movement of goods only apply to State activity in the context of product standards has been brought into question by the *Fra.bo* judgment,[124] concerning the practices of DVGW, a recognized German SSO in the water sector. Admittedly, this was not a simple private

[120] Case C-470/03 *AGM-COS.MET Srl v Suomen valtio and Tarmo Lehtinen* [2007] ECR I-2749, paras 65–66.

[121] See paras 67–73. See also *Commission v Germany* (n 118), where the Fund was unable to justify the 'German quality' mark by relying on the protection of geographical indications under the Art 36 exception on industrial and commercial property.

[122] See for example Schepel and Falke (n 11) 57 et seq.

[123] Case C-159/00 *Sapod Audic v Eco-Emballages SA* [2002] ECR I-5031, para 74.

[124] *Fra.bo* (n 17).

relationship either. The general sales conditions for the water sector, adopted as a State measure, granted a presumption of conformity to products certified under DVGW standards. While acknowledging the specificities of the 'legal and regulatory context', however, the judgment took a step forward by focusing directly on the effect of DVGW's standard as the only effective possibility to enter the German market.

Crucially, the free movement rules were not applied because of the special nature of DVGW as a non-profit making body charged with the public interest, but because of the actual opportunities for market entry. Due to the general sales conditions, and in the absence of harmonized standards for copper fittings, the Italian manufacturer Fra.bo could either have its fittings certified through DVGW or follow an entirely unclear, difficult, and costly procedure of appointing an expert to examine whether its fittings satisfy the essential requirements laid down by the Construction Products Directive and German legislation.[125]

The judgment is significant because it shows the Court breaking free of the need to show links with the State. While the presumption of conformity granted to DVGW standards by the State (by a measure that, it should be noted, was not actually binding since suppliers and consumers could in theory agree differently) was clearly relevant to the Court's analysis, it did not mean that DVGW's activities are 'State action'.[126] Rather, the Court asked whether they were comparable, in effect, with the activities normally undertaken by the State.[127] The answer to that question is that, due to the presumption of conformity and the absence of feasible alternatives, DVGW 'in reality holds the power to regulate the entry into the German market' and is therefore subject to the free movement rules in both its standardization and certification activities. Arguably, this leaves open the possibility of applying the free movement rules to an SSO with no particular links to the State that still, for any other reason, 'in reality' regulates access to the market of a Member State. It might be unlikely for a purely market-based SSO's activities to have such an impact, but it cannot be a priori excluded.

Unlike the AG's Opinion,[128] the *Fra.bo* judgment restricted itself to the scope of the questions referred: whether or not the free movement rules apply. It did not say anything on whether and why there might be a restriction and whether it could be justified. The referring German court, however, eventually found a violation of the free movement rules and breach of contract in DVGW's withdrawal of Fra.bo's certification, notably because it should have recognized the Italian

[125] The German legislation itself, of course, must respect the rules on free movement of goods. This is repeated in the text of the Construction Products Directive. ibid para 20.

[126] See para 24.

[127] Paragraph 26. Of course, this presupposes that we know what it is that the State does and why those activities are different from other activities. In the context of standard setting, the comparison may seem easier because the Court can make a relatively straightforward analogy with binding technical regulations. Indeed, the judgment refers to cases where Member States infringed the free movement of goods by insisting on national marks of conformity or refusing to recognize equivalent guarantees issued in another Member State (see para 23 and the case law cited therein).

[128] See the Opinion of AG Trstenjak, paras 51–60.

laboratory's test and because the 3,000-hour water submersion test that the standard required was unnecessary.[129]

It is questionable whether all of those findings are justified. For example, it is not obvious to what extent the free movement rules impose mutual recognition[130] on SSOs, that is whether they have to accept equivalent guarantees provided by other, similar standardization schemes. If this were the case, the whole standard-setting exercise could lose value, leading to a 'race to the bottom' where undertakings would have an incentive to satisfy the least demanding quality standard. Standardization and certification, whether performed by State-sanctioned or purely private SSOs, are inherently exclusionary in the sense that any undertaking that wants to obtain a standard will have to pass a number of hurdles and incur expenses. The reward for this is easy market access in the future. This cost-saving aspect of standardization would be put in question if undertakings could challenge the details of a standard on free movement grounds, or if those seeking compliance with a standard had to entertain case-by-case explanations by producers believing to have fulfilled equivalent guarantees.

It is therefore likely that, given the opportunity, the Court would employ a lighter touch when dealing with SSOs and formulate a test that focuses primarily on good governance criteria rather than on the substance of a standard. This would make sense from an institutional perspective: courts do not have the knowledge to effectively discuss the technical details of a standard. They are not well placed to decide whether copper fittings actually need to survive 3,000 hours of submersion in boiling water or not. An additional reason for light-touch review is that in the context of standardization it makes even more sense than in the context of straightforward public technical regulations to protect regulatory diversity, experimentation, and the ability of different SSOs to strive for varying levels and ways of protection through their standards.

On the other hand, an SSO's activities could be scrutinized in light of process criteria: whether they follow a sufficiently clear procedure, whether they are transparent and representative of all relevant stakeholders, whether there is any explicit or implicit discrimination between domestic and foreign producers etc. For recognized, official standard setting, it could be easier to pass this sort of test since their set-up and functioning is already to a large extent immersed into a political structure on the EU level.

For DVGW, this would mean that requiring the 3,000-hour test, in particular, is not very likely to actually restrict free movement. This is at odds with the approach of the Advocate General, as well as that of the referring court, both

[129] Oberlandesgericht Düsseldorf, VI-2 U (Kart), 14 August 2013 (2. Kartellsenat). For an extensive discussion, see Paul Verbruggen, 'Private Law Rights and Remedies under the Free Movement of Goods and Services' in Hans W Micklitz & Carla H Sieburgh, *Primary EU Law and Private Law* (forthcoming).

[130] This would go much further than the obligation that arises from international mutual recognition agreements (eg Agreement on mutual recognition between the European Community and the United States of America (1999) OJ L31/3): recognizing conformity assessment performed, according to the importing State's standards, by exporting State bodies.

of which largely followed the Court's traditional analysis of State measures and held DVGW's actions to be restrictive.[131] Generalizing that approach, however, would mean that every decision not to certify is a restriction of free movement. As I have argued, it makes little sense to analyse standards in this way. While their activities should not be exempted completely simply on the ground that they are private actors, mutual recognition should apply with weaker force than with State measures. Whether that translates into a form of *de minimis*, or into a test that explicitly focuses on governance criteria remains to be seen.

Following a more restrained approach, the only measure of the DVGW that seems problematic from the point of view of free movement is the refusal to recognize tests conducted by an Italian laboratory for certification purposes. Of course, allowing only accredited bodies to perform conformity assessment is a normal part of most standardization schemes. This refusal may therefore be justified (DVGW argued, for example, that the test report gave insufficient information) but could be *prima facie* suspect from the point of view of openness of DVGW's procedure and its disparate impact on foreign producers.

Another open question is the relationship between the State and the private regulator. In the context of *Fra.bo*, it could be argued that Germany is actually at fault for drafting its regulations in way that does not provide feasible alternatives to DVGW certification, such as explicitly recognizing certification by SSOs from other Member States or making the alternative procedure (risk assessment by appointed experts) accessible and affordable.

The most straightforward answer to that is that the Member State and the SSO are potentially liable for different activities. Germany's regulations, arguably, restrict free movement. On top of that, however, DVGW could be infringing certain distinct duties under the free movement rules, such as the duty not to discriminate between undertakings or test laboratories on grounds of nationality or the duty to conduct the standardization procedure in an open, transparent, and inclusive manner. Neither of those claims necessarily hinges on the other.

Finally, *Fra.bo* does not enter the justification stage. Even if the DVGW infringed free movement, on what grounds could it justify its measures?[132] It has been clear ever since *Bosman* that private bodies could invoke any of the aims laid down in the Treaty as well as the 'mandatory requirements' developed in the Court's case law. What is less clear is to what extent justifications by a private entity can go further, invoking, for example, freedom of association or the freedom to conduct a business in order to justify its regulatory choices directly from the point of view of private autonomy.

Again, judging from previous case law, those justifications are not likely to be decisive. The reason for this is the trade-off between private autonomy and

[131] See in particular para 36.

[132] The Opinion of AG Trstenjak, paras 36–39, entered into this discussion, splitting the possible justifications into four: written (Art 36 TFEU), unwritten (mandatory requirements), 'special grounds in the private interest', and 'objective considerations' (inspired by the *Angonese* judgment).

regulatory autonomy. If SSOs are indeed, as I have speculated, given a wide deference by the Court in terms of the substance of their measures, the price that has to be paid for that is openness to review—private autonomy gives way to a (broad) regulatory autonomy. The private autonomy argument is, thus, largely out of the way once a measure enters the justification stage.

5. Standard Setting and the Relationship Between Free Movement and Competition

A last issue which was raised but left open in *Fra.bo* was the relationship of free movement and competition law in analysing SSO measures. The national court asked if DVGW's conduct falls under the scope of the free movement or, alternatively, competition rules. Interestingly, it specifically linked the two questions: is there an impediment to trade under Art 101 TFEU, it asked, 'if the technical standard would not be applicable if it had been adopted directly by the national legislature because it infringes the principle of the free movement of goods?'[133]

In these two questions, then, we see a clear opportunity for the CJEU to choose what I have called a convergent reading, finding that a hypothetical public restriction of free movement morphs into a restriction of competition law when created by a private actor in an analogous situation, or a separation reading: applying both sets of rules independently.

There was, however, an even simpler way out. The questions were posed alternatively, that is if there is a restriction on free movement, the referring court did not want to further inquire about competition law. Like the AG, the Court took this invitation and dispensed with competition law analysis.

Keeping in mind the case law applying competition law to standardization, however, some conclusions can be drawn. Cases such as *Belasco* could easily fall under the free movement of goods as well as under the competition rules if assessed following the *Fra.bo* approach. The same would also be true of the standard in *EMC Development* were it not a case on European, but national standardization. Although there is no reason to exempt European standards bodies from free movement law in general, it is not easy to see how their standards would actually restrict trade *between* the Member States.

It seems that, in this context as well, the Court follows a kind of a separation narrative. This can be seen in *EMC Development*, where the Court was faced with an overlap not of the competition and free movement rules, but of the competition rules and the Construction Products Directive. The claimant was trying to persuade the Court into a convergent reading: the standard, claimed EMC, is frequently used in public procurement, preventing even competing products with CE marking from entering the market. This would violate the rules of the CPD which require the

[133] Paragraph 16.

Member States to allow all products with CE marking into their market and, more broadly, to respect free movement of goods. Moreover, the standard was, according to EMC, expressed in terms of composition rather than performance, which violated Art 7/2 of the CPD.[134] These violations, according to EMC, should have been taken into account in the competition law analysis of the standard.

In response, the General Court pointed out that violations of the Directive are, in substantive terms, a separate matter that does not enter the competition law analysis and, in procedural terms, an issue that cannot be dealt with by the Commission when it applies Art 101.[135] Indeed, the very existence of the Directive—an alternative, sector-specific set of rules—seems to speak against taking such arguments into account in competition law.[136]

Nevertheless, the overlap of the two sets of rules remains possible both when it comes to recognized and market-based standard setting. The Commission has at times made statements arguing that recognized standardization could fall under the rules on free movement of goods, whereas purely market-based standardization should be examined under competition law alone.[137] Were this to be explicitly confirmed, however, such a strict separation would be a break from the Court's case law in other domains, and certainly at odds with *Fra.bo*—if not with its outcome, then with its reasoning.

6. Conclusion

The application of EU law to private or co-regulatory standard-setting schemes shares some of the central features of its application to private regulators in other contexts.

Firstly, it shows the diminishing relevance of a public–private distinction. In the standardization context, given the growing diversity of its functions and aims, the different ways in which it is performed and the sheer quantity of areas where it is important, there is no wall between public and private bodies or public and private rules. Co-regulation, or at least *ex post* legal recognition of standards, is common. At the same time, market-based standardization and standardization by single powerful actors (such as private food safety standards set by large retailers) have become increasingly prominent. Some mechanisms to control the exercise of that private power are needed.

The growing importance of standard setting may explain the fact that the free movement and competition rules are increasingly applied to SSOs, a trend in

[134] *EMC Development* (n 76) paras 107 and 132. [135] ibid paras 135–37.

[136] ibid paras 120–22.

[137] In its answer to parliamentary question No. 835/82 (1983) OJ C93/1, it stated that national standards compliance with which is rendered obligatory *de iure* or *de facto* by state involvement would be considered under [Art 34 TFEU], while import restrictions stemming from an agreement between undertakings not to accept products not in accordance with national standards would be judged under competition law. See Schepel and Falke (n 11) 55.

which *Fra.bo* is the latest and most important step. As the general chapters suggested, this broad application of both the free movement and competition rules is driven by functionalism. Thus, product standards set by recognized SSOs are subject to EU internal market law not primarily because of the links between them and the Member States, but because their standards can be seen as '*de facto* mandatory' (*EMC Development*) or as *de facto* indispensable for market access (*Fra.bo*).

EU law is not, however, antagonistic to standard setting. Like with sports and professional regulation, the application of EU law is better described as an attempt to bring private regulators into the fold. Once the private autonomy argument is out of the way and the possibility of applying EU law is accepted, the actual scrutiny is not likely to be particularly deep or substantive. Rather, the competition and free movement rules will in most cases focus on the way SSOs are governed, with considerable deference to the substance of their standards. This makes sense from an institutional perspective. The very reason for the existence of standard-setting is the need to fill a gap in what traditional political processes can do. Political processes, courts, and competition enforcers are not well-equipped to supervise standardization in detail, but can keep it broadly in check through secondary legislation, competition, and free movement law, focusing their scrutiny on good governance criteria.

This can be seen from the case law, which is reluctant to address the substance of standards as long as the process of their development passes muster (*EMC Development*). Similarly, the rather detailed discussion of standard setting in the Horizontal Guidelines is dominated by process concerns, such as ensuring access to standard development and to standards as finished products, transparency, non-discrimination, IP disclosure, and FRAND licensing. The European Standardization Regulation imposes similar process requirements on national and European recognized SSOs.

Another way in which the case study of standard setting supports the conclusions of the general chapters is that this process-oriented approach, in particular through soft law instruments like the Horizontal Guidelines, enables reforms of the practices of SSOs. Thus, the Guidelines target the operating rules of SSOs as such, even though most of the case law in recent years dealt with single dominant undertakings that abused the standard-setting process. The SSOs are the gatekeepers of that process. It is therefore more effective to influence the rules they impose on participants, for example by inducing them to require IP disclosure and FRAND licensing, than to individually target cases of abuse of dominance. SSOs have responded to this, even if they have not been the main targets of scrutiny under Art 101 TFEU.

While this case study therefore conforms in many respects to the discussion presented in the general chapters of the book, there are certain specificities, and in some ways the conclusions differ. Firstly, while both are potentially subject to the free movement and competition rules, the distinction between recognized and market-based standard setting is important in EU law. This has to do with the fact that the system of recognized European and national SSOs is, in important ways, a creature of EU law and its 'new approach to harmonisation'. The impact of the free movement and competition rules is to some extent reduced because of the need to preserve what has become a sort of EU industrial policy. Formally recognized standards are not generally seen as restrictions of trade. The EU Standardization Regulation may further strengthen this role of standard setting on the EU level.

Secondly, like in other areas, competition and free movement law follow similar patterns and deal with similar arguments. The case law suggests that both sets of rules can be applied on their own. To date, however, there have not been many cases in which both sets of rules were applied to the same facts. One possible reason for that—and another specificity of this area—is that the free movement rules arrived to the stage quite late. Only after *Fra.bo* has the debate on the free movement liability of SSOs begun in earnest. Unlike with sports and the legal profession, the first significant forays of EU law took place under the competition rules. Today, on the other hand, the *Fra.bo* judgment and its follow-up by the German court may suggest that the free movement rules are about to become a more credible threat to the practices of standard-setting bodies.

Thirdly, there has so far been no equivalent to *Wouters* and *Meca-Medina* in the competition law treatment of standard setting. This may, to some extent, be explained by the fact that competition law has long been comfortable with reviewing the practices of undertakings (and, to a lesser extent, SSOs themselves) in the context of standard setting, and Art 101/3 may seem to be sufficient to accommodate the regulatory autonomy of SSOs. It is more likely, however, that the right case has not yet come. There is no particular reason why the 'inherent restriction' doctrine could be invoked by lawyers, accountants, sporting bodies, geologists, and road carriers, but not by standard-setting organizations.

Finally, this chapter has pointed to an important specificity of standard setting: its rather uncomfortable fit with the notion of mutual recognition that is central to free movement law. Simply transposing the principle of mutual recognition, as it has developed in relation to Member State measures, could seriously jeopardize the effectiveness of standard setting. In contrast to other areas, mutual recognition would seem to seriously reduce the value of the entire standard-setting exercise. Enabling a lawyer from one Member State to practise in another will, of course, incentivize some potential attorneys to study and qualify in the Member State with the lowest requirements. These are, however, always likely to remain a minority. On the other hand, making it clear that products certified by one SSO should automatically be recognized by another—especially in the context of recognized standard setting—would be a huge incentive for manufacturers to circumvent the more demanding rules. When difficult and technical issues are concerned, as is often the case with standards, asymmetries of information might lead consumers to select the cheapest option, and manufacturers would adapt accordingly. The case law of the CJEU does not yet sufficiently explain how mutual recognition should work in the standard-setting context, but it may soon be required to do so.

VIII
Conclusion

Sports, legal services, and standard setting are pertinent examples, but they barely scratch the surface. Increasingly, the rules by which we live are set, implemented, and enforced by private actors. This did not happen simply because the State decided to outsource some of its tasks. The reality is much more complex. Private actors are involved in regulation in a variety of ways, including delegation, *ex post* recognition, and co-regulation. Many of them, moreover, base their authority directly on the consent of others. They hold the power to set and enforce rules, settle disputes internally, and even impose sanctions on individuals, not because the State decided they should do so, but relying on the freedom of contract. Because contract law is public law, even these actors are in some sense acting 'in the shadow' of the State. To put it differently, State action is always present.[1] This, however, does not explain to what extent regulatory complexity should be reflected in the application of legal disciplines of EU law. To say that the State is everywhere is not useful, because it lumps all behaviour in one homogenous group.

This book has analysed how competition and free movement law, the two pillars of the EU's internal market, have tackled these issues. Because competition law controls private action that restricts competition, and free movement law controls regulatory action that restricts free movement, both could and do apply to private regulation. Because they are premised on a public–private divide—competition law applying only to undertakings and associations of undertakings, and free movement law applying largely to State measures—both are under pressure to realign their scope and content when faced with cases of private regulation.

It is perhaps not surprising that the drafters of the Treaties did not have the crumbling public–private divide and private regulation in mind during the 1950s. Even today, however, both academic discussions and the practical application of law seem often to be based on a simple version of a public–private distinction, with the market on one and the State on the other side. This is also true of the free movement and competition rules. In doubt, the traditional view of how these rules should be applied would fall back on the public–private distinction. It would classify conduct as public or private, regulatory or economic, State-like or

[1] Cass R Sunstein, 'State Action Is Always Present' (2002) 3 Chicago Journal of International Law 465.

market-like, public interest-driven or private interest-driven, and then apply the rules as they were originally designed.

Meanwhile, private regulation has itself been under pressure to conform to EU law scrutiny. This book has analysed the impact of EU internal market law on private regulation, particularly in the three case studies. In particular, it looked at the specific requirements imposed by the legal disciplines, and the way this has been reflected in the practice of EU institutions and in the development of various EU policies.

The conclusions of that analysis can therefore be divided in two groups: first, the impact of private regulation on competition and free movement law and, second, the impact of competition and free movement law on private regulation.

1. Adaptations: The Response of EU Law to Private Regulation

A common view of how EU free movement and competition law should respond to private regulation is to classify a certain activity as public or private, regulatory or economic, according to some predetermined benchmark, and then simply apply the appropriate legal discipline (normally, only one of the two). I have argued that this classification exercise is a dead end, and likely to get even worse as regulatory complexity grows. Arguments based only on the public–private divide are not helpful in understanding how EU law should deal with private regulation. They divert attention from the context and effects of the regulatory scheme that is challenged under EU law. They may also obscure the fact that both sets of rules have already adapted to private regulation in a number of ways.

The free movement rules have long been interpreted as having 'horizontal effect' in some circumstances. Those circumstances include all or most cases of co-regulation, such as private bodies created or supervised by the State,[2] or those that are relied upon to implement State measures.[3] Far from shielding the private actors from scrutiny, the hybrid public–private nature of those schemes made them vulnerable to judicial review. Other cases of private regulation, however, show that a strong link to the State is not a necessary ingredient. Actors that 'collectively' adopt rules on employment or service provision, such as sporting bodies[4] or industry associations,[5] are also subject to the free movement rules. From *Viking Line* and *Laval*, we also know that private actors can be said to be in regulatory roles even when they do not 'legislate' or adopt general rules. The case

[2] Case 249/81 *Commission v Ireland* [1982] ECR 4005; Case 222/82 *Apple and Pear Development Council v K.J. Lewis Ltd and others* [1983] ECR 4083; Case C-325/00 *Commission v Germany* [2002] ECR I-9977.

[3] C-341/05 *Laval un Partneri Ltd v Svenska Byggnadsarbetareförbundet, Svenska Byggnadsarbetareförbundets avdelning 1, Byggettan and Svenska Elektrikerförbundet* [2007] ECR I-11767.

[4] Case 36-74 *B.N.O. Walrave and L.J.N. Koch v Association Union cycliste internationale, Koninklijke Nederlandsche Wielren Unie and Federación Española Ciclismo* [1974] ECR 1405.

[5] Case C-411/98 *Angelo Ferlini v Centre hospitalier de Luxembourg* [2000] ECR I-8081.

law has gone even further. Most importantly, it has covered cases of direct and indirect discrimination against workers[6] (and, arguably but marginally, service recipients)[7] on the basis of nationality, even regardless of any regulatory role of the respective defendants. Juxtaposing this with the previously described case law, many commentators have expressed fears that all private behaviour now seems to fall within the rules.[8] Along with others, however, I have argued that this line of case law follows a distinct approach, focused on discrimination against persons and fundamental rights, and is largely congruent with clear prohibitions contained in secondary legislation.[9]

The *Fra.bo* judgment has indicated that all of the fundamental freedoms now have a similar scope, at least as far as private regulation is concerned. Even more interestingly, *Fra.bo* suggests that the free movement rules can apply whenever the actions of a private actor, in their economic and legal context, are capable of effectively restricting market access. I have argued that this test is appropriate, but that it should not be read as catching any action that has an impact on another individual's single exercise of free movement. Putting to one side cases of discrimination similar to *Angonese*, what should be disciplined is largely private regulation not subject to (regulatory) competition that has a market-partitioning effect. By taking the legal and economic context into account, the answer to the question of whether a private regulatory measure restricts free movement has to be more complex than is the case with Member States, whose measures can be more easily presumed to have an impact on market access.

The free movement rules have also adapted to private regulation at the justification stage. Here, the case law moves from discussing pure private autonomy to what I have called 'regulatory autonomy'. Private regulators normally cannot invoke blanket exemption from the free movement rules, but could invoke fundamental rights based on private autonomy, such as the freedom to conduct a business or the freedom of assembly. This mode of justification, however, is of little use once it is noted that the measures of private regulators affect third parties and touch upon substantive interests and policies like environmental protection, public health, or product safety. In those circumstances, justification naturally focuses on the substantive interests at issue. This shift towards substantive justification can also be described in terms of a trade-off: as private actors are seen to have broader regulatory autonomy, and thus the ability to invoke a margin of appreciation in pursuing public policies as a defence, they lose the ability to justify their measures by private autonomy in the narrow sense. Indeed, private regulators are, after *Bosman*, allowed to defensively invoke a wide variety of public

[6] Case C-281/98 *Roman Angonese v Cassa di Risparmio di Bolzano SpA* [2000] ECR I-4139.

[7] Case 251/83 *Eberhard Haug-Adrion v Frankfurter Versicherungs-AG* [1984] ECR 4277.

[8] See, for example, Harm Schepel, 'Who's Afraid of the Total Market? On the Horizontal Application of the Free Movement Provisions in EU Law' in Ioannis Lianos and Okeoghene Odudu (eds), *Regulating Trade in Services in the EU and the WTO—Trust, Distrust and Economic Integration* (Cambridge University Press 2012).

[9] See Chapter II section 2.3.

interests.[10] Moreover, the Court explicitly grants them a margin of discretion that is similar, if not broader than that granted to Member States. For example, the Court accepts structural and organizational justifications, such as the need to preserve the 'European sports model'.[11] It also allows private regulators to pursue their objective at their chosen levels of protection by reading the necessity test in a more flexible way, reflecting the more limited regulatory alternatives at the disposal of private actors.[12] All this, however, depends on legitimacy: private regulators can only defend their measures by invoking regulatory objectives that they actively pursue and protect.

The competition rules have also been forced to adapt. Dealing with private regulation leads them to a choice between a 'cleaner', narrow reading that fully exempts cases involving regulation and externalizes debates on public policy objectives to other institutions and areas of law, and a broader reading that accepts a role in supervising regulatory measures, while attempting to internalize a wider variety of public interests. I have argued that EU competition law can be said to follow the broad approach.

The case law has attempted, through a patchwork of legal constructs,[13] to ring-fence areas that the Member States have consistently and clearly organized on a non-market basis. For example, recent cases have more carefully distinguished between 'economic' and 'non-economic' aspects of a co-regulatory scheme.[14] Overall, however, it can be concluded that competition law reflects the hybridity of various co-regulatory schemes through a broad, functional definition of an undertaking and the possibility of applying its disciplines to the State (the 'useful effect' doctrine and the rules on special and exclusive rights). Instead of exempting State action, it explicitly applies to Member State measures that facilitate cartels or abuses of a dominant position, create exclusive rights, or delegate decision-making authority without adequate public review.[15] Instead of wholly rejecting private actors' defences based on public policies, whether under Art 101/3 TFEU or otherwise, as 'frontal assaults on the basic policy of EU competition law',[16] it has created new ways for private regulators to invoke broad public policy justifications. The most notable of these is the so-called 'inherent restriction' or 'regulatory ancillarity' test within Art 101/1 TFEU, first outlined in *Wouters*. While

[10] This does not seem to have assuaged the doubts of critics who argue that private actors do not, or should not, have access to public interest justifications under the free movement rules. See Chapter II section 4.2.

[11] Joined cases C-51/96 and C-191/97 *Christelle Deliège v Ligue francophone de judo et disciplines associées ASBL, Ligue belge de judo ASBL, Union européenne de judo (C-51/96) and François Pacquée* (C-191/97) [2000] ECR I-02549.

[12] See, by analogy, Case C-309/99 *J. C. J. Wouters, J. W. Savelbergh and Price Waterhouse Belastingadviseurs BV v Algemene Raad van de Nederlandse Orde van Advocaten, intervener: Raad van de Balies van de Europese Gemeenschap.* [2002] ECR I-1577, paras 105–07.

[13] See Chapter III section 4.

[14] Case C-138/11 *Compass-Datenbank GmbH v Republik Österreich* ECLI:EU:C:2012:449.

[15] See Chapter III section 3.2.

[16] A paraphrase of *National Society of Professional Engineers v United States* (1978) 435 US 679 section B.

this test was initially thought to be highly case- and context-specific, it has more recently seen something of a renaissance, and has even been used to justify a State restriction of competition.[17]

The consequence of these developments is that EU competition law can be applied to a wide range of cases of private regulation, even those that do not resemble standard categories of anticompetitive behaviour (eg the anti-doping procedures in *Meca-Medina* or bar exam committees in *Mauri*). Instead of searching for harm to consumer welfare, competition law scrutiny of such cases focuses on issues of governance, administration, or procedure. It does not ask, for example, how the application of anti-doping rules harms the welfare of viewers of swimming competitions. Instead, it might ask whether the anti-doping rules provided adequate opportunities for the accused athletes to defend themselves, or whether the evidentiary thresholds for 'adverse findings' are unreasonably strict.

Like in free movement cases, the Court has broadly followed the logic of 'regulatory autonomy'. The broad reading of competition law potentially covers many measures, but it applies a light-touch review to the substantive decisions of private regulators that it sees as representative, unbiased, and procedurally fair. While EU competition law is generally concerned with the lack of accountability of private regulators,[18] at the same time it recognizes them as legitimate in their respective fields and accords them a margin of discretion, as shown by the *Wouters* approach ('the bar association could have reasonably considered necessary'). At times, this has allowed defendants to invoke dubious regulatory objectives, such as to argue that setting prices in light of the 'dignity of the profession' is necessary in order to 'provide guarantees to the consumers of geologists' services'.[19] More important than these aberrations is the more general conclusion: in its application to private regulators, EU competition law does not simply balance competition against other values. Instead, it asks whether private regulators have overstepped a permissible margin of discretion when adopting or applying the relevant rules. While this is certainly an unnatural exercise for competition law to be engaged in, it allows for a more honest and inclusive debate than a 'classification' approach which would place conduct in the public or private box, depending on some apparently neutral criteria.

1.1 Distinct, but non-exclusive: Dealing with the overlap of free movement and competition law

The broad approach to both competition and free movement law, however, creates a problem: the increased likelihood that those rules will overlap. Private regulation is especially likely to be the culprit. In cases of overlap, the Court pursues neither

[17] See Chapter III section 3.1.3.

[18] Case C-171/05 P *Laurent Piau v Commission* [2006] ECR I-37.

[19] Case C-136/12 *Consiglio nazionale dei geologi v Autorità garante della concorrenza e del mercato and Autorità garante della concorrenza e del mercato v Consiglio nazionale dei geologi* ECLI:EU:C:2013:489.

full convergence nor full separation. While the two sets of rules are mutually reinforcing and both pursue the central aim of constructing an internal market, they are not just two parts of an indistinct 'seamless web'.[20] There is no requirement that conduct which escapes one must be caught by another. Nor is there, however, a requirement that conduct which is caught by one necessarily escapes the other.

The Court thus treats the rules as independent legal tests that are not mutually exclusive and can be applied simultaneously. This can lead to a number of problems, including increased complexity and higher likelihood of error. I have argued, however, that it is preferable to the alternatives: full convergence, or the adoption of some kind of selection principle to strictly separate the two sets of rules. Falling back on the public–private divide to handle the overlap, while tempting, would do more harm than good.

Differences not only in the substance and background context of the rules, but also in procedure, institutional set-up, and remedies argue in favour of applying either set of rules on its own terms, even when the same facts fall under both. Actively pursuing convergence by blending the rules or treating them interchangeably is therefore not feasible. The suggestion that overlap should be avoided altogether by strictly separating them also fails in either of its two (mutually contradictory) versions: doctrinal and factual. Doctrinal separation—classifying conduct as the subject matter of either competition or free movement law—would be question-begging and unhelpful, especially because there do not seem to be any clear criteria (broad vs. narrow, more vs. less strict, specialized vs. general) that would accurately describe the relationship between the two sets of rules. Moreover, the rules are not and cannot be factually separated, since by their own terms they clearly both apply to a range of situations at the same time. Indeed, if factual separation was possible, doctrinal separation would be unnecessary.

To offset the problems of the overlap, I suggest that the limits of both free movement and competition law should be clarified, that the overlap should be acknowledged and taken into account explicitly, and that 'hybrid' approaches such as translating liability under one set of rules into the other should be avoided.

Thus, when a national court refers questions on both sets of rules, the best approach for the Court of Justice would be to answer all of them. If the rules are independent, the outcomes under either could obviously go in any direction. When the Court, for example, finds liability under the free movement rules and then skips the competition rules, a national court or competition agency could come to the conclusion that there is automatically no violation, or indeed that there must logically also be a violation, of competition law. Therefore, while the Court's choice to prefer one set of rules over another may make sense from the point of view of judicial economy, it could have unforeseen procedural and remedial consequences. In addition, focusing on one set of rules over another may tacitly lead other actors to reinterpret the scope of the rules. For example, if decisions of sporting bodies on the licensing of individual athletes are

[20] See Chapter IV section 3.1.

routinely analysed as a free movement rather than a competition issue, competition enforcers including the Commission may decide to move their enforcement activities elsewhere.[21]

2. Regulatory Autonomy: The Impact of EU Law on Private Regulation

Both EU free movement and competition law have adapted in order to create a margin of discretion for private regulators, allowing them to pursue a wide range of regulatory objectives at their chosen levels of protection.[22] The bargain is, however, that their measures are rarely fully excluded from EU law scrutiny. This reflects a shift from pure private autonomy to regulatory autonomy. These general conclusions feed into the three case studies: the regulation of sports, legal services, and standard setting. A closer look into those three areas shows not only how free movement and competition law adapt to private regulation, but also better illustrates the specific disciplines that are imposed on private regulators.

In broad terms, I have argued that the two sets of rules are used as a sort of accountability mechanism[23] for private regulators. While ostensibly focused on competition and trade, judicial and agency review under EU internal market rules opens up their actions to more general scrutiny. Rather than directly weighing their regulatory objectives against the values of competition, this scrutiny actively holds private regulators to standards of good governance and fair procedures. In all three areas, the competition and free movement rules can in some sense be described as tools of 'meta-regulation': they leave it to private regulators themselves to formulate answers to particular problems, as long as they do so in a way that is acceptable from the point of view of good governance.

2.1 Focus on governance and procedure

The three case studies differ in many respects. The extent to which State regulation is intertwined with private regulation ranges from relatively low (sport, market-based standard setting) to very high (the legal profession). The rationales for regulation and the historical context differ. Private regulation also takes place on different levels. In sports and standard setting, it occurs both nationally and transnationally, whereas the legal profession is largely regulated on the national level (with some notable, but not legally binding exceptions such as the CCBE Code of Conduct). The broader legal context is also different. Extensive

[21] An example of that is the apparent attempt to limit the free movement rules to discrimination of individual athletes on the basis of nationality in Commission, 'Developing the European Dimension in Sport' (Communication) COM(2011) 12 final.

[22] See n 11 and n 12.

[23] Richard B Stewart, 'Remedying Disregard in Global Regulatory Governance: Accountability, Participation, and Responsiveness' (2014) 108 American Journal of International Law 211, 233–34.

EU legislation governs the legal profession, but is almost totally absent from the sport sector.

Despite these differences, the scrutiny of private regulators in the three case studies, under either set of rules, follows similar lines. The free movement and competition analysis tends to focus on the institutional and procedural characteristics of private regulatory schemes, such as conflicts of interest (*MOTOE*, *GB-Inno-BM*, *OTOC*, *EMC Development*), the effectiveness of appeal mechanisms (*Wilson*, *FIA*), proportionality of sanctions (*Meca-Medina*), the composition of decision-making bodies (*EMC Development*, *Mauri*, or even *Pechstein*), or effective supervision by the State in co-regulatory schemes (the '*effet utile*' case law). In standard setting, competition law has scrutinized the opportunities for competitors to participate in the development of standards and to access a standard once developed, and has led to the imposition of IP disclosure and FRAND licensing duties by standard-setting organizations. The principles of proportionality and non-discrimination in decision-making are imposed on bar associations even in the absence of a specific legal requirement to that effect.[24] In the legal profession, the scrutiny over rules on market access has been stricter than that over rules on conduct, which can be seen as an attempt to reinforce participation in decision-making and eliminate biases in favour of incumbents.[25] EU legislation that directly addresses private regulators also imposes a number of governance and procedural disciplines, such as the rules on the participation and voting rights of attorneys from other Member States,[26] or the European Standardization Regulation's rules on transparency, consultation, participation, and access.[27]

On the other hand, the substance of product standards, the rules on attorney conduct, or the organization of a sports league are far less likely to be questioned. From the point of view of the benefits of private regulation, a relatively light-touch approach on substantive issues may make sense. The best example is standard-setting, where competition agencies and courts are poorly placed to decide on the justification of substantive decisions. In the legal profession, the Court's stricter approach to entry rules in comparison with conduct rules could also reflect the informational advantages of the bar associations.

It is true that the broad application of the free movement and competition rules has exposed many private regulatory measures to scrutiny even though their overall market effect—beyond the impact on the market opportunities of the individuals directly concerned—is not obviously restrictive. It is odd to describe strict anti-doping rules or the composition of a bar examiners' board as an agreement to restrict competition. This is, however, a consequence of the broad, regulatory autonomy approach. On the other hand, private regulators also stand to benefit in their confrontation with EU law. Extended free movement and competition scrutiny can actually reinforce private regulation and recognize its legitimacy. In *Piau*,

[24] Case C-225/09 *Edyta Joanna Jakubowska v Alessandro Maneggia* [2010] ECR I-12329.

[25] See Chapter VI section 8.

[26] See Chapter VI section 4.3.

[27] See Chapter VII section 2.2.

for example, the fact that FIFA is the only authority effectively regulating players' agents served both as a trigger for competition law scrutiny and as a basis to defer to FIFA's measures. In *Gullung*, the Court largely deferred to the authority of a bar association to decide on the consequences of past ethical violations, even when that barred an attorney from another Member State from accessing the market. In *EMC Development*, the fact that a recognized European SSO followed its own procedures in developing a standard was a strong argument against competition law liability.

2.2 Negotiated approaches: Free movement and competition law as leverage for reform

EU law's potential to legitimize private regulation is reflected not only in the case law, but also in the strategies of the EU institutions. Free movement and competition law are not just used as a weapon, but as a way of bringing private regulators into the fold and influencing limited reforms. In standard setting, for example, it is the rules of the non-binding Horizontal Guidelines rather than direct Commission case work that have influenced the practices of SSOs. In the legal profession, the Court does not show much appetite for de-regulating, but the Commission and national competition authorities have been successful in promoting voluntary reform.

The two sets of rules are used, not always in a fully strategic manner, to steer the activities of private regulators. By finding some of their measures contrary to EU law, the Court and the Commission have imposed a measure of 'market accountability'.[28] For example, they have forced sporting bodies to allow cross-border movement of athletes, prevented restrictions on the establishment of foreign attorneys by bar associations, and required standard-setting organizations to open participation to competitors. This outright application of free movement and competition law was built upon by policy initiatives that went further, pushing for more detailed reforms that were not necessarily explicitly required by the case law: see, for example, the Commission's policy documents on sports starting from the 2007 White Paper, the 2004 Report on competition in professional services, or the 2011 Horizontal Guidelines' instructions for standard-setting bodies.[29]

In the long run, free movement and competition law serve as a launch-pad for the development of EU policies in the sectors where private regulation is dominant. The Commission and national authorities were far more successful in influencing reforms of the liberal professions by a competition advocacy process in the Member States than through the direct enforcement of free movement and competition law against Member States and professional bodies. In the area of sports, aggressive enforcement of free movement law by the Court has, at times, contravened the

[28] Colin Scott, 'Self-Regulation and the Meta-Regulatory State' in Fabrizio Cafaggi (ed), *Reframing Self-Regulation in European Private Law* (Kluwer Law International 2006) 141–42.

[29] Commission, 'Guidelines on the applicability of Article 101 of the Treaty on the Functioning of the European Union to horizontal co-operation agreements' (Communication) (2011) OJ C11 section 7.

negotiations between the Commission and sporting bodies, but has also provided the Commission with a basis for constructing a sort of a sports policy despite a lack of EU competences in that field. In all three sectors, in different ways and to a different extent, case-by-case application of the competition and free movement rules has given way to negotiated, voluntary, or soft-law mechanisms.

The relationship between the EU institutions and private regulators veers between antagonism and partnership. For example, the Commission has supported some measures of sporting bodies that were later found to violate EU law,[30] deferred to the decisions of other Commission departments in favour of standard-setting schemes (*EMC Development*), and largely abstained from casework against the legal profession in favour of competition advocacy and voluntary domestic reforms.

This negotiated approach may seem to be a sign of weakness or disregard for the requirements of EU law. It could, on the other hand, also be portrayed as constructive. Soft law and informal negotiated instruments can be used to support broader EU policies in areas where the EU has limited legislative competence and where private actors set the main rules. Frequently, this means that case-by-case enforcement is foregone in favour of 'softer' methods of influencing private actors to adopt the measures favoured by the Commission. This may, of course, be challenged on grounds of democratic legitimacy, as it tacitly shifts power both to an EU-level executive and to private actors. From the point of view of market integration, however, it may not be a bad strategy—even if some of the previous examples of negotiations, such as the agreement that preceded *Bosman*, were probably not justified by such concerns.

2.3 Institutional choices and legal doctrine

The application of free movement and competition law in the three sectors yields further insights. Firstly, in all three case studies, both the overlap of and the differences between the free movement and competition rules have been a result of institutional choices, not just of legal doctrine as such. For example, the dominance of competition law in recent discussions has less to do with what the law actually requires, and more with the strategies of the Commission and other actors. The enforcement tools it provides, such as the acceptance of commitments, more serious remedies, the ability to rely on national competition authorities in competition advocacy efforts, and to adopt non-binding guidance documents with detailed regulatory requirements (eg the rules on standardization agreements in the *Horizontal Guidelines* or the *Report on competition in professional services*) make competition law a much more useful tool. It is therefore likely that the majority of cases dealing with private regulation will be handled through competition law, even though the initial ground-breaking judgments of the Court, at least in sports and the legal profession, were mostly based on the free movement rules.

[30] See, most famously, Case C-415/93 *Union royale belge des sociétés de football association ASBL v Jean-Marc Bosman, Royal club liégeois SA v Jean-Marc Bosman and others and Union des associations européennes de football (UEFA) v Jean-Marc Bosman* [1995] ECR I-4921.

On the other hand, a convergent reading of the two sets of rules may also be a helpful tool for the Commission and others that seek review of the measures of private regulators. Thus, for example, the 2004 Report on Competition in Professional Services and the 2007 White Paper on Sport both, to some extent at least, mix and match the requirements of free movement and competition law to explain why and how private regulators should reform their practices along the lines of a general requirement of proportionality.[31]

Another conclusion emerging from the case studies is that the extent of judicial intervention may depend on the capacity of the EU political process. Thus, it could be argued that the Court was more assertive in cases dealing with sport than in the cases on the legal profession or standard setting because of, respectively, the existence of EU legislation on the service provision and establishment of lawyers and EU-wide co-regulatory schemes that involve recognized national standard-setting bodies. On the other hand, the Court may defer to the measures of private regulators because of the inadequacies of domestic political processes: thus, FIFA's rules on players' agents were legitimized in part because of the absence of laws governing their conduct (*Piau*).

3. An Effective Accountability Mechanism?

I have suggested that free movement and competition law could be described as a legal accountability mechanism[32] that could address some of the risks of private regulation while preserving its benefits. Private regulators are not systematically subject to legal challenges in the same way that, for example, a State body would be in a system of administrative law. This is why alternative mechanisms of judicial review, and especially EU law, have become so important and, possibly, why their scope is interpreted so broadly. Their potential to improve the practices of private regulators is significant.[33] Their case-by-case application has, as described, resulted in enhanced requirements of reason-giving, transparency, participation, neutrality, non-discrimination, etc.

For several reasons, however, neither judicial review nor EU internal market law more broadly should be seen as a panacea. Judicial review is sporadic and reactive, and is only able to deal with a very small number of measures.[34] Individuals will not frequently have an incentive to pursue litigation and might be pressured by private regulators to abstain from it—as, for example, with the internal dispute settlement procedures in sport. The free movement and competition rules, given

[31] See Chapter V section 6 and Chapter VI section 5.2. [32] See n 23.

[33] As Stewart notes, 'even episodic court decisions finding global regulatory bodies' decision-making procedures deficient can stimulate adoption of changes that will promote greater regard for the disregarded'. Stewart (n 23) 250.

[34] See Mary Elizabeth Magill, 'Courts and Regulatory Capture' in Daniel Carpenter and David A Moss (eds), *Preventing Regulatory Capture: Special Interest Influence and How to Limit It* (Cambridge University Press 2013).

their relatively limited content and focus, cannot deal with all the challenges posed by the growth of private regulation. The best they can do is to accommodate it and partly discipline some of its excesses.

Moreover, extensive application of the free movement and competition rules may be destructive. It could reduce regulatory experimentation and block the benefits of private regulation. One example of that is the notion that standard-setting organizations should apply the principle of mutual recognition, for example by certifying products that have already been certified under other 'equivalent' standards. The tools created under the two sets of rules in order to grant a margin of discretion to private regulators and recognize their regulatory autonomy could also be stretched too far. Price-fixing in order to protect the 'dignity of geologists' should not be seen as an equally valuable regulatory project as, for example, protecting the independence of attorneys. As the Court seems to have recognized in recent case law, a broad recognition of private regulators' legitimacy requires a serious analysis of the proportionality and coherence of their measures.

For these and other reasons, the case law still has some way to go in order to find a *modus vivendi* with private regulation. The first step would be to let go of the idea that everything can be solved by finding exactly where the public–private distinction should lie and classifying cases accordingly. The risks and benefits of private regulation should be addressed more explicitly on a case-by-case basis, with attention to the context of a particular sector as well as the surrounding legal framework. The opportunities for doing so are sure to increase, with private actors taking on regulatory roles in a variety of areas on the national and transnational level. The story of EU competition and free movement law's encounter with private regulation will, therefore, undoubtedly continue.

Bibliography

MONOGRAPHS

Allison JWF, *A Continental Distinction in the Common Law: An Historical and Comparative Perspective on English Public Law* (Oxford University Press 2000)

Amato G, *Antitrust and the Bounds of Power: The Dilemma of Liberal Democracy in the History of the Market* (Hart 1997)

American Bar Association Section on Antitrust Law, *Handbook on the Antitrust Aspects of Standards Setting* (American Bar Association 2004)

Baquero Cruz J, *Between Competition and Free Movement: The Economic Constitutional Law of the European Community* (Hart 2002)

Barnard C, *The Substantive Law of the EU: The Four Freedoms* (3rd edn, Oxford University Press 2010)

Bellamy & Child, *European Community Law of Competition* (Roth P and Rose V eds, 6th edn, Oxford University Press 2008)

Blind K, *The Economics of Standards: Theory, Evidence, Policy* (Edward Elgar 2004)

Bobbio N, *Democracy and Dictatorship: The Nature and Limits of State Power* (Polity 1989)

Bork RH, *Antitrust Paradox: A Policy at War with Itself* (Simon & Schuster 1993)

Breyer S, *Regulation and Its Reform* (Harvard University Press 1984)

Buendia Sierra JL, *Exclusive Rights and State Monopolies under EC Law* (Oxford University Press 2000)

Burrage M, *Revolution and the Making of the Contemporary Legal Profession: England, France, and the United States* (Oxford University Press 2006)

Büthe T and Mattli W, *The New Global Rulers: The Privatization of Regulation in the World Economy* (Princeton University Press 2011)

Calliess G-P and Zumbansen P, *Rough Consensus and Running Code: A Theory of Transnational Law-Making* (Hart 2010)

Claessens S, *Free Movement of Lawyers in the European Union* (Wolf Legal Publishers 2008)

Dixit AK, *Lawlessness and Economics: Alternative Modes of Governance* (Princeton University Press 2004)

Donnelly CM, *Delegation of Governmental Power to Private Parties: a Comparative Perspective* (Oxford University Press 2007)

Ehlermann C-D and Atanasiu I (eds), *European Competition Law Annual 2004: The Relationship Between Competition Law and the (Liberal) Professions* (Hart 2006)

Elhauge E and Geradin D, *Global Competition Law and Economics* (Hart 2011)

Ellickson R, *Order without Law: How Neighbors Settle Disputes* (Harvard University Press 1994)

Förster P, *Die unmittelbare Drittwirkung der Grundfreiheiten: zur Dogmatik des Adressatenkreises von Pflichten aus EG-Grundfreiheiten* (Lang 2007)

Geradin D, *Remedies in Network Industries: EC Competition Law vs. Sector-Specific Regulation* (Intersentia Publishers 2004)

Geradin D, Layne-Farrar A, and Petit N, *EU competition law and economics* (Oxford University Press 2012)

Gerber DJ, *Law and Competition in Twentieth Century Europe: Protecting Prometheus* (Oxford University Press 2001)

Guzdek K, *Binnenmarkt, unverfälschter Wettbewerb und Marktversagen: zur Parallelität der Einschränkungsmöglichkeiten im Rahmen der Grundfreiheiten sowie der Wettbewerbs- und Beihilferegeln des EU-Rechts* (Stämpfli 2012)

Hale RL, *Freedom Through Law: Public Control of Private Governing Power* (Columbia University Press 1952)

Hatzopoulos V, *Regulating Services in the European Union* (Oxford University Press 2012)

Heremans T, *Professional Services in the EU Internal Market: Quality Regulation and Self-regulation* (Hart 2012)

Hindelang S, *The Free Movement of Capital and Foreign Direct Investment: The Scope of Protection in EU Law* (Oxford University Press 2009)

Hovenkamp H, *The Antitrust Enterprise: Principle and Execution* (Harvard University Press 2005)

Jaensch M, *Die unmittelbare Drittwirkung der Grundfreiheiten: Untersuchung der Verpflichtung von Privatpersonen durch Art. 30, 48, 52, 59, 73b EGV* (Nomos 1997)

Kaplow L and Shavell S, *Fairness Versus Welfare* (1st edn, Harvard University Press 2002)

Komesar NK, *Imperfect Alternatives: Choosing Institutions in Law, Economics, and Public Policy* (University of Chicago Press 1994)

Komesar NK, *Law's Limits: The Rule of Law and the Supply and Demand of Rights* (Cambridge University Press 2001)

Krisch N, *Beyond Constitutionalism: The Pluralist Structure of Postnational Law* (Oxford University Press 2010)

Larouche P, *Competition Law and Regulation in European Telecommunications* (Hart Publishing 2000)

Lengauer A-M, *Drittwirkung Von Grundfreiheiten* (Springer 2011)

Maduro MP, *We the Court: The European Court of Justice and the European Economic Constitution: A Critical Reading of Article 30 of the EC Treaty* (Hart 1998)

Majone G, *Dilemmas of European Integration. The Ambiguities and Pitfalls of Integration by Stealth* (Oxford University Press 2005)

Monti G, *EC Competition Law* (Cambridge University Press 2007)

Nascimbene B and Bergamini E, *The Legal Profession in the European Union* (Kluwer Law International 2009)

Nazzini R, *The Foundations of European Union Competition Law: The Objective and Principles of Article 102* (Oxford University Press 2011)

Odudu O, *The Boundaries of EC Competition Law: The Scope of Article 81* (Oxford University Press 2006)

Oliver D, *Common Values and the Public–Private Divide* (Butterworths 1999)

Pound R, *Lawyer from Antiquity to Modern Times* (West Publishing 1953)

Preedy K, *Die Bindung Privater an die europäischen Grundfreiheiten: zur sogenannten Drittwirkung im Europarecht* (Duncker & Humblot 2005)

Prosser T, *The Limits of Competition Law: Markets and Public Services* (Oxford University Press 2005)

Rodriguez Iglesias GC and Ortiz Blanco L (eds), *The Judicial Application of Competition Law: Proceedings of the FIDE XXIV Congress Madrid 2010 Vol. 2* (Facultad de Derecho Universidad Complutense 2010)

Rousseva E, *Rethinking Exclusionary Abuses in EU Competition Law* (Hart 2010)

Ruffert M (ed), *The Public–Private Law Divide: Potential for Transformation?* (British Institute of International and Comparative Law 2009)

Sabel CF and Zeitlin J, *Experimentalist Governance in the European Union: Towards a New Architecture* (Oxford University Press 2010)

Sauter W and Schepel H, *State and Market in European Union Law: The Public and Private Spheres of the Internal Market Before the EU Courts* (Cambridge University Press 2009)

Schepel H, *The Constitution of Private Governance: Product Standards in the Regulation of Integrating Markets* (Hart 2005)

Schepel H and Falke J, *Legal Aspects of Standardisation in the Member States of the EC and EFTA: Comparative Report*, vol 1 (Luxembourg: Office for Official Publications of the European Communities 2000)

Snell J, *Goods and Services in EC Law: A Study of the Relationship Between the Freedoms* (Oxford University Press 2002)

Sykes AO, *Product Standards for Internationally Integrated Goods Markets* (Brookings Institution Press 1995)

Tamanaha BZ, *Law as a Means to an End: Threat to the Rule of Law* (Cambridge University Press 2006)

Ten Brink P, *Voluntary Environmental Agreements: Process, Practice and Future Use* (Greenleaf Publishing 2002)

Townley C, *Article 81 EC and Public Policy* (Hart 2009)

Tryfonidou A, *Reverse Discrimination in EC Law* (Kluwer Law International 2009)

Van Bael I and Bellis J-F, *Competition Law of the European Community* (5th edn, Kluwer Law International 2009)

Van den Bergh R and Camesasca P, *European Competition Law and Economics: A Comparative Perspective* (2nd edn, Sweet & Maxwell 2006)

Van der Meulen B (ed) *Private Food Law: Governing Food Chains Through Contract Law, Self-Regulation, Private Standards, Audits and Certification Schemes* (Wageningen Academic Publishers 2011)

Van Rompuy B, *Economic Efficiency: The Sole Concern of Modern Antitrust Policy?* (Kluwer Law International 2012)

Weatherill S, *European Sports Law: Collected Papers* (T.M.C. Asser Press 2007)

Wendt IE, *EU Competition Law and Liberal Professions: an Uneasy Relationship?* (Martinus Nijhoff Publishers 2012)

Whish R and Bailey D, *Competition Law* (7th edn, Oxford University Press 2012)

Woods L, *Free Movement of Goods and Services within the European Community* (Ashgate 2004)

CHAPTERS IN EDITED VOLUMES

Baldwin R and Cave M, 'Self-Regulation' in Baldwin R and Cave M (eds), *Understanding Regulation: Theory, Strategy and Practice* (Oxford University Press 1999)

Barbou des Places S, 'Self-Regulation and the Professions: A Perspective from Regulatory Competition Theory' in Cafaggi F (ed), *Reframing Self-Regulation in European Private Law* (Kluwer Law International 2006)

Cherednychenko O, 'Subordinating Contract Law to Fundamental Rights: Towards a Major Breakthrough or Towards Walking in Circles?' in Grundmann S (ed), *Constitutional Values and European Contract Law* (Kluwer Law International 2008)

Claes M, 'The European Union, its Member States and their Citizens' in Leczykiewicz D and Weatherill S (eds), *The Involvement of EU law in Private Law Relationships* (Hart 2013)

Coglianese C and Mendelson E, 'Meta-regulation and self-regulation' in Cave M, Baldwin R and Lodge M (eds), *The Oxford Handbook of Regulation* (Oxford University Press 2010)

Davies G, 'Freedom of Contract and the Horizontal Effect of Free Movement Law' in Leczykiewicz D and Weatherill S (eds), *The Involvement of EU Law in Private Law Relationships* (Hart 2013)

Forrester IS, 'Where Law Meets Competition: Is Wouters Like a Cassis de Dijon or a Platypus?' in Ehlermann C-D and Atanasiu I (eds), *Competition Law Annual 2004: The Relationship Between Competition Law and the (Liberal) Professions* (Hart 2006)

Gerard DMB, 'A Global Perspective on State Action' in Lianos I and Sokol DD (eds), *The Global Limits of Competition Law* (Stanford University Press 2012)

Gilliams H, 'Competition Law and Public Interest: Do We Need to Change the Law for the (Liberal) Professions?' in Ehlermann C-D and Atanasiu I (eds), *European Competition Law Annual 2004: The Relationship Between Competition Law and the (Liberal) Professions* (Hart 2006)

Gyselen L, 'The emerging interface between competition policy and environmental policy in the European Union' in Cameron J, Demaret P and Geradin D (eds), *Trade and the Environment: The Search for Balance* (Cameron May 1996)

Hancher L and Larouche P, 'The Coming of Age of EU Regulation of Network Industries and Services of General Economic Interest' in Craig P and de Búrca G (eds), *The Evolution of EU Law* (2nd edn, Oxford University Press 2011)

Hartkamp AS, 'Fundamental Rights, Fundamental Freedoms and Contract Law' in Grundmann S (ed), *Constitutional Values and European Contract Law* (Kluwer Law International 2008)

Herberg M, 'Global Legal Pluralism and Interlegality: Environmental Self-Regulation in Multinational Enterprises as Global Law-Making' in Dilling O, Herberg M and Winter G (eds), *Responsible Business: Self-Governance and Law in Transnational Economic Transactions* (Hart 2008)

Huber PM, 'Zur Drittwirkung von Grundrechten und Grundfreiheiten' in Ruffert M (ed), *Dynamik und Nachhaltigkeit des öffentlichen Rechts: Festschrift für Professor Dr Meinhard Schröder zum 70 Geburtstag* (Duncker & Humblot 2012)

Jarvis M, 'Scope: Persons Bound' in Oliver P (ed), *Oliver on Free Movement of Goods in the European Union* (Hart 2010)

Jenny F, 'Regulation, Competition and the Professions' in Ehlermann C-D and Atanasiu I (eds), *European Competition Law Annual 2004: The Relationship Between Competition Law and the (Liberal) Professions* (Hart 2006)

Joerges C, 'A Renaissance of the European Economic Constitution' in Neergaard UB, Nielsen R and Roseberry LM (eds), *Integrating Welfare Functions into EU Law: From Rome to Lisbon* (Djoef Publishing 2009)

Kaplow L, 'On the Choice of Welfare Standards in Competition Law' in Zimmer D (ed), *Goals of Competition Law* (Edward Elgar 2012)

Kennedy D, 'A Transnational Genealogy of Proportionality in Private Law' in Brownsword R and others (eds), *The Foundations of European Private Law* (Hart 2011)

Kerber W, 'Should Competition Law promote efficiency? Some Reflections of an Economist on the Normative Foundations of Competition Law' in Drexl J, Idot L and Monéger J (eds), *Economic Theory and Competition Law* (Edward Elgar 2007)

Lane R, 'The Internal Market and the Individual' in Niamh Nic S (ed), *Regulating the Internal Market* (Edward Elgar 2006)

Larouche P, 'Contrasting Legal Solutions and the Comparability of EU and US Experiences' in Leveque F and Shelanski HA (eds), *Antitrust and Regulation in the EU and US: Legal and Economic Perspectives* (Edward Elgar 2009)

Leible S, 'Fundamental Freedoms and European Contract Law' in Grundmann S (ed), *Constitutional Values and European Contract Law* (Kluwer Law International 2008)

Lianos I, 'Competition Law in the European Union After the Treaty of Lisbon' in Ashiagbor D, Countouris N, and Lianos I (eds), *The European Union after the Treaty of Lisbon* (Cambridge University Press 2012)

Lindh P, 'The Influence of Competition Law on Free Movement Rules' in Kanninen H, Korjus N and Rosas A (eds), *EU Competition Law in Contest: Essays in Honour of Virpi Tiili* (Hart 2009)

McArdle D, 'CAS 2009/A/1912–1913 *Pechstein v International Skating Union*' in Anderson J (ed), *Leading Cases in Sports Law* (Springer 2013)

Magill ME, 'Courts and Regulatory Capture' in Carpenter D and Moss DA (eds), *Preventing Regulatory Capture: Special Interest Influence and How to Limit it* (Cambridge University Press 2013)

Marenco G, 'The Birth of Modern Competition Law in Europe' in *European Integration and International Co-ordination: Studies in Honour of Claus-Dieter Ehlermann* (2002)

Marx A, 'Global Governance and the Certification Revolution: Types, Trends and Challenges' in Levi-Faur D (ed), *Handbook on the Politics of Regulation* (Edward Elgar 2011)

Mataija M, 'Competition Law Implications of Private Regulation in Lifestyle Policy' in Alemanno A and Garde A (eds), *Regulating Lifestyle Risks: The EU, Alcohol, Tobacco and Unhealthy Diets* (Cambridge University Press 2014)

Mavroidis PC and Infantino G, 'Inherit the Wind: A Comment on the *Bosman* Jurisprudence' in Maduro MP and Azoulai L (eds), *The Past and Future of EU Law: The Classics of EU Law Revisited on the 50th Anniversary of the Rome Treaty* (Hart 2010)

Mavroidis PC and Neven DJ, 'The White Paper: A Whiter Shade of Pale—Of Interest and Interests' in Ehlermann C-D and Atanasiu I (eds), *Competition Law Annual 2000: The Modernisation of EC Antitrust Policy* (Hart 2001)

Michelon C, 'The Public Nature of Private Law?' in Michelon C and others (eds), *The Public in Law: Representations of the Political in Legal Discourse* (Ashgate 2012)

Miettinen S, 'Policing the Boundaries Between Regulation and Commercial Exploitation: Lessons from the MOTOE case' in Parrish R, Gardiner S and Siekmann R (eds), *EU, Sport, Law and Policy: Regulation, Re-regulation and Representation* (T.M.C. Asser Press 2009)

Miettinen S, 'Regulating Sports Services in Community Law' in Parrish R, Gardiner S, and Siekmann R (eds), *EU, Sport, Law and Policy: Regulation, Re-regulation and Representation* (T.M.C. Asser Press 2009)

Monéger J, 'Competition, Regulation and System Coherence' in Ullrich H (ed), *The Evolution of European Competition Law: Whose Regulation, Which Competition?* (Edward Elgar 2006)

Nafziger JAR, 'International Sports Law' in Nafziger JAR and Ross SF (eds), *Handbook on International Sports Law* (Edward Elgar 2011)

Novitz T, 'The Impact of Viking and Laval: Contesting the social function and legal regulation of the right to strike' in Ales E and Novitz T (eds), *Collective Action and Fundamental Freedoms in Europe: Striking the Balance* (Intersentia 2010)

Nowak WJ, 'Public-Private Governance: A Historical Introduction' in Freeman J and Minow M (eds), *Government by Contract: Outsourcing and American Democracy* (Harvard University Press 2009)

O'Donoghue R, 'Verbalizing a General Test for Exclusionary Conduct under Article 82 EC' in Ehlermann C-D and Marquis M (eds), *European Competition Law Annual 2007: A Reformed Approach to Article 82 EC* (Hart 2008)

O'Keefe D and Bavasso AF, 'Four Freedoms, One Market and National Competence: In Search of a Dividing Line' in O'Keefe D and Bavasso AF (eds), *Judicial Review in European Union Law – Liber Amicorum in Honour of Lord Slynn of Hadley*, vol 1 (2000)

Odudu O, 'Economic Activity as a Limit to Community Law' in Barnard C and Odudu O (eds), *The Outer Limits of European Union Law* (Hart 2009)

Ogus A, 'Self-regulation' in *Encyclopedia of Law and Economics*, vol 5 (2000)

Pound RW and Clarke K, 'Doping in sport' in Nafziger JAR and Ross SF (eds), *Handbook on International Sports Law* (Edward Elgar 2011)

Reich N, 'Balancing in Private Law and the Imperatives of the Public Interest: National Experiences and (Missed?) European Opportunities' in Brownsword R, Micklitz H-W, Niglia L and Weatherill S (eds), *The Foundations of European Private Law* (Hart 2011)

Reich N, 'The Impact of the Non-discrimination Principle on Private Autonomy' in Leczykiewicz D and Weatherill S (eds), *The Involvement of EU Law in Private Law Relationships* (Hart 2013)

Rostain T, 'Self-regulatory authority, markets, and the ideology of professionalism' in Baldwin R, Cave M, and Lodge M (eds), *The Oxford Handbook of Regulation* (Oxford University Press 2010)

Roth W-H, 'Drittwirkung der Grundfreiheiten?' in Due O and others (eds), *Festschrift für Ulrich Everling*, vol 2 (Nomos 1995)

Roth W-H, 'Strategic competition policy: a comment on EU competition policy' in Ullrich H (ed), *The Evolution of European Competition Law: Whose Regulation, Which Competition?* (Edward Elgar 2006)

Schepel H, 'Who's afraid of the total market? On the horizontal application of the free movement provisions in EU law' in Lianos I and Odudu O (eds), *Regulating Trade in Services in the EU and the WTO—Trust, Distrust and Economic Integration* (Cambridge University Press 2012)

Schweitzer H, 'European Standard-Setting Policy and the Role of Competition Law' in Baudenbacher C (ed), *Current Developments in European and International Competition Law 15th St Gallen International Competition Law Forum (ICF) 2008* (Helbing & Lichtenhahn 2009)

Schweitzer H, 'Efficiency, Political Freedom and the Freedom to Compete—Comment on Maier-Rigaud' in Zimmer D (ed), *The Goals Of Competition Law* (Edward Elgar 2012)

Scott C, 'Self-Regulation and the Meta-Regulatory State' in Cafaggi F (ed), *Reframing Self-Regulation in European Private Law* (Kluwer Law International 2006)

Scott C, 'Reflexive Governance, Regulation and Meta-Regulation: Control or Learning?' in de Schutter O and Lenoble J (eds), *Reflexive Governance: Redefining the Public Interest in a Pluralistic World* (Hart 2010)

Sheldon I, 'Food Standards and International Trade' in Roosen J, Lusk JL and Shogren JF (eds), *The Oxford Handbook of the Economics of Food Consumption and Policy* (Oxford University Press 2011)

Siekmann R and Soek J, 'Models of Sport Governance within the European Union' in Nafziger JAR and Ross SF (eds), *Handbook on International Sports Law* (Edward Elgar 2011)

Siragusa M, 'Critical Remarks on the Commission's Legal Analysis in its Report on Competition in Professional Services' in Ehlermann C-D and Atanasiu I (eds), *European Competition Law Annual 2004: The Relationship Between Competition Law and the (Liberal) Professions* (Hart 2006)

Snell J, 'Private Parties and the Free Movement of Goods and Services' in Andenas M and Roth WH (eds), *Services and Free Movement in EU Law* (Oxford University Press 2002)

Spaventa E, 'The Horizontal Application of Fundamental Rights as General Principles of Union Law' in Arnull A and others (eds), *A Constitutional Order of States?: Essays in EU Law in Honour of Alan Dashwood* (Hart Publishing 2011)

Stephen FH, 'The Market Failure Justification for the Regulation of Professional Service Markets and the Characteristics of Consumers' in Ehlermann C-D and Atanasiu I (eds), *European Competition Law Annual 2004: The Relationship Between Competition Law and the (Liberal) Professions* (Hart 2006)

Stuyck J, 'Libre circulation et concurrence: les deux piliers du Marché commun' in Dony M and de Walsche A (eds), *Mélanges en hommage à Michel Waelbroeck* (Bruylant 1999)

Szyszczak E, 'Competition and the Liberalised Market' in Shuibhne NN (ed), *Regulating the Internal Market* (Edward Elgar 2006)

Temple Lang J, 'European Competition Policy and Regulation: Differences, Overlaps, and Constraints' in Shelanski HA and Lévêque F (eds), *Antitrust and Regulation in the EU and US* (Edward Elgar 2009)

Teubner G, 'Global Private Regimes: Neo-Spontaneous Law and Dual Constitution of Autonomous Sectors in World Society?' in Ladeur K-H (ed), *Globalization and Public Governance* (Ashgate 2004)

Van den Bergh R, 'Towards Efficient Self-regulation in Markets for Professional Services' in Ehlermann C-D and Atanasiu I (eds), *European Competition Law Annual 2004: The Relationship Between Competition Law and the (Liberal) Professions* (Hart 2006)

Van Rompuy B and Pauwels C, 'The Recognition of the Specificity of Sport in the European Commission's Article 81 EC Decisional Practice Related to Sports Media Rights' in Parrish R, Gardiner S, and Siekmann R (eds), *EU, Sport, Law and Policy: Regulation, Re-regulation and Representation* (T.M.C. Asser Press 2009)

Veljanovski C, 'Economic Approaches to Regulation' in Baldwin R, Cave M, and Lodge M (eds), *The Oxford Handbook of Regulation* (Oxford University Press 2010)

Verbruggen P, 'Private Law Rights and Remedies under the Free Movement of Goods and Services' in Micklitz H-W and Sieburgh CH, *Primary EU Law and Private Law* (forthcoming)

Waelbroeck D, 'Les rapports entre les règles sur la libre circulation des marchandises et les règles de concurrence applicables aux entreprises dans la CEE' in Capotorti F and Pescatore P (eds), *Du droit international au droit de l'intégration: liber amicorum Pierre Pescatore* (Nomos 1987)

Wathelet M, 'Sport Governance and EU Legal Order: Present and Future' in Gardiner S, Parrish R and Siekmann RCR (eds), *EU, Sport, Law and Policy: Regulation, Re-Regulation and Representation* (T.M.C. Asser Press 2009)

Weatherill S, 'EU Sports Law: the effect of the Lisbon Treaty' in Biondi A, Eeckhout P and Ripley S (eds), *EU Law after Lisbon* (Oxford University Press 2012)

Weatherill S, 'The Elusive Character of Private Autonomy in EU Law' in Leczykiewicz D and Weatherill S (eds), *The Involvement of EU Law in Private Law Relationships* (Hart 2013)

Weintraub J, 'The Theory and Politics of the Public/Private Distinction' in Weintraub J and Kumar K (eds), *Public and Private in Thought and Practice: Perspectives on a Grand Dichotomy* (University of Chicago Press 1997)

Yeung K, 'Competition Law and the Public/Private Divide' in Auby J-B and Freedland M (eds), *The Public Law/Private Law Divide: Une Entente Assez Cordiale?* (LGDJ 2004)

JOURNAL PAPERS

Akerlof GA, 'The Market for "Lemons": Quality Uncertainty and the Market Mechanism' (1970) 84 Quarterly Journal Of Economics 488

Andreff W, 'Some Comparative Economics of the Organization of Sports: Competition and Regulation in North American vs. European Professional Team Sports Leagues' (2011) 8 European Journal of Comparative Economics 3

Angeli M, 'Willing to Define Willingness: The (Almost) Final Word on SEP-Based Injunctions In Light of Samsung and Motorola' (2015) 6 Journal of European Competition Law & Practice 221

Azoulai L, 'The Court of Justice and the Social Market Economy: The Emergence of an Ideal and the Conditions for its Realization' (2008) 45 Common Market Law Review 1335

Bernstein L, 'Opting Out of the Legal System: Extralegal Contractual Relations in the Diamond Industry' (1992) 21 Journal of Legal Studies 115

Böhm F, 'Privatrechtsgesellschaft und Marktwirtschaft' (1966) 17 ORDO 75

Bomhoff J, 'Lüth's 50th Anniversary: Some Comparative Observations on the German Foundations of Judicial Balancing' (2008) 9 German Law Journal 121

Bomhoff J and Meuwese A, 'The Meta-regulation of Transnational Private Regulation' (2011) 38 Journal of Law and Society 138

Bradley C, 'Consultation and Legitimacy in Transnational Standard-Setting' (2011) 20 Minnesota Journal of International Law 480

Brenncke M, 'Case C-58/08, *Vodafone Ltd and Others v Secretary of State for Business, Enterprise and Regulatory Reform*, Judgment of the Court of Justice (Grand Chamber) of 8 June 2010' (2010) 47 Common Market Law Review 1793

Brophy AL and Ghosh S, 'Whistling Dixie: The Invalidity and Unconstitutionality of Covenants Against Yankees' (1999) 10 Villanova Environmental Law Journal 57

Bruner CM, 'States, Markets, and Gatekeepers: Public-Private Regulatory Regimes in an Area of Economic Globalization' (2008) 30 Michigan Journal of International Law 125

Budzinski O, 'Monoculture Versus Diversity in Competition Economics' (2008) 32 Cambridge Journal of Economics 295

Budzinski O, 'The Institutional Framework for Doing Sports Business: Principles of EU Competition Policy in Sports Markets' (2012) 11 International Journal of Sport Management and Marketing 44

Cafaggi F and Janczuk A, 'Private Regulation and Legal Integration: The European Example' (2010) 12 Business and Politics 1

Cengiz F, 'Multi-level Governance in Competition Policy: The European Competition Network' (2010) 35 European Law Review 660

Choper JH, 'Thoughts on State Action: The Government Function and Power Theory Approaches' (1979) Washington University Law Quarterly 757

Christiansen A and Kerber W, 'Competition Policy with Optimally Differentiated Rules Instead of "Per Se Rules vs Rule of Reason"' (2006) 2 Journal of Competition Law and Economics 215

Coase RH, 'The Problem of Social Cost' (1960) 3 Journal of Law and Economics 1

Cohen MR, 'Property and Sovereignty' (1927) 13 Cornell Law Quarterly

Craven R, 'Football and State aid: too important to fail?' (2014) 14 International Sports Law Journal 205

Dalton C, 'An Essay in the Deconstruction of Contract Doctrine' (1985) 94 Yale Law Journal 997

Danielsen D, 'How Corporations Govern: Taking Corporate Power Seriously in Transnational Regulation and Governance' (2005) 46 Harvard International Law Journal 411

Davies ACL, 'One Step Forward, Two Steps Back? The Viking and Laval Cases in the ECJ' (2008) 37 Industrial Law Journal 126

Davies G, 'Freedom of Movement, Horizontal Effect, and Freedom of Contract' (2012) 3 European Review of Private Law 805

Davies G, 'Understanding Market Access: Exploring the Economic Rationality of Different Conceptions of Free Movement Law' (2010) 11 German Law Journal 671

Delimatsis P, '"Thou Shall Not ... (Dis) Trust": Codes of Conduct and Harmonization of Professional Standards in the EU' (2010) 47 Common Market Law Review 1049

Devlin A, 'Antitrust as Regulation' (2012) 49 San Diego Law Review 823

Diller JM, 'Private Standardization in Public International Lawmaking' (2012) 33 Michigan Journal of International Law 481

Duval A, 'Lex Sportiva: A Playground for Transnational Law' (2013) 19 European Law Journal 822

Easterbrook FH, 'Limits of Antitrust' (1984) 63 Texas Law Review 1

Elhauge ER, 'The Scope of Antitrust Process' (1991) 104 Harvard Law Review 667

Emons W, 'Credence Goods and Fraudulent Experts' (1997) 28 RAND Journal of Economics 107

Engle E, 'Third Party Effect of Fundamental Rights (Drittwirkung)' (2009) 5 Hanse Law Review 165

Farrell H, 'Regulating Information Flows: States, Private Actors, and E-Commerce' (2006) 9 Annual Review of Political Science 353

Fischer-Lescano A and Teubner G, 'Regime-Collisions: The Vain Search for Legal Unity in the Fragmentation of Global Law' (2003) 25 Michigan Journal of International Law 999

Fox EM, 'Competition Law and the Agenda for the WTO: Forging the Links of Competition and Trade' (1995) 4 Pacific Rim Law & Policy Journal 1

Froomkin AM and Lemley MA, 'ICANN and Antitrust' (2003) University of Illinois Law Review 1

Fuchs D, Kalfagianni A and Havinga T, 'Actors in Private Food Governance: The Legitimacy of Retail Standards and Multistakeholder Initiatives With Civil Society Participation' (2009) 28 Agriculture and Human Values 353

Gal MS and Faibish I, 'Six Principles for Limiting Government-Facilitated Restraints on Competition' (2007) 44 Common Market Law Review 69

García B and Weatherill S, 'Engaging With the EU in Order to Minimize its Impact: Sport and the Negotiation of the Treaty of Lisbon' (2012) 19 Journal of European Public Policy 238

Gardiner S and Welch R, 'Bosman—There and Back Again: The Legitimacy of Playing Quotas under European Union Sports Policy' (2011) 17 European Law Journal 828

Goebel RJ, 'Lawyers in the European Community: Progress Towards Community-Wide Rights of Practice' (1991) 15 Fordham International Law Journal 556

Goldberg PK and Verboven F, 'Market Integration and Convergence to the Law of One Price: Evidence From the European Car Market' (2005) 65 Journal of International Economics 49

Grundmann S, 'The Concept of the Private Law Society: After 50 Years of European and European Business Law' (2008) 4 European Review of Private Law 553

Harlow C, '"Public" and "Private" Law: Definition Without Distinction' (1980) 43 Modern Law Review 241
Hatzopoulos V, 'The Economic Constitution of the EU Treaty and the Limits between Economic and Non-economic Activities' (2012) 23 European Business Law Review 973
Havinga T, 'Private Regulation of Food Safety by Supermarkets' (2006) 28 Law & Policy 515
Horowitz HW, 'The Misleading Search for State Action under the Fourteenth Amendment' (1956) 30 Southern California Law Review 208
Hovenkamp H, 'Standards Ownership and Competition Policy' (2007) 48 BCL Rev
Ibáñez Colomo P, 'On the Application of Competition Law as Regulation: Elements for a Theory' (2010) 29 Yearbook of European Law 261
Ibáñez Colomo P, 'Rules of Purely Sporting Interest and EU Competition Law: Why the Wouters Exception is Not Necessary' (2012) 8 Competition Law International 54
Inman RP and Rubinfeld DL, 'Making Sense of the Antitrust State-Action Doctrine: Balancing Political Participation and Economic Efficiency in Regulatory Federalism' (1996) 75 Texas Law Review 1203
Jaffe LL, 'Law Making by Private Groups' (1937) 51 Harvard Law Review 201
Joliet R, 'The Free Circulation of Goods: The Keck and Mithouard Decision and the New Directions in the Case Law' (1994) 1 Columbia Journal of European Law 436
Jones A, 'Regulating the Legal Profession: Article 81, the Public Interest and the ECJ's Judgment in Wouters' (2008) 19 European Business Law Review 1079
Jr. RJG and Nowak JE, 'A Functional Analysis of the Fourteenth Amendment State Action Requirement' (1976) 1976 Supreme Court Review 221
Jurav L and Veit F, 'The Slovak Antimonopoly Office holds that several provisions of the lawyers' rules of professional conduct breach both Slovak and EU competition provisions (Slovak Bar Association)' (2005) 452 e-Competitions
Katz A, 'Taking Private Ordering Seriously' (1996) 144 University of Pennsylvania Law Review 1745
Kennedy D, 'Form and Substance in Private Law Adjudication' (1976) 89 Harvard Law Review 1685
Kennedy D, 'The Stages of the Decline of the Public/Private Distinction' (1982) 130 University of Pennsylvania Law Review 1349
Kienapfel P and Stein A, 'The Application of Articles 81 and 82 EC in the Sport Sector' (2007) 3 Competition Policy Newsletter 6
Kingston S, 'Integrating Environmental Protection and EU Competition Law: Why Competition Isn't Special' (2010) 16 European Law Journal 780
Krenn C, 'A Missing Piece in the Horizontal Effect "Jigsaw": Horizontal Direct Effect and the Free Movement Of Goods' (2012) 49 Common Market Law Review 177
Kumm M, 'Who is Afraid of the Total Constitution?: Constitutional Rights as Principles and the Constitutionalization of Private Law' (2006) 7 German Law Journal 341
LeRoy MH, 'The Narcotic Effect of Antitrust Law in Professional Sports: How the Sherman Act Subverts Collective Bargaining' (2011) 86 Tulane Law Review 860
MacGowan N and Quinn M, 'Could Article 30 impose obligations on individuals?' (1987) 12 European Law Review 163
Maher I, 'Competition Law and Transnational Private Regulatory Regimes: Marking the Cartel Boundary' (2011) 38 Journal of Law and Society 119
Manning B, 'Corporate Power and Individual Freedom: Some General Analysis and Particular Reservations' (1960) 55 Northwestern University Law Review 38

Marenco G, 'Competition between National Economies and Competition between Businesses–A Response to Judge Pescatore' (1987) 10 Fordham International Law Journal 420
Mataija M, 'Internal Situations in Community Law: An Uncertain Safeguard of Competences within the Internal Market' (2010) 5 Croatian Yearbook of European Law and Policy 31
Michelman FI, 'W(H)ither the Constitution' (1999) 21 Cardozo Law Review 1063
Mnookin RN and Kornhauser L, 'Bargaining in the Shadow of the Law: The Case of Divorce' (1979) 88 Yale Law Journal 950
Monti G, 'Article 81 EC and Public Policy' (2002) 39 Common Market Law Review 1057
Monti G, 'Managing the Intersection of Utilities Regulation and EC Competition Law' (2008) 4 Competition Law Review 123
Mortelmans K, 'Towards Convergence in the Application of the Rules on Free Movement and on Competition?' (2001) 38 Common Market Law Review 613
Nelson P, 'Information and Consumer Behavior' (1970) 78 Journal of Political Economy 311
O'Loughlin R, 'EC Competition Rules and Free Movement Rules: An Examination of the Parallels and their Furtherance by the ECJ Wouters Decision' (2003) 24 European Competition Law Review 62
Odudu O, 'The Wider Concerns of Competition Law' (2010) 30 Oxford Journal of Legal Studies 599
Ogus A, 'Rethinking Self-Regulation' (1995) 15 Oxford Journal of Legal Studies 97
Oliver P and Roth WH, 'The Internal Market and the Four Freedoms' (2004) 41 Common Market Law Review 407
Orbach B, 'The Antitrust Consumer Welfare Paradox' (2011) 7 Journal of Competition Law & Economics 133
Parret L, 'Shouldn't We Know What We are Protecting? Yes We Should! A Plea for a Solid and Comprehensive Debate about the Objectives of EU Competition Law and Policy' (2010) 6 European Competition Journal 339
Parrish R, 'The Politics of Sports Regulation in the European Union' (2003) 10 Journal of European Public Policy 246
Pearson G, 'Sporting Justifications Under EU Free Movement and Competition Law: The Case of the Football "Transfer System"' (2015) 21 European Law Journal 220
Pelkmans J, 'The New Approach to Technical Harmonization and Standardization' (1987) 25 Journal of Common Market Studies 249
Pera A, 'Changing Views of Competition, Economic Analysis and EC Antitrust Law' (2008) 4 European Competition Journal 127
Pescatore P, 'Public and Private Aspects of European Community Competition Law' (1986) 10 Fordham International Law Journal 373
Petit N and Rato M, 'The Commission's Non Contractual Liability in the Field of Merger Control—Don't Use a Hammer When You Need a Screwdriver' (2007) Global Competition Policy
Prechal S, 'Free Movement and Procedural Requirements: Proportionality Reconsidered' (2008) 35 Legal Issues of Economic Integration 201
Prechal S and de Vries S, 'Seamless Web of Judicial Protection in the Internal Market?' (2009) 34 European Law Review 5
Prosser T, 'Competition Law and Public Services: From Single Market to Citizenship Rights?' (2005) 11 European Public Law 543

Regan DH, 'The Supreme Court and State Protectionism: Making Sense of the Dormant Commerce Clause' (1986) 84 Michigan Law Review 1091

Reich N, 'The "November Revolution" of the European Court of Justice: Keck, Meng and Audi Revisited' (1994) 31 Common Market Law Review 459

Rincón A, 'EC Competition and Internal Market Law: On the Existence of a Sporting Exemption and its Withdrawal' (2007) 3 Journal of Contemporary European Research 224

Roda J-C, 'Sport et droit de la concurrence: L'exemple du football professionnel' (2012) 3 Concurrences 71

Rose J, 'The Legal Profession in Medieval England: A History of Regulation' (1998) 48 Syracuse Law Review 1

Sauter W, 'Containing Corporatism: EU Competition Law and Private Interest Government' (2015) 36 European Competition Law Review 187

Scharpf FW, 'The Asymmetry of European Integration, or Why the EU Cannot be a "Social Market Economy"' (2010) 8 Socio-Economic Review 211

Schepel H, 'Delegation of Regulatory Powers to Private Parties Under EC Competition Law: Towards a Procedural Public Interest Test' (2002) 39 Common Market Law Review 31

Schepel H, 'Constitutionalising the Market, Marketising the Constitution, and to Tell the Difference: On the Horizontal Application of the Free Movement Provisions in EU Law' (2012) 18 European Law Journal 177

Schepel H, 'Freedom of Contract in Free Movement Law: Balancing Rights and Principles in European Public and Private Law' (2013) 5&6 European Review of Private Law 1211

Schoenhard PM, 'A Three-Dimensional Approach to the Public-Private Distinction' (2008) Utah Law Review 635

Schweitzer H, 'Competition Law and Public Policy: Reconsidering an Uneasy Relationship: The Example of Art. 81' EUI Working Papers LAW No 2007/30

Seidman LM, 'The State Action Paradox' (1993) 10 Constitutional Commentary 379

Semmelmann C, 'The European Union's Economic Constitution Under the Lisbon Treaty: Soul-Searching Shifts the Focus to Procedure' (2010) 35 European Law Review 516

Shaffer GC, 'How Business Shapes Law: A Socio-Legal Framework' (2009) 42 Connecticut Law Review 147

Shelanski HA, 'The Case for Rebalancing Antitrust and Regulation' (2011) 109 Michigan Law Review 683

Simon WH, 'Who Needs the Bar: Professionalism without Monopoly' (2002) 30 Florida State University Law Review 639

Snyder DV, 'Private Lawmaking' (2003) 64 Ohio State Law Journal 371

Sørensen KE, 'Non-Harmonized Technical Regulations and the Free Movement of Goods' (2012) 23 European Business Law Review 163

Stephen FH, 'Regulation of the Legal Professions or Regulation of Markets for Legal Services: Potential Implications of the Legal Services Act 2007' (2008) 19 European Business Law Review 1129

Stewart RB, 'Remedying Disregard in Global Regulatory Governance: Accountability, Participation, and Responsiveness' (2014) 108 American Journal of International Law 211

Stone Sweet A and Mathews J, 'Proportionality Balancing and Global Constitutionalism' (2008) 47 Columbia Journal of Transnational Law 68

Stucke ME, 'Reconsidering Antitrust's Goals' (2012) 53 Boston College Law Review 551

Sunstein CR, 'State Action Is Always Present' (2002) 3 Chicago Journal of International Law 465

Szyszczak E, 'Competition and Sport' (2007) 32 European Law Review 95

Terry LS, 'The European Commission Project Regarding Competition in Professional Services' (2009) 29 Northwestern Journal of International Law & Business 1

Townley C, 'Which goals count in Article 101 TFEU? Public Policy and its Discontents: The OFT's Roundtable Discussion on Article 101(3) of the Treaty on the Functioning of the European Union' (2011) 32 European Competition Law Review 441

Trachtman JP, 'Trade and ... Problems, Cost-Benefit Analysis and Subsidiarity' (1998) 9 European Journal of International Law 32

Trachtman JP, 'Fragmentation, Coherence and Synergy in International Law' (2011) 2 Transnational Legal Theory 505

Tryfonidou A, 'Further steps on the Road to Convergence Among the Market Freedoms' (2010) 35 European Law Review

Turner C, 'State Action Problems' (2013) 65 Florida Law Review 281

Tushnet M, 'The issue of State Action/Horizontal Effect in Comparative Constitutional Law' (2003) 1 International Journal of Constitutional Law 79

Van de Gronden JW, 'The Internal Market, the State and Private Initiative: A Legal Assessment of National Mixed Public-private Arrangements in the Light of European Law' (2006) 33 Legal Issues of Economic Integration 105

Van Gestel R and Micklitz H-W, 'European Integration Through Standardization: How Judicial Review is Breaking Down the Club House of Private Standardization Bodies' (2013) 50 Common Market Law Review 145

van Leeuwen B, 'PIP Breast Implants, the EU's New Approach for Goods and Market Surveillance by Notified Bodies' (2014) 3 European Journal of Risk Regulation 338

van Leeuwen B, 'Private Regulation and Public Responsibility in the Internal Market' (2014) 33 Yearbook of European Law 277

Van Rompuy B, 'The Impact of the Lisbon Treaty on EU Competition Law: A Review of Recent Case Law of the EU Courts' (2011) 1 CPI Antitrust Chronicle

Verbruggen P, 'Does Co-Regulation Strengthen EU Legitimacy?' (2009) 15 European Law Journal 425

Vogel D, 'Private Global Business Regulation' (2008) 11 Annual Review of Political Science 261

Waelbroeck M, 'Competition, Integration and Economic Efficiency in the EEC from the Point of View of the Private Firm' (1983) 82 Michigan Law Review 1439

Weatherill S, 'Anti-doping Revisited—The Demise of the Rule of "Purely Sporting Interest"' (2006) 27 European Competition Law Review 645

Wilks S, 'Agencies, Networks, Discourses and the Trajectory of European Competition Enforcement' (2007) 3 European Competition Journal 437

Williamson OE, 'Economies as an Antitrust Defense: The Welfare Tradeoffs' (1968) 58 The American Economic Review 18

Witt AC, 'Public Policy Goals under EU Competition Law—Now is the Time to Set the House in Order' (2012) 8 European Competition Journal 443

Wyatt D, 'Horizontal Effect of Fundamental Freedoms and the Right to Equality after Viking and Mangold, and the Implications for Community Competence' (2008) 4 Croatian Yearbook of European Law and Policy 1

Zacharias FC, 'The Myth of Self-Regulation' (2009) 93 Minnesota Law Review 1147

Zittrain J, 'Internet Points of Control' (2003) 43 Boston College Law Review 1

Zumbansen P, 'Neither "Public" nor "Private", "National" nor "International": Transnational Corporate Governance from a Legal Pluralist Perspective' (2011) 38 Journal of Law and Society 50

ONLINE AND WORKING PAPERS

Azoulai L, 'Sur un sens de la distinction public/privé dans le droit de l'Union européenne' in Robin-Olivier S, Odudu O and Azoulai L (eds), *The Public/Private Divide in European Union Law* WP 2010/7 (CEJEC 2010)

Balassa BA, 'Types of Economic Integration' (International Bank for Reconstruction and Development Bank Staff Working Paper No. 185, 1974)

Baumé T, 'Notion of undertaking and association of undertakings, exercise of the powers of a public authority and application of the Wouters derogation to a regulatory measure adopted by a professional association' (2013) Journal of European Competition Law & Practice, published online May 19, 2013 <http://jeclap.oxfordjournals.org/content/early/2013/05/19/jeclap.lpt023.full>

Cafaggi F, 'Rethinking Private Regulation in the European Regulatory Space' EUI Working Paper LAW 2006/13

Cafaggi, 'Product safety, private standard setting and information networks' EUI Working Paper LAW 2008/17

Cafaggi, 'Private Regulation in European Private Law' EUI RSCAS WP 2009/31

Cafaggi, 'Private regulation, supply chain and contractual networks: The case of food safety' EUI RSCAS WP 2010/10

Cafaggi, 'The architecture of transnational private regulation' EUI Working Paper LAW 2011/12

Calliess G-P, 'Lex mercatoria' (2015) ZenTra Working Papers in Transnational Studies 52/2015

Calliess G-P, Mertens J, and Renner M, 'Privatizing the Economic Constitution—Can the World Market Reproduce its own Institutional Prerequisites?' Osgoode CLPE Research Paper 11/2012 <http://ssrn.com/abstract=2056625>

Duval A, 'The Pechstein Ruling of the OLG München (English Translation)' (6 Feb 2015) <http://ssrn.com/abstract=2561297>

Duval A, 'SV Wilhelmshaven: a Rebel with a cause! Challenging the compatibility of FIFA's training compensation system with EU law' (Asser International Sports Law Blog, 24 February 2015) <http://www.asser.nl/SportsLaw/Blog/post/sv-wilhelmshaven-a-rebel-with-a-cause-challenging-the-compatibility-of-fifa-s-training-compensation-system-with-eu-law>

Fallon M and Gerard D, 'Trailing the trailers in search for a typology of barriers: Sketching a scale of relative gravity and exploring its implications' Cahiers du CeDIE Working Paper No 2012/6

Hatzopoulos V, 'The concept of "economic activity" in the EU Treaty: from ideological dead-ends to workable judicial concepts' College of Europe Research Paper in Law 06/ 2011 <http://www.coleurope.eu/sites/default/files/research-paper/researchpaper_6_2011_hatzopoulos.pdf>

Joerges C, Schepel H and Vos E, 'The law's problems with the involvement of non-governmental actors in Europe's legislative processes: the case of standardisation under the "New Approach"' EUI Working Paper LAW No 99/9

Komárek J, 'Institutional dimension of constitutional pluralism' Eric Stein Working Paper No 3/2010

Krzeminska-Vamvaka J, 'Horizontal Effect of Fundamental Rights and Freedoms—Much Ado About Nothing? German, Polish and EU Theories Compared After Viking Line' Jean Monnet Working Paper 11/09

Lamadrid de Pablo A and Ortiz Blanco L, 'Nullity/Voidness: An Overview of EU and National Case Law' 49199 e-Competitions

Lemley MA, 'Intellectual Property Rights and Standard-Setting Organizations' 90 California Law Review online (2002)

Lianos I, '"Lost in Translation": Towards a Theory of Economic Transplants' Jean Monnet Working Paper 08/09 <http://papers.ssrn.com/sol3/papers.cfm?abstract_id=1485378>

Maduro MP, 'The Chameleon State: EU Law and the Blurring of the Private/Public Distinction in the Market' <http://ssrn.com/abstract=1575542>

Mariniello M, 'European Antitrust Control and Standard Setting' Bruegel Working Paper 2013/01

Marx A and Cuypers D, 'Halting Deforestation and Forest Certification: What is the Macro-Impact of the Forest Stewardship Council?' (2010) Leuven Centre for Global Governance Studies Working Paper No 56

Micklitz H-W, Svetiev Y and Comparato C (eds), 'European Regulatory Private Law – The Paradigms Tested' (2014) EUI LAW Working Paper 2014/4

Milner-Moore GR, 'The Accountability of Private Parties under the Free Movement of Goods Principle' Jean Monnet Working Paper 9/95

Montesa Lloreda A and Givaja Sanz A, 'The Spanish Supreme Court firmly protects price competition in the liberal professions and gives a controversial view on the interaction between EC and national competition Law (Ricardo)' (2008) 23835 e-Competitions

Muris TJ, 'State Intervention/State Action – A U.S. Perspective' George Mason University School of Law Law & Economics Working Paper Series <http://ssrn.com/abstract_id=545163>

Semmelmann C, 'The Public-Private Divide in European Union Law or an Overkill of Functionalism' (2012) Maastricht European Private Law Institute Working Paper 2012/12

Semmelmann C, 'Theoretical Reflections on the Public–Private Distinction and their Traces in European Union Law' Oñati Socio-legal Series [online] 2(4) 25

Sunstein CR and Vermeule A, 'Interpretation and Institutions' University of Chicago Law & Economics, Olin Working Paper No 156

Van den Bergh R, 'Towards Better Regulation of the Legal Professions in the European Union' Rotterdam Institute of Law and Economics (RILE) Working Paper No 2008/07 <http://ssrn.com/abstract=1113310>

Vedder HHB, 'Voluntary Agreements and Competition Law: What Are, and What Should be the Boundaries to VA's Imposed by Competition Law?' FEEM Working Paper No 792000 <http://ssrn.com/abstract=253333>

Wouters J, Marx A and Hachez N, 'Private standards, global governance and transatlantic cooperation: The Case of Global Food Safety Governance' Leuven Centre for Global Governance Studies Working Paper

Index